Introducing Character Animation with Blender

SECOND EDITION

Introducing Character Animation with Blender

SECOND EDITION

TONY MULLEN

Wiley Publishing, Inc.

Acquisitions Editor: Mariann Barsolo
Development Editor: Stephanie Barton
Technical Editor: Terry Wallwork
Production Editor: Eric Charbonneau
Copy Editor: Kim Wimpsett
Editorial Manager: Pete Gaughan
Production Manager: Tim Tate
Vice President and Executive Group Publisher: Richard Swadley
Vice President and Publisher: Neil Edde
Book Designer: Caryl Gorska
Compositor: Chris Gillespie, Happenstance Type-O-Rama
Proofreader: Nancy Bell
Indexer: Ted Laux
Project Coordinator, Cover: Katherine Crocker
Cover Designer: Ryan Sneed
Cover Images: Alligator image copyright © Julia Korbut
Sintel image copyright © Blender Foundation | www.sintel.org
Big Buck Bunny image copyright © Blender Foundation | www.bigbuckbunny.org

Copyright © 2011 by Wiley Publishing, Inc., Indianapolis, Indiana

Published simultaneously in Canada

ISBN: 978-0-470-42737-8 (pbk)
ISBN: 978-1-118-09065-7 (ebk)
ISBN: 978-1-118-09063-3 (ebk)
ISBN: 978-1-118-09064-0 (ebk)

For general information on our other products and services or to obtain technical support, please contact our Customer Care Department within the U.S. at (877) 762-2974, outside the U.S. at (317) 572-3993 or fax (317) 572-4002.

Wiley also publishes its books in a variety of electronic formats. Some content that appears in print may not be available in electronic books.

Library of Congress Cataloging-in-Publication Data is available from the publisher.

10 9 8 7 6 5 4 3 2 1

Dear Reader,

Thank you for choosing *Introducing Character Animation with Blender, Second Edition.* This book is part of a family of premium-quality Sybex books, all of which are written by outstanding authors who combine practical experience with a gift for teaching.

Sybex was founded in 1976. More than 30 years later, we're still committed to producing consistently exceptional books. With each of our titles, we're working hard to set a new standard for the industry. From the paper we print on, to the authors we work with, our goal is to bring you the best books available.

I hope you see all that reflected in these pages. I'd be very interested to hear your comments and get your feedback on how we're doing. Feel free to let me know what you think about this or any other Sybex book by sending me an email at nedde@wiley.com. If you think you've found a technical error in this book, please visit http://sybex.custhelp.com. Customer feedback is critical to our efforts at Sybex.

Best regards,

Neil Edde
Vice President and Publisher
Sybex, an Imprint of Wiley

To Beni Nitha Mullen

Acknowledgments

As always, I am grateful to the dedicated Blender developers around the world who devote their time and effort to improving Blender. I would like to thank my editor Mariann Barsolo, editorial manager Pete Gaughan, development editor Stephanie Barton, technical editor Terry Wallwork, production editor Eric Charbonneau, and the rest of the team at Sybex who made this book happen. I would also like to thank the Blender user community for its support and particularly those readers of the first edition of this book who offered their comments on how it could be improved. Lastly, I am grateful to my wife, Yuka, and my daughters, Hana and Beni, for their love and support.

About the Author

Tony Mullen, PhD, has a broad background in CG-related work. He teaches at Tsuda College and Musashino Art University, where his courses have included modeling and animation with Blender and programming with Python. Mullen has been a cartoonist and an illustrator; his screen credits include writer, co-director, and lead animator on several short films, including the award-winning live-action/stop-motion film *Gustav Braustache and the Auto-Debilitator.* He is the author of five Blender-related books from Sybex including *Blender Studio Projects: Digital Movie-Making* (with Claudio Andaur) and *Bounce, Tumble and Splash! Simulating the Physical World with Blender 3D.*

CONTENTS AT A GLANCE

Foreword ▪ **xvii**

Introduction ▪ **xix**

PART I ■ **CREATING A CHARACTER WITH BLENDER 1**

Chapter 1 ▪ Blender Basics: Interface and Objects **3**

Chapter 2 ▪ Working with Meshes **27**

Chapter 3 ▪ Completing the Model with Materials, Textures, and Hair **87**

Chapter 4 ▪ Armatures and Rigging **121**

Chapter 5 ▪ Shape Keys and Facial Rigging **159**

PART II ■ **BRINGING IT TO LIFE: ANIMATION 205**

Chapter 6 ▪ Basics of Animation **207**

Chapter 7 ▪ Armature Animation **223**

Chapter 8 ▪ Facial Animation and Lip Sync **261**

Chapter 9 ▪ Animation for Production **277**

Chapter 10 ▪ Further Issues in Character Animation **299**

Chapter 11 ▪ Lighting, Rendering, and Editing Your Animation **321**

Chapter 12 ▪ Python Scripts and Add-Ons **341**

PART III ■ **BLENDER IN PRODUCTION 347**

Chapter 13 ▪ The Fruits of Freedom: Open Movies and Open Content **349**

Chapter 14 ▪ A Look Inside the Blender Open Movies **359**

Chapter 15 ▪ Behind the Scenes with *Sintel* **381**

Chapter 16 ▪ Feifi the Canary—*Plumiferos* Takes Wing **407**

PART IV ■ **BLENDER AND BEYOND 419**

Chapter 17 ▪ Other Software and Formats **421**

Chapter 18 ▪ Resources for Further Learning **427**

Index ▪ **433**

Contents

Foreword   xvii

Introduction   xix

PART I ■ CREATING A CHARACTER WITH BLENDER   1

Chapter 1 ■ Blender Basics: Interface and Objects   3

Work Areas and Window Types   4

Navigating the 3D Space   9

Objects and Datablocks   18

User Preferences   23

Chapter 2 ■ Working with Meshes   27

Polygons and Subsurfacing   28

Poly-by-Poly Modeling and Box Modeling   33

Common Problems and Solutions in Mesh Modeling   81

Chapter 3 ■ Completing the Model with Materials, Textures, and Hair   87

Materials and Material Slots   88

Material Properties   91

Textures and UV Mapping   98

Working with Particle Hair   115

Chapter 4 ■ Armatures and Rigging   121

Blender Armature System   122

Building a Simple Armature   123

Rigging Captain Blender with Rigify   135

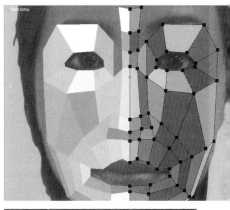

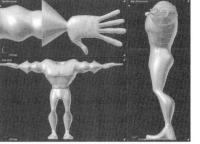

Chapter 5 ■ Shape Keys and Facial Rigging   **159**

Shape Key Basics   160

Building a Shape Key Set for
Captain Blender   172

Facial Bones and Controls   187

Improved Mesh Deformations Using
Driven Shape Keys   200

PART II ■ BRINGING IT TO LIFE: ANIMATION   **205**

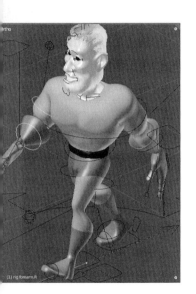

Chapter 6 ■ Basics of Animation   **207**

Keyframes and Function Curves   208

Using the Graph Editor: Bouncing a Ball   210

Interpolation and Extrapolation   217

Chapter 7 ■ Armature Animation   **223**

Posing and Keyframing with the
DopeSheet and Action Editor   224

Walk and Run Cycles   237

Pose-to-Pose Animation   250

Chapter 8 ■ Facial Animation and Lip Sync   **261**

Facial Posing   262

Lip Sync   267

Playback   273

Chapter 9 ■ Animation for Production   **277**

Working with Proxies   278

Using the NLA Editor   283

NLA in Action   289

**Chapter 10 ■ Further Issues in Character
Animation**   **299**

Interacting with Props   300

Lattices and Mesh Deformers   306

Softbodies and Metaballs   314

Chapter 11 ■ Lighting, Rendering, and
　　　　　　　Editing Your Animation　　321

　　Lighting Basics　　322

　　Rendering Your Animation　　334

　　Editing in the Sequence Editor　　336

Chapter 12 ■ Python Scripts and Add-Ons　　341

　　Using Add-Ons　　342

　　The Blender Python API　　345

　　Learning More about Blender
　　Python Scripting　　346

PART III ■ BLENDER IN PRODUCTION　　347

Chapter 13 ■ The Fruits of Freedom: Open
　　　　　　　Movies and Open Content　　349

　　The Blender Institute　　350

　　The Blender Open Movie Project　　350

　　Free and Open Licenses for Software
　　and Content　　355

Chapter 14 ■ A Look Inside the Blender
　　　　　　　Open Movies　　359

　　Learning from *Elephants Dream*　　360

　　Nonhuman Rigs in *Big Buck Bunny*
　　and *Sintel*　　370

　　The Production Pipeline　　375

Chapter 15 ■ Behind the Scenes with *Sintel*　　381

　　From Durian to *Sintel*　　382

　　The *Sintel* Open Content　　383

　　Sintel Artists in Their Own Words　　387

Chapter 16 ■ Feifi the Canary—*Plumiferos*
　　　　　　　Takes Wing　　407

　　Introducing Feifi　　408

　　Facial Deformations with Lattices　　410

　　Rigging a Cartoon Bird　　411

PART IV ■ BLENDER AND BEYOND   **419**

  Chapter 17 ■ Other Software and Formats   **421**

      Importing and Exporting Other
File Formats   422

      Useful Open Source Software for
Blender Artists   422

      Blending into the (Near) Future   425

  Chapter 18 ■ Resources for Further Learning   **427**

      Selected Blender Resources   428

      Recommended Non-Blender-Specific Books   430

      On Becoming a Blender Master   432

  Index   **433**

Foreword

Truth be told, the first time I downloaded Blender I didn't know what I was getting into. I thought this animation stuff would be easy! I was about 14 years old when I first tried Blender, and if I remember correctly, it was probably about a year after the software was released as open source. That first day I spent about eight hours trying to model a cube, vertex by vertex. When I ended up with something that more closely resembled a scrambled egg, I wiped Blender from my hard drive out of frustration. I was not ready for Blender, and Blender was not ready for me. It was clunky and intimidating and hard on the eyes.

But when I came back to it only a couple months later, with a bit more patience and determination, I fell in love.

I feel in a way that I have grown up with Blender. As I have matured as an artist, I have witnessed Blender mature. Over the years I have been astonished at the rate of its development and the increasing breadth of its feature set. Blender has always been a capable 3D tool, but I think it's only recently that it truly stands its ground next to its commercial counterparts. It has been my privilege to watch the software and the Blender community grow.

Like many others, I was awed and impressed by *Elephants Dream* and *Big Buck Bunny.* In addition to being great films in their own rights, both projects spearheaded massive improvements in Blender and have proven its viability in a more serious (and fully open source!) production environment. As an aspiring filmmaker, I was greatly motivated by those projects. It's really possible to *make movies* with entirely free software! It was a dream come true for me to become involved in the third Blender Open Movie Project, *Sintel.*

If I learned anything on the project, it's that making movies is hard. 3D animation is an incredibly complex process, and every step can be a struggle on both an artistic and a technical level.

There's a lot to learn. And learning takes time.

There are a myriad of training materials out there, of varying clarity and quality. I know I've personally sifted through dozens of written tutorials, wiki docs, and videos, trying to figure out how to approach my personal animation projects. Tony Mullen's book *Character Animation with Blender* is the authoritative guide on the technical side of animation in Blender. From an introduction of using the interface to the nitty-gritty details of setting up drivers for facial shape keys, this book will guide you through the complex landscape of Blender's animation tools and ultimately help you do the work you aspire to do.

I wish everyone reading this the best of luck!

— *Colin Levy*
Director, *Sintel*
www.colinlevy.com

Introduction

It's been five years since the first edition of *Introducing Character Animation with Blender* came out, and a lot has changed in the world of Blender. Interest in Blender has exploded. When the first edition of this book came out, it was the only English-language book on Blender in print. Now, as this second edition of the book arrives, there are well over a dozen books that I can think of offhand, to say nothing of commercial training DVDs and professional online tutorial services, none of which were around five years ago. Clearly somebody has begun to sit up and take notice.

It's clear why, too. Blender has been making its mark in ways that are increasingly hard to ignore. The first Blender Open Movie Project movie, *Elephants Dream*, premiered as the first edition of this book was being written. Since that time, two more movies, *Big Buck Bunny* and *Sintel*, have been released to increasing fanfare. Each of the movies has been more ambitious than the first, and each has fulfilled its ambitions impressively. In addition to the movies, the Blender Institute has released a complete game and a half dozen professional training DVDs by some of the world's top Blender creators. When I wrote the first edition of this book, I felt I had something to prove. Now, five years later, it is clear that Blender is proving itself.

In addition to the prolific content output of the Blender Institute, the coding of Blender has progressed at a rapid pace. Between the release of *Big Buck Bunny* and *Sintel*, the underlying event-handling and data-handling frameworks of Blender were entirely rewritten. This made it possible to completely re-conceive the user interface and Python scripting API, both of which were also rewritten as part of the overhaul. The result is a completely revamped application that has managed to earn kudos both from longtime Blender users and from longtime critics alike.

If you're new to Blender, there's never been a better time to learn. Although there will always be a learning curve to acquiring 3D graphics skills, the new interface is more intuitive and user friendly than ever before. If you're coming from other software, you'll be pleased to see that the interface is fully configurable (there is even an option for Maya-style interface presets accessible directly in the splash screen).

The new Blender has been a long time coming, and it is designed to last. Now that it is finally stable and ready for professional use, adoption of Blender by users of all kinds, from young hobbyists to old pros, is bound to continue even more rapidly.

The Open Source Advantage

Blender is a powerful 3D modeling and animation software package available for Windows, Macintosh, and Linux. Like other similar packages such as Lightwave, 3ds Max, and Maya, Blender offers a wide range of modeling, animation, and rendering tools. It also has a number of distinguishing features of its own, including its excellent cross-platform portability, the ability to run scripts in the Python programming language, a unique and intuitive user interface for efficient workflow, and extraordinary flexibility in importing and exporting files, scenes, and objects for use with other programs, including a variety of high-quality ray tracers. It has advanced physics simulators, and its new, lightning-fast implementation of UV unwrapping has already become the envy of the industry. These features alone are enough to make Blender a strong competitor in the world of 3D tools, but its biggest single distinguishing feature is that it's free.

That's not simply to say that somebody is giving out free samples that you can use in some capacity without paying for. Blender is licensed under the GNU Public License, the foremost license for open source software. This means Blender source code is freely available for anybody to download, use, copy, alter, and distribute for any purpose, provided they abide by the guidelines laid out in the GPL. These guidelines require that changes made to the code be explicitly identified and that resulting released code remain open and freely available. In short, Blender is truly, fully free, and the license is designed to make sure it stays free for good.

For people with a computer science background, the idea that top-quality software can be free is not new. Open source projects such as the GNU/Linux operating system, the Apache web server, and the MySQL database have amply demonstrated the robustness and quality possible with an open source development model. All of those are examples of widely used, high-quality, and *commercially viable* free software. Furthermore, software such as the TeX/LaTeX typesetting package, widely used for academic typesetting in technological fields, stands as a clear testament to the potential for innovation in open source software; TeX/LaTeX remains unrivaled in what it does by any proprietary consumer-oriented software package. Richard Stallman, the author of the GPL and longtime advocate of free software, likes to emphasize the notion of "free as in free speech, not as in free beer," and many Blender users are quick to stress that their fondness for Blender is not based on cost.

Nevertheless, in the realm of consumer-oriented and graphics software, it remains true that most of the best industrial-strength software applications are proprietary. Even the best open source applications in these areas tend to come across largely as underdog imitations of their proprietary counterparts. For this reason, it is reasonable to wonder what the catch is with something like Blender. And the good news is that as far as the software is concerned, there really is no catch. Blender is a robust, fully fleshed out piece of software, remarkably free of bugs, and more stable than some proprietary packages with similar functionality. Its development is rapid, with new features and fixes being released at a steady clip. Development is overseen by Ton Roosendaal, the creator of Blender and head of the Blender Foundation, and the core programming team is passionate and committed to holding the Blender code to high standards. The Blender Foundation regularly participates as a mentoring organization in Google's Summer of Code program, in which young programmers are given the opportunity to contribute to an open source project. So in the case of Blender, as with the best open source programs, being free does not imply a lack of quality in the software itself.

Furthermore, in addition to allowing programmers from all over the world the ability to contribute code and bug fixes to the software, the open source model also encourages a sense of community among users. The free nature of the software encourages users to share their expertise and abilities where they can. Aside from the core programmers, there are numerous users contributing useful Python scripts to the community, to say nothing of the countless high-quality tutorials created by users.

What we are left with is a first-rate, professional-quality 3D animation package that is available to everybody completely free. You don't have to pay thousands of dollars for the software and commit to many more for upgrades, you don't have to risk getting nabbed pirating software, you don't have to worry about your chosen package falling out of favor or the vendor going out of business, and you don't have to mess around with watermarks on your work or hobbled, semi-functional shareware. With Blender, *you're* free to get right down to what's important: creating.

Depending on your needs, Blender may be the only 3D animation package you ever have to bother with. If you are a hobbyist, a freelancer, or the head of your own production company, you may be able to do fine without ever touching another 3D modeling and animation application. However, Blender in its current incarnation as a first-tier 3D animation tool is comparatively new. Before the recent recode of the armature system in version 2.40, Blender suffered from a number of shortcomings as an animation tool. Even then, it was highly regarded for its modeling abilities and its versatility, but with the recent improvements in its animation capabilities, Blender has come into its own in the realm of animation. It is now fully capable of producing high-quality animation, and with time it will surely begin to be adopted into more and more professional studios and production houses impressed by its flexibility and workflow.

Currently, of course, Blender is not the industry standard. If you are hoping to get work in the field of animation, it would be a good idea to aim for basic proficiency in at least one other 3D application. You can't really predict which application you may be asked to use within a job setting, but prospective employers will appreciate that you are familiar with more than one environment. Even so, there are advantages to using Blender. For building portfolio pieces and show reels, any quality software will do, and the freedom and flexibility of Blender are as much an advantage for students and job-seekers as they are for anybody else. Most of the skills you will need in the industry are general 3D and animation skills, and these can be learned with any fully functional software package. The skills you master in Blender will transfer to other software packages and greatly speed up your ability to pick up new applications.

Who Should Buy This Book

As the title implies, this book is intended for people who want to learn to create quality character animation using the Blender 3D software package. Such people probably fall into three basic groups:

- Blender users who have experience with modeling and rendering but have not yet seriously explored Blender's character animation capabilities. It is likely that a lot of Blender users fall into this category, since Blender has been heavily used for years as a 3D illustration tool.

- Experienced character animators who are considering making a transition to using Blender instead of, or in addition to, another software package. These people can expect to be quite familiar with the concepts dealt with in this book but need to know how the concepts are implemented in the Blender software.

- Highly motivated newbies to both Blender and the field of character modeling and animation. These are the people who will be picking the bones of this book. I hope to supply these readers with all they need to use Blender to get started in character modeling and also to give them some good pointers on where to go from here to develop their skills more fully.

For all of these people, the learning curve can be long. When the first edition of this book was written, very little professional learning material was available. Blender learners had to rely on wiki pages and scattered web tutorials (some of which were excellent) to learn. A cohesive introduction to Blender was not available. For this reason, I took a very broad view of what the topic of character animation encompasses. Modeling, texturing, and animation were all part of what I covered, and most of the information in the book applied to other forms of modeling and animation than character animation. The book was very well-received, and in this second edition I have stayed with the same basic formula.

Likewise, although it is very much part of this book, I do not go into great depth on the art of animation per se. In Chapter 18, I recommend several books to help you deepen your knowledge and skills in this regard.

With this second edition of *Introducing Character Animation with Blender*, I aim to provide a clear, cohesive overview of character creation and animation as implemented in Blender. I hope that this encourages people to make the most of Blender's capabilities, to exercise their own creativity, and to support the fantastic community that has developed around this software.

You can use this book in several ways. The most straightforward (and demanding) is to start at the beginning and follow all the steps to model and animate the rigged character described over the course of the book. Alternately, you can skip around from chapter to chapter and follow only the steps of the individual chapters. For this, `.blend` files are available for download from the book's companion website to help: `www.sybex.com/go/introducingblender`.

What's Inside

Here is a glance at what's in each chapter.

In **Part I: Creating a Character with Blender**, I take you through the Blender program, its tools, and the complete foundational process of building a character.

Chapter 1: Blender Basics: Interface and Objects introduces you to the Blender desktop and shows you how to navigate the various windows you'll be using throughout the book. This chapter also explains the basics of how Blender handles 3D objects and what this will mean to you as you work with them.

Chapter 2: Working with Meshes covers the most important mesh modeling tools and shows several approaches to organic modeling. The chapter culminates with the completion of the Captain Blender character mesh, which you will use throughout the rest of the book for animation tutorials and examples.

Chapter 3: Completing the Model with Materials, Textures, and Hair continues with modeling the Captain Blender mesh, now focusing on creating clothing, skin, and hair using such tools as material shaders, UV mapped textures, and the particle system for hair.

Chapter 4: Armatures and Rigging introduces the armature system with simple examples and then moves on to creating a high-quality armature for the Captain Blender character using the new Rigify automatic rigging add-on.

Chapter 5: Shape Keys and Facial Rigging moves beyond the basics of armature deformations to show how more precise animation of mesh shapes can be accomplished with shape keys and how the behavior of these can be associated to armature poses to create easily controllable facial expressions and improved joint deformations.

In **Part II: Bringing It to Life: Animation**, you will turn to animating the character you created in Part I.

Chapter 6: Basics of Animation looks at the simple example of a bouncing ball to introduce the ideas of animation function curves (F-Curves) and keyframes, which are the underlying components of all animation in Blender.

Chapter 7: Armature Animation shows how posing, keyframing, and F-Curves work with the character rig you created in Part I to create your first real character animations. You will create actions such as jumping, walking, running, and others.

Chapter 8: Facial Animation and Lip Sync turns your attention to the facial rigging you did in Chapter 5. Using these methods of facial posing, you will see how the character can be made to express emotion and how lip movements can be created to sync with a sound file.

Chapter 9: Animation for Production looks at tools for animating within the context of a larger production, specifically, using Blender's armature proxy system and its powerful Non-Linear Animation Editor.

Chapter 10: Further Issues in Character Animation covers a number of worthwhile topics in character animation that have not been addressed in other chapters, such as interacting with props and using features such as lattices and the Mesh Deform modifier, soft body simulation, and metaballs.

Chapter 11: Lighting, Rendering, and Editing Your Animation tells you what you need to know to output your animations to fully realized, finished works using

Blender's built-in rendering engine. In this chapter, you will learn how to use the Sequence Editor to edit separate animated segments together to create a complete animation.

Chapter 12: Python Scripts and Add-Ons shows you how to use Blender's powerful Python-based add-on system and highlights some of the most useful add-ons. In this chapter, you'll also learn the basics of how the Python API works.

In **Part III: Blender in Production**, you will look at real-world cases of Blender being used in professional-level animation projects.

Chapter 13: The Fruits of Freedom: Open Movies and Open Content introduces the two best-known Blender-based animation projects: the world's first "open movie," *Elephants Dream*, and the eagerly anticipated CG feature film from Argentina, *Plumiferos*.

Chapter 14: A Look Inside the Blender Open Movies peeks into the *Elephants Dream* production files to see how the characters of that film are modeled and rigged and highlights some of the interesting approaches to character animation taken by the creators of the film.

Chapter 15: Behind the Scenes with *Sintel* takes a closer look at the production of *Sintel*. This chapter includes in-depth interviews with members of the *Sintel* creative team.

Chapter 16: Feifi the Canary—*Plumiferos* Takes Wing presents a very special look at a fascinating character rig from *Plumiferos*, an inspiring behind-the-scenes glimpse at this exciting project.

Part IV: Blender and Beyond wraps up by giving you some pointers to where you can go to continue deepening your skills and understanding, beyond what's contained in this book.

Chapter 17: Other Software and Formats gives a brief overview of the import and export possibilities of Blender to and from other 3D formats and surveys a variety of open source software that will likely be of interest to Blender animators.

Chapter 18: Resources for Further Learning directs you to some recommended books, tutorials, and other resources for deepening your knowledge of animation and CG techniques in general.

Online Companion Files

On the book's companion website, www.sybex.com/go/introducingblender, you'll find the project files you'll need to jump in at any point with the book's tutorials and exercises, organized into folders by chapter. Among these are the .blend files for the Captain Blender character you see throughout the book.

You can download Blender 2.5 any time from the Blender website at www.blender.org. Note that future versions of the software may have slight changes and deviate from descriptions in this book. This is no problem. Either you can adapt the lessons to the new versions yourself or you can download version 2.5 from the older versions archive on the Blender website. All Blender versions remain permanently available.

How to Contact the Author

I welcome feedback from you about this book or about books you'd like to see from me in the future. You can reach me by writing to blender.characters@gmail.com. You can also find me among the regular posters in the BlenderArtists forum at http://blenderartists.org/forum.

Sybex strives to keep you supplied with the latest tools and information you need for your work. Please check the book's website at www.sybex.com/go/introducingblender, where I'll post updates that supplement this book if the need arises.

Creating a Character with Blender

Before you do *any actual character animation, you need a character to animate. The goal of the first part of this book is to get you comfortable enough with the modeling and rigging tools in Blender to translate your own ideas into actual 3D characters. Blender has powerful mesh modeling tools and a very flexible system for creating materials and textures. It also boasts a state-of-the-art armature system that will enable you to create complex, highly poseable rigs for your characters. By the end of this part of the book, you will have a fully rigged character completed, which you can use to follow the animation tutorials in the following part. More importantly, you will have gained the skills to create your own character.*

CHAPTER 1 ■ **BLENDER BASICS: INTERFACE AND OBJECTS**

CHAPTER 2 ■ **WORKING WITH MESHES**

CHAPTER 3 ■ **COMPLETING THE MODEL WITH MATERIALS, TEXTURES, AND HAIR**

CHAPTER 4 ■ **ARMATURES AND RIGGING**

CHAPTER 5 ■ **SHAPE KEYS AND FACIAL RIGGING**

Blender Basics: Interface and Objects

The first hurdle in learning any complex piece of software is to become familiar with the interface. In the past, this was especially true of Blender, which had until recently garnered a reputation for an idiosyncratic and often perplexing interface. With the release of the long-awaited Blender 2.5, this reputation may change. Blender 2.5 is the result of thousands of hours of designing, debugging, and coding, from a complete recode of Blender's low-level event-handling system to a top-to-bottom redesign of the graphical user interface (GUI). Users coming from other 3D software will feel especially welcomed by the improved organization of the interface and by its high degree of customizability.

Much of this customizability is the result of an overhaul of Blender's Python API, which enables advanced users to have near total control over all aspects of the interface (as well as access to most 3D data) via the Python scripting language. For users familiar with the ideas behind object-oriented programming, many aspects of Blender's organization will be especially intuitive, such as the use of objects, function overloading, and the reuse of datablocks. Getting a good feel for these ideas and how they are implemented in Blender will greatly increase your proficiency at accomplishing what you want. Going further to master Python scripting will give you a great deal of added power over your Blender environment. Nevertheless, it's not necessary to be a programmer to use Blender, and this book doesn't assume any programming knowledge.

Blender 2.5's strengths begin with its interface, and so will this book. Mostly, you'll learn by doing over the course of this book, but in this chapter, you'll take a quick look at the most salient points of the Blender interface.

- ■ **Work Areas and Window Types**
- ■ **Navigating the 3D Space**
- ■ **Objects and Datablocks**
- ■ **User Preferences**

Work Areas and Window Types

When you first open Blender, one or two windows will open on your system's desktop, depending on the operating system you use. In Windows, your main Blender window appears in front of the Blender console window. In Linux, the console is hidden unless you open Blender from the command line in a terminal window, in which case the Blender console is the terminal. In Mac OS X, the console does not appear initially, but you can access it from within the Applications/Utilities directory. In Windows, the console is a solid black window with white text. It should read something like Found Bundled Python and the path of the Python installation. The console displays output from Python scripts and other plug-ins and integrated software, such as renderers. For the purposes of the material in this book, however, you need only know that you should not close the console. If you do, Blender shuts down unceremoniously, and you may lose some of your work.

Figure 1.1

Blender desktop

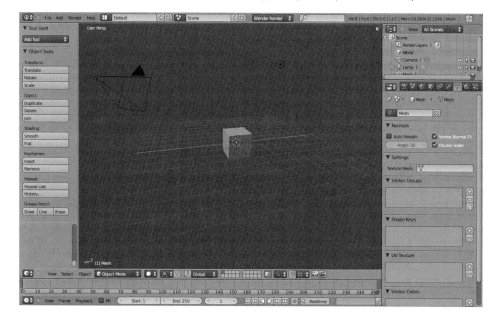

Blender does not prompt you to save changes before closing. If you accidentally close Blender without saving, simply open a fresh session and select File → Recover Last Session. The most recent Blender session is automatically saved in a file in your /tmp directory by default. Be aware, however, that on Mac OS X this default directory is deleted whenever you restart your machine.

The other window is the main Blender window (shown in Figure 1.1). If it's not already maximized, maximize it. Blender can use all the screen real estate you can give it.

You are now looking at your Blender desktop, which should appear a lot like Figure 1.1. The Blender desktop consists of a nonoverlapping configuration of windows. By default, the windows are arranged as shown in Figure 1.2. As you can see, five windows appear in this configuration. Each window holds a different editor type as identified in the figure. The darker gray areas indicate the placement of each window's header. Headers can be displayed at the top of a window, at the bottom of the window, or not at all. You'll see what each editor type is for shortly.

Figure 1.2

The default window arrangement

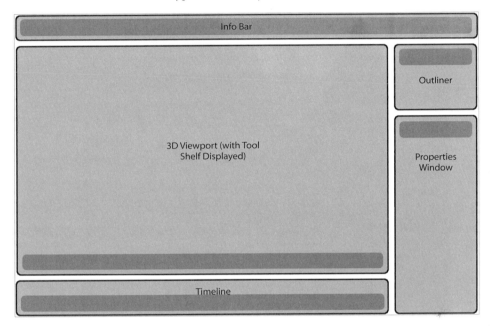

You can resize each window by clicking one of the window's borders and dragging to enlarge or reduce the size of the window, as illustrated in Figure 1.3. You can split a window into two identical windows by clicking the upper-right or lower-left corner of the window and dragging in the direction that you want the window to be split, as shown in Figure 1.4. You can also merge windows that share a complete border by clicking the upper-right or lower-left corner and dragging across the border that you want to be eliminated, as shown in Figure 1.5. In this way, you can arrange the windows on your Blender desktop with a great deal of freedom.

Obviously, splitting a window into two identical windows is of limited use unless you can change the content of the windows, which of course you can. All windows are created equally in Blender; any window can display any editor type. The editor type displayed in a particular window is determined by the icon at the leftmost corner of the window's header. You can select which editor type is displayed by choosing it from the menu shown in Figure 1.6.

Figure 1.3

Dragging borders to resize windows

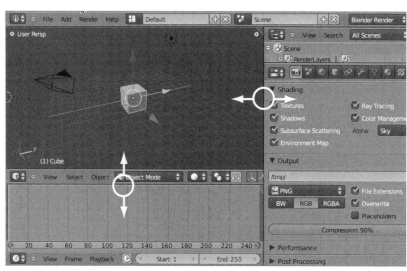

Figure 1.4

Splitting a window into two identical windows

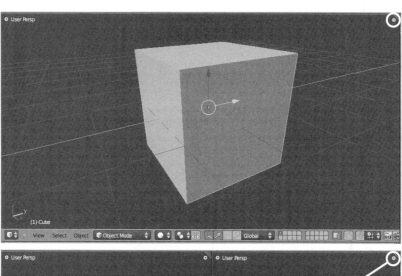

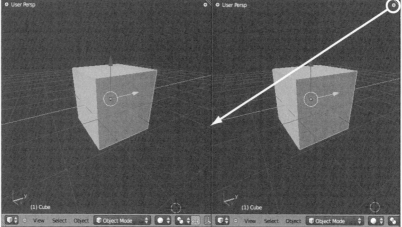

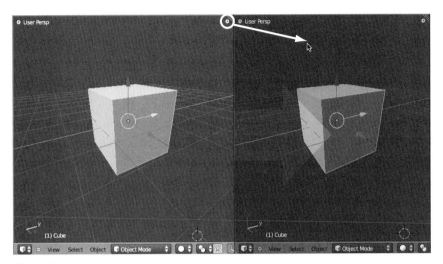

Figure 1.5
Merging two windows

Figure 1.6
The Editor Type menu

The editor types are as follows:

3D View Displays 3D objects and scenes in various modes, including the Object, Edit, and Pose modes. This editor allows a variety of viewing options, including toggled perspective/orthographic drawing (Numpad 5). The shortcut for accessing the 3D view is Shift+F5.

Timeline Displays the progress through time of an animation. With this editor, you can start, stop, and scrub through the animation, and you can directly input the start, end, and current frames.

Graph Editor Lets you select and edit animation function curves (F-Curves) and drivers. Previous versions of Blender dealt with this functionality by means of Ipo curves, but the old system has been replaced by a more generalized and powerful F-Curve framework. You can access the Graph Editor with Shift+F6.

DopeSheet Provides an organized overall view of an animated scene, enables sequences of armature poses to be stored together as actions for subsequent use in nonlinear animation, and lets you view and edit shape key animations. You can access the DopeSheet with Shift+F12.

NLA Editor Lets you combine actions and other animations in a nonlinear way to form complex animations.

UV/Image Editor Lets you edit UV mapping information and image-based textures. You access the UV/Image Editor with Shift+F10.

Video Sequence Editor Enables nonlinear editing, compositing, and playback of video sequences. It can take still-frame or video sequences as input. You can access the Video Sequence Editor with Shift+F8.

Text Editor Enables text editing. You often use this editor type as an area for notes about the blend file or for Python scripting. You can execute Python scripts from the Text Editor using the Alt+P hotkeys. The shortcut for accessing the Text Editor is Shift+F11.

Node Editor Lets you edit and configure material, texture, and composite nodes. You can access the Node Editor with Shift+F3.

Logic Editor Enables editing of real-time interactive logic for use in the Blender Game Engine. You access the Logic Editor with Shift+F2.

Properties Lets you view and edit property values for a wide variety of contexts and entities including objects, scenes, render contexts, simulations, modifiers, constraints, materials, textures, lamps, and cameras. The Properties window largely replaces the functionality found in the "Buttons area" of older Blender versions. You can access the Properties window with Shift+F7.

Outliner Enables a graphical overview of all datablocks and the links between them, with multiple display options. You can access the Outliner with Shift+F9.

User Preferences Lets you specify look-and-feel preferences, language preferences, file location defaults, and other preferences. You can bring up a pop-up User Preferences window by pressing Ctrl+Alt+U.

Info Provides a header bar with general-purpose menus for file handling, object addition, rendering, help, window configuration, and scene selection. Info also displays diagnostics about scene content and render progress, among other information. The Info window does not contain any functionality other than what is displayed in its header.

File Browser Lets you open files from the hard drive and import or append Blender datablocks from within files on the hard drive.

Console Provides a fully functional Python command-line interpreter with access to the Python API. You can access the console with Shift+F4.

> Your operating system may have hotkeys that override the Blender hotkeys. Mac OS X in particular uses the F keys for various desktop management functionality. If you want to use the default Blender keyboard shortcuts, you will need to disable the OS X shortcuts first. See your OS X documentation about how to do this. Some Linux desktops also have built-in hotkeys that need to be disabled for Blender to work right, so please consult the documentation for your system's desktop manager.

In this book, the term *window* usually refers to a window with a specific editor type active. For example, the term *3D view window* will mean a window with the 3D View editor type selected. It's perfectly possible to have more than one instance of the same editor type open in separate windows doing different things at the same time. For example, you can have two or more 3D view windows open at once looking at your 3D scene from different directions.

Properties Window

With the Properties editor, you can access a lot of information about many aspects of Blender's functionality, and as such, it's a place where you'll spend a lot of time. The information is fairly dense, so it's worthwhile to get a general sense of what's going on there before going much further.

The Properties editor can display any of up to 11 *contexts* at a time. These contexts correspond to the icons in the header of the Properties window (not all 11 are available at the same time). The possible properties contexts are as follows:

- Render
- Scene
- World
- Object
- Object Constraints
- Modifiers
- Object Data
- Material
- Texture
- Particles
- Physics

Which contexts are available depends on what type of object is selected in the 3D viewport. Throughout the course of this book, you will dip into each of these contexts. In this book, I will usually shorten the terminology by referring to *Render properties* rather than *the Render context of the Properties editor*.

Context-Sensitive Menus

Blender contains a number of menus that you can access in certain window types and in specific modes. Throughout this book, you will use these menus to add objects in Object mode, to perform special operations in Edit mode, and to key values for animation, among other things.

Navigating the 3D Space

As with any 3D application, you first need to get used to navigating the 3D space in Blender. The following are the three main tools to do this:

Middle Mouse Button (MMB) Freely rotates the 3D space. By default, the 3D space is rotated around the origin (in other words, zero point) of all axes. You can choose to have it rotate around the active object by setting the Rotate Around Selection option in the Interface user preferences in the User Preferences window.

Ctrl+MMB (or mouse wheel) Zooms in and out in the 3D space.

Shift+MMB Pans 3D view.

If the Emulate 3 Button Mouse option is selected on the Input tab of the user preferences, you can emulate the middle mouse button by Alt+clicking. This can be useful for laptops that have no middle button or whose "middle button" is a difficult-to-push combination of right and left buttons. In the case of a one-button Mac mouse, the mouse click is equivalent to clicking. The middle button is Alt+mouse, and you simulate the right mouse button with Apple(⌘)+mouse. This is not ideal. Do yourself a favor and spring for a three-button model with a good, solid, mechanical mouse wheel.

In many cases, hotkeys and mouse movements have analogous results in different contexts. A good example is the behavior of the Ctrl+MMB and Shift+MMB hotkeys. As just mentioned, these keys allow zooming and panning in the 3D window. However, if the mouse is over the Properties window, they have results analogous to zooming and panning. Pressing Ctrl+MMB lets you enlarge or reduce the vertical size of the Properties display. MMB lets you drag the Properties display within the window.

Figure 1.7

The 3D cursor

You will use the 3D cursor frequently (see Figure 1.7). You can position it by clicking where you want it in the 3D viewport.

Blender Units

Blender uses one unit of measurement, unsurprisingly called a Blender unit (BU). A Blender unit is the size of a single square on the background grid in the Blender 3D viewport. If you are working on scale models, you need to decide what real-world measurement to assign to a single BU and then proportion your work accordingly. Some simulations assume a BU is equal to 1 meter, as does the Metarig functionality that you will see in Chapter 4, so it's worthwhile to keep this scale in mind, but there's nothing strict about it. A BU can equal whatever real-world measurement you want. For precision users, Blender 2.5 also has access to metric and imperial unit measurements as well as custom measurement scales.

Using Hotkeys

You will notice that Blender favors the use of a lot of hotkeys. Memorizing and becoming comfortable with the various hotkeys and their specific configurations on your own machine is one of the first hurdles to learning to work with Blender. Table 1.1 and Table 1.2 list the most important Blender hotkeys. You can configure all Blender hotkeys in the user preferences, but if you plan to use Blender frequently, particularly if you plan to use multiple installations of Blender, then I recommend getting used to the defaults where you can.

HOTKEY	ALL MODES
Spacebar	Function search
R	Rotate
S	Scale
G	Translate (move)
X	Delete
A	Select all/deselect all
B	Border select
C	Circle select
Ctrl+P	Make parent
Alt+P	Clear parent
Shift+D	Duplicate
I	Insert animation key
Alt+C	Object conversion menu
Right arrow	Move forward one frame
Left arrow	Move backward one frame
Up arrow	Move forward 10 frames
Down arrow	Move backward 10 frames
Shift+right arrow	Go to the last frame
Shift+left arrow	Go to the first frame
0–9/Alt+0 through Alt+9	Show corresponding layer
F12	Render
F11	Display rendered image
W	Specials menu
X, Y, Z	Constrain transformation to (selected global axis)
XX, YY, ZZ	Constrain transformation to (selected local axis)
Shift+X, Shift+Y, Shift+Z,	Constrain transformation to take place in the selected plane by global coordinates
Shift+XX, Shift+YY, Shift+ZZ	Constrain transformation to take place in the selected plane by local coordinates
N	Display transform properties
Shift+S	Snap menu
Numpad 1, 3, 7	Front, side, and top view
Numpad 0	Camera view
Ctrl+Alt+Numpad 0	Move camera to current view
Ctrl+Numeric 0	Use selected object for camera view

Table 1.1

Hotkeys common to all modes

	HOTKEY	OBJECT MODE	EDIT MODE
Table 1.2	Tab	Go into Edit mode	Go into Object mode
Hotkeys specific to object and edit modes	F		Make Edge/Face
	P	Play game	Separate mesh selection into new object
	L		Select linked vertices
	M	Move object to new layer	
	U		Undo
	E		Extrude
	V		Rip mesh
	K		Loop cut/Knife menu
	Ctrl+J	Join meshes/curves	
	Ctrl+A	Apply scale and rotation	
	Alt+R, Alt+G, Alt+S	Clear rotation, clear translation, clear scale	
	Ctrl+N	Reload startup file	
		Make normals consistent; recalculate normals outside	
	Ctrl+E		Edges
	Alt+S		Fatten/shrink
	Ctrl+S		Shear

You can find information about hotkeys and edit them in the keymap configuration area of the Input tab in the User Preferences window. For users of laptops or one- or two-button mouse devices, some further key combinations are also necessary. The instructions in this book assume you have a three-button mouse and a separate number keypad, but I will point out how to simulate the key combinations if you don't. With a little time following the instructions in this book, the hotkeys will begin to come naturally, and the speed and ease with which you can work with Blender will greatly increase. If you've done animation in other 3D software, you probably have a good idea which of these keys you'll use most often. If you're new to the field, expect to become very familiar with the R, S, and G keys for rotating, scaling, and moving things around, as well as with the I key for keying frames for animation.

Layers

In the header of the 3D viewport there are 20 small square buttons, divided into 4 rows of 5 buttons. These buttons toggle the visibility of individual layers in a scene.

Layers let you separate objects in your 3D view so that you can see some objects but not others. The terminology is somewhat arbitrary; layers in Blender are groupings used to hide or show specific objects and to control which objects interact with certain simulations and lighting effects. They can be useful to organize your work during editing and also during animation. You can restrict lights to illuminate only objects on the same layer as the light, which is an indispensable tool in lighting. Also, you can limit forces such as wind effects, curve guides, and collision effects (discussed later in this book) to affect only those objects on their own layer.

You can toggle the layers that are visible in the 3D viewport and to the renderer by using the buttons mentioned previously or by using the keyboard number keys (not the numeric keypad). You can toggle multiple layers at once by Shift+clicking the buttons. The top row of layers corresponds to the keyboard number keys 1 through 0. The bottom row of layers corresponds to Alt+1 through Alt+0. In general, you use the numeric keypad to change views, and you use the keyboard numbers to change layers. You can use either to input numbers into a text field, for example.

> If you accidentally press a keyboard number key other than the layer you are working in, it may be a shock when all the objects suddenly disappear from the 3D view window! Don't panic; simply return to viewing the layer your work was on by using the layer buttons.

You can send an object to a different layer by selecting the object and pressing the M key. A dialog box displays with the layer buttons in the same order as they appear in the 3D viewport header. Simply click the layers you want to send the item to, holding Shift to select multiple layers, and click OK. An object can reside on as many layers as you choose.

Views and Perspective

There are various ways to view your scene. When you open Blender initially, default view shows the scene in perspective view, in which lengths and sizes are affected by their distance from the viewer and things farther away appear smaller, just as in nature. To toggle into orthographic mode, press 5 on the numeric keypad. This mode gives a less realistic orthographic view that can be easier to work with.

> It is possible to zoom too far forward in perspective view and find yourself trapped. If your viewpoint seems frozen or difficult to control, this is probably the problem. Simply press 5 on the numeric keypad to toggle into orthographic view, and then zoom your viewpoint out. You can also press the Home key to bring the entire scene into view.

Using the number pad, you can switch your view to follow the x-, y-, or z-axis. The numeric 1 key changes the view to look down the y-axis (front view), and numeric 3 will change the view to follow the x-axis (right view). Holding down the Ctrl key while you press these numbers changes the view to their respective opposites, looking up the axis from the negative direction. Numeric 2 and 8 rotate the scene vertically with respect to the 3D viewport, and numeric 4 and 6 rotate the scene horizontally.

> If you use a laptop without a numeric keypad, setting the Emulate Numpad user preference will let you switch views using the ordinary keyboard numbers. If you select this, the keyboard numbers will no longer switch visible layers. I rarely if ever use keyboard numbers to set layer visibility, so I always choose this option.

The 0 key on the numeric pad switches to the active camera viewpoint. A dotted rectangle frames the view, indicating the video-safe area, as you can see in Figure 1.8. If the camera is on a visible layer, a solid rectangle also appears, representing the camera. You can right-click this rectangle to select the camera, like any other object. From other views, you can place the camera at the current view by pressing Ctrl+Alt+Numeric 0, which will also put you automatically into camera view. You can also use Ctrl+Numeric 0 to place *any object* in the active camera. You can use this shortcut to switch cameras, but you can also use it to check on the *viewpoint* of other objects, which can be useful for directional objects such as spotlights.

Figure 1.8

Camera view

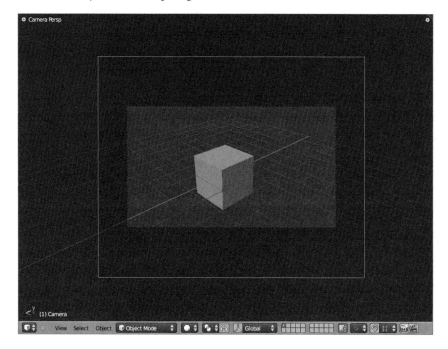

Interacting with 3D Objects

In the header bar of the 3D view window, there is a drop-down menu for selecting the mode. The default mode to begin with is Object mode, in which you can select and manipulate objects and relationships between them.

You can select objects in several ways. The simplest way to select a single object is by right-clicking it. If you hold Shift, you can add individual objects to the selection. Selected objects are outlined in shades of orange. The last object you selected is outlined in a lighter orange, indicating that it is active. To make one of the other selected objects the currently active object, Shift+right-click it. Shift+right-click the active object to remove it from the selection. By pressing the Z key, you can toggle between the wireframe and solid views. In solid view, you cannot select objects that are completely obscured from the view by other objects. You must either move your view to a place where you can get to the object or enter wireframe view. Alt+right-clicking a spot with more than one selectable object lets you select from a list of those objects.

You can also select objects with the Box Select tool, accessed by pressing the B key once. With this tool, you drag a box over an area of the screen and then select all visible objects within the box. Hold down the left mouse button while dragging the box to cover the selection. Pressing the B key and then dragging the box with the middle mouse button uses the box for deselection. There are several ways to manipulate the location, rotation, and size of objects, and it is entirely a matter of personal preference which one to use.

Hotkeys

The following are some hotkeys that might be helpful:

- To rotate, press the R key once, and rotate the object with the mouse. The default rotation axis is the current angle of the 3D view. After you rotate the object the way you like it with the mouse, click to accept the new rotation; otherwise, right-click to quit the rotation without making the change.

- To translate or change an object's location in 3D space, the hotkey is G (for "grab"). Press this key once, and move the object around with the mouse. As with rotation, clicking finalizes the move, and right-clicking aborts it.

- To scale an object, the hotkey is S. When you have pressed the S key, moving the mouse closer to the pivot point reduces the scale of the object, and moving the mouse farther from the pivot point enlarges the object. Again, clicking finalizes; right-clicking aborts.

Motion Manipulators

Blender also provides the manipulator widgets shown in Figure 1.9 for rotating, translating, and scaling. You can toggle these three manipulators on and off independently of each other by using the buttons in Figure 1.10. To use a manipulator, click the colored portion of the manipulator of the axis along which you want to perform the operation. In the case of translation, click the colored arrow on the appropriate axis; in the case of scaling, click the colored rectangle; in the case of rotation, click the colored curve that circles the axis you want to rotate the object around.

Figure 1.9

The manipulator widgets: (a) rotation, (b) translation, (c) scale

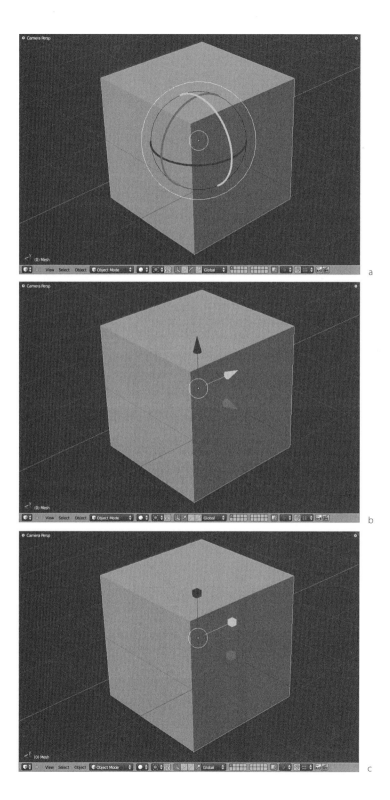

Restricting to Axes

When you rotate, translate, or scale, you often want to restrict the operation to a particular axis or to fix one axis while operating in the other two. To select an axis to rotate, scale, or translate along, press X, Y, or Z after pressing the R, S, or G key. This restricts the operation to the global axis. Press the axis key twice to restrict the operation along the object's local corresponding axis. To scale or translate along a plane, press Shift and the key corresponding to the axis you do not want changed. For example, to scale an object along its x- and y-axes, press S followed by Shift+Z.

Figure 1.10

The manipulator selection buttons

Pivot Point

The *pivot point* is the point around which rotations are calculated, and it is also used as a reference point for scaling. You can choose the point to use as your reference point in the drop-down menu shown in Figure 1.11. The default, Median Point, is a point calculated to be in the center of your entire selection. If you have multiple objects selected, the median point is somewhere in between them all. You can choose to have objects rotate independently around their own centers, around the active object, around the 3D cursor, or around the center of the object's bounding box. The default median point pivot, which you can set with the Shift+comma hotkey, is the most commonly used, but in this book you will occasionally switch the pivot point to be the 3D cursor for specific purposes, which you can set with the keyboard period key.

Figure 1.11

Pivot selection drop-down menu

Object Centers

Every object has a center. The *center* is the point around which the object rotates by default, and the location of the center is considered to be the location of the object. When you translate and rotate in Object mode, the actions are carried out on the entire object. However, in Edit mode, you can move the 3D portion of the object (for example, in the case of a Mesh object, by selecting and moving the entire mesh in Edit mode) without moving the center. When you do a lot of editing, this can easily happen and cause poorly placed centers that can cause unexpected behavior with objects. You can set the origin either by using the Tool Shelf button or by using the hotkey Shift+Ctrl+Alt+C over the 3D viewport region, which will open a menu of options for setting the origin.

Parenting

Parenting is an important way to create relationships between objects (and some other entities). You will use parenting often in modeling, animating, and texturing. When one object is *parented to* another, you can refer to the first object as the *child* and the second object as the *parent*. In this case, the child object's movements are all considered only in relation to the parent. When you translate, rotate, or scale the parent object, you do the same to the child object. However, the relationship is not symmetrical. Like a moon around a planet, the child object can move or rotate in relation to the parent object without influencing the parent object. To define a parent relationship, select more than one object. The *active* object is the last object selected, and by default it is highlighted with a lighter orange than the previously selected objects. Press Ctrl+P to parent all selected objects to the active object; that is to say, the selected objects all become child objects to the active object. Put another way, the object you selected last will become the parent of the other objects. In the case of two objects, the first object you select is parented to the second object. To delete a parent relationship, select the objects and press Alt+P to open a menu of options for clearing parent relations.

Parenting is not restricted to just object/object relationships. Vertices or bones can be parents to objects. There are two types of *vertex parenting*: single-vertex parenting and triple-vertex parenting. With *single-vertex parenting*, the parented object follows only the location of the parent vertex. *Triple-vertex parenting* allows the object to follow both the location and the rotation of the vertex triad to which it is parented. You will see an example of vertex parenting in Chapter 3.

Similarly, *bone parenting* allows an object to be in a parent relationship with a single bone in an armature. In bone parenting, the parented object inherits the location, rotation, and other qualities (such as squash and stretch) from the parent bone. You will see examples of bone parenting in Chapter 4.

Objects and Datablocks

Objects and datablocks are the fundamental building blocks for everything you will do in Blender. It's not a complicated system, but understanding how it all hangs together makes it easier to work efficiently. This chapter describes objects and object data and introduces the ideas of datablocks and linking. Later in the book, you'll see a lot more of datablocks—indeed, just about everything you see will be some kind of a datablock—so it helps to have an idea of what the concept means in Blender.

You must often make adjustments to the modeling of a character in the middle of an animation. You might want to do this for a number of reasons. To reduce animation or rendering time, you might want to block a scene with a simpler version of the character you will ultimately use. You might need to fix texturing or modeling problems that you didn't notice before beginning to animate. Also, with involved, team-based animation projects, a certain degree of flexibility is probably required in terms of task ordering—so that all the participants can make efficient use of their time. Allowing animators to work with armature deformations of Mesh objects, while other artists are modeling, rigging, and refining the meshes themselves, can save considerable time. In particular, using linked datablocks can eliminate the need to reedit or reappend the same datablock into different scenes or shots. For these reasons, an understanding of Blender's underlying object and datablock organization can be very useful.

In Blender, the basic 3D entity is an *object*. There are a number of different types of objects, each of which has different characteristics and different kinds of data associated with it. All objects have the characteristics of location, rotation, and size.

In addition to location, scale, and rotation, each 3D object is associated with a datablock of specific information to its type. In the case of the Empty object, there is no other information besides this basic 3D object information.

3D object types include the following:

- Meshes
- NURBs curves/surfaces
- Bezier curves
- Meta objects
- Armatures
- Lattices
- Text objects
- Empties
- Cameras
- Lamps

All objects have certain properties. Every object has a *location*, which is the point in space of the object's center. Every object has a *size* defined in terms of the percent of its size at the time of its creation. Every object has a *rotation*, which is the difference between the angles of its local axes and the global axes of the 3D space.

All objects of a particular type also have type-specific *datablocks* associated with them. A Mesh object requires a Mesh datablock, for example, and a Lamp object requires a Lamp datablock. This datablock contains information pertinent to the thing itself. The properties specific to a mesh, such as the placement of its vertices and faces, are contained in the Mesh datablock. A Lamp object datablock likewise contains information about the kind of light source and its properties.

Meshes and Mesh Objects

It is easy to get confused between the object and the object's type-specific datablock, but the distinction is important. It is common shorthand, for example, to refer to a Mesh object simply as a *mesh*, but strictly speaking, a mesh in Blender refers to the *Mesh datablock* associated with the *Mesh object*.

To see an example of Mesh objects and their datablocks, open Blender and split the Properties window into two. Select the default cube in the 3D viewport by right-clicking the cube. In one Properties window, choose the Object properties context, and in the other Properties window, look at the Object Data context, as shown in Figure 1.12. The highlighted fields in that figure indicate the object name and the name of the Mesh data-block. They both read Cube. Because objects and datablocks have separate namespaces, it is not a problem for them to be named identically; in fact, most of the time, it is intuitive, so they should be named identically.

Now, in Object mode, click to place your 3D cursor off to one side of the default cube, press Shift+A to open the Add menu, and add a cone mesh, as shown in Figure 1.13. Select the Cap Ends option in the Tool Shelf when adding the cone so that the cone is a closed solid mesh. Note that the mesh name and the object name, predictably enough, are Cone, as you can see in Figure 1.14. (If you add another object of the same type, Blender automatically appends the suffix .001 to the end of the new name and increments for each subsequent new object.)

Select the Cube Mesh object by right-clicking it. Click the small triangle mesh icon to the left of the datablock's name in the Object Data's Properties window, as shown in Figure 1.15; a drop-down menu appears with the available mesh names. In the drop-down menu, Cone will be an option. Select this option, and your Cube object is now a cone! Not only is it a cone, but it's the *same cone* as the Cone object. If you edit the mesh on one of these objects, both objects' meshes will be edited, as you can see in Figure 1.16.

Figure 1.12
Viewing object properties and object data properties

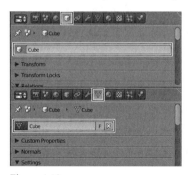

Figure 1.13
The Add menu (Shift+A)

Figure 1.14
The object and datablock names visible in the Properties windows

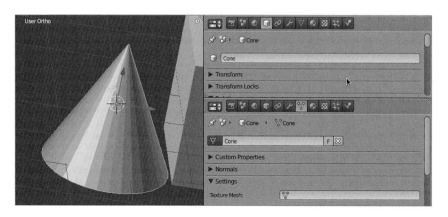

Although the mesh data is identical, the objects are still very much independent. To see this, in Object mode, select the Cube object. Press S, and scale the object to about twice its size. Now you have a big cone and a small cone. This is because mesh edits are made to the Mesh datablock, which is now shared between the objects, whereas the overall scale is an object-level property. Go back to the mesh drop-down menu on the Cube object and look at the options.

In the drop-down menu, there are two options: Cone and Cube. Select the Cube mesh from the drop-down menu. Now your Cube object is again associated with a Cube mesh. However, the cube is now twice the size that it was before because the scaling you did in Object mode applied to the object instead of the mesh.

Exploiting this distinction between Mesh objects and the meshes themselves can be very useful for character animation because it helps maintain a flexible and modular workflow. An armature modifier, as you will see later in the book, operates on a Mesh object, which means you can replace the mesh in the middle of an animation simply by swapping a new Mesh data-block in as the object data for the animated object.

You will learn more about these meshes in Chapter 2, so it is a good idea to save this .blend file now so that you can return to it later.

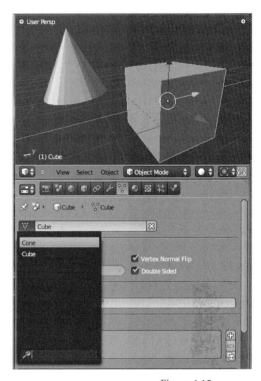

Figure 1.15

The datablock name drop-down menu

Figure 1.16

Editing the mesh

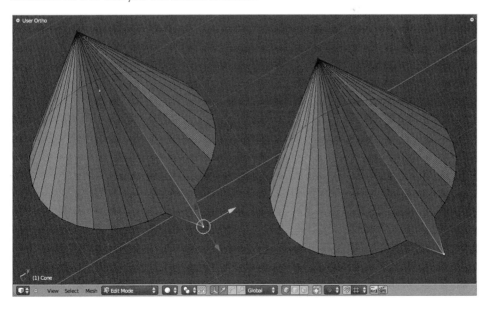

Managing Datablocks

Datablocks describe most aspects of modeling and animation in Blender. Materials, textures, Ipo curves, and actions are all examples of datablocks that can be freely associated with any number of different objects after they're created (see Figure 1.17).

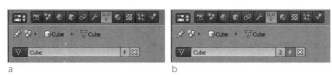

Figure 1.17

(a) The default Cube mesh has one user, the Cube object. If it is unlinked from this object, it is not persisted after the file is closed because it has no users. (b) By toggling the F button, a fake user is added (the 2 refers to the number of users for that datablock). Now, even if there are no real users of the datablock, it persists because its user count is not zero.

In the preceding example, the Cube mesh datablock is no longer associated with any object. Blender discards unused datablocks when it shuts down, so if you save the file and then shut down and restart Blender with things in that state, this mesh is gone. In fact, there is no way to actively delete such datablocks; they remain "alive" until Blender quits. If you want to purge unused datablocks without completely quitting Blender, you can save and then reopen your file.

Sometimes, you want to keep a datablock on hand even though it does not have a *user* object. If you want an unused datablock to persist after saving, you must create a *fake* user for it. For datablocks that can be retained in this way, including the ones mentioned previously, there is be a button next to the datablock drop-down menu with the letter *F*, as shown in Figure 1.17. Selecting the datablock you want to make persistent and clicking F creates a fake user for the datablock so that it will not be discarded at shutdown.

Outliner Window

In some cases, such as actions, Blender creates a fake user automatically when the datablock is created. In this case, you may want to remove a fake user to delete the undesired datablock. To do this, you use the Outliner window in Datablocks view. Datablocks are organized by type. You can navigate to the datablock you want to toggle and choose whether it should have a fake user using the appropriate check box. Figure 1.18 shows the check box for the Cube mesh in the Datablocks view of the Outliner. In many cases, an F icon is shown beside mentions of a datablock. In these cases, you can remove fake users by clicking the F icon.

Figure 1.18

Datablocks view in the Outliner window

The Outliner window also provides several other organized views of the data in your `.blend` file. By default, it opens with the All Scenes view selected, as shown in Figure 1.19, but you can select from different types of information to view using the drop-down menu.

To the right of each 3D object in the scene view are three icons: an eye, an arrow, and a camera. The eye icon toggles visibility of the object in the 3D viewport. The arrow icon toggles selectability in the 3D viewport. The camera icon toggles whether the object will be rendered.

Accessing Data from Different Files

You often need access to objects or datablocks from other files. Animation projects can quickly get far too big to store in single .blend files, and yet many different scenes and shots may share the same main elements. You can access datablocks between separate files in Blender in several ways.

The first and simplest way is to use *append*. To append a datablock from another file, select Append from the File menu or press Shift+F1. A File Browser window opens, in which you can access .blend files stored on your computer and their contents. In the File Browser window, when you click the name of a .blend file, you see a list of datablock types, just as if they were directories. Enter the appropriate type directory; you see a list of the datablocks of that type available for appending. Here is another place to be aware of the difference between objects and object type datablocks. If you want to append a Mesh object from another file, for example, you find the object in the Object type directory instead of the Mesh type directory.

Figure 1.19

The Outliner window displaying all scene information

Another approach to using data across separate files is by linking the datablocks. Linking can be done similarly to appending, except that in the File Browser header, the Link button is selected instead of Append and the Tool Shelf area to the left of the browser contains options related to linking. In this case, the data can be edited only in the file from which it was originally linked, and all edits appear in the files that linked to the data. The hotkey for linking is Ctrl+Alt+O.

Groups

Objects can be collected together into named groups using the Add To Group button in the Object Properties area, as shown in Figure 1.20. Groups themselves can then be treated as an object type when appending, allowing you to append whole collections of objects easily.

User Preferences

You can access the User Preferences window in several ways. Because it is an ordinary editor type, you can select it in any window using the Editor Type menu. You can also access it in a window of its own either by accessing the File menu in the Info header or by pressing Ctrl+Alt+U.

Figure 1.20

Add To Group button

The User Preferences window is organized into seven panels, accessed by buttons along the top of the window, as shown in Figure 1.21.

Interface Gives you options related to Blender's GUI and interaction with the 3D space. Some of these options are self-explanatory, and

they are all a matter of taste, so experiment with different settings. I recommend you check the Rotate Around Selection option, particularly if you plan to do mesh modeling. This ensures that whatever you are working on stays centered on your screen when you rotate the space.

Figure 1.21

The User Preferences window

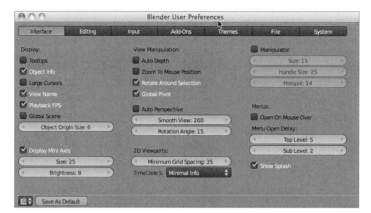

Editing Presents options for editing objects, animation curves, grease pencil sketches, and other kinds of editing. Settings for the Undo feature are also accessed in this panel. You can adjust these settings to save memory, but I recommend keeping your undo steps as high as your resources allow.

Input Presents options related to user input. You can find the options for Emulate 3 Button Mouse and Emulate Numpad in this panel. You can switch between trackball and turntable orbit styles for rotating the 3D space. Blender's default setting is Trackball, which can be disorienting for users of other 3D software that uses the more constrained turntable style of 3D orbiting.

This panel is also where you can set your preferences for hotkey combinations. The hotkeys are organized in a functionality-based tree structure. You can access the hotkey settings for each area of functionality by clicking the triangle next to the functionality label to reveal the full list of hotkeys related to that functionality. Figure 1.22 shows the hotkey settings for saving a Blender file revealed under the Window functionality list. The default hotkey for saving is Ctrl+S. As you can see in the figure, both the pressed key and the help keys can be edited in this panel, as well as some options specific to the functionality. In addition, the Python call related to this function is also shown, making this panel a handy quick reference for scripters also.

Add-Ons Enables you to select which add-ons will be available in your Blender environment. Add-ons provide additional functionality coded in Python, and they integrate seamlessly into the Blender interface. For example, some mesh add-ons provide a selection of additional mesh primitives available through the Add menu.

Themes Enables you to tweak the colors and some other properties of visual elements of Blender. The visual elements of all editor types can be adjusted in this way.

File Enables access to file-related preferences including default file paths and options for how many backup versions to save and how often to autosave.

System Gives you access to some miscellaneous prefer-ences such as sound-handling preferences, OpenGL lighting and clipping in the 3D window, the color picker type, custom weight paint range, and lower-level operating-system-related preferences. As a new Blender user, you will probably not have much cause to vary these settings from the defaults.

Figure 1.22

Editing the hotkey combination for saving a Blender file

After you have the configuration the way you like it, press Ctrl+U or click Save As Default at the bottom of the User Preferences window. When you do this, the *entire current state* of Blender (except for the User Preferences window itself) will be saved as the default state when you open Blender. This means any model or scene in your 3D viewport will also be loaded as the default state of Blender. To return your start state to the original default, choose File → Load Factory Settings in the Info header. You can save that state again by pressing Ctrl+U.

You should experiment with user options. There's a lot to play around with, in terms of look and feel. As long as you don't press Ctrl+U, all settings will return to their defaults on your next startup. For the rest of this book, we assume most things to be in their default configuration, and the figures will all show the default theme.

Now that you've looked at the basics of the Blender interface and the datablock system, you're ready to get your hands dirty and begin modeling.

CHAPTER 2

Working with Meshes

In Blender as in many 3D animation programs, the basic object type in character modeling is the mesh. Two of Blender's main tools of character animation, armatures and shape keys, are best suited for use with meshes. For this reason, although you can use other modeling techniques—such as NURBS, Bezier curves, and metaballs—animated characters that use these tools are typically created as polygon meshes in Blender. Perhaps because of this, Blender's mesh modeling tools have attained a higher level of usability than its other modeling tools.

This chapter covers Blender's main tools for organic mesh modeling. You'll look at several different approaches, and by the end you will have built a fairly complex character mesh, which you will texture, rig, and animate in later chapters. If you prefer to skip these modeling tutorials and get straight to the next step, check the DVD for the appropriate `.blend` file to start with. The tutorials in this chapter should result in the same mesh that you will find in the `CB-Model-base_mesh.blend` file, so you can use that file to start on the next chapter's tutorials. However, if you are interested in learning to model characters in Blender, follow the tutorials in this chapter before moving on, and use the `.blend` file as an additional reference.

- ■ **Polygons and Subsurfacing**

- ■ **Poly-by-Poly Modeling and Box Modeling**

- ■ **Common Problems and Solutions in Mesh Modeling**

Polygons and Subsurfacing

Polygon modeling refers to modeling shapes defined as collections of vertices connected by straight edges, which in turn form polygonal faces. These shapes are called *meshes*. Editing a mesh involves adding, removing, or moving vertices, edges, and faces.

The time it takes the computer to calculate 3D information about a mesh depends primarily on the number of vertices (*verts*) in the mesh. Therefore, you should use the fewest possible vertices to accurately represent the desired shape of your mesh. You also want to do this because meshes with fewer vertices are easier to edit. If you have too many vertices, it becomes difficult to keep the surfaces of your mesh as smooth and even as with fewer vertices.

Because you need a large number of flat polygons and straight edges to give the illusion of rounded, organic surfaces, Blender uses another method of calculating the surface of a mesh based on its polygon structure, called Catmull-Clark subdivision surfacing (also called *subsurfacing* or simply *subsurfing*). Subsurfacing in this manner involves computing a curvature based on the polygon structure to greatly increase the appearance of smoothness of the surface. The calculations are simple enough that the computer can do them on the fly much more quickly than it would take it to keep track of an equivalent number of real vertices.

Let's return to the two objects from Chapter 1, Cube and Cone, and their associated meshes. Select the Cube object. You do subsurfacing in Blender by adding a subsurface modifier to a Mesh object. On the Modifiers tab in the Buttons window, click Add Modifier, and select Subdivision Surface from the drop-down, as shown in Figure 2.1.

As you can see, with the subsurf modifier turned on with its view subdivisions value at 1, the cube's surface takes on a different, smoother shape. In the View field under Subdivisions on the subsurf modifier panel, change the value to 2. Now you have something that begins to resemble a sphere. Optimal values for subsurfacing are 2 or 3 for the View field under Subdivisions and 3 or 4 for the Render field under Subdivisions, depending on the speed of your computer. Setting subsurfacing to be smoother when you actually render is a good idea. Higher values for these fields are unnecessary for the purposes of this book and can lead to serious slowdowns and even freeze your computer.

Figure 2.1

Adding a subsurf modifier

Although the cube now looks a lot smoother than it did before, it still looks like flat surfaces forming a sphere. To change this, you do not need to add more subsurface levels. Rather, you can simply change the way Blender calculates shading, giving the illusion of a smooth surface, by selecting Smooth rather than Flat under the Shading option on the Tool Shelf of the 3D viewport, as shown in Figure 2.2. Do this on the Cube object, and you will see how much smoother it appears.

Let's try the trick from Chapter 1 again, replacing the Cube mesh data with the Cone mesh data on the Cube object. A couple of things are worth noting. First, the Cone shape is now subsurfaced. The subsurf modifier acts on the Mesh *object*, and therefore swapping in new mesh data will not change the subsurfacing. You now have a subsurfaced Cone shape.

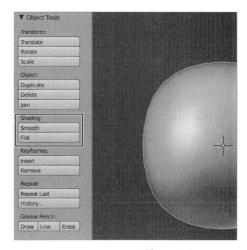

Figure 2.2

Shading options on the Tool Shelf

Second, you'll notice that this subsurfaced Cone shape doesn't look very good. At any rate, it's not what you would call smooth, as you can see in Figure 2.3. This is an illustration of a problem that one often hears about with regard to triangles and subsurfacing. Because of the nature of the subsurfacing calculation, triangles often do not subsurface smoothly, and the more elongated the triangles are, the more pronounced this problem is.

In general, conventional polygon modeling wisdom holds that triangles are to be avoided. As you can see in Figure 2.4, the same cone subsurfaces much more smoothly when you make some cuts and change the geometry to quads. In fact, equilateral triangles subsurface reasonably well in many situations, but the reality of mesh deformations means that any triangle on your mesh in a place that is animated cannot stay equilateral all the time. For this reason, triangles should be avoided in visible places on your mesh that you intend to animate. At the time of this writing, polygons of more than four sides, known as *n-gons*, are not supported in Blender. A project is underway to extend Blender's mesh modeling capabilities in this and other ways, but currently, quads and triangles are the only polygons that Blender supports. That means you'll be using a lot of quads.

Figure 2.3

A subsurfaced cone made of triangles

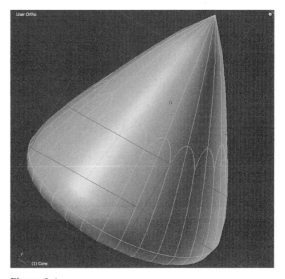

Figure 2.4

A cone modeled with quads

Blender Modifier System

As you just saw in the case of subsurfacing, you can impose certain qualities on a Mesh object by using modifiers. Modifiers let you alter an object in a nondestructive way. If you remove a modifier from a mesh, the mesh simply returns to its unmodified state. A wide variety of modifiers are available to create special effects, but in this book you will mainly be interested in the modifiers most pertinent to character modeling and animation. These modifiers include the following:

Subdivision Surfaces This modifier, often referred to as *subsurf*, adds virtual subdivisions to a mesh according to one of two algorithms. The default method of subsurfing uses an algorithm called *Catmull-Clark* to create rounded, smoothly curved surfaces from low polygon meshes. This method of subsurfacing is very important for organic mesh modeling.

Mirror This modifier displays a virtual mirror image of the mesh across a selected axis (the default is x). Mirrors are very useful for modeling symmetrical objects such as faces and bodies.

Lattice This modifier associates a mesh with a Lattice object, allowing for simple deformations of the mesh. A Lattice modifier is often used for distorting the shape of a mesh in unrealistic ways, and it is useful for cartoon effects such as stretching and squashing and bugging eyes.

Armature This modifier associates a Mesh object with an armature object for figure posing. Armatures enable more precise and constrained deformations than a Lattice modifier.

Mesh Deform Like Lattice and Armature modifiers, the Mesh Deform modifier is a tool for deforming a mesh. Mesh Deform modifiers let you deform one mesh by means of another Mesh object. The effect obtained with a Mesh Deform modifier is something between a Lattice and an Armature.

The concept of modifiers has expanded in recent Blender versions to include things that are usually dealt with elsewhere in the interface. For example, physics simulations and particles are all processed by Blender now as modifiers, but their settings are controlled in their own panels. They are modifiers insofar as their effect on the mesh is calculated according to the order they appear in the modifier stack, which you will learn more about in later chapters. Modifiers are also "nondestructive" in the sense that they can be deleted, leaving the mesh in its original, unmodified state.

The "traditional" modifiers you deal with directly as modifiers share certain options. You can toggle the display of the modified form of the mesh with these buttons, which are located to the immediate right of the modifier's name.

The leftmost button toggles the display of the modified mesh in the rendered view, the next button to the right toggles the display in the 3D view window, the second button from the right specifically toggles the display of the modifier in the 3D view in Edit mode, and the rightmost button toggles whether the modifier is applied to the *editing cage* (the term for the visual representation of edges and vertices that you edit in Edit mode).

Most modifiers also have the options to copy and apply the modifier. The Copy function creates an identical modifier at the same place in the modifier stack as the original. The Apply function deletes the modifier and applies its effects to the mesh, creating a new, unmodified mesh, which is identical to the modified form of the original mesh. Be careful with this option. You usually do not need to apply a subsurface modifier, for example, and you should apply a Mirror modifier only when you have finished all edits that need mirroring.

As you create modifiers, they appear in order in a stack, which determines the order in which the modifiers' effects are calculated. The up and down arrow buttons on the Modifier panel let you move the modifier up or down in the stack.

NURBS MODELING

Nonuniform rational B-splines (NURBS) are a way to define curved lines and surfaces that are more precise, more compact, and more restrictive in terms of modeling than subsurfaced meshes. NURBS is an older method for creating organic shapes using computer graphics, but since the rise of subsurface modeling, NURBS modeling has fallen from favor somewhat for character modeling purposes, depending upon the specific 3D application. Current uses of NURBS tend to focus on industrial design, where precision is more important than it is in character animation. (Precision measurement in general is not a strong suit of Blender, making it inadequate as a specialized CAD application.)

Blender has NURBS modeling capabilities, but it has much better support for mesh modeling. The only real reasons for a character modeler to use NURBS in Blender are to apply specific, personally preferred modeling methods and to follow habits acquired using more NURBS-oriented software. Another drawback of using NURBS for character modeling in Blender is the limitation on armature modification available for NURBS. Although NURBS surfaces can take armature modifiers, you cannot create vertex groups or do weight painting on NURBS surfaces, and armatures are limited to using envelopes to influence the surface. I'll talk more about what this means and why it is so restrictive in Chapter 4. For now, it should suffice to say that meshes in Blender can be much more responsive to armatures than NURBS surfaces are.

There has been talk about improving Blender's NURBS editing functionality for years, but I wouldn't advise anybody to hold their breath for it. Even if such improvements are made, it is unlikely that this would significantly affect how character modeling is best done in Blender.

You can create NURBS primitives by pressing Shift+A to add an object and selecting Surface or Curve. The tools available for modeling with NURBS are broadly analogous to those available for mesh modeling (although there are far fewer).

Modifier Effects

To see an example of how the resulting mesh can differ according to the order in which the modifiers are applied, create a new file in Blender, and select the default cube. On the Modifiers tab, choose Add Modifier → Mirror.

On the Modifier panel, select the Clipping option. Now enter Edit mode. By default, all vertices should be selected. Move the entire cube one Blender unit (BU) to the right along the x-axis. To do this, press G and X in succession, and hold down Ctrl while you move the object with the mouse to turn on incremental snapping.

As you move the cube to the right, you will see the cube's mirror image moving to the left. When you have moved the cube half its own width, the cube and its mirror image will be flush with each other, as in Figure 2.5(a).

Figure 2.5

The effect of modifiers on meshes: (a) a mirrored cube; (b) the cube mirrored and then subsurfaced; (c) the cube subsurfaced and then mirrored; (d) the mesh with the modifiers applied

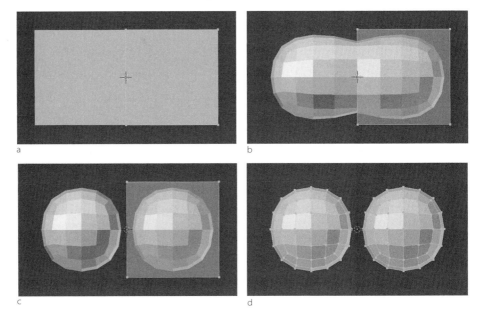

Now, add a subsurface modifier in the same way you added the Mirror modifier. Set the View subdivision level to 2. You should end up with the peanut-like shape you see in Figure 2.5(b). This is because the mesh being subsurfaced is not the original cube but the mirror-modified cube.

If you want to subsurface the original cube and mirror-modify the resulting mesh, you need to bump the subsurface modifier up so it is calculated before the Mirror modifier. Do this by clicking the up arrow on the subsurface modifier (or the down arrow on the Mirror modifier). The resulting modified mesh, as you can see in Figure 2.5(c), is two separate sphere shapes.

You can now try applying the modifiers. You must be in Object mode to apply modifiers, so tab into Object mode first. Also, be sure to apply the top modifier first, or your results may be unexpected. If you apply both of these modifiers, you wind up with a single Mesh object, whose mesh consists of two sphere shapes, as in Figure 2.5(c). If you edit this object, you will see that each vertex is an independent, fully editable, real vertex.

You will look more closely at the various modifiers and their uses later in the book.

VERTEX SIZE

You might notice that the vertices shown in the illustrations here are larger than the ones on your computer. This is done for legibility in print, but if you want to change the vertex size on your own computer, you can do this on the Themes tab of the User Preferences window. Scroll down to the bottom of the Themes settings to find the Vertex Size field.

Poly-by-Poly Modeling and Box Modeling

You can take several approaches to modeling. Broadly speaking, the various approaches fall into two main classes: *poly-by-poly modeling* and *box modeling.* In poly-by-poly modeling, the modeler starts with a small portion of a model—which could be a polygon, an edge, or even just a vertex—and works outward from this starting point using extrusion and other tools. In box modeling, the modeler begins with a simple 3D object, often a cube, and uses subdivision and cuts to mold the shape into the desired model.

These approaches are not mutually exclusive. In fact, when you construct even a marginally complex model, you usually incorporate elements of both approaches. All polygon modeling uses extrusion and subdivision, so drawing a clear distinction between these modeling approaches is of limited value. Nevertheless, although it is largely a matter of personal preference, whether you choose to start with a cube to build your model or start with a single polygon or vertex will determine the subsequent steps you need to take to create your model. Because the two methods differ in the emphasis they place on various tools, it is good practice to go through concrete examples of both.

For the remainder of this chapter, we will work on step-by-step tutorials, in which you'll follow instructions to create models. It's important to realize that the specific steps and their order in these tutorials are arbitrary. For the most part, I chose steps for ease of explanation. In reality, mesh modeling is no more a strict step-by-step endeavor than painting a picture or sculpting in clay. When you do go on to do your own models, you can forget all about these specific steps. The important goals for learning to model are to master the tools to the point that you can create whatever kind of mesh topology you want and to understand mesh topology and its relationship to deformations so that you know what kind of topology will work for the kind of model you want to make. So, wing it here if you need to, and focus on getting to know the tools. Your study of organic topology for animation will take you well beyond the covers of this book and will involve a lot of firsthand experience of your own as well as studying models with good mesh topology whenever you can.

Modeling a Human Head with Poly-by-Poly Modeling

In poly-by-poly modeling, you are free to choose where you place vertices at the beginning of the modeling process. In this example, you can trace the outline of a photograph closely.

First you need to set up the work areas so that you can see the background images you want to use to guide your modeling. For this tutorial, you'll mostly want to look at the model from the front and from the left side, so you'll need two 3D viewports for that. Once you've opened Blender, split the 3D viewport vertically by clicking your mouse in the upper-right corner of the 3D viewport window and dragging to the left, as you learned in Chapter 1. With your mouse over the leftmost viewport, press 1 on the number pad to change the view to front view, and then press 5 on the number pad to toggle this view into orthogonal view. When editing, you'll usually find orthogonal view easier to work with than perspective view.

Now put your mouse over the right 3D viewport and press 3 on the number pad followed by 5 on the number pad to get an orthogonal view from the user's (your) right side. Your 3D viewports should look as shown in Figure 2.6. The label in the upper-left corner of the right window reads "Right Ortho." It's a little confusing, because this is in fact a view of the cube's left side, but the labeling is based on the viewer's perspective. You can enter the reverse view of each of the number pad views by holding Ctrl while you press the number pad key.

To add a background image to a 3D viewport, you need to access the Properties Shelf for the viewport, which you can do either by clicking the small round button in the upper-right corner of the viewport or by toggling the shelf with the N key. In the Properties Shelf, you'll find a Background Images check box. Drill down into the panels here with the triangular icons until you've found the Open button, as shown in Figure 2.7.

Figure 2.6

Two viewports in front and side orthogonal views

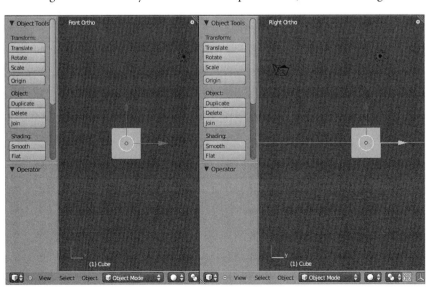

Click Open, and you will see a file browser. Navigate to the image you want on your hard drive, and click Open. For the left viewport, use the image front.jpg from the book's companion DVD. Make adjustments to the X offset value on the Background Images tab so that the centerline of the 3D viewport is as close as possible to the middle of the face, as shown in Figure 2.8, where the X offset value has been adjusted to 0.1. For the right viewport, follow the same steps but use side.jpg. The resulting viewports should look like Figure 2.9. Note that in the figure I have hidden both the Properties Shelf and the Tool Shelf for both viewports. You can toggle these shelves' visibility with the N key and the T key, respectively, or just drag them out of view with the mouse.

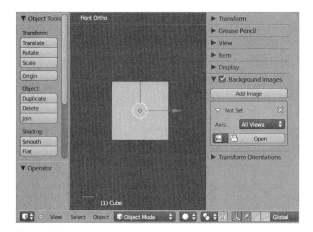

Figure 2.7

Accessing the Background Image panel in the viewport Properties shelf

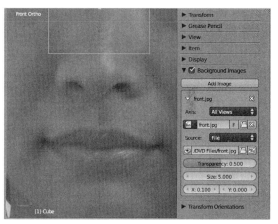

Figure 2.8

Adjusting the X offset value of the background image to center the face

Figure 2.9

3D viewports with back-ground images

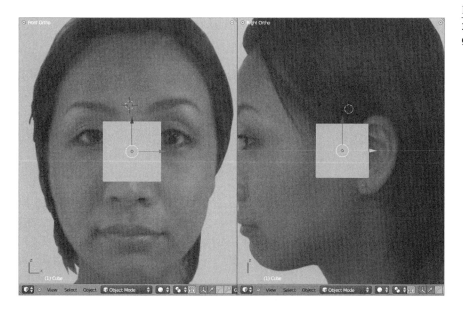

Because you will begin modeling with a Mirror modifier, the model will be perfectly symmetrical. Real faces are not perfectly symmetrical, so over the course of the modeling, it might be necessary to adjust this X offset to account for the difference and to keep the model as close to the overall face as possible. Nonsymmetrical modeling has to be done later.

If you plan to create your own background images, keep in mind that Blender calculates the default size based upon the width of the photograph. For this reason, it is simplest to work with photographs with the same height and width. The best thing is to crop your background image in an image manipulation program such as Gimp or Photoshop in such a way that the eye line, nose, and lips line up as closely as possible. There will almost always be inconsistencies in the view caused by perspective and slight shifts in the position of the subject. Another alternative is to put both front and side views on the same image, as you'll see done in the Captain Blender tutorial later in this chapter.

Now that you have the background image in place and the views organized, you can get started modeling. You won't be using the manipulator while modeling, so you can toggle it off in the 3D viewport header to get it out of the way. Pressing Ctrl+spacebar will also toggle the manipulator visibility.

To edit the mesh, first select the Mesh object by right-clicking it, and then tab into Edit mode. The cube's vertices are now selectable and editable.

You'll begin by deleting the back face of the cube, leaving you with just the front face pane. This is best done in the side view viewport, in transparent, or in *wireframe* view mode. To toggle wireframe view mode, press the Z key, which toggles between wireframe and solid display mode.

HOTKEY: Z key toggles between wireframe and solid display mode.

When you are in wireframe mode, vertices that would not be visible in solid mode are visible and selectable. The A key toggles selection between all vertices and no vertices. To select the back face of the cube, first ensure that no vertices are selected by toggling with the A key, and then press the B key to initialize box selection and drag your mouse so as to surround the vertices with the selection box. The resulting selection will look like Figure 2.10.

HOTKEY: B key initializes box selection.

Select all vertices with the A key. Still in the side view viewport, scale the selected portion of the mesh down by pressing the S key and moving the mouse.

HOTKEY: A key toggles all items in the view selected and unselected.

HOTKEY: S key scales the selection.

When you have scaled to the size you want, click to confirm the transformation. Then move the selection to the bridge of the nose, as shown in Figure 2.11, by pressing the G key and moving it with the mouse. Click to confirm the transformation.

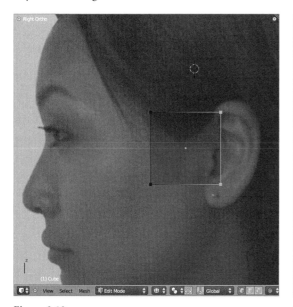

Figure 2.10

Selecting the rear face of the cube

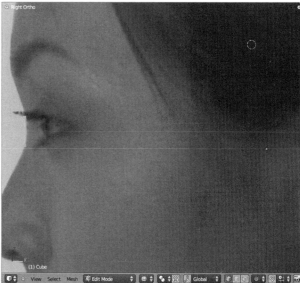

Figure 2.11

The selection scaled and moved

The process of rotating, scaling, and grabbing (moving/translating) vertices, edges, or faces is analogous to performing those transformations on objects. The hotkeys are R, S, and G, respectively, and you can constrain the transformations to the x-, y-, or z-axis by pressing the corresponding hotkeys. As in the case of objects, the left mouse button confirms the transformation, and the right mouse button cancels it.

When modeling things such as faces or human bodies that are largely symmetrical, it helps to be able to model only one half and to let Blender mirror the model automatically. You do this by using the Mirror modifier mentioned previously.

You can activate the Mirror modifier now by clicking Add Modifier in the Modifier properties panel, as shown in Figure 2.12. When the drop-down menu appears, select Mirror, as shown in Figure 2.13. Leave most of the Mirror modifier settings at their default values, but select Clipping, as shown in Figure 2.14. This option clips the seam between the two mirrored halves of the model together, preventing the model from splitting or overlapping along the center line. As you will see later in the modeling process, there are times when you want this and times when you don't.

In the 3D viewport, looking at the scene from the front view, select the vertices of the plane with the A key if they aren't already selected, and move the plane to your right, away from the center by pressing the G key and dragging them with the mouse, as shown in Figure 2.15. You will see the mirrored mesh move the opposite direction. Note that no matter how far you pull the vertices from the center, the centermost vertical edge between the mirrored half remains clipped to the center. This happens because Clipping is active on the Mirror modifier.

Now you'll begin modeling with extrusion. This is the heart of poly-by-poly modeling. Make sure all vertices are deselected with the A key, and then select the top edge of the plane by holding the Shift key and right-clicking the two top vertices. In the side view window, extrude this top edge by pressing the E key. Extrude again to follow the contour of the forehead, as shown in Figure 2.16.

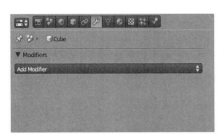

Figure 2.12
The Modifier properties panel

Figure 2.13
Adding the Mirror modifier

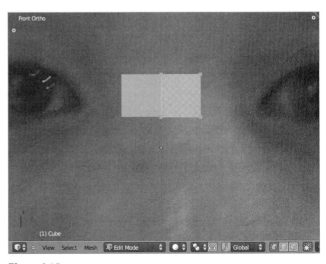

Figure 2.14
Mirror modifier settings

Figure 2.15
Moving the mirrored plane away from the center

HOTKEY: E key extrudes new geometry from selected geometry.

Next, do the same thing with the bottom edge of the plane, extruding downward 10 times to follow the contours of the face down past the chin, as shown in Figure 2.17. Do these steps in the side view, but keep an eye on the front view to make sure everything is where it should be from all angles.

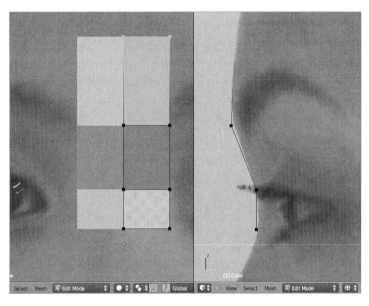

Figure 2.16

Extruding the top edge over the forehead

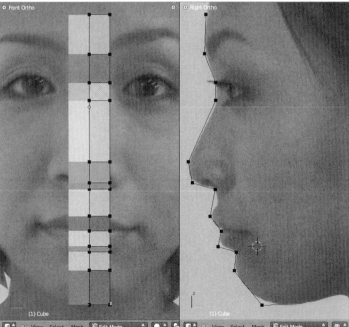

Figure 2.17

Extruding the bottom edge over the lower part of the face

In the front view, adjust the position of the vertices around the mouth. Select the single vertex at the top edge of the lip, and extrude (E key or Ctrl+click) four new vertices around the edge of the mouth from the top of the lip. You can add an edge between any two vertices by selecting both vertices and pressing the F key. Do this to connect the last of the four extruded vertices to the bottom edge of the mouth. Figure 2.18 shows the result.

HOTKEY: F key in Edit mode creates an edge between two selected vertices and creates a face when three or four vertices are selected.

Figure 2.18

Modeling the shape of the mouth

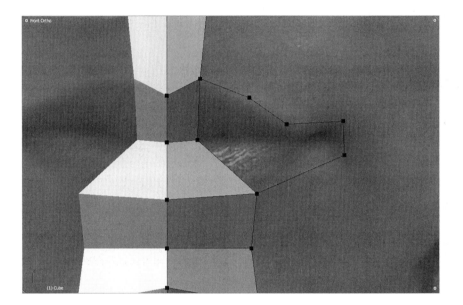

When you are extruding the lip outline, you might not see your changes mirrored on the left side of the model. If this is the case, you are probably viewing in Solid mode, which displays only mirrored faces. Pressing the Z key shows the wireframe model properly mirrored. If the modifier is set to apply to the editing cage during Edit mode, then the wireframe model will always be visible.

With the drop-down in the header of the 3D viewport, activate Proportional Editing with a Sharp falloff so that the selected icons appear as shown here.

Proportional editing causes unselected vertices within an area of influence to respond to edits on selected vertices. The influence diminishes according to the curve of the falloff type you select for the Proportional editing tool. The area of influence is represented by a circle and can be adjusted with your mouse wheel. You can turn proportional editing on and off with the O key and iterate through falloff types by pressing Shift+O.

With proportional editing active, select the vertices at the corner of the mouth and pull them back along the y-axis by pressing the G key to grab them and then the Y key to constrain the translation to the y-axis. As you can see in Figure 2.19, the vertices of the entire mouth should move in conformance with the proportional editing curve. If too many or too few other vertices move, adjust the circle of influence of the proportional editing tool with your mouse wheel.

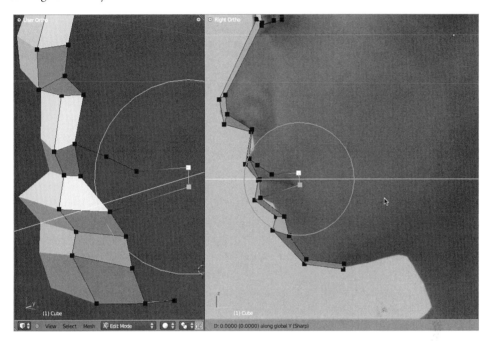

Figure 2.19

Translating the edge of the mouth along the y-axis with proportional editing

Now that you know how to extrude vertices with the E key or Ctrl+click and how to create an edge between two vertices with the F key, you should have no trouble adding some more geometry to the mesh.

Disable proportional editing, and add the vertices and edges shown in Figure 2.20. Be sure to keep an eye on both the front and side views so that the shape stays accurate from all angles. From time to time it's a good idea to check your work from other angles, as shown in Figure 2.21.

Hold the middle mouse button to rotate your view, and then press 1 or 3 on the number pad to get back to the front or side view, respectively. When you leave the orthogonal views, your background image will disappear, but don't worry, it will appear again when you get back into the front and side view modes.

Take note of the geometry you've begun to construct at this point. You have already established several important features, which are important regardless of what modeling technique you use. Both the eyes and the mouth are already being constructed of loops. As you continue to model, you will keep the eyes and mouth in this form. When you model a different character later using box modeling, you will still make sure that the mouth and eyes are loops and that the loops extend and overlap in a way that includes the nose and cheeks within an unbroken pattern of loops. This is important from an animation perspective. You might be able to get away with different underlying geometry for a still model, but if you intend to animate facial expressions, you'll find that the human face is unforgiving in terms of the necessary geometry.

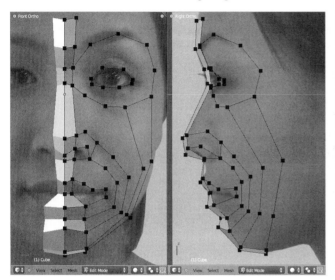

Figure 2.20
Adding vertices and edges

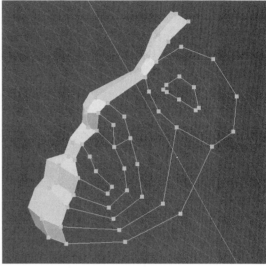

Figure 2.21
Checking the work from various angles

You need to make the eye outline now. To do this, create a vert in front view by Ctrl+clicking with no verts selected, as shown in Figure 2.22. You can extrude from this vert to create the outline of the eye, as in Figure 2.23. Complete the last edge by selecting the first and last vertices and pressing the F key. Once again, the number of verts shown is important because you will later need to connect the eye to rest of the face, so be sure to follow the example exactly.

Figure 2.22

Adding a single vertex at the inner corner of the eye

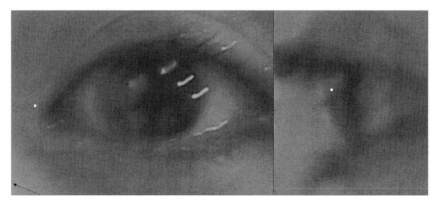

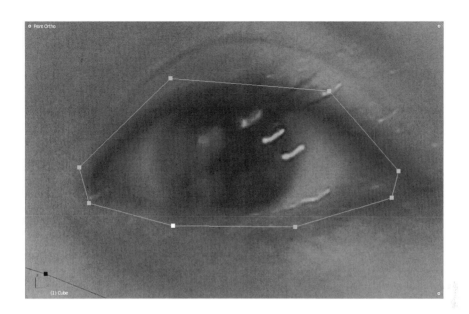

Figure 2.23

Outlining the eye with vertices

GEOMETRY, TOPOLOGY, AND LOOPS

The term *geometry* refers to the vertices that make up a mesh and specifically their placement in the 3D space. The term *topology* refers to the structure created by the edges and faces that connect the vertices. Identical-looking meshes can have different underlying topological structures, and for beginning modelers it is easy to get caught up in making the shape look right, at the expense of paying attention to the actual structure. When making models for animation, however, it is very important to consider the topology of the mesh because it will determine how the mesh deforms when you begin to add shapes or poses.

Topology is important because of the way the edges and vertices provide "tension" by holding the surface in place. Think of an umbrella: an open umbrella is shaped something like a hemisphere, made of cloth and held in its shape by a topology of edges extending from the tip. You can construct a similar hemisphere of cloth by using concentric rings, for example, but such a structure clearly does not fold like an ordinary umbrella. This is somewhat analogous to how edges influence the deformation of a mesh. To get the correct topology, you must consider what deformations you want from the mesh.

Loops are continuous sequences of edges (*edge loops*) or faces (*face loops*) that define the surface of a subdivided form. Loops might completely encircle some section of the mesh, but this is not necessarily the case. Not all edges or faces are part of a loop. You can select edge loops in their entirety by using Alt+RMB; you should try selecting a few edges in your model in this way to get a sense for what Blender recognizes as edge loops. Loops are very important in facial modeling; without correct loop structure in the face, it is very difficult to get good facial deformations. Good loop structure is especially critical in the mouth and nose area.

For the best deformations, the flow of the loops should approximately follow the shape of the muscles of the face because they determine how the shape of the face will change and the directions along which the skin will stretch. As you progress through this tutorial, you should pay close attention to the way edges and faces create loops. Further study of facial anatomy and musculature can also be very helpful.

Fix the shape of the eye outline to follow the eye in the background image by translating the appropriate verts along the y-axis, as with the rest of the face.

Next, begin to fill in the faces. To fill in a face, you select its four vertices and press the F key, as shown in Figure 2.24.

Figure 2.24

Adding a face between four vertices

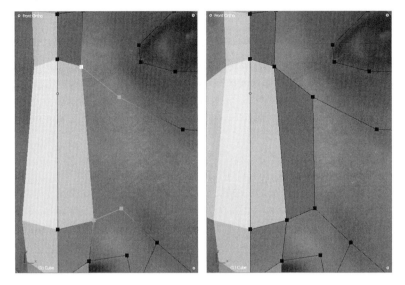

Figure 2.25

More faces filled in

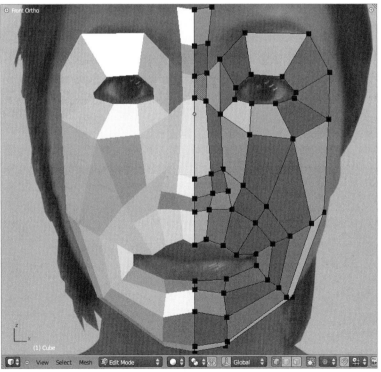

The faces you fill in will also appear in the mirrored portion of the model. Fill in the faces, four verts at a time. Fill in the faces as shown in Figure 2.25.

At any point in the process, you can add a Subdivision Surface (subsurf) modifier to generate a smoother, more rounded mesh. In most cases, you can model equally easily with or without subsurfing, so it is a matter of personal preference at what point you add the modifier. Try adding it now.

To add the subsurf modifier, go to the same Modifier Properties area in which you added the Mirror modifier, and select Subdivision Surface from the Add Modifier drop-down menu, as shown in Figure 2.26. The modifier will appear in the modifier stack below the Mirror modifier, as shown in Figure 2.27. In the fields below the Subdivisions label, change the View value to 2 and the Render value to 3. These values

Figure 2.26

Adding a subsurf modifier

determine how smoothly the model will be displayed in the 3D viewport and during rendering. The values 2 and 3, respectively, are usually ideal.

When you add a subsurf modifier after editing a mesh's geometry, you may find that ugly black artifacts appear, such as those shown in Figure 2.28. The location of these artifacts depends on factors such as the order in which the faces were created, so it's likely that artifacts on your model will be different. These artifacts are caused by inconsistent normals; adjoining faces are facing opposite directions. To fix this, enter Edit mode, select all the vertices with the A key, and press Ctrl+N to make the normals consistent.

Figure 2.27

Settings on the subsurf modifier

Figure 2.28

Artifacts caused by inconsistent normals

Continue with the model by extruding the edges of the forehead, as shown in Figure 2.29, and the side of the face, as shown in Figure 2.30. Connect the geometry with a face, as shown in Figure 2.31.

Figure 2.29

Extruding the fore-head geometry

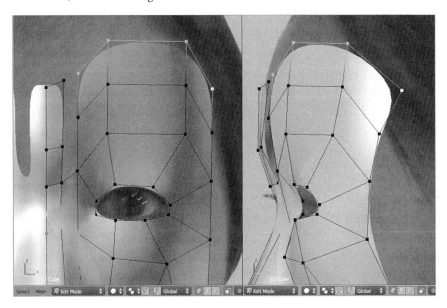

Figure 2.30

Extruding geometry for the side of the face

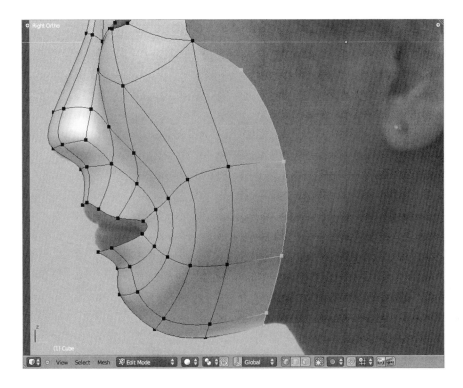

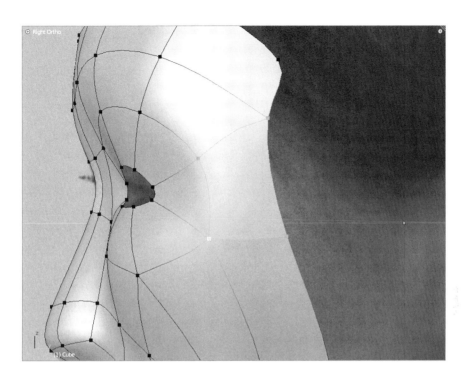

Figure 2.31
Adding a face at the temple area

Now turn to modeling the nose. Begin by selecting the faces shown in Figure 2.32 and extruding them with the E key, as shown in Figure 2.33.

To form the nostrils, you need to adjust your Mirror modifier settings. Currently, you have Clipping selected. With Clipping selected, mirrored faces extrude together, as they did when you extruded the tip of the nose a moment ago.

Figure 2.32
Selecting the faces that make up the tip of the nose

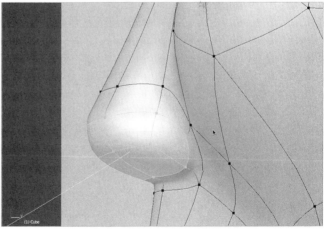

Figure 2.33
Extruding the tip of the nose

For the nostrils, however, you want to extrude mirrored faces as individual faces. So, uncheck Clipping in the Mirror modifier properties panel, and then extrude the faces as shown in Figure 2.34 to begin forming the nostrils. Scale them down slightly. Extrude again, viewing from the side as shown in Figure 2.35, and pull the inner faces up and inward. Scale them down slightly to complete the basic modeling of the nostrils. Once you've done this, go back to the Mirror modifier properties and turn Clipping back on.

When you have the basic topology done, you can push the vertices around until you're satisfied with the shape of the nose, which should look something like Figure 2.36.

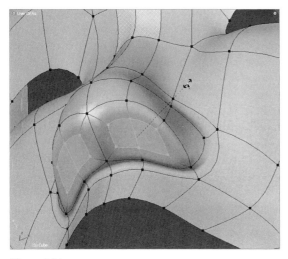

Figure 2.34
Extruding and scaling the nostrils

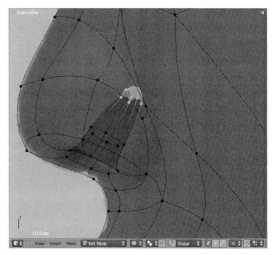

Figure 2.35
Extruding the nostrils inward

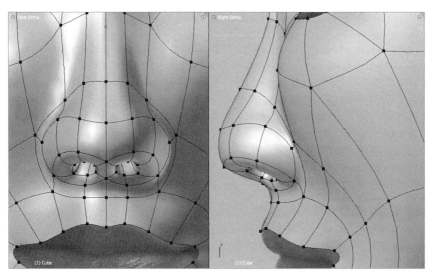

Figure 2.36
The finished nose

Next you'll turn to the lips. To model the lips, you'll use the 3D cursor as a pivot for scaling. To place the 3D cursor where you want it, select the middle vertices at the top and bottom edge of the lips, and then press Shift+S to display the snap menu and choose Cursor To Selection, as shown in Figure 2.37. Be careful not to inadvertently place your 3D cursor somewhere else by clicking. If you do this, you'll need to select these vertices again and snap the 3D cursor back where you want it.

HOTKEY: Shift+S key brings up the Snap menu.

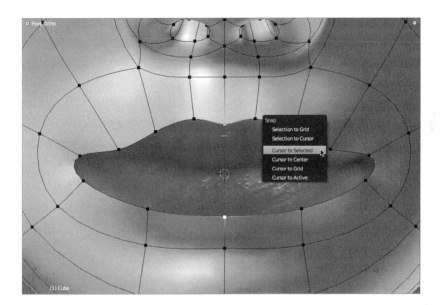

Figure 2.37

Snapping the 3D cursor to the point between two vertices

Select the edge loop around the lips by holding the Alt key and right-clicking any edge in the edge loop, and then extrude a total of three times to create the lip geometry shown in Figure 2.38. Each time you extrude, you will need to scale down slightly by pressing the S key and then scale down slightly more along the z-axis (vertical) by pressing the S key followed by the Z key. Move the vertices as necessary to create a pleasing shape for the lips.

To model the eyes, begin by cutting a loop around the eye using Ctrl+R, as shown in Figure 2.39. Then extrude the edge of the eye three times, as shown in Figure 2.40. The sharp edge of the eyelid is formed by extruding, scaling down slightly, and then extruding again and translating along the y-axis slightly. The last extrusion brings the edge farther into the head where it will be hidden by the eyeball.

HOTKEY: Ctrl+R initializes the Loop Cut tool in Edit mode.

Figure 2.38

Extruding, scaling, and translating edge loops to form the lips

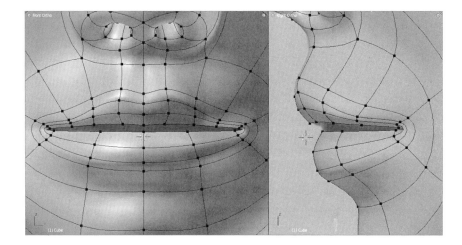

Figure 2.39

Cutting a new loop around the eye

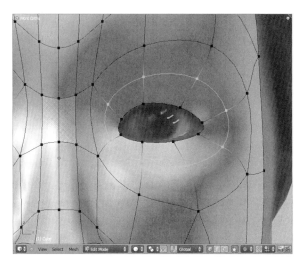

Figure 2.40

Extruding the loop of the eyelids

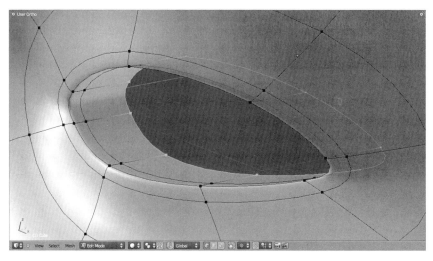

You can't do much more modeling around the eye area without knowing exactly where they eyeball will be positioned, so now is a good time to add the eyeballs. Do this in Object mode so the eyeballs will be a separate object from the head mesh. In the front-view 3D viewport, add a sphere by pressing Shift+A and selecting UV Sphere. Set the values for Segments and Rings at 12 in the fields on the Tool Shelf to the left of the 3D viewport, and select Align To View, as shown in Figure 2.41. If the object is not already centered, then center it by pressing Alt+G. Alt+G places the object so that its center point is in the origin of the 3D space.

HOTKEY: Alt+G clears the transformation for the selection.

Add a Mirror modifier to the sphere, leaving Clipping off. Add a subsurf modifier to the eyeballs also, with the same settings as the one on the head mesh. In Edit mode, scale the mesh down and move it into place, as shown in Figure 2.42. The eyeballs will probably not fit perfectly in the face, but place them where you think they belong. You will need to enter Object mode, select the head mesh, and enter Edit mode to edit the mesh around the eyes in order to make the face fit the eyeballs properly, as shown in Figure 2.43.

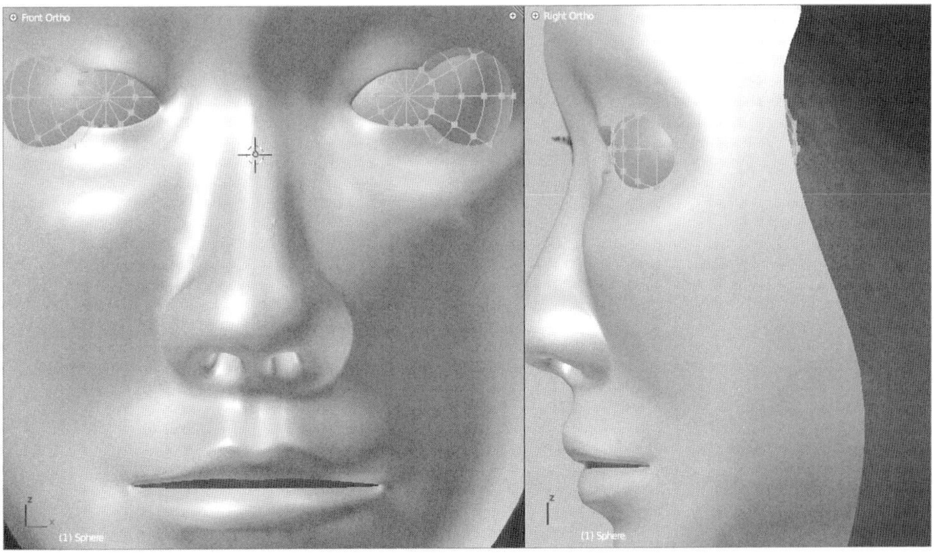

Figure 2.41

Adding a sphere for the eyeballs

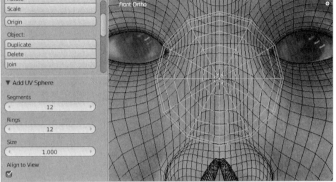

Figure 2.42

Mirroring and positioning the eyeballs

Figure 2.43

**Adjusting the face
mesh to accommo-
date the eyeballs**

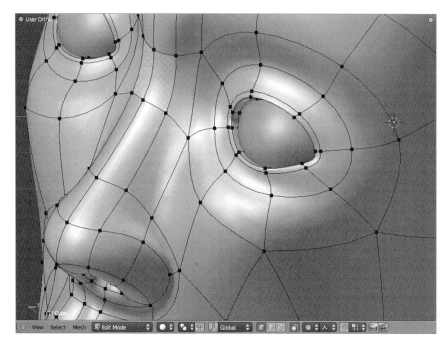

Extrude some geometry for the neck down from the chin as shown in Figure 2.44, and then add a face to the forehead as shown in Figure 2.45. With the geometry as it is so far, it is straightforward to extrude and model the remainder of the head, as shown in Figure 2.46 and Figure 2.47. When you've finished with all these steps, your model should look like Figure 2.48.

Figure 2.44

**Extruding the front
of the neck**

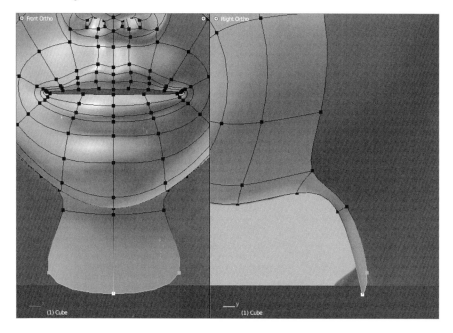

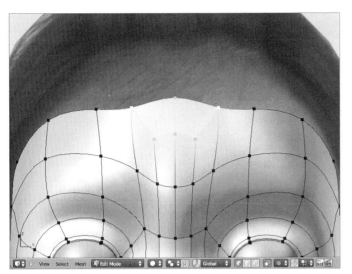

Figure 2.45
Adding a face to the forehead

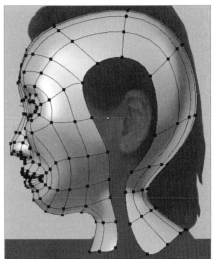

Figure 2.46
Extruding the forehead to create the shape of the head

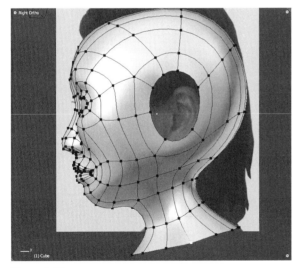

Figure 2.47
Filling in remaining geometry

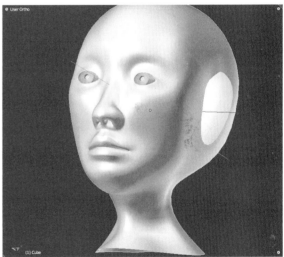

Figure 2.48
The finished model

There's not enough room in this book to go into detail about modeling ears for this character, so I'll leave that as an exercise for you to experiment on your own. Look at photographs and your own ears in the mirror, and try to create mesh ears with topology that follows the shape you want to model. There's no right way to do it; if it looks good, it is good. Also, remember that ears are not usually animated, and there are lots of hidden nooks and crannies where you can hide the odd triangle, so it's OK to take some liberties.

The Mirror modifier works by making a mirrored duplicate of the mesh you're working on. After you apply it, these vertices become real. Adding another Mirror modifier creates a new set of mirrored verts. If this is edited, the original unmirrored mesh remains unchanged, resulting in a variety of mesh problems. For this reason, it is not advisable to add a new Mirror modifier after you have already applied one. One way around this limitation is to delete half the mesh before applying the second Mirror modifier. However, it's a good idea to try to get all your symmetrical editing done before applying the Mirror modifier. If you're not sure you've done this, it might be best to save a backup file before applying the modifier.

Introducing Captain Blender: From Mild-Mannered Cube to Superhero

In the next section, you will create a whole comic book–style character using box modeling; you will then have the basis for the character model that you will work with and build on throughout the book.

Although you can use some variation of poly-by-poly modeling, because you want to focus on the overall shape of the body early on, box modeling is a good option. In contrast with the previous tutorial's example of starting with the details of the face and working outward to the shape of the head, box modeling lets you quickly work out the proportions and then focus on smaller and smaller areas of detail.

Note again that these methods are not exclusive to each other. You can model the head using poly-by-poly modeling, model a body using box modeling, and then attach the head to the body. After you become accustomed to mesh modeling in Blender, you will find your own favorite approaches to modeling various kinds of objects and characters.

Getting Started: Legs and Feet

To create Captain Blender, you'll begin in the same way you did when you modeled the face, with two 3D viewports—one in orthogonal front view and one in orthogonal side view. A small difference is that in this case, there is only one image file for the background, which includes both front and side views of Captain Blender, as shown in Figure 2.49. You'll load the same file as the background image in your front and side views, but in the side view you will need to adjust the x-axis offset for the background image so that the profile image is properly lined up with the cube when shown from the side, as shown in Figure 2.50.

Figure 2.49

Front and side view character sketches

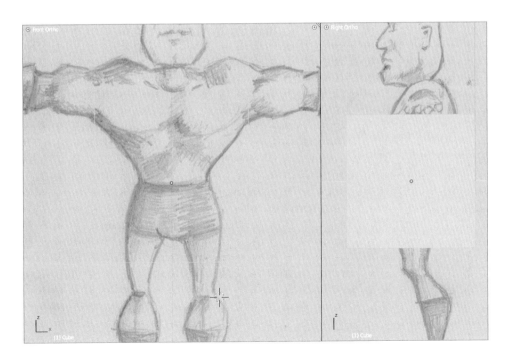

Figure 2.50

Front and right ortho views with background images

When box modeling, I find that a smooth, subdivided cube is a great way to start. Tab into Edit mode, select all the vertices of the default cube by pressing the A key, and then press the W key to bring up the mesh Specials menu. Select Subdivide Smooth, as shown in Figure 2.51. The result will be a slightly rounded subdivided cube, as shown in Figure 2.52. This shape will form the basis of the torso, so scale and translate it to fit approximately to the torso of the character. You scale with the S key and translate with the G key. Remember that you can scale along a specific axis by pressing the S key followed by the key of the axis you want to scale along. So to elongate the shape vertically, press the S key, and then press the Z key. Scale and translate the mesh as shown in Figure 2.53.

HOTKEY: W key brings up the Specials menu specific to the mode you're in.

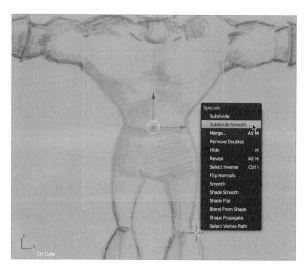

Figure 2.51

The Subdivide Smooth operator in the mesh Specials menu

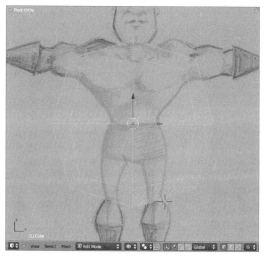

Figure 2.52

The subdivided cube

Next, you'll begin modeling a leg. To do this, you'll extrude the two faces on your right on the bottom of the subdivided cube. To select both the front-facing and back-facing faces, be sure that the mesh view is wireframe (transparent) in your front-view 3D viewport, and select the vertices using the Box Select tool. You access the Box Select tool by pressing the B key and dragging the mouse so that the dotted box surrounds the vertices you want to select. If you do this in solid (opaque) view mode, only the front-facing, visible vertices will be selected. In this case, you want the vertices on the back to be selected too. When you've selected the two faces in this way, press the E key to extrude the base of the leg, as shown in Figure 2.54.

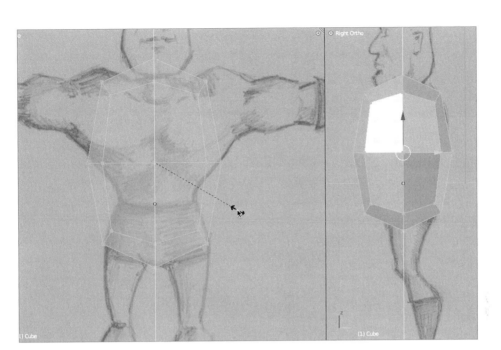

Figure 2.53

Adjusting the location and scale of the mesh

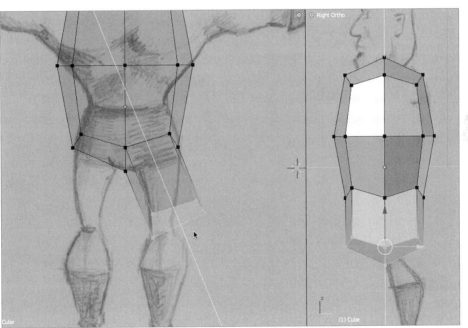

Figure 2.54

Extruding a leg

Now that you've extruded the base of one leg, it's almost time to add the Mirror modifier. Before doing this, however, you need to delete half the mesh so that the mirrored portion will not overlap. Do this by selecting the vertices on the left side using the Box Select tool and pressing the X key (select Vertices from the Delete menu), as shown in Figure 2.55. Be sure to select the vertices in wireframe view so that you delete all vertices in the front and back. Add the Mirror modifier in the same way you did for the head model in the previous section, and select the Clipping option. Figure 2.56 shows the resulting mirrored mesh.

HOTKEY: X key deletes the selection.

Figure 2.55

Deleting half the mesh

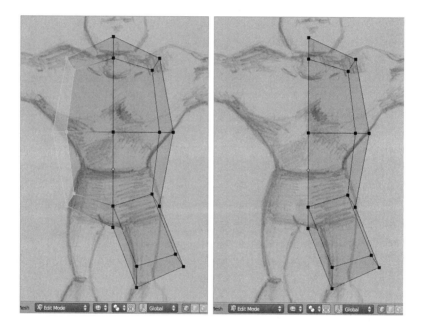

This is a good time to add the subsurf modifier also. Add the modifier in the same way you did in the previous section with the head model. In Object mode, select the Smooth shading option in the Tool Shelf, as shown in Figure 2.57. Tab back into Edit mode to continue editing the mesh.

Cut a vertical loop in the mesh using the Loop Cut tool. You access Loop Cut with Ctrl+R, and you set the location of the loop by moving your mouse over an edge perpendicular to where you want the loop cut. When you do this, a purple loop cut indicator will appear, as shown in Figure 2.58. You can adjust the number of cuts made by this tool using the mouse wheel, but just one cut is fine here. Confirming the cut with the left mouse button will cut the mesh and add the new vertices, as shown in Figure 2.59.

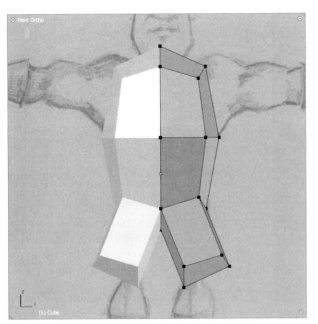

Figure 2.56
The mirrored mesh

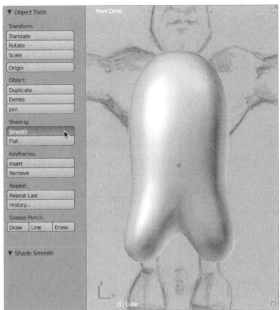

Figure 2.57
The subdivided mesh with smooth shading

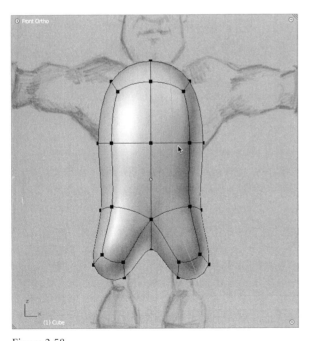

Figure 2.58
Making a loop cut

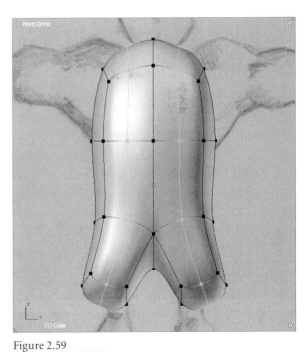

Figure 2.59
The resulting mirrored loop cut

Select the faces at the end of the extruded leg, as shown in Figure 2.60, and extrude them twice to the ankles, scaling as you go, to get them shaped, as shown in Figure 2.61. Adjust the location of the vertices of the leg to round off the shape, as shown in Figure 2.62.

Extrude three more times downward to create a base from which to extrude the foot. Select the front faces of this shape, as shown in Figure 2.63, and extrude four times forward along the y-axis. Shape the mesh as shown in Figure 2.64 to create the feet. To flatten the soles of the feet, select the bottom faces of the feet and extrude with the E key, as shown in Figure 2.65. Scale the extruded vertices to 0 along the vertical axis by pressing the S key followed by the Z key followed by 0. This has the effect of flattening the geometry vertically.

Adjust the vertices of the legs, as shown in Figure 2.66, to form the knees and calves. Remember that you can select complete edge loops by holding the Alt key while right-clicking an edge in the loop. Being able to scale, rotate, and move a whole edge loop at once is very useful in making these kinds of adjustments. In the same way, shape the rest of the legs so that you end up with something similar to what's shown in Figure 2.67.

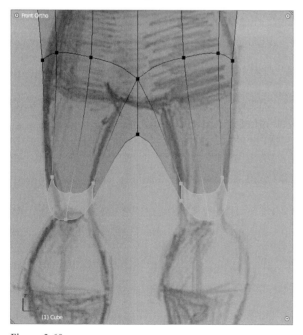

Figure 2.60

Moving the leg vertices downward

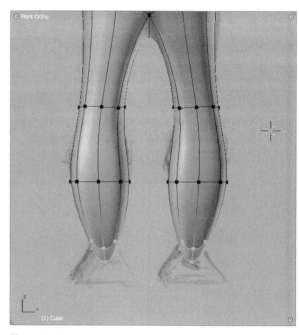

Figure 2.61

Extruding the lower legs

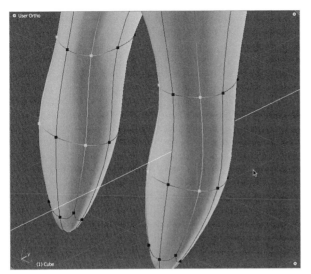

Figure 2.62

Shaping the legs

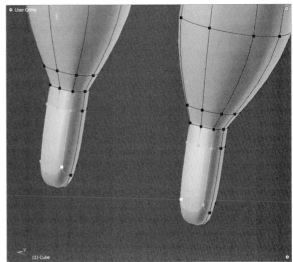

Figure 2.63

Preparing to extrude the feet

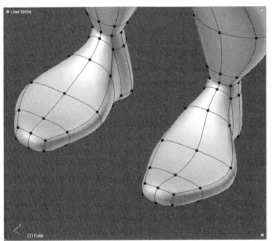

Figure 2.64

The extruded and shaped feet

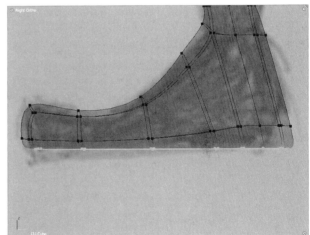

Figure 2.65

Extruding the soles of the feet

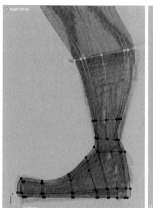
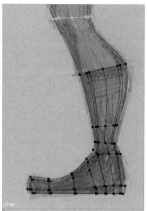

Figure 2.66

Tweaking the leg shape

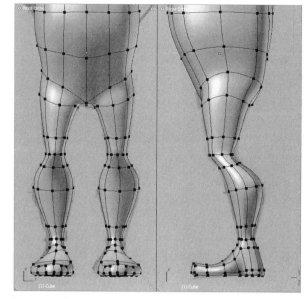

Figure 2.67

The legs so far

Torso and Arms

This section will focus on Captain Blender's upper body. As before, you will make a lot of use of loop cuts and extrusions. Keep in mind what kinds of deformations you will want from the character when you come to animating him. This decision will influence how you model the arms.

To begin with, you'll need to add some new geometry to the torso to give you something to work with. Do this by cutting a loop around the belly, as shown in Figure 2.68, and another loop around the chest, as shown in Figure 2.69. Remember that the Loop Cut tool is accessed by pressing Ctrl+R and then putting your mouse over an edge perpendicular to the loop you want to cut.

Select the eight faces that make up the front of the abdomen, extrude with the E key, and then scale with the S key, as shown in Figure 2.70. This is another way to add vertices to work with.

Select the shoulder faces (both front and back), as shown in Figure 2.71. Extrude six times, bringing the extruded vertices down the length of the arm and scaling the circumference of the mesh arm appropriately, and then activate proportional editing and twist the tip of the arm around the x-axis using rotation (R key), as shown in Figure 2.72.

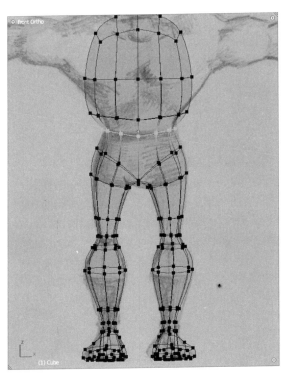

Figure 2.68

A loop cut at the belly

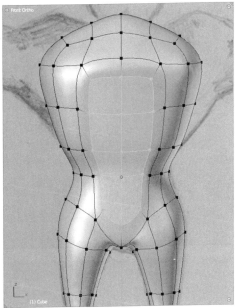

Figure 2.69

A loop cut at the chest

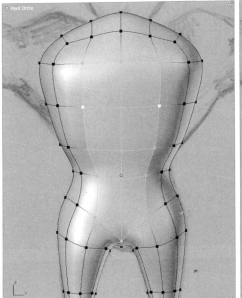

Figure 2.70

Selecting and extruding faces on the abdomen

Figure 2.71

Preparing to extrude the arms

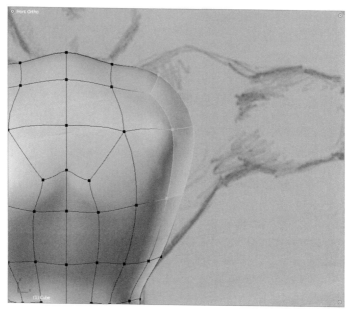

Figure 2.72

Extruding the arms and twisting with the proportional editing tool

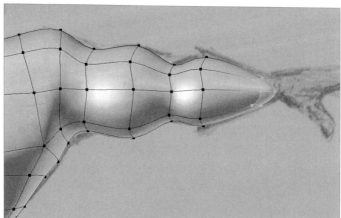

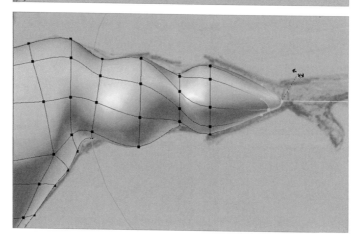

Hands and Gloves

This section looks at the details of creating the hands and the flared gloves. Once again, you will use all the techniques of the previous sections, while adding a few new ones, such as separating polys using the Rip tool and stitching mesh segments again by creating faces.

Continue where you left off at the tip of the arm, and extrude the base shape of the hand. This consists of five extrude operations from wrist to where the base of the fingers will be, as shown in Figure 2.73.

Scale the width of the hand along the y-axis by pressing the S key followed by the Y key. Figure 2.74 shows this operation viewed from above (notice the Top Ortho label in the upper-left corner of the figure). You can enter the top ortho view by pressing 7 on the number pad. Extrude and scale the base of the thumb as shown in Figure 2.75. Extrude three more times to the full length of the thumb, and move the vertices around to adjust the shape of the thumb. Then delete the vertex at the very tip of the appendage so that the mesh at the base of the fingers is open, as shown in Figure 2.76.

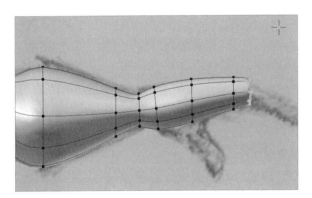

Figure 2.73
Extruding the basis of the hand

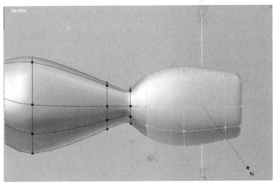

Figure 2.74
Scaling the shape of the hand along the y-axis

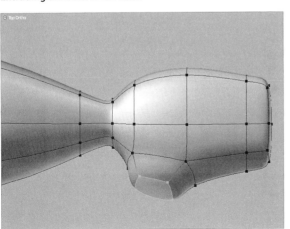

Figure 2.75
Extruding the thumb

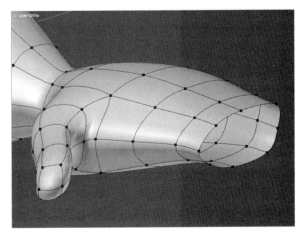

Figure 2.76
Deleting the endmost vertex

Again in top view, select the four topmost faces on the back of the hand, and cut them in a U-shape, as shown in Figure 2.77 with the knife tool. Access the knife tool by pressing and holding the K key while click-dragging the mouse over the edges in the mesh you want to cut. When you've made the cut on the back of the hand, view the mesh from below by holding Ctrl and pressing 7 on the number pad (all number pad views can be reversed by holding Ctrl when you choose them). Select the eight faces that make up the palm of the hand, and cut them in a U-shape, as shown in Figure 2.78.

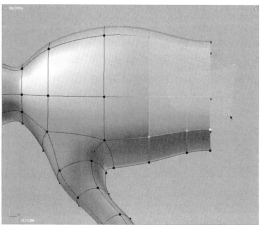

Figure 2.77

Cutting vertices into the back of the hand with the knife tool

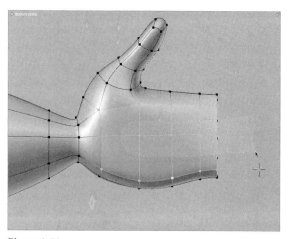

Figure 2.78

Cutting the palm of the hand with the knife tool

Close the open end of the hand with faces, as shown in Figure 2.79. As you should recall from the poly-by-poly modeling example previously, you create faces by selecting four vertices at a time (Shift+right-click) and pressing the F key. You will select these eight new faces two by two to form the basis of the four fingers.

Select each pair of faces, and extrude nine times along the length of the fingers. Scale the circumference of each finger appropriately. You can adjust the rotation of each finger by selecting all of its vertices and rotating the whole finger with the R key. Likewise, the G key will let you grab and move the geometry to get the placement just right. The resulting fingers should look something like the ones shown in Figure 2.80.

HOTKEY: R key rotates the selection.

To create the flared glove, you'll need to rip the mesh. Select the edge loop just up from the wrist by holding Alt and right-clicking an edge in the loop. Rip the mesh by pressing the V key. This will separate the edge loop into two, as shown in Figure 2.81. Extrude from there to create the glove flare, as shown in Figure 2.82. Extrude again and scale down slightly to give the glove some thickness, and then extrude once more and pull the new loop in to double back inside the glove, where it will be hidden by the arm mesh, as shown in Figure 2.83.

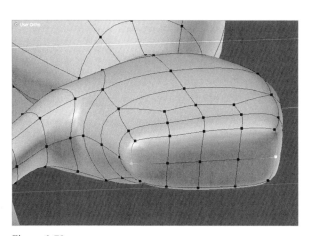

Figure 2.79

Filling in the end of the hand with faces

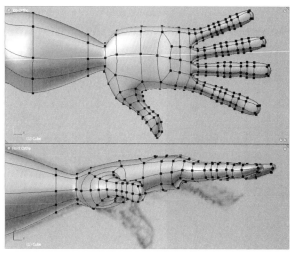

Figure 2.80

Extruded fingers

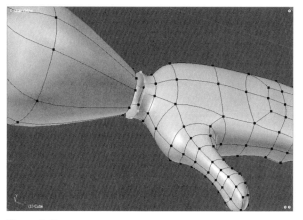

Figure 2.81

Ripping edges at the wrist to create the glove

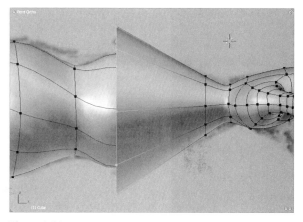

Figure 2.82

Extruding the glove

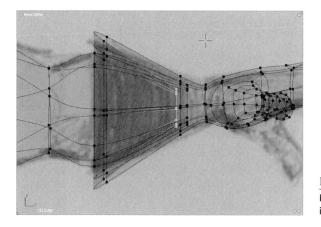

Figure 2.83

Extruding the glove inward

Collar and Belt

In this section, you'll model the collar and the belt. The collar will give you the chance to see how you can use extrusion to create tightly creased forms, such as the place where Captain Blender's neck meets his suit. The belt will be a separate Mesh object.

To create the collar area, delete the vertex at the top of the mesh, where the neck of the character should be, as shown in Figure 2.84. Select the edge loop around the hole where the vertex has been removed, extrude, and then scale downward, as shown in Figure 2.85. Extrude three more times: on the first extrusion scale down slightly, on the second extrusion drag the edge loop downward slightly along the z-axis, and on the third extrusion drag the extruded loop down farther, where it will eventually be hidden by the neck of the character.

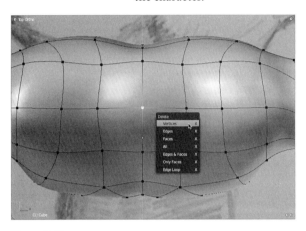

Figure 2.84
Deleting the vertex at the neck

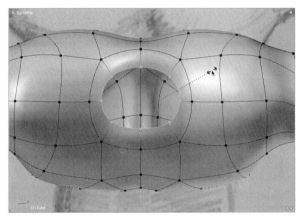

Figure 2.85
Extruding and scaling vertices around the neck

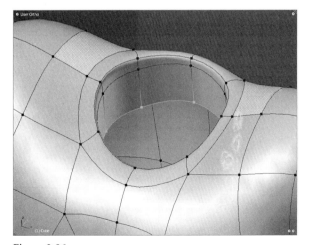

Figure 2.86
Extruding and translating vertices to complete the neck of the costume

At this point, you're finished with the main body Mesh object for Captain Blender. Other parts of the character will use separate objects. It is no problem to use multiple objects for a single character; in fact, it is often much easier to treat separate items of clothing or body parts as separate objects.

Before you go on to modeling other objects, take a look at the model you have, and compare it with the model in Figure 2.87. Make sure that the shapes look right and the geometry is all there. Add edge loops if necessary.

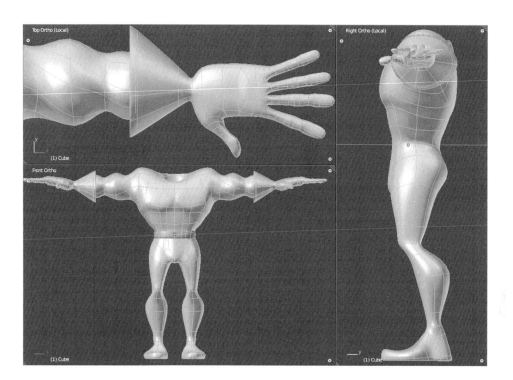

Figure 2.87

Views of the body

Captain Blender's trusty utility belt is made of an extruded circle. Scale the belt to fit as shown in Figure 2.88. In the same way that you can constrain transformations to particular axes by pressing X, Y, or Z, you can constrain the transformations to particular planes by pressing Shift+X, Shift+Y, or Shift+Z to constrain to the plane perpendicular to the specified axis.

So, in order to constrain your scaling to the xy plane, as illustrated in Figure 2.88, use Shift+Z. When you have the belt the right side, extrude the whole thing to give some thickness and scale down again on the xy plane. Delete the inside faces of the belt.

When you've finished modeling the belt, enter Object mode, select the body mesh, and apply the Mirror modifier. This makes the virtual, mirrored vertices real, and they are now independently editable. After you have applied the Mirror modifier, select the belt object, and then hold Shift while selecting the body object. The order of selection is

Figure 2.88

Modeling the belt from a circle

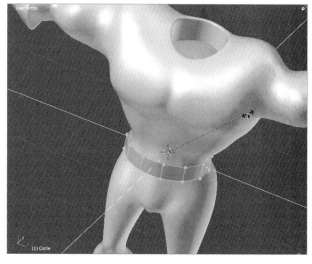

important here because the last object selected will be the object that everything else is joined to. Press Ctrl+J to join the two meshes.

That takes care of the body. You'll model the head as a separate object in the next section.

Modeling the Head

Now let's turn to the head. As mentioned previously, the head will be a separate object. To concentrate on modeling this object without getting distracted by the modeling you've already done, you can do this work on a separate layer.

Blender's layer functionality lets you create visibility groups that you can toggle on and off as you like. The default scene is all located in the first layer, and only the first layer is set to be visible by default. Switch to the second layer by clicking the second button in the layers button bank on the header of the 3D viewport, as shown in Figure 2.89.

Figure 2.89

Switching to layer 2

Add a new cube by pressing Shift+A and choosing Mesh → Cube from the Add menu. Press Alt+G and Alt+R if necessary to clear any translation or rotation from the new object. Tab into Edit mode, and subdivide-smooth the mesh in the same way that you did previously to begin modeling the body (the W key will open the mesh Special tools menu when you have a mesh-type object selected and are in Edit mode). Grab and scale the subdivided cube, and place it over the head in the background image, as shown in Figure 2.90.

Use the Loop Cut tool to create more geometry to work with. Figure 2.91 shows the mesh after four new horizontal loops have been cut.

Select the front faces where the eyes will be, extrude once, and then scale down, as shown in Figure 2.92. Make two vertical loop cuts as shown in Figure 2.93.

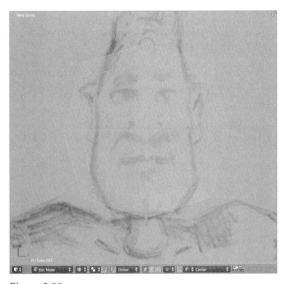

Figure 2.90

A new cube after the Subdivide Smooth tool

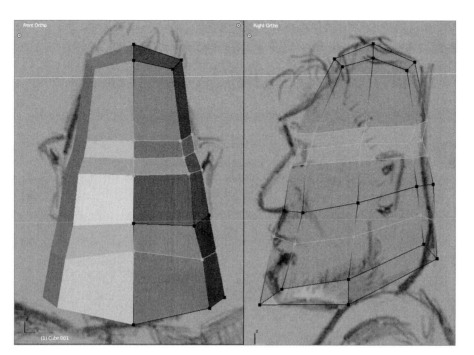

Figure 2.91

Four newly cut edge loops

Select the seven faces shown in Figure 2.94, and draw the knife tool through them by holding the K key and the left mouse button and moving the mouse across the faces as shown. The result should look like the second image in Figure 2.94. Note that the quad in the eye area has been converted into triangles to conform to the newly created geometry. This is fine. Later, you're going to delete these triangles anyway.

Select the nine faces that make up the front of the nose and mouth area, and extrude and scale them twice, adjusting the location of the vertices to get a result, as shown in Figure 2.95. Select the six faces on the bottom of the mesh, and delete them with the X key, as shown in Figure 2.96.

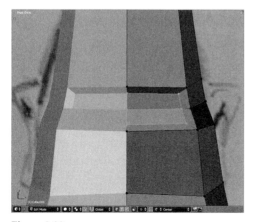

Figure 2.92

Extruding the eye area

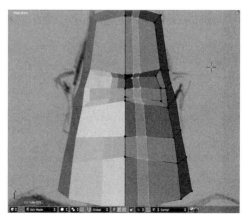

Figure 2.93

Two more loop cuts

Figure 2.94

Making a cut with
the knife tool
and the resulting
topology

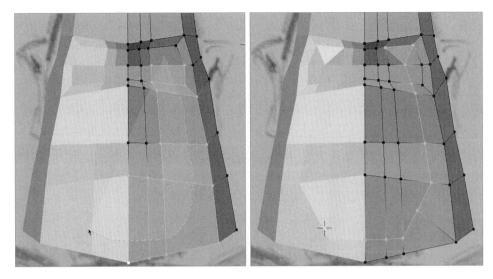

Figure 2.95

Extruding the nose
and mouth
area twice

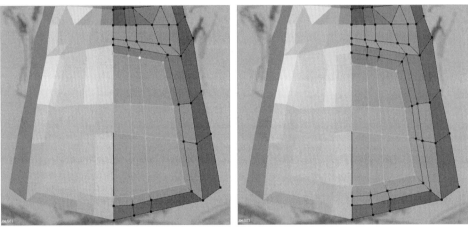

Figure 2.96

Deleting faces at the
bottom of
the model

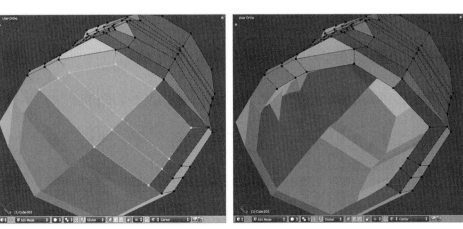

At this point, you should be comfortable enough with the tools to do a little bit of solo flying. Follow the images in Figure 2.97 to continue modeling the head and face.

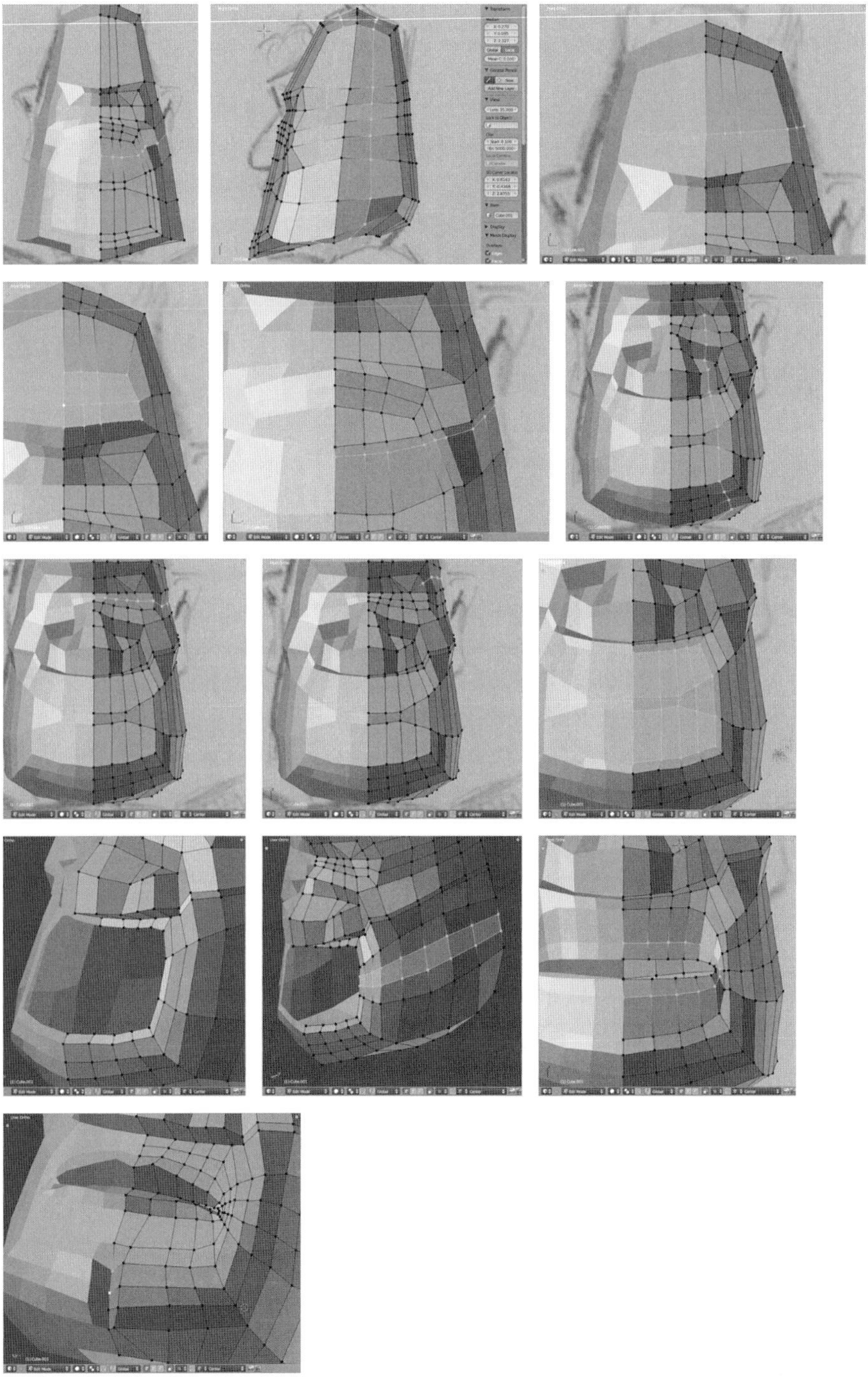

Figure 2.97

Modeling the face with cuts and extrusion

Now you turn your attention to the eye area. You need to reorganize the faces in the eye area slightly by deleting some faces and making some others with the F key. Then you need to make a few cuts and extrude inward to create the eye sockets, as shown in Figure 2.98.

Figure 2.98

Modeling the eye-lids and eye sockets

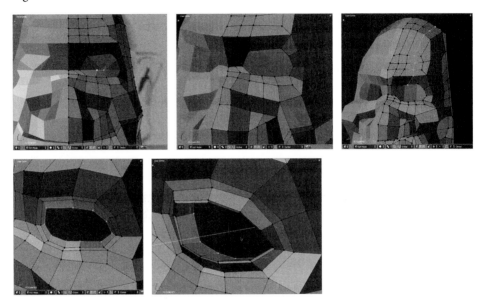

At this point, add a subsurf modifier to get a better sense of how the model will look when it's finished. The model so far should look something like the one shown in Figure 2.99. You can also check what you have against the model in the .blend file for this chapter on the book's downloadable companion files.

Figure 2.99

The model so far, with subsurfing

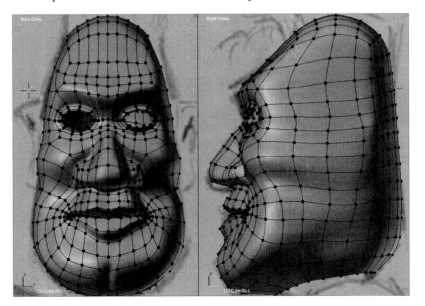

Later, when you add hair to the character, it will be helpful to have the hair-emitting portion of the scalp modeled in an intuitive way. To achieve this, you'll make some adjustments to the topology of the head. But before that, extrude the basis of the ears as shown in Figure 2.100 so that you have a better idea of where the hairline should be located.

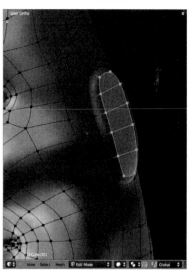

Figure 2.100

Extruding the basis of the ear

A very handy tool for adjusting the topology of a model is the Rotate Edge tool, which is accessed from the Mesh menu in the 3D viewport header (this menu is present only when a mesh is selected in Edit mode). Select the two vertices shown in Figure 2.101, and choose Mesh → Edge → Rotate CCW to rotate the edge counterclockwise in the mesh as shown in the figure. Use the Rotate Edge tool again to rotate the edge shown in Figure 2.102.

Merge the two vertices shown in Figure 2.103 into a single vertex. The Merge tool can be found in the mesh Specials menu (W key) or activated directly with Alt+M. Choose At Center when prompted to choose where the vertices should merge. This will merge the vertices at a midpoint between the two original vertices.

Continue in this manner, by rotating edges and merging vertices, to model the hairline into the mesh, as shown in Figure 2.104.

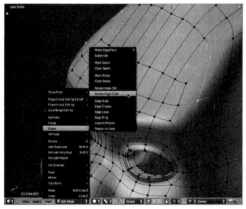

Figure 2.101
Rotating an edge within the mesh

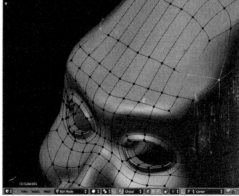

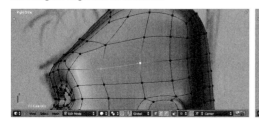

Figure 2.102
Rotating another edge

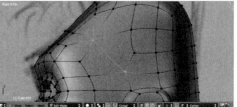

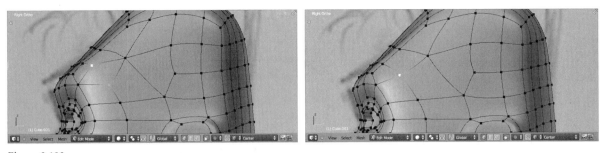

Figure 2.103

Merging two vertices

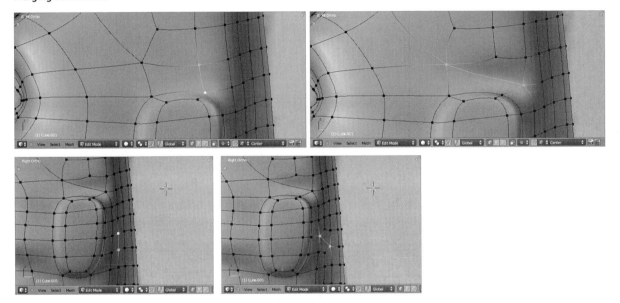

Figure 2.104

More edge rotations and vertex merges to create a hairline

Once you are finished with the basic outline of the hairline, it's a good idea to clean up the topology of the scalp a bit. Follow the images in Figure 2.105 to do this. When you've finished, add another edge loop around the hairline with the Edge Loop tool (Ctrl+R), as shown in 2.106.

Now you can return to finishing the ear. From the base you extruded previously, extrude, scale, and translate the faces to create a rough ear shape, as shown in Figure 2.107. Select the faces shown in Figure 2.108, and smooth them using the Smooth tool in the mesh Specials menu (W key). Turn the smoothing iterations up all the way to 100 in the corresponding field in the Tool Shelf, as shown in the figure.

From this basis and with the skills you've picked up so far in this chapter, you should be able to use the Extrude tool, and scale, rotate, and translate in order to finish the ear model, as shown in Figure 2.109.

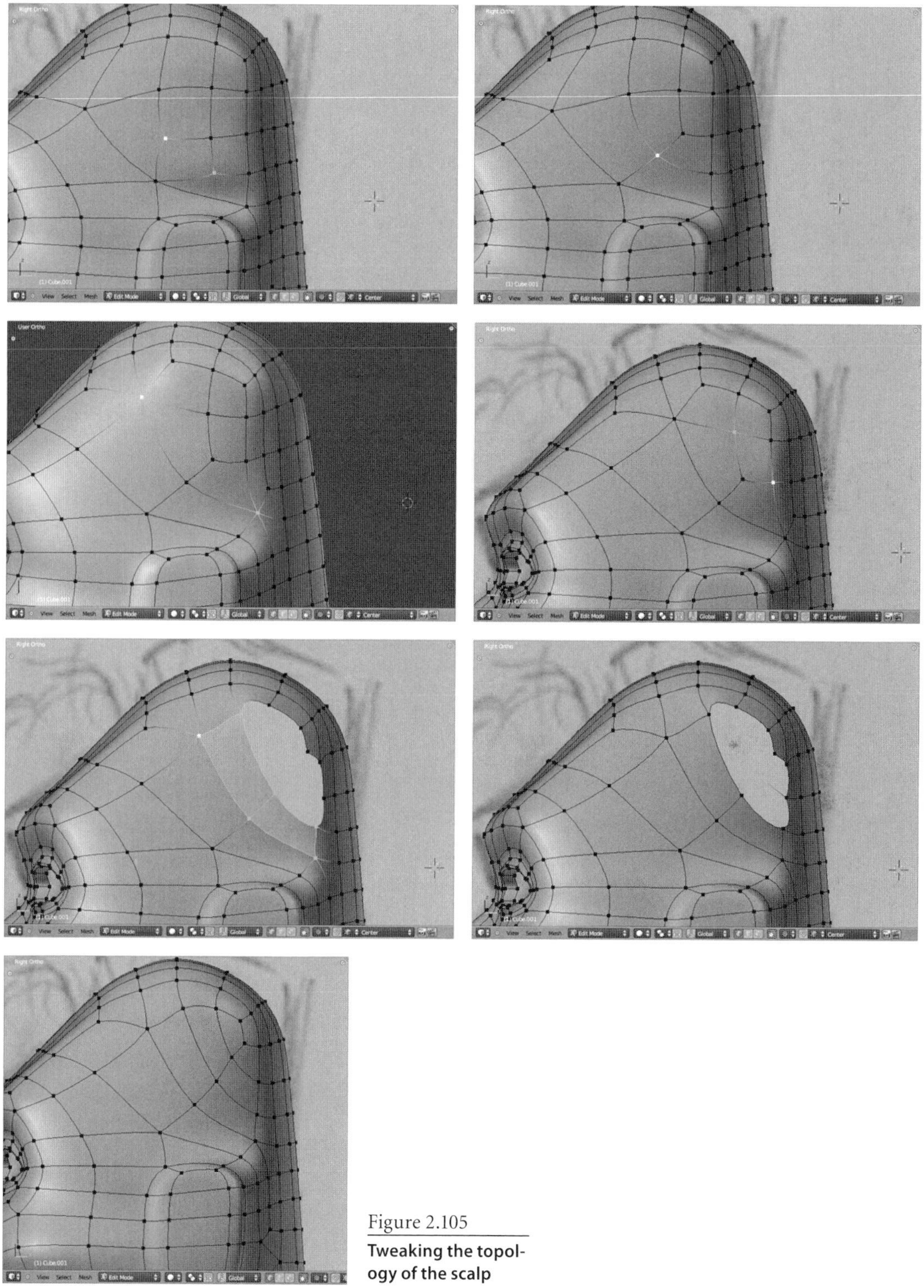

Figure 2.105

Tweaking the topol-
ogy of the scalp

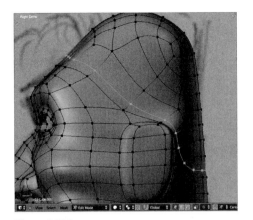

Figure 2.106

Adding an edge loop around the scalp area

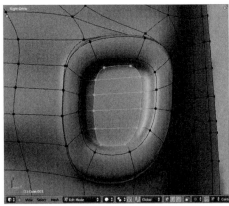

Figure 2.107

Extruding more ear geometry

Figure 2.108

Smoothing the base of the ear

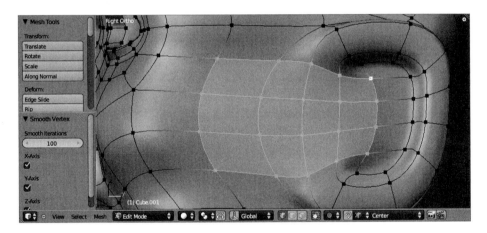

Figure 2.109

Finishing the ear

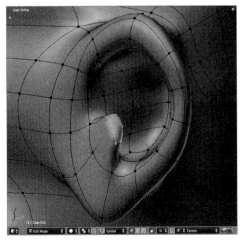

All that is left to do on this model in terms of new geometry is to add a few vertices to the base of the head, as shown in Figure 2.110, and to extrude the neck, as shown in Figure 2.111.

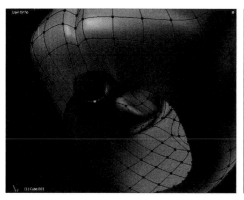
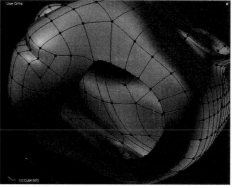

Figure 2.110

Adding some faces to the neck area

Once you've gotten this far, toggle the body visible by holding Shift+clicking the first layer button in Object mode to see how the head and body fit together. Make any necessary adjustments to get them to fit nicely together, as shown in Figure 2.112. This is also a good time to add eyes to the model just as you did in the "Poly-by-Poly Modeling and Box Modeling" section of this chapter and to make the necessary adjustments to the shape of the face to accommodate the eyeballs.

For any animation that will involve the character opening its mouth, of course you will also need to have the mouth modeled. This includes the oral cavity, the tongue, and the upper and lower rows of teeth. Figure 2.113 shows a simple mouth setup that you can use for this character, and Figure 2.114 shows its placement inside the head. Be sure that it does not poke through the surface of the face.

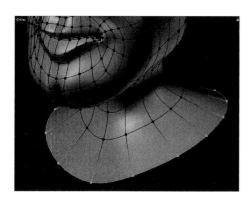

Figure 2.111

Extruding the neck

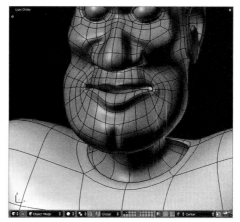

Figure 2.112

The head and body together

Figure 2.113
Modeling the inner mouth

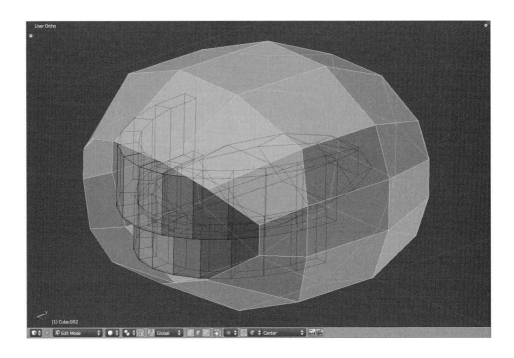

Figure 2.114
Placement of the inner mouth

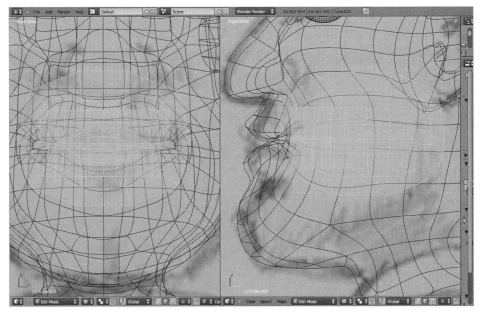

Once you have all this finished, take a break! You've finished the complete Captain Blender model, and you're ready to move on to adding materials and textures to make the model more convincing. Figure 2.115 shows a simple render of the completed Captain Blender mesh.

Figure 2.115

The finished Captain Blender model

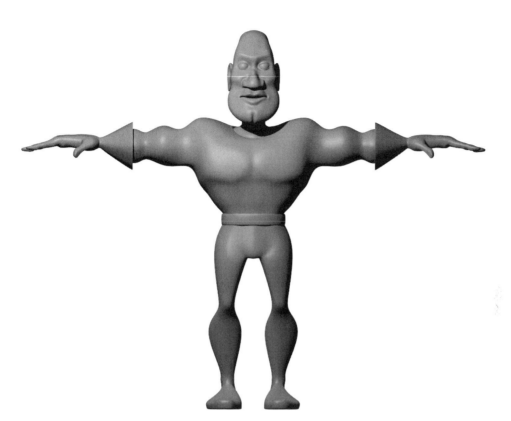

Common Problems and Solutions in Mesh Modeling

Many of the most common problems that arise during mesh modeling are easy to spot and have straightforward solutions. This section covers a few that are sure to arise if you do extensive mesh modeling.

Inconsistent Normals

A telltale ugly black shadow-like seam like the one in Figure 2.116 indicates mismatched normals. In the Properties Shelf (press the N key over the 3D viewport) on the Mesh Display panel, you can select to display face normals. If you do this, you can see which direction the normals in your mesh point, as in Figure 2.117 (normals are displayed in blue by default in Blender). Most often, normals point outward, and in all cases they should be consistent throughout a mesh. In this instance, the normals on the left half of the mesh are pointing outward, as they should be. Because the mesh in the figure is in solid view, you cannot see the normals on the right side because they are reversed and are pointing inward.

This problem is simple to solve. Select all verts, and hit Ctrl+N. The problem should vanish. If it doesn't, there could be more serious problems with the structure of your mesh.

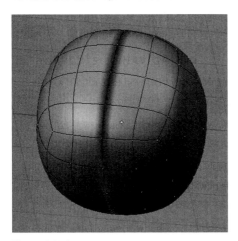

Figure 2.116

Inconsistent normals

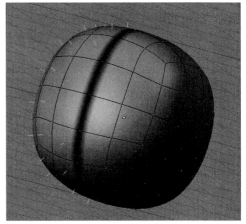

Figure 2.117

With Draw Normals turned on, they don't all point outward.

Overlapping Faces

The problem of overlapping faces is often not apparent in the 3D window in Blender; it becomes visible only when the image is rendered, showing up as a pattern of dark artifacts on the surface of the mesh, as in Figure 2.118. This problem is caused by multiple faces sharing the same coordinates. It is most often the result of inadvertently duplicating a mesh or portion of a mesh and leaving the duplicated portion in the same spot as the original.

There are two likely possibilities. First, you might have duplicated the object. In Object mode, right-click the Mesh object once, and move it with G to see whether it is a duplicate, as in Figure 2.119. If it is a duplicate object, delete the unwanted copy.

If it is not a duplicate object, the verts and faces of the mesh were probably accidentally duplicated in Edit mode. This might show up as a strange pattern of selected edges, as in Figure 2.120, but it might also not be evident at all. In any case, the solution is to select all verts in the mesh, press the W key to display the Specials menu, and select Remove Doubles.

Figure 2.118

Overlapping faces create artifacts when rendered.

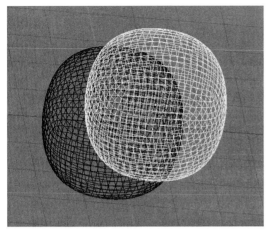

Figure 2.119

Move an object aside to see whether it is hiding an identical object.

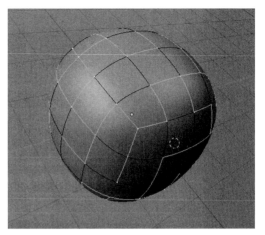

Figure 2.120

A strange selection pattern in Edit mode might indicate overlapping faces.

Internal Faces

Unwanted pinching in your mesh is often the result of having unnecessary faces connecting parts of the mesh that should not be connected. Generally, a mesh should be hollow, without separate compartments inside it. The pinched mesh in Figure 2.121 is a result of having internal faces connecting the middle loop of vertices.

You can solve this problem by selecting all unwanted internal faces (see Figure 2.122) and deleting them with the X key, choosing Faces from the Delete menu.

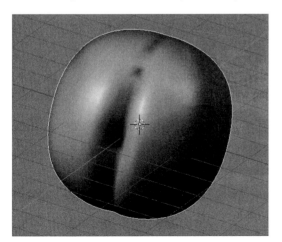

Figure 2.121

A pinched effect caused by internal faces

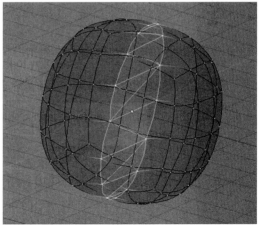

Figure 2.122

Delete unwanted internal faces to solve the problem.

Unwanted Doubles

Another common problem is the appearance of a creased seam on your mesh, as in Figure 2.123, which is usually caused by doubled edges.

Use the Box Select tool (B) to select the seam, as in Figure 2.124, and select Remove Doubles (this can be accessed from the W specials menu). If the vertices are not exactly in the same place, it might be necessary to adjust the Merge Threshold value in the Tool Shelf operator panel when Remove Doubles is carried out. Raising this value increases the area within which verts are considered doubles of each other. Raising this value too high results in merging vertices that should not be merged, so be careful.

In some cases, if there is a seam in which the corresponding verts are too far from each other to be merged using remove doubles, it might be necessary to "weld" the seam shut two verts at a time. Select the two verts you want to merge, press W, and choose Merge. You might need to do this for all the verts in the seam in some cases.

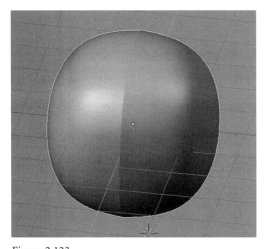

Figure 2.123

An unwanted crease caused by doubled-up verts

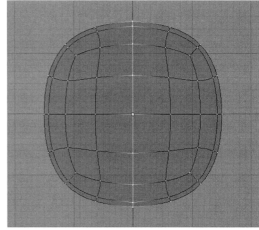

Figure 2.124

Select all verts in the offending area using the Box Select tool.

Unwanted Extrusions

Accidentally pressing Ctrl+LMB with a single vertex selected is a common cause of unwanted extrusions, which can show up in a mesh in a variety of ways, creating pimples and pockmarks on the surface of your mesh, depending on the nature of the extrusion. You can see the surface results of this problem in Figure 2.125. The cause of the problem is clearer when the mesh is viewed in wireframe mode, as in Figure 2.126.

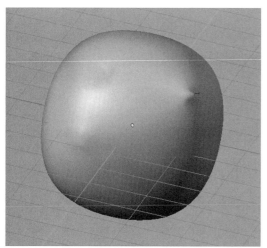

Figure 2.125
Problems caused by unwanted extrusion

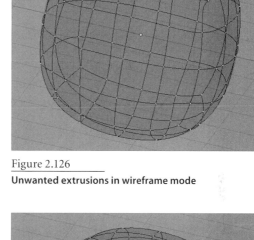

Figure 2.126
Unwanted extrusions in wireframe mode

The solution is simply to delete the extruded verts. In the cases in which the verts have been extruded far enough to be clearly identifiable, as in the top two cases where the verts are extruded into and out from the surface of the mesh, the verts can be selected and deleted.

In the more subtle case in Figure 2.127, the extruded vert was not displaced and so resides at the same coordinate as the original vert. This is actually just another case of unwanted doubles, and the solution is to select the doubled vert using the Box Select tool and to remove doubles.

Now that you understand the basics of mesh modeling and have created the mesh of the character, you can begin to add details. The next chapter will cover creating materials and textures and using static particles to make hair.

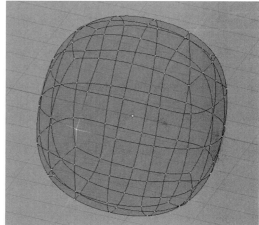

Figure 2.127
A doubled vertex

CHAPTER 3

Completing the Model with Materials, Textures, and Hair

Previous chapters covered the basics of using Blender's various modeling tools to build organic shapes. But this is only the first step of creating characters. By default, all the shapes you build begin as a uniform, dull gray, slightly glossy material. To make characters interesting and lifelike, or even just to change their color, you need to delve into the world of materials, textures, and particle hair to complete the model.

- **Materials and Material Slots**
- **Material Properties**
- **Textures and UV Mapping**
- **Working with Particle Hair**

Materials and Material Slots

In Blender, the visible properties of objects are determined by the objects' *materials*. Materials contain information about color, transparency, reflectivity, and other qualities that determine how objects appear and how they respond to light. Materials also contain information about *textures*, which enable more refined control over the surface properties of objects. Blender associates materials with objects by means of material *slots*. The distinction between a material and the slot it occupies on an object is important, so this chapter will begin by looking at that relationship.

Figure 3.1
Materials and material slots

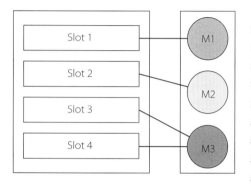

Each mesh object can have a virtually unlimited number of material slots associated with it. Each material slot is assigned to zero or more faces on the mesh. Likewise, each material slot is associated with a single material. In this way, materials are assigned to faces on the mesh. The relationship between material slots and materials is not necessarily one-to-one. A single material can be shared by two different material slots. Figure 3.1 shows a possible arrangement of slots and materials. In this figure, four slots are shown represented by rectangles on the left, and three materials are shown, represented by circles on the right. Slots 3 and 4 both link to the third material, labeled M3. In practice, this means that if you edit M3 by changing its color or other properties, the parts of the mesh with slots 3 and 4 assigned will change.

In fact, slots in Blender are not explicitly numbered. Past Blender versions used explicitly numbered material indices, but now there is simply a stack of slots. The numbered labels I use in the figures here are simply counting from the top.

To take a look at material slots directly, fire up Blender, and select the default cube. Look at the Material Properties window, as shown in Figure 3.2. The material slots for this object are shown in the panel near the top of the window with the plus and minus icons to the right of it. By default, the cube is associated with a single material slot containing a material with the name Material. Conceptually, what you're seeing represents the slot/material relationship shown in Figure 3.3.

Click the Diffuse color field to bring up a circular color picker, and set the diffuse color of the material in this slot, as shown in Figure 3.4. I've set this material to green.

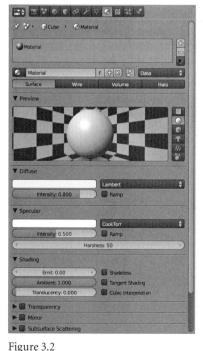

Figure 3.2
The Materials Properties window

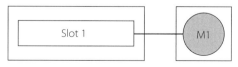

Figure 3.3
The default material arrangement

To have more than one material on a mesh, you need to first add a new material slot to hold the new material. You do this by clicking the + sign to the right of the material slots stack. When you do this, a new slot will appear, as shown in Figure 3.5. This material slot is also labeled Material. This means that the new material slot is associated with the same material as the first slot. Conceptually, the arrangement is as shown in Figure 3.6. There is still only one material to work with. Rename the Material something meaningful, like Green, by entering the new name in the material field just below the stack panel. As you can see in Figure 3.7, the name in both slots changes to Green.

Look again at the field where you entered the name. To the right of the material's name in this field is the number 2, the letter *F*, a plus symbol, and an X symbol. The 2 means that this material is associated with two *users*. In this case, this means that the material is being used by two slots. The F button toggles a *fake user* for the material. This is useful if you have a material with no slots using it that you would like to save. The plus symbol creates a new material, and the X symbol deletes the material from this slot.

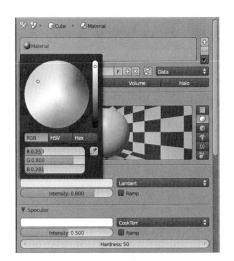

Figure 3.4

Changing the diffuse color

Figure 3.5

Adding a new material slot

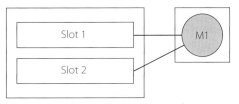

Figure 3.6

The new slot sharing a material

As you can probably guess by now, you want to click the plus symbol to create a new material in this slot. Another way to do the same thing is to click the button with the 2 written on it, which will have the effect of making the material a "single-user" material. When you click either of these symbols, the second slot will change, as shown in Figure 3.8. Blender has created a new, distinct material that is an exact copy of the original Green material and named it Green.001 according to Blender's automatic naming conventions. Any time Blender needs to name an element using an already-used name, it appends a three-digit index to the name, beginning with .001 and iterating as necessary. The situation now is illustrated in Figure 3.9.

Figure 3.7

The material renamed

Figure 3.8

The newly created material

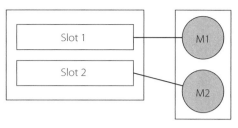

Figure 3.9

The relationship between the two slots and the two materials

The important point here is that Green.001 is now a completely separate material. You can change this material's properties without affecting the original Green material. Try it now by changing the color of the new material. I've made mine purple and renamed the material Purple, as shown in Figure 3.10.

If you've followed the steps so far, you should have two material slots on the object, with unique materials in each, one Green and the other Purple. However, the object

Figure 3.10

Green and Purple materials

in your 3D viewport, the default cube, is only green. This is because all the faces on the cube are still associated with the first material slot.

To assign a material to a face, simply tab into Edit mode, select the face or faces you want to assign the material to, and click Assign on the Material slots panel with the material slot selected. In Figure 3.11, you can see the cube with the top face selected (the object is shown in wireframe to more clearly show the selection). With Purple selected in the material slots stack, click Assign, and the top face of the cube turns purple, as shown (in black and white, of course) in Figure 3.12.

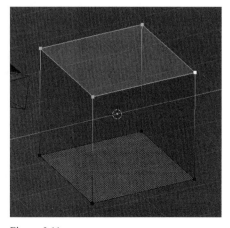

Figure 3.11

The cube with the top face selected

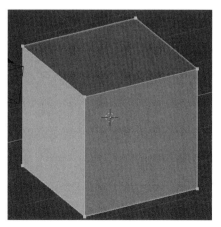

Figure 3.12

The cube with two materials assigned

You can control which materials are associated with which slots by selecting the slot and choosing a material from the material field drop-down menu, as shown in Figure 3.13. If you choose the top slot and choose Purple from the drop-down menu, the entire cube will become purple. The top face and the rest of the cube are still associated with separate slots, but the slots both point to the same material.

Material Properties

Now that you've seen how to associate materials and material slots with parts of your mesh, let's look more closely at what you can do with these materials. For the purposes of this book, it's enough to think of materials as essentially colors and shading properties. You will learn more about texturing, but you will not be looking at some of the more exotic material properties and functions available in Blender. For more exhaustive information on materials, as with all subjects, you should consult the official documentation.

Figure 3.13

Selecting which material the slot will point to

As you saw in the first section, one important property of a material is the color. You can set R, G, and B values in the color picker widget by clicking the color wheel, by using the RGB sliders, or by clicking the value and editing the values directly or using the color sampler represented by the little dropper icon.

Shaders influence how light reflects from the surface of an object. In nature, this is determined by the physical properties of the material's surface. Shaders are algorithms for simulating the reflective effects of these physical properties. There are separate shading algorithms to handle *diffuse* shading and *specular* shading.

Diffuse shading deals with light that reflects off objects in all directions, creating a uniform, matte surface color. Specular shading deals with light that reflects at a specific angle to the surface of the object, creating highlights. This is not a distinction that exists in reality; in reality, light is light. However, in computer graphics, it is an important distinction. Most materials have both a diffuse and a specular component. Shiny materials have a higher specular component, and matte materials have a lower specular component. Typically what you think of as the color of an object is the color of its diffuse component; the specular component is generally white.

In Blender, the color and the shader for the diffuse component and the specular component are set separately, as shown in Figure 3.14, where the drop-down menu for the diffuse shader is revealed to show the list of shader options for diffuse shading.

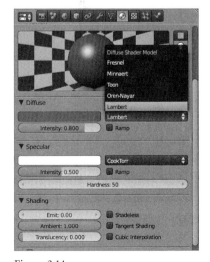

Figure 3.14

Shader information in the Material Properties window

TOON AND ANIME STYLE SHADING

You generally use a shader to create a realistic simulation of some specific physical surface. In character animation, one common exception to this use of shaders is in toon shading, which creates a cartoon or traditional 2D anime-style appearance. Toon shaders divide gradations into several levels of shading that can be smoothed together, resulting in a sharp, cartoony distinction between lit parts and shaded parts of the object. Toon shaders are often used in conjunction with the Edge feature in the Render buttons panel, which adds an outline around the object as part of the rendering process, further enhancing the traditional 2D look.

In the image shown here, the old man rendered on the right is made of toon-shaded materials with the Edge feature turned on, in contrast with the more realistically shaded and rendered old man model on the left. In this case, the materials in the old man on the right were all set to toon shading for both diffuse and specular shaders, with the Smooth value set to 0 for maximal sharpness between shaded and nonshaded areas. Specularity and size values varied between the materials, and you should experiment for the effect you want.

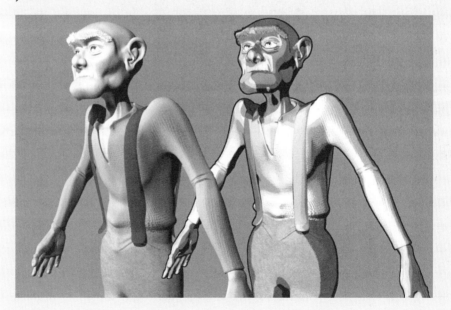

MATERIAL NODES

Blender has a powerful node system that you can use to create materials and to do advanced image compositing. Nodes behave similarly to the way layers behave in some 2D image-processing applications, enabling effects and inputs to be laid over one another and be combined in various ways. Nodes are much more powerful than layers in this sense because they can be combined in nonlinear ways. With material nodes, you can have complete control over every aspect of a material by combining fundamental components of materials and shaders in a flexible way. Nodes form a network of linked inputs and outputs, which you can view and edit in the Node Editor window; the basic node setup for the default material is shown here.

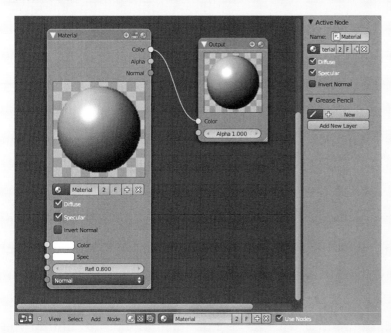

You will see a simple example of working with nodes in this chapter, but the knowledge you gain by working with Blender's ordinary materials system will also not be wasted when you move on to using material nodes more heavily. Materials that use nodes are always composed of at least one basic (non-node) material that is the input to the network of nodes. The understanding you have of color, shaders, mirroring, transparency, and textures will all remain pertinent when you work with nodes. In this sense, material nodes do not replace the basic material system but rather extend it.

Shading and Materials for Captain Blender

Let's return to the superhero model you were working on in the previous chapter. You want to now give him a colorful suit, not to mention some skin and hair.

Orange seems like a good color for Captain Blender's tights, and blue is good for his gloves, boots, and britches. For variety, you'll make his belt black. Click the plus symbol next to the material slots panel twice to create two new slots.

You can do the next few steps in any order. You need to associate vertex groups on the mesh with material slots, and you have to create and name a new material for each slot. By default, the entire mesh is assigned material slot1, which will be the orange material. Let's begin by selecting the portions of the mesh you want to be blue in Edit mode, as shown in Figure 3.15.

Figure 3.15

Selecting the parts of the mesh to make blue

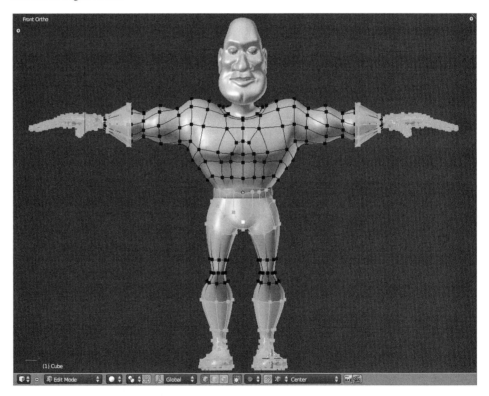

Click the second material slot, and click Assign. Then click the plus symbol next to the material name field to create a new material. The new material's name will be automatically generated to Material.001. Rename this material Blue. Rename the first material Orange.

For the Blue material, set the RGB values as R: 0.2, G: 0.2, and B: 0.6. In Blender, color values range from 0 to 1. If you are accustomed to working with a scale of 0 to 255, you should simply think of 1 as the equivalent of 255, the maximal value of the color, with

0 the same in both cases. Captain Blender's gloves, boots, and britches are made out of super-strength PVC, and Lambert and Wardiso shaders are good for plastics, so you'll use a Lambert diffuse shader with intensity set at 0.8; for the specular shader, you'll use the Wardiso shader with specularity set at 0.6 and Slope set at 0.2.

For Orange, set the RGB values to 1.0, 0.3, and 0.0, respectively. Captain Blender spends a lot of time in this suit, and it needs to be easy on the skin, so you'll give it a nice velvety surface by using a Minnaert shader with the darkness value set to 0.4. There's very little specularity on this material, so for the specularity shader, you'll stick with the default CookTorr shader with specularity set to 0.01.

Run a render by pressing F12 to see how these shaders are looking on your mesh. (On Mac, you will have to adjust your Mac keyboard shortcuts not to override this Blender hotkey, but you'll be glad you did.) Check Chapter 11 for tips on how to set up your camera and lighting for a good-looking render.

Now select Captain Blender's belt. To do this, place the mouse near one of the vertices of the belt, and press L. Because the belt is not connected by any edges to the rest of the mesh, it can be easily selected in this way. Assign the belt to the third slot, and then add a new material to this slot by pressing the plus symbol. Rename this material to Black. Set the color and shaders for the belt (you can experiment a bit with the settings).

You'll need to do the same thing with the inside of Captain Blender's mouth and his teeth, which are a separate object. You can select the individual mesh pieces with the L key. Keep the color dark and reflectivity low on the inside of the mouth because it will be noticeable if it is too bright.

Basic Texturing

No superhero's outfit is complete without a big splashy logo across his chest. To do this, you will use an image texture in a way analogous to a decal. To control the position, size, and rotation of the decal, you will use an Empty object. Go into Object mode, press Shift+S to snap the 3D cursor to the grid, and add an Empty object with Shift+A. Place the Empty object squarely in front of the chest by moving the empty with the G key and constraining the movement to the appropriate axes with the Y and Z keys. Rotate the Empty object by pressing the R key followed by the X key and then inputting the number **90** directly via the keyboard to rotate the Empty object 90 degrees counterclockwise around the x-axis so that the Empty object 's z-axis points outward away from Captain Blender's chest, as shown in Figure 3.16.

Figure 3.16

Placing the Empty object in front of the chest

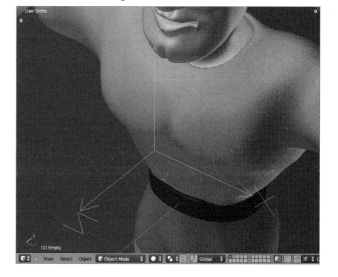

You'll want this Empty object to follow the movement of the mesh when Captain Blender poses. To do this, you will use a special kind of parenting called *vertex parenting.* More specifically, you'll use *three-vertex parenting.* This lets you parent an object not to another object but to actual vertices (or triples of vertices) in the second object. To do this, select the Empty object, and then hold Shift and right-click the Captain Blender mesh. Press Tab to enter Edit mode, and select three vertices around the middle of Captain Blender's chest, near the location of the Empty object. Press Ctrl+P, and choose Make Vertex Parent. In this case, you need three vertices to make sure that the Empty object follows that of Captain Blender's chest, even when the mesh is deformed. In cases where you only need an object's location to be influenced by a vertex, you can use single-vertex parenting. Single-vertex parenting and three-vertex parenting are the only options for vertex parenting. If you try to vertex parent with another quantity of vertices selected, Blender will complain.

Figure 3.17

Adding the Logo texture

You'll put the texture directly onto the Orange material, so make sure the appropriate material slot is active. Go to the Texture Properties window, and add a new texture if there is not one already on the material. Name the texture Logo, and choose Image or Movie as the texture type, as shown in Figure 3.17. In the Image panel in the Texture Properties window, select the source file from your hard drive, as shown in Figure 3.18. You'll find the logo.tif source file in the downloadable resources directory for this book.

In the Influence panel, you can choose how the texture is to be used, that is, what characteristics of the texture will influence the surface appearance of the mesh. In this case, you want to use the texture's color, so Color should be checked with the value set at the full value of 1. Also, you'll have the texture influence the specularity of the mesh with a value of 0.8. This will make the logo on the mesh a bit shiny, like a crisp new iron-on patch. (How else do you think a superhero gets the logo on his costume?) Figure 3.19 shows the influence settings for this texture.

Finally, you need to set the Mapping values as shown in Figure 3.20. Mapping settings define the relationship (mapping) of points on the texture to points on the surface of the mesh. In this case, you will be using the coordinate system of the Empty object that you just added to determine the coordinates of the texture.

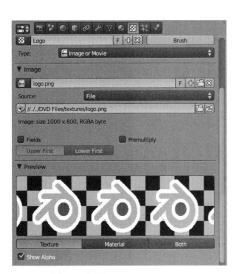

Figure 3.18

Setting the image for the texture

When the Empty object moves, rotates, or scales, the texture will do the same on the surface of the mesh. Select Object in the coordinates drop-down menu, and enter **Empty** in the field that appears. In the Image Mapping panel just below, select

Clip Cube. This controls whether the image will be repeated or whether it will be projected through the entire mesh. With Clip Cube selected, the image will appear only once and will appear only within a cube shaped area around the Empty object. This will keep it from projecting onto the character's back also.

Once you've made these adjustments, view the result by rendering with F12. You'll need to make sure to place the camera so that it can see the texture and put a light in place so that you can see what it looks like.

How does it look? If the logo is too large or small, you can adjust the size by scaling the Empty object. If it's in the wrong place, you can move it around by moving the Empty object. Of course, you can also rotate the image by rotating the Empty object. Figure 3.21 shows a render of the full model with materials so far.

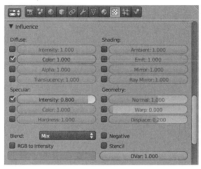

Figure 3.19

Influence settings for the texture

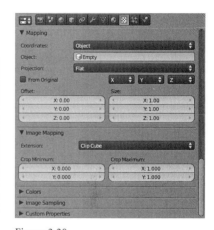

Figure 3.20

Mapping values for the texture and image

Figure 3.21

A render of the materials so far

Textures and UV Mapping

With the logo example, you saw a very simple way to map a texture to a mesh. Clearly, object mapping does not offer enough precise control to work for sophisticated textures that need to follow the shape of a complex mesh. To see an example of how to do this, you'll turn to Captain Blender's head and face.

Using material and shader options is not really enough to give you the kind of look you want for human skin. The best way to get convincing-looking skin is by applying two-dimensional textures to the surface of the mesh, much as you did with the logo, although you'll need to use a more sophisticated approach to mapping. In the case of Captain Blender, you're not going for an especially realistic look, but you can apply the same methods you'll use here to creating more realistic styles. Of course, a realistic style requires more detailed textures than a cartoony style.

UV mapping provides a way to apply a two-dimensional image or texture onto the surface of a three-dimensional object. The name *UV* refers to the two-dimensional coordinates, U and V, which are mapped into the 3D (X, Y, and Z) coordinate space. Blender has powerful tools for creating this mapping, which make it fairly straightforward to map a 2D image to any 3D object when you get the hang of it.

The first step of UV texturing an object is to create a representation of the surface you want to apply the texture to in UV coordinate space—similar to the way maps of the world are sometimes represented in a flattened, orange-peel style. Creating this 2D image is called *unwrapping*. By default, Blender uses a method of unwrapping called *angle-based flattening*.

For working with UV textures, you will want one window open to the UV/Image Editor window type. Split your Blender desktop up in a way you feel comfortable with, and make sure that one window shows the UV/Image Editor and another window shows the 3D viewport.

Because Captain Blender's head is more or less a closed surface, you need to prepare the object for unwrapping by providing seams along which it can be split. The unwrapper will first cut the surface along these seams and then flatten it.

Create seams in Edit mode by selecting the edges that should be seams and pressing Ctrl+E for the Edge Specials menu. Select Mark Seam. Do this for the edges shown in Figure 3.22. In general, it is a good idea to try to mark the seams in places that are likely to be unobtrusive later, such as parts of the mesh that are covered by hair, are visible only from behind, or that conform to creases or concealed places in the mesh. It's also best to try to keep your seams symmetrical on a symmetrical mesh. Finally, try to put seams in places most likely to be distorted by flattening. Real-life seams in clothing are a great reference for how seams should be created on a mesh. Think about clothing items with sleeves, hoods, collars, pockets, and the like. Consider why the seams on those items are in the places they are.

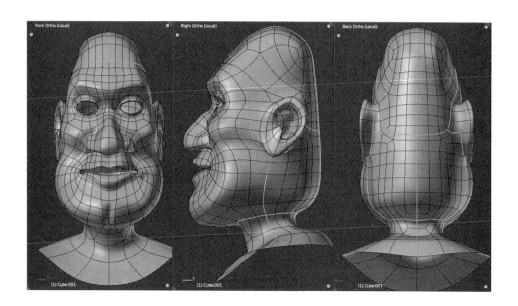

Figure 3.22
**Marking seams for
UV unwrapping**

Before you can create an actual UV texture mapping, you need to add a slot for it on your mesh. You do this in the UV Texture panel in the Mesh Properties window. Note that you can add more than one UV texture. Unfortunately, multiple UV textures are beyond the scope of this book, but you should be aware that multiple UV textures are possible. You can also bake textures from one UV texture with one mapping to a different UV texture with a different mapping, which can be useful for removing visible seams. For now, simply click the + symbol once to create a single UV texture slot, as shown in Figure 3.23.

Next, still in Edit mode, select the entire head by pressing the A key. Move your mouse over the UV/Image Editor, and unwrap the mesh by pressing the E key. If your mesh structure and seam placement are exactly as described so far, then you should see mesh islands similar to the ones shown in Figure 3.24. Their positions, sizes, and rotations may be different from those shown, but you can adjust this later.

Figure 3.23

**Adding a new UV
texture to the mesh**

From the Image menu in the UV/Image Editor, select New. In the dialog box that pops up, select the check box next to the UV Test Grid label. Leave the other values the same and create the image.

Figure 3.24

**The unwrapped
UV mapping**

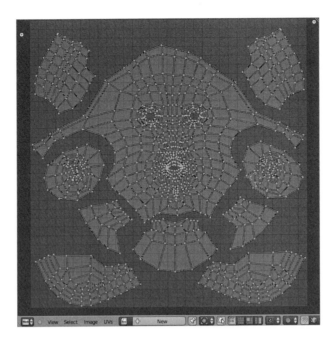

You should see a gray checkerboard pattern with small colored crosses appear behind your UV map. In the 3D viewport header, choose the Textured Viewport Shading option from the drop-down menu to the right of the Mode menu. You should see the test grid texture mapped to Captain Blender's head, as shown in Figure 3.25. At this point, you should save the image directly by choosing Save in the Image menu of the UV/Image header.

> Note that changes to an image are not automatically saved when you save Blender. You must save edited or new images explicitly as images. As a hint to the user, an image that has not yet been saved will have an asterisk shown to the right of its name in the menu bar entry.

You can now begin to paint your texture using Blender's Texture Paint functionality. To do this, simply enter Texture Paint mode with the drop-down menu in the 3D header. You can find the texture painting tools in the Tool Shelf of the 3D viewport by pressing T or by clicking the little plus sign widget in the upper-left corner of the 3D viewport. On the tool panel you can choose the type of brush by clicking directly on the brush-type icon at the top of the panel, you can choose the color of your texture paint with the color picker, and you can set the strength, size, and jitter level of the brush in the corresponding value fields. Brush strength and size can also be adjusted with the Shift+F and F hotkeys, respectively. Figure 3.26 shows texture painting in progress.

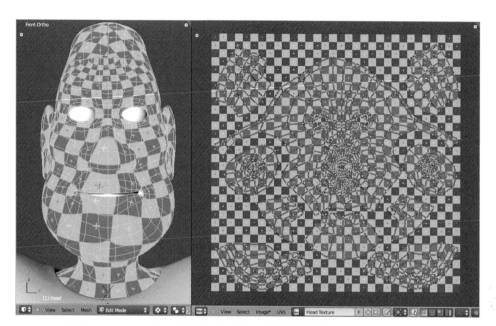

Figure 3.25

The mesh in with the default grid texture applied

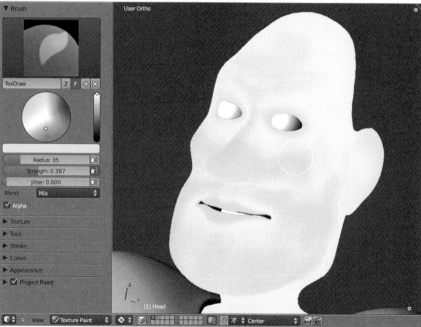

Figure 3.26

Painting in Texture Paint mode

As powerful as texture paint is, sometimes you may want to do more advanced texture work, using photographs, alpha channels, more sophisticated brushes, or other effects. For these situations, you can edit your texture in the image-editing software of your choice.

To refer to the UV map pattern while editing, you can export the UV map pattern using the Export script included in Blender. This is found under the UV menu in the UV/Image Editor header in Edit mode. The output of the exporter is an image file showing the UV mapping, as shown in Figure 3.27. You can choose which kind of image file to export, but the default PNG format is a good choice. This can be imported into GIMP as a layer. Setting the layer to Divide mode will give you an overlay of white guidelines over the texture image, as shown in Figure 3.28, so you can know exactly where the image corresponds to the mesh structure.

Figure 3.27

The exported UV map pattern

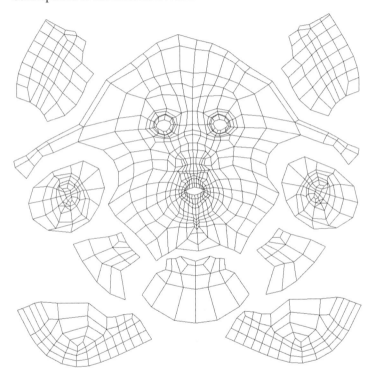

Getting back to Captain Blender, it's now time to add another texture. The first texture you added was to control the mesh's color, but color is only one of many surface characteristics that can be controlled with texture. You can control specularity, transparency, light emittance, and other characteristics with textures. One important use of textures is to control bump effects. This enables you to give the impression of bumpiness to a surface that is actually smooth.

In photorealistic skin texturing, bump mapping is used to create wrinkles, pores, bumps, and other skin irregularities that are far too small to model with actual vertices. With Captain Blender, you're going for a much less realistic effect, so you'll just use bump mapping for the eyebrows as an example of the process.

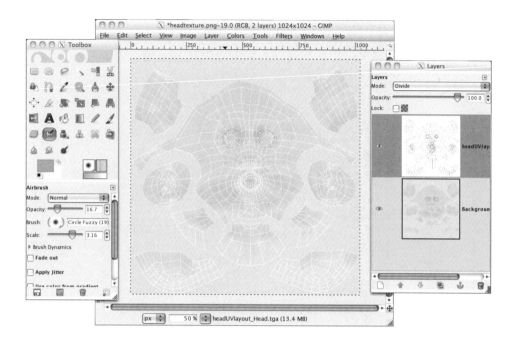

Figure 3.28

**Editing the texture
in GIMP**

Begin by creating a new image in the UV/Image Editor. Do this in exactly the same way you created the color texture image, except rather than selecting the UV Test Grid option, leave the check box blank and create a plain black image, as shown in Figure 3.29. Save the image with an indicative filename so that you know by sight that it is the bump map image.

Figure 3.29

**Adding a new all-
black image texture**

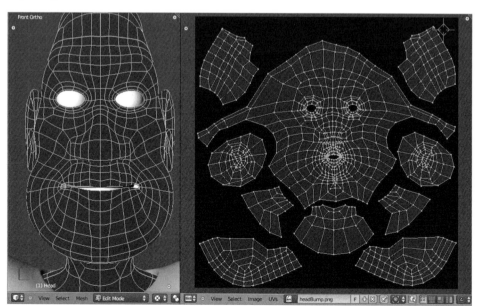

Once again, enter Texture Paint mode, and paint the texture. Use a fine brush size and white paint to paint eyebrows, as shown in Figure 3.30. When you finish, save the texture.

Figure 3.30

Painting a bump map for the eyebrows

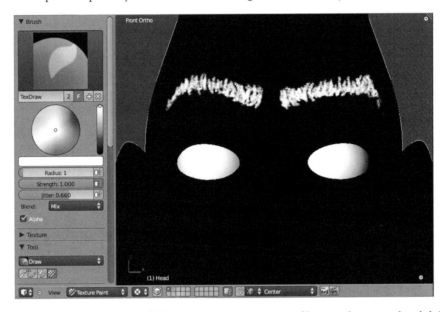

At this point, you should have two separate texture files saved on your hard drive: the bump map texture for the eyebrows and the color texture for the face, shown in Figure 3.31 and Figure 3.32, respectively.

Figure 3.31

The finished bump map texture

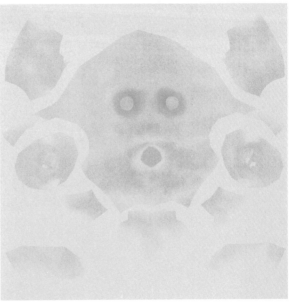

Figure 3.32

The finished color texture

If you were to render an image now, you would find that Captain Blender's head is the same dull gray that it was to begin with. You've created textures, but you have not applied them to a material, so the renderer cannot access them. To render these textures, first create a new material for the head just as you did for the body previously (if a material is already active on the mesh, you can just use that one).

With the material slot selected, enter the Texture Properties window, and add a new texture slot (again, if there is already a texture slot there, use that one). Name the texture Color, and choose Image or Movie from the Type drop-down menu. In the Image panel, find the color texture that you saved on your hard drive. Figure 3.33 shows the Texture Properties window with all this done.

Scroll down the Texture Properties window to the Mapping panel, and choose UV from the drop-down menu.

You'll do the same with the bump map, placing it in the second texture slot and naming this slot Bump, as shown in Figure 3.34. This texture's Mapping value should also be set to UV. However, for the bump map, you must also adjust the Influence values. In the Influence panel, uncheck Color, and check Specular: Intensity and Geometry: Normal. Set those fields with values −0.8 and −0.6 respectively, as shown in Figure 3.35. This will do two things: it will make the mesh shinier in the places where the texture is white (eyebrow hair is shinier than skin), and it will cause the white areas to appear to bump out from the surface of the mesh. Figure 3.36 shows the material values for the head material. Notice that the preview shows the texture applied.

Figure 3.33
Applying the color image texture to the material

Figure 3.34
Applying the bump image texture to the material

Figure 3.35
Influence settings for the bump texture

Figure 3.36
The material preview with the texture applied

Subsurface Scattering

No matter how realistic the color, bump, and specularity on a model is, there are certain characteristics of skin and tissue that cannot be represented with surface textures alone. In fact, skin and animal tissue (as well as many other substances such as wax, vegetable matter, milk, and certain kinds of synthetics) are slightly translucent and exhibit a property called *subsurface scattering* (SSS).

Subsurface scattering occurs when not all of the light that strikes a material's surface gets reflected exactly at the surface. Some of the light penetrates the surface slightly and is reflected from a point within the surface. This creates a blurring (or scattering) effect. Real-life subsurface scattering is the main reason why a wax statue at Madame Tussauds is more lifelike than a plastic mannequin at Target.

In Blender, you access subsurface scattering on the Material panel on the Subsurface Scattering panel. For the Captain Blender model, check the Subsurface Scattering check box, and choose the Skin2 preset, as shown in Figure 3.37. I turned down the Color influence somewhat for this model. You should experiment with rendering with SSS activated to see the kind of results it produces. Getting a highly realistic SSS effect can be tricky, but it is an important effect if you're looking for lifelike character models.

At this point, with the textures applied and SSS turned on, the rendered mesh should appear as shown in Figure 3.38.

Figure 3.37

Adding subsurface scattering

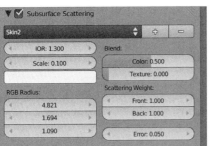

Eyelashes

Figure 3.38

The mesh so far

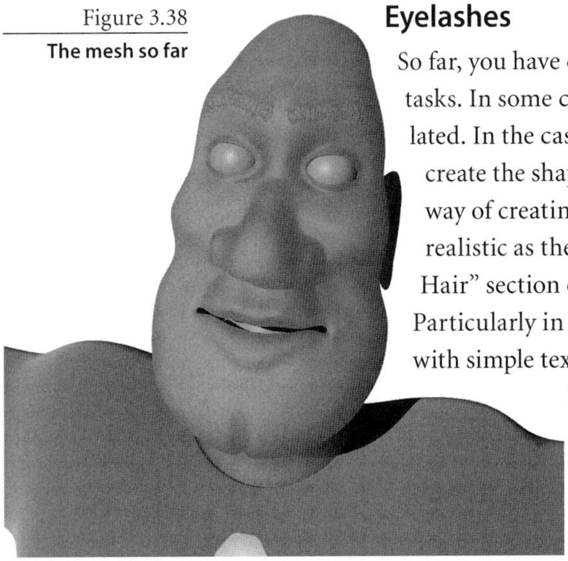

So far, you have considered mesh modeling and texturing to be separate tasks. In some cases, however, the two tasks become especially interrelated. In the case of eyelashes, for example, you can use a texture itself to create the shape of the lashes. Using a 2D texture on planes is a common way of creating many hair effects. It doesn't usually result in hair as realistic as the particle hair that you'll see in the "Working with Particle Hair" section of this chapter, but it can be much easier to manage. Particularly in a simple case such as eyelashes, the benefits of working with simple textures often outweigh those of using particles.

Because you must apply a texture to a mesh, you need to return briefly to mesh modeling to create a surface on which to apply the texture. You'll start by selecting and duplicating the edge loops around the eyelids, which will be approximately where you want the lashes to be.

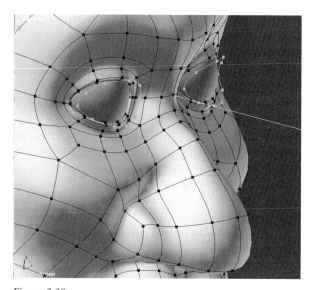

Figure 3.39

Copying edge loop geometry to begin creating eyelashes

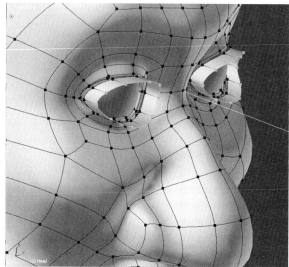

Figure 3.40

Extruding the eyelashes

Select the loop by holding Alt while right-clicking an edge in the loop, and then copy the loop by pressing Shift+D. Move the duplicated edges out a bit along the y-axis to make them easier to work with, as shown in Figure 3.39. Next, you'll extrude the edge along the y-axis to give you the surface, as shown in Figure 3.40.

You'll do a little tweaking now, separating the outer edges of the surface by selecting each edge and pressing the V key. Also, move the faces back toward the face and shape them in the way you want the eyelashes to be. Another important step here is to select all the faces and press Ctrl+N to recalculate the normals outside. Your results should look like Figure 3.41.

Select only the lashes by pressing the L key with your mouse over a vertex in each lash, top and bottom, right and left. The L key enables you to select connected pieces of mesh. Be sure not to select the entire head mesh; you've already unwrapped that part, and you don't want to remap it. With only the lashes selected, press the E key in the UV/Image Editor to unwrap the lashes, as shown in Figure 3.42.

Figure 3.41

Selecting the fully modeled eyelashes

HOTKEY: L key selects a single connected section of mesh based on proximity with the mouse pointer in Edit mode.

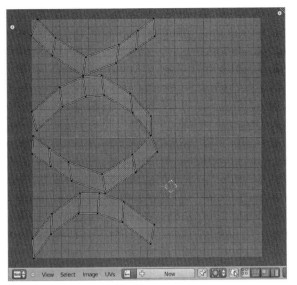

Figure 3.42

UV unwrapping the eyelashes

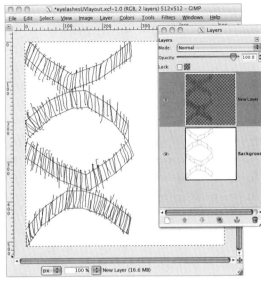

Figure 3.43

Drawing the eyelash texture

Export the UV map as described previously, and open the image in your 2D image-editing application. Add a new transparent layer and draw some simple eyelash lines on the new layer, as shown in Figure 3.43. Save only the transparent layer with the lashes drawn on as your texture. Save the file as a PNG file.

Figure 3.44

The eyelash texture

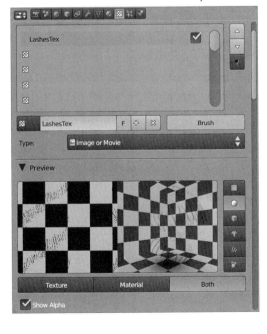

Create a new material and assign it to the mesh of the lashes, just as you have done several times so far in this chapter. Set the material color to Red: 0.615, Green: 0.289, Blue: 0.0. This will give us the reddish-brown color of the eyelashes. Set Specular Intensity to 0. Check the Transparency check box, and in the Transparency panel set the Alpha value to 0. Add an image texture to the material and load the PNG file you just created as the texture image. Choose UV for the Mapping type. If you check the Show Alpha check box on the texture preview, the resulting texture preview will appear as shown in Figure 3.44. Set the Influence value of the texture to Alpha, with full (1.0) influence.

The lashes material is now finished, but you need to make a change to the head material to enable it to respond correctly to the shadows cast by a transparent or partially transparent material. Choose the head material slot, and in the Shadow panel for the head material select the Receive Transparent check box. The Receive Transparent option is necessary so that the mesh can take shadows from transparent objects correctly. By default, all shadows are treated as though they are cast by opaque objects, so in this case, the eyelash meshes would cast solid black shadows. Note that although transparency is a property of the eyelashes, the ability to receive transparent shadows from transparent meshes is a property of the object onto which the shadows are cast. When you've done this, the result should render out to look similar to Figure 3.45.

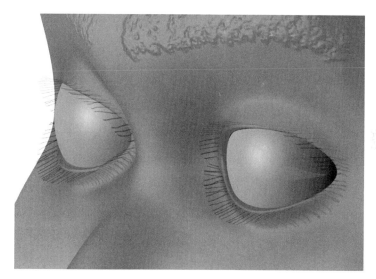

Figure 3.45

The finished eyelashes

Controlling Materials with Nodes

When you briefly revisit the method described here to make the eyebrows, there's something that doesn't quite sit right. The bump-mapped eyebrows in themselves aren't too bad, but the fact that the SSS effect on the head material is also being applied to the eyebrows is a little bit wrong. The result of this makes the eyebrows look more waxy and fake than they ought to look.

Unfortunately, you cannot control SSS with just a surface texture. However, using Blender's powerful material node system, you can mix two completely separate materials on one mesh and use a texture to determine where each material is used.

To do this, first create a copy of the head material by selecting its slot and clicking the plus symbol to the right of the material slots field in the Material Properties window. Click the 2 next to the new material's name to make it a single-user material. Rename it HeadMaterialNoSSS. Uncheck Subsurface Scattering, as shown in Figure 3.46. Otherwise, leave the settings for the material the same.

Add yet another material slot by clicking the plus symbol to the right of the slots. Once again, separate the material on this slot into its own single-user material by clicking the 2 next to it. This time, click the nodes button shown highlighted in Figure 3.47 to make the material a node material. A node material is a material whose characteristics are the final output of a node graph. The node graph can take multiple other materials or textures as inputs.

Figure 3.46

Creating a copy of the head material without SSS

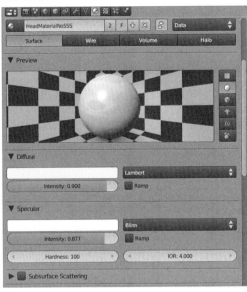

The hotkeys for adding and deleting nodes are analogous to adding and deleting elements in the 3D viewport. Shift+A brings up a menu of possible node types to add, and the X key deletes a node. When you create the node material, two nodes will automatically be created, a Material node and an Output node. The Material node is an input that can be an ordinary non-node-based material, and the Output node determines the characteristics of this node-based material.

For this example, choose the original head material from the drop-down menu on the Material node. Add a second Material node by pressing Shift+A and selecting Input → Material. From the drop-down menu on this node, choose the HeadMaterialNoSSS material. Add a Texture node by pressing Shift+A and selecting Input → Texture. Select the Bump texture from the drop-down menu. Finally, press Shift+A and select Color → Mix to add a Mix node.

Figure 3.47

Adding a new node-based material

The idea is to mix the two materials together using the texture as a mix factor. Remember that the texture corresponds to the eyebrows, so it should describe exactly where the two materials should apply. The node network should be set up as shown in Figure 3.48.

This is a very simple use of material nodes, but it should begin to give you an idea of how powerful they can be for creating complex materials and for mixing materials in a seamless and smooth way on a mesh. To delete a link between two nodes, hold Ctrl and the left mouse button, and drag your mouse across the link.

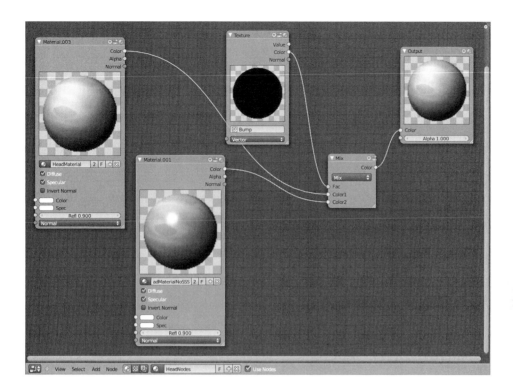

Figure 3.48

Mixing the two materials with nodes

Modeling Eyes

So far, our hero has been lacking one of the most important parts of a convincing human face: eyes. Now you'll replace the blank gray orbs he currently has with some actual eyeballs. This process also involves a few additional steps of mesh modeling.

You'll begin with those very orbs, because they are already the right size. To view the eyeballs on their own, select them in Object mode, and press the slash key on the numeric keypad to enter Local mode. You'll now view only the eyeballs, and you can work with them without seeing anything else until the next time you press the slash key on the number pad.

Also, you'll make only one eye and then copy it, so you can remove the Mirror modifier and recenter the object center on the single orb object. To remove the Mirror modifier, simply click the x in the upper-right corner of the modifier on the Modifiers tab. To position the object center, refer to "Object Origins" in Chapter 1.

So, now you're working with a single UV sphere with 12 segments and 12 rings. Enter Edit mode to begin editing the mesh. Use the Loop Cut tool (Ctrl+R) to make a loop cut around where the iris will be.

The eyeball consists of two spheres, one inside the other. The outer sphere is transparent and models the clear lens in front of the iris and the specularity over the surface of the eyeball. The inner sphere will contain the colors and textures you want for the various parts of the eye. To make the two spheres, go back into Object mode, and duplicate the orb with Shift+D. Scale the new sphere down 1 percent by pressing S and immediately entering **.99**.

You'll work with one sphere at a time, so let's put them on separate layers for the time being. Enter Object mode, select the outer sphere, press M, and select any of the currently invisible layer buttons to put the sphere on that layer.

With the inner sphere selected, go into Edit mode, and create a concave indentation where the iris will be. Make sure you have proportional editing turned on with the drop-down menu in the 3D window header and set to Sphere Falloff. Then select the vertex at the pole of the sphere and use G, Y to move the point inward. Make sure to adjust the influence of the proportional editing tool with the mouse wheel so that only the nearest vertices are affected. You can see the influence of the proportional editing tool as a very light gray circle.

If you try to move the vertex and the whole eyeball moves, it is because the proportional editing tool's field of influence is very wide. It might be too wide for you to see the circle in the 3D viewport. You might need to move the view out a bit to see the circle. Also, remember that you can adjust the proportional editing tool's field of influence only while you are actually editing. You must press the G key first; then you can adjust the size of the circle. You should wind up with an indentation like the one shown in Figure 3.49.

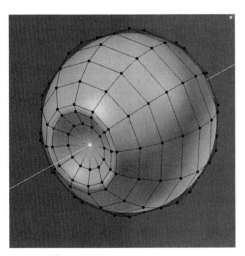

Figure 3.49

Modeling an indentation for the iris

That's all the modeling you need to do on the inner eye. The real work here is done in the material, and specifically in textures. Create a new material slot, and name it **EyeBall** in the materials editing area. Turn the RGB values all up to 1, making the eyeball pure white. In the Specular panel, set Intensity to 0.

The iris and pupil will consist of three procedural textures layered on top of each other, which will together create the color, texture, and lightness and darkness of the eye. You'll start with the basic color. Create a new texture in the top texture slot, and name it **Iris**. Set the texture type to Blend, as shown in Figure 3.50.

You'll use the color ramp to control the color variation from the center of the pupil to the edge of the iris. Check the Ramp box in the Colors panel of the Texture Properties window and set your color ramp similarly to the one shown in Figure 3.51.

You can add stops in the color ramp by clicking Add and adjust their color and alpha values with the color picker. The rightmost stop should be solid black, because it will be the iris. The leftmost stop should be white and should have an alpha value of zero. The colors in between are up to you, but I gave Captain Blender greenish eyes that blend into brown around the edges of the iris.

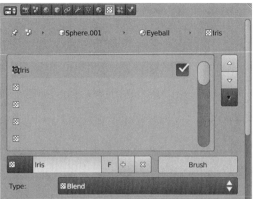

Figure 3.50
Adding the Iris texture

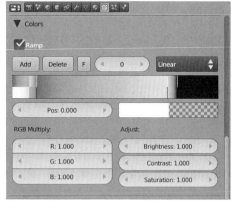

Figure 3.51
Adjusting the color ramp for the Iris texture

For the Mapping values, use Generated mapping and Sphere projection, as shown in Figure 3.52. Also follow that figure in setting the projection coordinates to Y, X, and X. On the Blend panel, set the Progression value as Spherical. The resulting texture preview will look as shown in Figure 3.53. Be sure to click the Both button under the preview window to see a preview of both the texture and the material it's on side by side.

What you have so far is close but still lacks some character as an eyeball texture. Even from a distance, human irises do not look like smooth color gradations. You can fix this by adding an element of noise in the form of a cloud texture. Place this texture in the second texture slot. Adjust the Size value of the cloud texture to get an effect like the one shown in Figure 3.54. Use the color ramp on this texture too to control the color and the steepness of the texture, as shown in Figure 3.55.

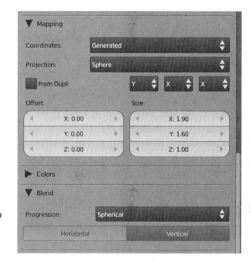

Figure 3.52
Mapping settings for the Iris texture

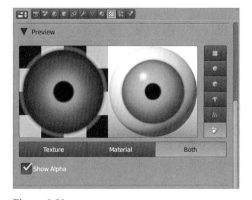

Figure 3.53
Preview of the Iris texture and material

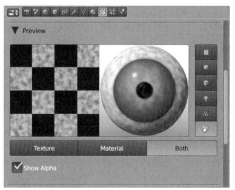

Figure 3.54
The cloud texture

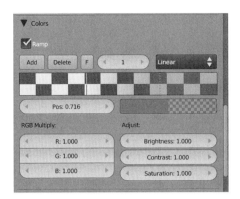

Figure 3.55

Color ramp for the cloud texture

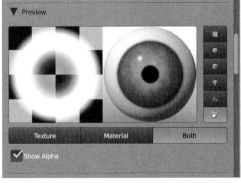

Figure 3.56

A stencil texture

Figure 3.57

Shaping the outer sphere of the eyeball

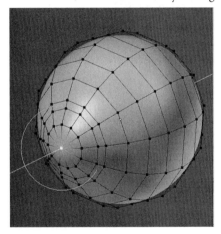

Obviously, the problem here is that the cloud texture covers the whole eyeball, which is clearly not right. To fix this, copy the original Iris blend texture so that it is in the second texture slot, below the original blend texture and above the cloud texture. Adjust the ramp to be solid white, with the left and right sides both at Alpha 0. Check the Stencil box on the Influence tab. Figure 3.56 shows the stencil texture, alongside its effect. Notice that the cloud pattern on the eyeball is visible only in the area corresponding to the opaque portion of the stencil texture.

You'll now turn to the outer sphere of the eyeball. In Edit mode, with proportional editing turned on (the field of influence should be about the same as it was the last time you used it), select the pole vertex over the iris area, and pull it outward along the y-axis to create the slight bump of the eye's lens, as shown in Figure 3.57.

Create a new material for this object, and name the material OuterEye. Check Transparency, and set the Alpha value to 0. Use a Wardiso specularity shader with intensity at around 0.4 and a slope of about 0.12.

Your finished product should look something like Figure 3.58 when you render it. You can join the outer mesh and inner mesh by selecting both in Object mode and hitting Ctrl+J. Name the object Eyeball.L, and place it in the left eye socket. Then copy the object with Shift+D, and press the X key to move the new eyeball directly over to the right eye socket. Place it properly, and make sure it has the correct name.

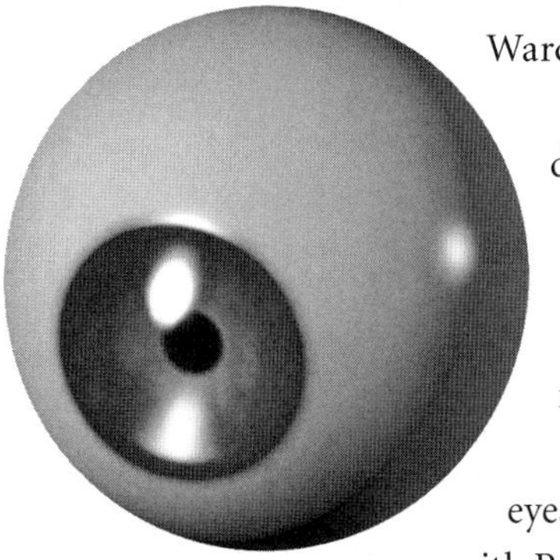

Congratulations. Your Captain Blender model now has clothing, skin, and eyes, as shown in Figure 3.59. Something is still missing, though. In the "Working with Particle Hair" section of this chapter, you'll see how to give your character convincing hair with Blender's particle functionality.

Figure 3.58

The finished eyeball lit and rendered

Working with Particle Hair

Blender's particle system is a powerful tool with a wide variety of uses. Particles let you represent and animate clusters of objects that are too small to be practical to simulate in other ways. Dust, powder, swarms of insects, and the like are often suited to simulation with particles.

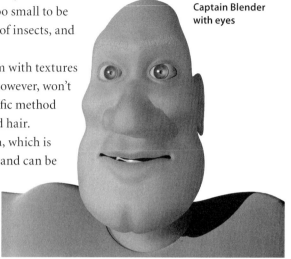

Figure 3.59

Captain Blender with eyes

You can also give particles a blurry quality and use them with textures to create convincing flame and smoke effects. This book, however, won't look at these uses of particles. Instead, it focuses on a specific method of using particles to effectively generate convincing fur and hair.

Like all particles, hair particles are emitted from a mesh, which is referred to as the *emitter*. The emitter can be visible or not and can be made of any material. The particles also have a material. You can control many qualities of the hair using particle settings in conjunction with textures and vertex groups, and you can style the hair in any way you like using the styling tools available.

Setting Up a Particle System

There are a variety of ways to create hair for a character. You could model the hairstyle directly with a mesh and use texturing to give it a convincing appearance. A common way to make hair is to layer many textured planes together. With what you've learned so far about texturing and mesh modeling, you should be able to come up with some interesting approaches to doing hair in this way. However, the most realistic method of creating hair in Blender is by using particles, which is what you'll do here.

Figure 3.60

Selecting the scalp mesh

Recall that when you originally modeled the head mesh in the previous chapter, you went out of your way to model the hairline around the edge of the scalp. Now you're going to take advantage of that by selecting the scalp portion of the mesh, as shown in Figure 3.60.

In the Mesh Properties window, scroll down to the Vertex Groups panel, and click the plus symbol to add a vertex group to the mesh. Name the group Hair Density, as shown in Figure 3.61. Click the Assign button to assign the selected vertices to this vertex group. You will use this vertex group to control where the hair will "grow" from.

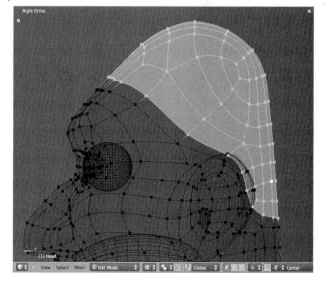

Figure 3.61

Adding a vertex group

To set up the particle system, enter the Particle Properties window, as shown in Figure 3.62, and add a new particle system by clicking the plus symbol, and then rename the particle system **Hair** as shown in that figure. Change the number of particles in the Emission panel from 1000 to 500. Your mesh should sprout hair, as shown in Figure 3.63. Now it's just a matter of bringing it under control!

Figure 3.62

Adding the hair particle system

First, you need to constrain where on the mesh the hair emits from. For this, you'll use the HairDensity vertex group you just created. Scroll down to the Vertexgroups panel, and enter **Hair Density** in the Density field, as shown in Figure 3.64.

Notice that you can control any of seven different hair characteristics with vertex groups. Density refers to how many hair particles emit from faces based on their vertex group value. In this case, all the values for the HairDensity vertex group are 1 or 0, so either the faces will fully emit hair or they won't emit any hair at all.

After you set the density vertex group, you should see the hair emit only from the scalp. Scroll back up to the Velocity panel, and change the Normal value from 1.0 to 0.2. This controls the length of the hair extending from the emitter face. After making these adjustments, Captain Blender's hair should look more like Figure 3.65. You'll do further refining of the hair style directly in Particle mode.

Before you continue on to styling, activate child particles by scrolling down to the Children panel and

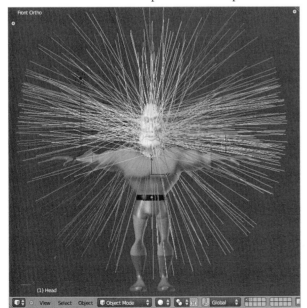

Figure 3.63

The new hair

Figure 3.64

Controlling hair density with the Vertex group

clicking the Faces button. This will cause child particles to be emitted from the same faces that the actual particles are emitted from, increasing the apparent density of the particle system. Although 500 is really not enough particles to give the appearance of a full head of hair on their own, with child particles, it is more than enough. Set Display to 5 and Render to 80. This determines how many child particles per strand are shown in the 3D viewport in Object mode and how many are rendered.

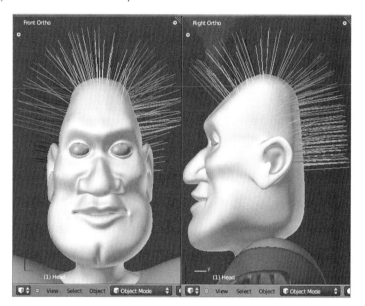

Figure 3.65

A more reasonable starting point for hair styling

Styling Hair

You can style hair with a great deal of control in Blender's Particle mode. However, once you begin styling the hair, many of the particle settings will be fixed, and you can change them only by discarding the edits you've made in Particle mode. You can adjust the number of child particles, for example, but you cannot change the number of actual particles without losing any hairstyling you've done.

Enter Particle mode using the mode drop-down menu in the 3D viewport header. Press the T key to open the Tool Shelf on the left side of the 3D viewport.

Hairstyling in Particle mode is simple, but it takes a little getting used to. You can select a "brush" type from the list in the Tool Shelf. A good one to start with is the Comb, as shown in Figure 3.66. As you might imagine, this brush shapes the particle hair in a way analogous to the way a real comb shapes real hair. You must keep in mind that your edits are all happening in the plane orthogonal to the user's perspective, so rotate your model frequently and style the hair from multiple different perspectives as you progress. If you spend all your time in orthogonal side view and get the hair looking just right, you may be surprised at how things look from the front.

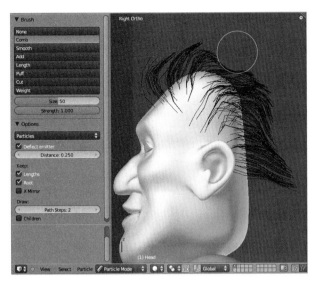

Figure 3.66

Styling hair in Particle mode

The other brushes are Smooth, Add, Length, Puff, Cut, and Weight. All of these have to do with the shape or amount of hair except for Weight, which enables you to do weight painting directly on the hair. This is useful for softbody effects on hair. The Size and Strength fields affect the size and influence of the brush. The Deflect Emitter option keeps the hair from penetrating the mesh that emits it (some penetration can still happen, so be sure to make test renders and adjust the hairstyling where necessary). Keep Lengths and Keep Root will hold the lengths or root fixed when combing. If you uncheck Root, you will be able to comb the hair right off of the head.

In the 3D viewport header, you can select from three different selection modes. The default mode is Path Edit mode, which enables you to comb, grow, and edit the hair as a whole. The other two are Point Select mode and Tip Select mode.

In Point Select mode, points along the length of the hair are visible as vertices, and you can select them in the same way that you select vertices in Edit mode. Furthermore, you can select individual hair particles using the L key. When particles are selected, only the selected particles are affected by the hairstyling tools. Figure 3.67 shows a few particles selected in this way, being styled to form a curlicue lock of hair over the forehead of the character. Without being able to select individual particles, it would be very tricky to achieve such an effect.

Figure 3.67

Selecting individual strand particles to edit

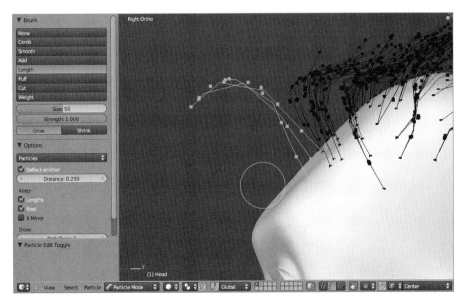

The third mode, Tip Select, is similar to Point Select except that you can select only the tips of the hair.

Hair Material and Texture

Hair particles will give you the shape and the density of the hair, but for really convincing hair, you need to be able to use materials and textures correctly.

Create a new material slot, make the material single user, and rename the material just as you have several times before in this chapter. Name the newly created material HairMaterial. Add a blend type texture to this material called HairTex.

Figure 3.68 shows the HairTex texture preview. Select Show Alpha, and select the Strand material preview to see how the texture will show up on hair particles.

The blend gradation itself is defined in the Color panel, similarly to how you created the Iris texture for the eyes. Enable the color ramp by checking the Ramp check box.

The ramp stops vary in Color and Alpha values from left to right representing the alpha and color change from the root to tip of each strand of hair. For Color, I have the hair beginning with a darker brown root and lightening to an orangish blond color to the right.

The Alpha value is more important. The Alpha value must taper off gradually to the right to give a sense of wispiness to the tips of the hair. On the left, there should be a more sudden—but not too sharp—gradation from alpha 0 to 1. This has the effect of softening the appearance of the roots where the particles emerge from the scalp. If this didn't have

an alpha gradation, the roots would look very abrupt, giving the appearance of something more like bad hair plugs. The Influence settings of the texture should be full influence for Color and Alpha values. Figure 3.69 shows the Ramp and Influence panels.

To receive the full alpha range from the texture, the material needs to have Transparency enabled and its own Alpha value set to 0, as shown in Figure 3.70. Both Specular and Diffuse intensity values are turned up to 0.9, with Lambert set as the Diffuse shader and Blinn set as the Specular shader. You can experiment with these values until you find the effect you like best. Note again the Strand material preview.

Figure 3.68

A blend texture for the hair material

Figure 3.69

The color Ramp and Influence panels for the blend texture

The material you just created is the third material on the head object. To set the hair particles to render with this material, you must select the corresponding material index in the Material field of the Render panel for the particles. This panel is part of the Particle Properties window and is shown in Figure 3.71. Be sure that Emitter is selected (otherwise the Emitter object, Captain Blender's head, will not be rendered) and choose Strand render, which will greatly speed up and improve the appearance of rendered hair.

That's all there is to it. When you render the head, you should see something similar to what's shown in Figure 3.72.

You've now finished modeling and texturing your character. The next chapter will take you into the next phase of preparing your character for animation, as you are introduced to armatures and rigging.

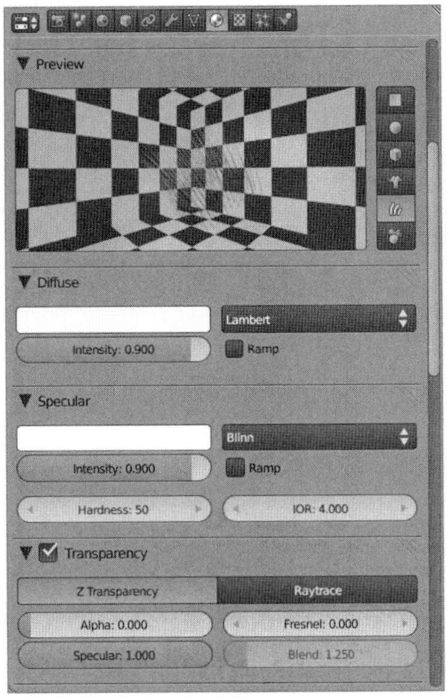

Figure 3.70

The hair material

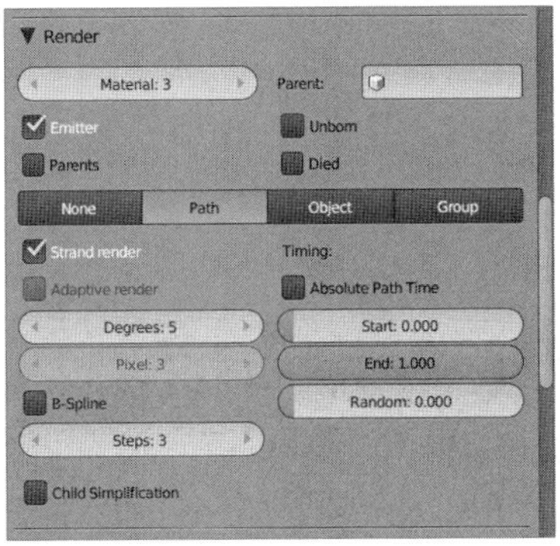

Figure 3.71

Render settings for the hair

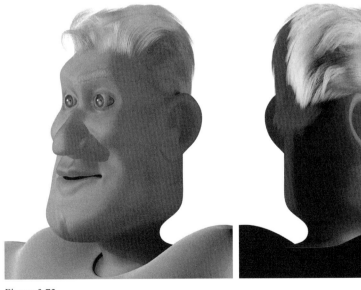

Figure 3.72

The mesh rendered with hair

CHAPTER 4

Armatures and Rigging

Most 3D character animation, both CG and traditional, relies on armatures to manipulate the characters' body parts. Armatures behave as the characters' skeletons, and their segments are referred to as *bones*. Of course, the mechanics of motion and posing are very different for a 3D mesh than they are for a flesh-and-blood human, so the bones of a CG character do not generally correspond to actual bones in a live person. Nevertheless, they are very similar conceptually. Building an armature can be very simple or very complicated, depending upon how much control the animator wants over the character's body parts and how many constraints and restrictions are desired on the character's movement. An armature in which the knees can be bent sideways, for example, is likely to be a simpler armature than one in which the joints have natural limitations. The degree of complexity necessary in an armature depends upon the requirements of the animation. A good armature should result in an easy-to-manipulate character with convincing movements.

The process of *rigging* a character means setting up an armature and its associated constraints. *Skinning* refers to connecting a mesh to an armature so that manipulating the armature results in the desired deformations of the mesh. The mesh should follow the movement of the armature in the appropriate way. Simply put, this is accomplished by having each bone influence the movement of certain vertices. There are several ways to assign influence to vertices, which are discussed in this chapter.

- ■ **Blender Armature System**

- ■ **Building a Simple Armature**

- ■ **Rigging Captain Blender with Rigify**

Blender Armature System

An armature in Blender consists of bones and their parent relationships, connections, and the various constraints that control their motion and interaction. You can use a well-put-together armature to create very realistic poses quickly and easily. You will now look briefly at the basic types of bones and constraints used in creating sophisticated armatures.

Bones

The armature system in Blender includes options for the behavior and display of bones. Depending on the role the bone will play in the rig, you can identify a number of basic bone classes used in rigging.

Control Bones   Control bones are the bones that the animator uses to control the rig. The control bone setup and display should be as simple and intuitive as possible. Typically the animator and the rigger or technical director are different people. The animator wants to pose the model and does not want to be bothered with the underlying behavior of the rig.

Deform Bones   Deform bones are the bones that influence the vertices of a mesh. When the deform bones move or rotate, the mesh they are associated with also moves or rotates.

Function Bones   For lack of a better term, I call the other bones in the rig *function bones*. These are bones that are neither control bones nor deform bones, but they play some other role in making the rig work. These bones include constraint targets or solvers such as inverse kinematics (IK) targets or solvers discussed in this chapter.

All bones in a rig belong to at least one of these classes. A bone may belong to more than one of the classes or even to all three. Professional rigs divide up this functionality in a way that makes the finished product easy to use for animators by displaying only what is necessary for animation.

A variety of options exist for bone display and editing. Many of these options are discussed in this chapter.

Bone Constraints

Bone constraints are essentially restrictions and controls that make movements by an object or bone dependent on another object or on some other factor. Setting up an armature with well-applied bone constraints can make posing the armature much easier than simply controlling every bone's movement completely by hand.

Important bone constraints in armature design include the following:

IK Constraint   Works with an IK solver to create a chain of bones whose position can be determined by the location of the tip.

Copy Location/Rotation/Scale   Restricts the location, rotation, or scale of one bone or object to that of another.

Track-to Constraint Forces an object or bone to point in the direction of ("track to") a specified object. This is useful for eye tracking and also to control the movement of the camera by tracking the camera to an Empty.

Floor Constraint Defines an object or bone beneath which another object or bone won't go. This is often used in conjunction with IK solvers to prevent feet from going beneath the level of the ground.

Stretch-to Constraint Causes a bone or object to stretch or squash to an object or bone that is set as the target constraint. It can also manage the displacement of volume, which results from the stretching or squashing.

Action Constraint Enables a bone's movement to control an action that has been animated in advance.

Building a Simple Armature

To get a look at the basics of building, displaying, and posing an armature, you'll build a quick and simple armature for the figure shown in Figure 4.1. If you followed the modeling tutorials in Chapter 2, you should have no problem box-modeling the figure yourself. If you prefer to skip the modeling, you can find the mesh of this figure on the accompanying DVD, in the file figure.blend. In the following example, front view is the view displayed by pressing 1 on the number pad, top view is the view by pressing 7 on the number pad, and pressing 3 on the number pad displays the view of the figure from the user's right, as in the other examples in this book.

Later in this chapter, you'll see a much faster and easier way to create sophisticated rigs using Blender's Rigify system. However, in this simple example, you'll build the rig from scratch in order to understand the basics of how armatures work.

The first step is to create the armature. The 3D cursor should be placed at the center of the Mesh object. In Object mode, press Shift+A, and select Add → Armature → Single Bone, as shown in Figure 4.2. If the cursor was not in the

Figure 4.1

A simple 3D figure

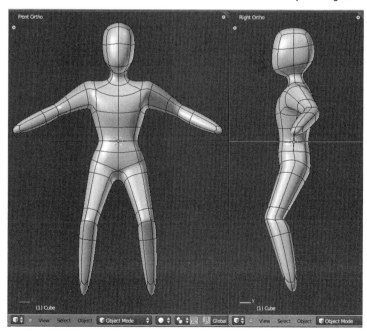

center of the space when you added the object, simply press **Alt+G** to move the object to the origin of the 3D space.

Figure 4.2

**Adding the arma-
ture object**

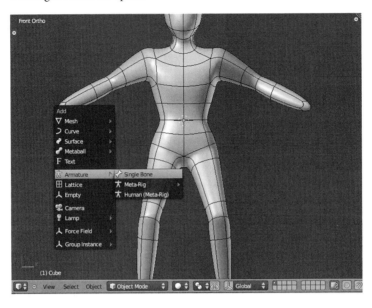

Figure 4.3

**Setting the object
properties to X-Ray
display**

Although the armature is there, you will not be able to see it in solid view mode, because it is located inside the mesh. With the armature object selected, select the X-Ray box in the Object Properties panel, as shown in Figure 4.3. This will ensure that the armature is visible even if other objects such as the character mesh cover it. When you've done this, the bone should be visible, as shown in Figure 4.4.

Editing armatures and bones is analogous to editing most kinds of objects in Blender. The G, R, and S keys have the same effect of translation, rotation, and scaling as they do elsewhere. Likewise, the E key is used to extrude when in Edit mode, which in the case of bones creates a new connected bone from the tip or the root of the original bone. To begin editing the armature, enter Edit mode either by using the menu in the 3D viewport header or by pressing the Tab key.

HOTKEY: Pressing E extrudes new bones in an armature in Edit mode.

In Edit mode, switch to side view (Numpad 3), select the whole bone by clicking its middle portion, and rotate the bone 90 degrees counterclockwise by pressing the R key and entering **-90** directly, as shown in Figure 4.5. Press the G key to grab and move the bone so that the tip of the bone is about where the base of the character's spine would be, as shown in Figure 4.6.

In Edit mode, you can select bones in three different ways. You can select the base of the bone (the small ball at the wide end of the bone) or the tip of the bone (the small ball at the narrow end of the bone), or you can select the whole bone by right-clicking the middle of the bone. To extrude from the tip of the bone, select the tip by right-clicking it.

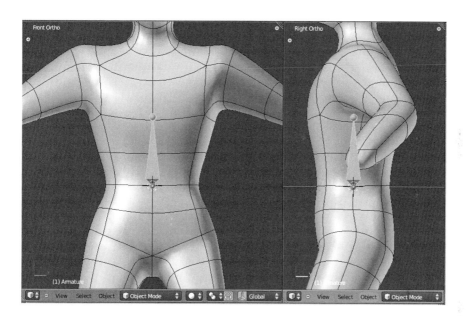

Figure 4.4

The armature in X-Ray display mode

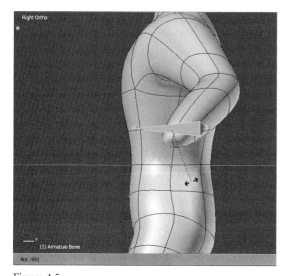

Figure 4.5

Rotating the bone

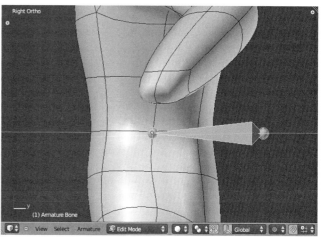

Figure 4.6

Placing the bone at the base of the torso

Extrude the first child of the bone by pressing the E key followed by the Z key to pull the extruded bone directly upward along the z axis, as shown in Figure 4.7. Do this again three more times to create bones for the chest, neck, and head, as shown in Figure 4.8.

Figure 4.7

Extruding a new bone

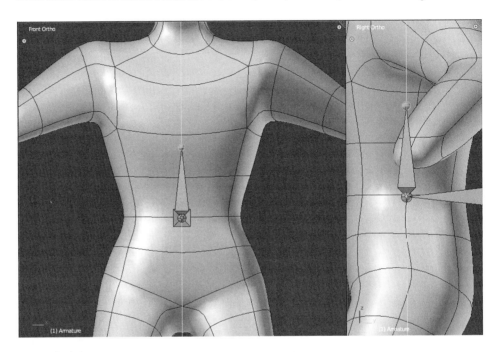

Figure 4.8

Extruding bones for the chest, neck, and head

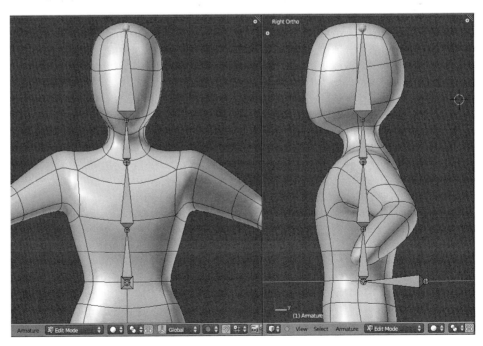

Next, you will extrude bones for the shoulders. However, to do this, you will use X-Axis Mirror so that you will not need to duplicate your efforts. Turn on X-Axis Mirror by clicking the check box in the Tool Shelf to the left of the 3D viewport (the Tool Shelf is accessed either by pressing the T key with the mouse over the 3D viewport or by clicking the little plus sign in the upper left of the 3D viewport), as shown in Figure 4.9.

HOTKEY: Pressing T over the 3D viewport accesses the Tool Shelf.

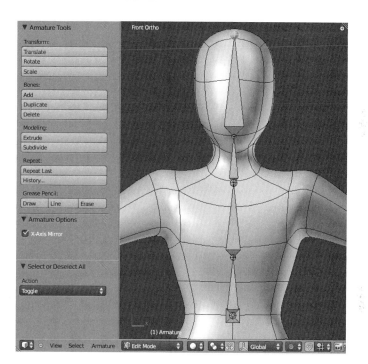

Figure 4.9

**Activating
X-Axis Mirror**

When you have activated X-Axis Mirror, select the joint at the base of the neck by right-clicking the bone node there. Do a mirrored fork extrude by pressing Shift+E to extrude the shoulders, as shown in Figure 4.10. Use the plain E key to extrude two more times to form the rest of the arms, as shown in Figure 4.11. Because the shoulders were fork-extruded with Shift+E and X-Axis mirror is active, edits you make on the arms will be automatically mirrored.

HOTKEY: Pressing Shift+E performs a forked extrude on armatures in Edit mode when X-Axis Mirror is active.

Figure 4.10

Mirror-extruding the shoulders with Shift+E

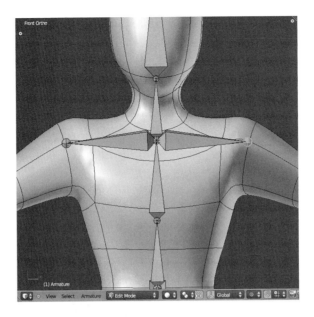

Figure 4.11

Extruding the arms

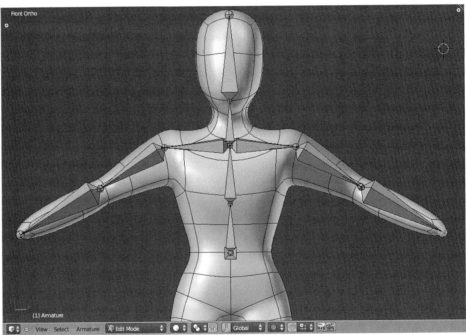

You've finished with the top half of the body. Now select the tip of the root bone (the first bone you added), and mirror-extrude downward with Shift+E to make the hips. From there, extrude two more times downward to make the bones of the legs, as shown in Figure 4.12.

Enter side view by pressing 3 on the number pad. Select the knee joints, grab them with the G key, and move them forward along the y-axis, as shown in Figure 4.13, so that they are slightly bent and conform to the shape of the mesh. Do the same with the elbows.

It helps to have arms and legs bent slightly in their rest position to facilitate proper bending during IK posing. You should bear this in mind when modeling your mesh and when setting up your armature.

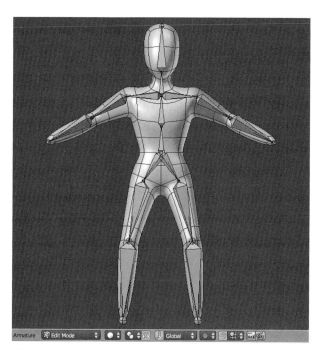

Figure 4.12
Extruding the leg bones

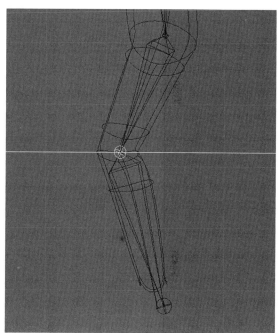

Figure 4.13
Bending the legs slightly at the joints

Inverse Kinematics

There are two main ways to pose characters, *forward kinematics* (FK) and *inverse kinematics* (IK). These will be discussed in more detail in later chapters, but it's important to have an idea of the difference. FK is the simplest way to pose a character. It is analogous to the way you would usually pose a jointed doll. When you rotate the upper arm of a doll, the forearm and hand follow that motion. IK posing is done by moving the tip of a chain of bones. The computer automatically calculates the rotation of the other bones in the chain appropriately.

As you'll see later in this book, FK posing is good for animating graceful arcs, and for this reason it is appropriate for free-swinging limbs. IK posing is best suited for cases when the endpoint of a limb (for example, the hand or foot) is fixed in place or moved by an external force. A classic example is walking, in which each foot is fixed on the ground while the rest of the body moves. When you try to animate a character walking by using only freely rotating legs, you get the appearance of sliding feet. For this reason, IK posing is often used for feet. A fully functional, flexible rig for general-purpose character animation requires that all limbs be poseable in either IK or FK. You'll see how this is done in the next section of this chapter, when you work with the Captain Blender armature.

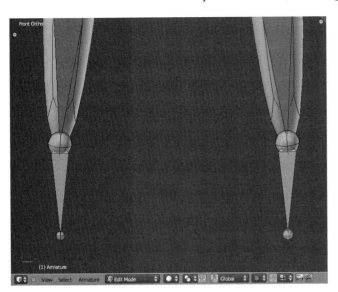

Figure 4.14

Extruding function bones to act as IK targets

To enable IK posing for the legs in this simple example rig, you need to add IK bone constraints on the lower leg bones. However, before doing this, you need to add function bones to act as the constraints' targets. Create these bones by extruding once more downward from the tips of the legs. These bones will extend beyond the edge of the mesh, as shown in Figure 4.14.

These bones will be used to control the movement of the leg, so they must be independent of the leg. Select one of the bones (be sure the whole bone is selected, not just the tip or the root), press Alt+P, and choose Clear Parent to remove the parent-child relationship between the bones, as shown in Figure 4.15. This also disconnects the bones so that the tip bones can be moved freely of the legs.

HOTKEY: Pressing Alt+P brings up a menu to clear parent relationships between objects or bones.

Bone constraints are dealt with in Pose mode. So far, you've seen the armature in Edit mode, which is analogous to Edit mode for meshes, and Object mode, which is identical to Object mode for other 3D objects. Armatures also have another mode that can be used: Pose mode. As the name suggests, Pose mode is the mode in which the completed armature is posed. You can rotate and move bones in a way analogous to the way you would control a doll or puppet, subject to whatever bone constraints you have in place. You can't add new bones or change the way the bones are connected to each other like you can in Edit mode.

To create the IK constraint, enter Pose mode using the drop-down menu in the 3D viewport header, as shown in Figure 4.16, or by pressing Ctrl+Tab.

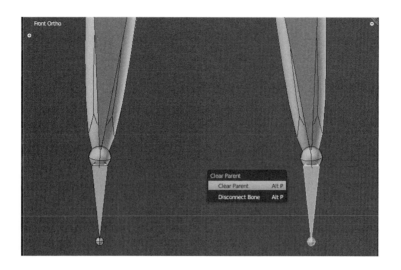

Figure 4.15

Removing the parent-child relationship with Alt+P

HOTKEY: Pressing Ctrl+Tab toggles between Pose mode and Object mode when an armature is selected.

In Pose mode, select the target bone first and then hold Shift and select the shin bone of the left leg. The order of selection is important to ensure that the constraint is applied to the correct bone. Press Shift+I, and choose To Active Bone to add the IK constraint, as shown in Figure 4.17.

Figure 4.16

Entering Pose mode

HOTKEY: Pressing Shift+I adds an IK constraint to the active (last selected) bone targeted to the previously selected bone in Pose mode.

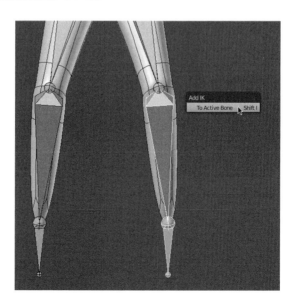

Figure 4.17

Adding an IK constraint

When you've done this, the shin bone should be displayed in yellow, and a dotted line should extend from the tip of the IK chain to the base of the root bone, as shown in Figure 4.18.

Figure 4.18

The IK constraint displayed

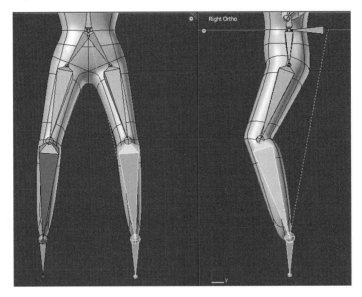

You can adjust the parameters of this constraint directly in the Bone Constraints panel of the Properties window, as shown in Figure 4.19. Set the Chain Length value to **2**, as shown in that figure. This ensures that IK posing is calculated only for the bones of the leg up to the hip. You don't need to worry about the number of the bone in the Bone field as long as the constraint is on the shin bone. The important thing in this figure is the chain length value.

Figure 4.19

Adjusting the parameters of the IK constraint

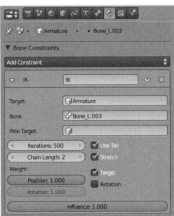

The default chain length is defined as 0, which actually means that the entire chain of bones, up to the root, is included in the IK chain. This is often not what you want and can lead to strange behavior of the armature when you pose the IK solver. Be sure to set your Chain Length value to end at the point where you want your IK chain to stop.

And with this, the IK constraint is in place on the left leg. Follow the same steps to add an IK constraint to the right leg. To pose the legs, move the IK target bones and observe the effect, illustrated in Figure 4.20. If you want to return the armature to its rest position, select the bones that have been moved, and press

Alt+G. If you've posed bones in the upper body by rotating them, return them to the rest pose by pressing Alt+R.

Skinning

The armature can now be posed, but it doesn't affect the mesh. To make it affect the mesh, you need to skin the rig, that is, assign bone influence to each vertex of the mesh. This influence is represented by vertex groups for each bone. Each vertex group contains weights ranging from 0 to 1 for every vertex that is a member of the group. If a vertex has a weight of 1 for a particular bone, then the bone's movement will have the maximum influence on the location of the vertex.

This may sound a little complicated, but fortunately there are a lot of tools for working with these weights and even setting them automatically.

In this example, you'll use the automatic weighting functionality. To skin the rig, enter Object mode, select the Mesh object, and then hold Shift and right-click to select the Armature object (as usual, the order you select these objects is important). Press Ctrl+P to set up a parent relationship. Choose Armature Deform With Automatic Weights, as shown in Figure 4.21, and presto—you're done! That wasn't so painful, was it? Try posing the armature now in Pose mode. The mesh should deform as shown in Figure 4.22.

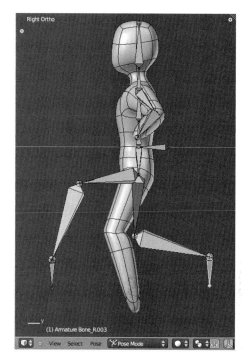

Figure 4.20

Posing the legs with IK

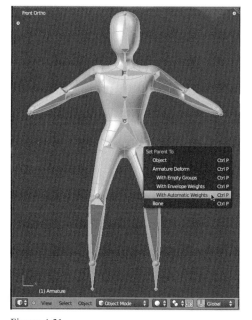

Figure 4.21

The IK constraint displayed

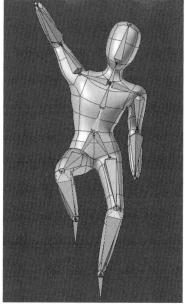

Figure 4.22

The rigged mesh

Actually, there's still one more simple thing to do to make the deformation as nice as possible. Take a look at the Modifiers panel in the Properties window, as shown in Figure 4.23. You'll see some familiar modifiers; there's the Mirror modifier used in modeling the mesh, the Subsurf modifier used to smooth the mesh, and now, at the bottom of the modifier stack, the Armature modifier, which as you can guess deforms the mesh according to the armature pose. However, recall the discussion about modifier order in Chapter 2. It would make more sense to have the armature deformation calculated *before* the resulting mesh was smoothed using the Subsurf modifier. To make this happen, simply move the Armature modifier up one position by clicking the up arrow icon in the upper right of the Armature modifier's widget. As you can see in Figure 4.24, you get considerably nicer deformations.

Figure 4.23

The Modifier stack

Figure 4.24

Improving deformations by correcting modifier stack order

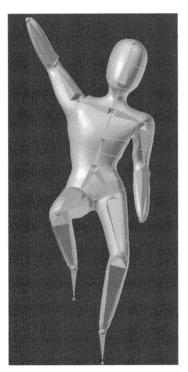
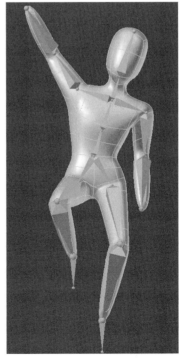

You can now pose your model freely, as shown in Figure 4.25. Experiment with this rig, and note the difference between how the IK posing of the legs and the FK posing of the rest of the limbs works.

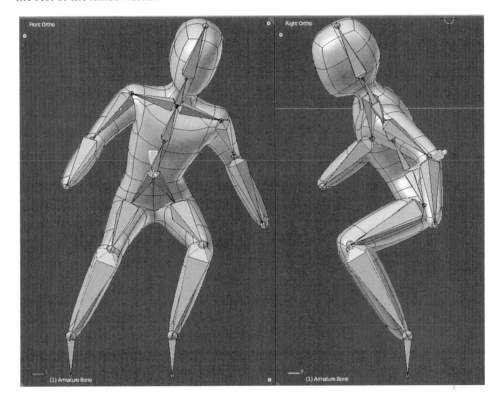

Figure 4.25

Posing the finished rig

Rigging Captain Blender with Rigify

Now that you've learned some of the most basic concepts of armatures and rigging, it's time to return to your Captain Blender model and get down to putting together a high-quality, full-featured rig to control him. If you prefer, you can start with the character model file in the downloadable archive for this chapter.

Rigging is a complex and tedious job, all the more so when you consider that all human or biped characters require largely the same functionality in their rigs. For this reason, unlike in the previous example, you're not going to build this rig yourself. You're going to let Blender do the hard work for you, using a meta-rig and the Rigify system newly introduced in Blender 2.5.

The Rigify Add-on

To use the automatic rig-generating system Rigify, you'll need to learn a little bit about Blender's system of add-ons, which is how you access Rigify. Add-ons are optional extensions to core Blender functionality. Typically, add-ons are written in the Python programming language, but unlike more traditional Blender Python scripts, the functionality of add-ons is usually seamlessly integrated into Blender. Activating an add-on simply enables Blender to do things that it wouldn't do if the add-on were not active.

The Add-Ons panel is accessible in the Blender User Preferences window, as shown in Figure 4.26. I recommend you spend a little time browsing this panel and seeing what kinds of things are available. For example, there are add-ons for the Add Mesh functionality that enable you to expand the variety of mesh primitives you can add to a scene and add-ons to enable you to use a variety of measuring systems.

The add-on you want right now is Nathan Vegdahl's Rigify add-on, which you'll find by scrolling down and looking for the Rigging: Rigify entry, as shown in Figure 4.27. Click the check box to the right of that add-on, and click the Install Add-On button. Now you're ready to rigify.

Figure 4.26

The Add-Ons panel

Figure 4.27

Installing the Rigify add-on

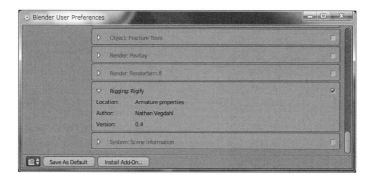

Creating a Meta-rig

The first step in making the Captain Blender rig is to add a meta-rig armature. The reason this armature is referred to as a meta-rig is that although it is an ordinary armature object, you will not be using it as your actual rig. Rather, you will use this armature to create a guide or template to tell the Rigify algorithm how to create the actual rig that you

Figure 4.28

Adding a meta-rig

will use to pose your character. The meta-rig will represent the locations of the joints and the rotations of the bones appropriate to the individual character you are rigging. Once you set up the meta-rig, the rigging itself will be almost completely automatic.

In Object mode, you'll add an armature just as you did in the previous example. However, this time, you won't just add a single bone. Instead, you'll select Human (Meta-Rig) from the menu, as shown in Figure 4.28. Press Alt+G to make sure the object is centered in the 3D space.

Assuming that your model is the same as the one described so far in this book, the resulting armature will look something like what you see in Figure 4.29. Clearly, the scale of the armature and the scale of the Mesh objects do not match, so they will need to be changed.

Figure 4.29

The armature and meshes do not match in scale.

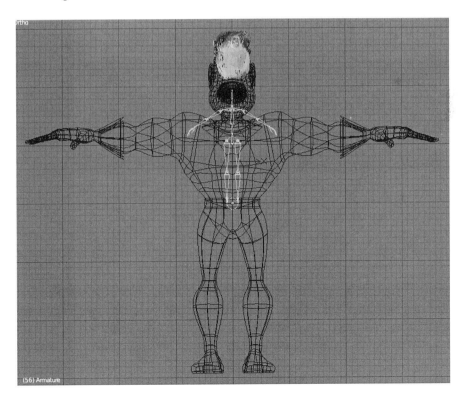

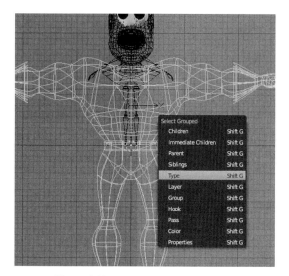

Figure 4.30

Selecting all the meshes in the scene with Select Grouped

In this case, you'll resize the meshes. Select the body mesh in Object mode, and then press Shift+G to bring up the Select Grouped menu; choose Type as shown in Figure 4.30 in order to select all the meshes in the scene. This will select the head, mouth, and eyes objects in addition to the body object. Scale them down so that the size of the character mesh is roughly the same as the size of the armature, as shown in Figure 4.31.

HOTKEY: Pressing Shift+G brings up the Select Grouped menu to enable you to select all objects with shared characteristics, such as all objects that belong to a group or all objects that share a type.

After you've scaled the meshes, you should apply the new scale. This sets the current size of the object as the unaltered scale of the object. For the body, eyes, and mouth, do this by simply selecting the object, pressing Ctrl+A, and choosing Apply Scale.

In the case of the head, it's not quite so simple because applying the scale here changes parameters for the hair particles in complicated ways. If you apply the scale on the head, your hair particles may behave in unexpected ways.

Figure 4.31

Scaling the meshes to match the armature

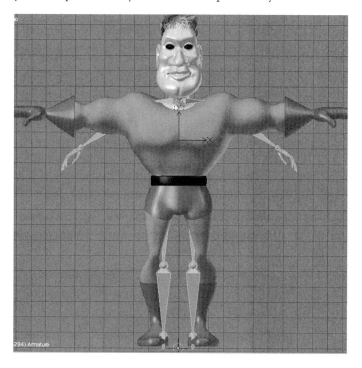

The way to apply a new scale to an object with hair particles is to disconnect the hair first, then apply the scale, and then reconnect the hair. To disconnect the hair, click the Disconnect Hair button on the Particles panel for the hair particle system, as shown in Figure 4.32. Then apply the scale to the head object with Ctrl+A, as shown in Figure 4.33. Finally, return to the Particles panel, and click Connect Hair.

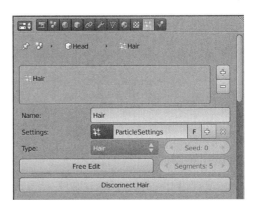

Figure 4.32

Disconnecting the hair particles

In some cases, you may find that the mesh jumps some distance from where it was previously when you do this. This is a trivial bug in the version of the software I'm working with right now. If this happens, simply select all the vertices of the mesh in Edit mode with the A key, and move the entire mesh to its original placement.

Once you've finished scaling the mesh, you can return to setting up your meta-rig. In the Armature properties panel under Display, select the X-Ray box as shown in Figure 4.34 so that your armature will be displayed through the mesh. This makes it much easier to see what you are doing when editing the

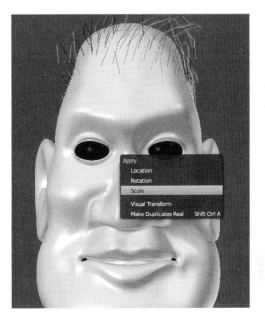

Figure 4.33

Applying the scale of the head object

armature. Also, turn on X-Axis Mirror in the Tool Shelf, as shown in Figure 4.35, so that you can edit only one side of the armature and the other side will automatically mirror the changes.

Next, in Edit mode, edit the armature to match the mesh. You'll have to do this on your own by selecting bones and joints and moving, rotating, and scaling them as necessary. Try to do as much as you can by selecting groups of bones together, for example selecting the whole hand with Box Select (B key). Stick to the front, side, and top orthogonal views and constrain your transformations to the x-, y-, or z-axis when you can. The important thing is to get the joints in the right places for your mesh and make sure that the bones are all where they ought to be and rotated correctly. Think of the armature as your character's skeleton, and place the bones appropriately to wind up with something along the lines of the armature shown in Figure 4.36.

Figure 4.34

Setting the X-Ray display option

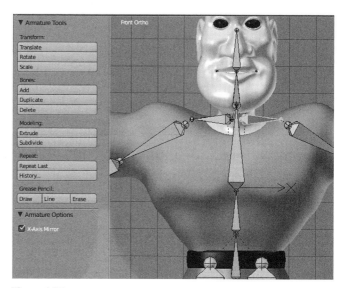

Figure 4.35

Turning on X-Axis Mirror

Figure 4.36

**Bone placement
for the Captain
Blender meta-rig**

Once you've placed the bones and joints in the correct locations, it's time to look a little closer at some crucial bone rotations. In particular, the *roll* of the bone—the rotation around the bone's local y-axis (lengthwise)—determines how the bone will bend at joints. To adjust the roll properly, you will want to set the armature Display settings to display bone axes, as shown in Figure 4.37. When you set this, each bone will show a representation of the directions of its three axes.

Figure 4.37

**Displaying
bone axes**

Rigify will generate a rig with joints that rotate around the x-axis of bones where relevant, with the joint's "inside" rotation being in the direction of the drawn z-axis in the bone axes representation. Figure 4.38 shows an example of how the bones' roll should look in the case of fingers. Note that the joints of the fingers will now naturally bend around the x-axes of the bones and with the inner angle in the direction of the positive z-axis, as shown in the display. Adjust the bone roll value directly in the Roll field of the Transform Properties shelf, as shown in Figure 4.39. You can access the Transform Properties shelf by pressing the N key in the 3D viewport (or by clicking the small plus sign in the upper-right corner of the 3D viewport).

Figure 4.38

**Bone roll angles
for the fingers**

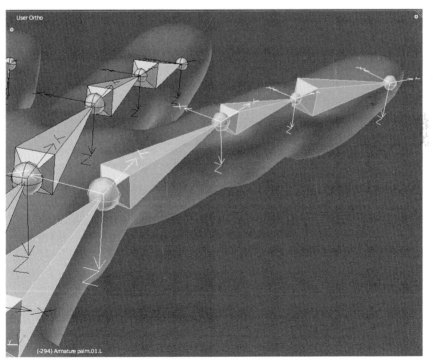

Figure 4.39

**Transform
properties**

Other important places to get your bone rolls right are at the elbows and wrists, shown in Figure 4.40, and the knees, shown in Figure 4.41. If the bone rolls are off, you'll find that the final rig's joints will bend wrong. Don't worry too much about getting this perfect, though. You can always delete a generated rig, adjust the rolls, and generate again after testing.

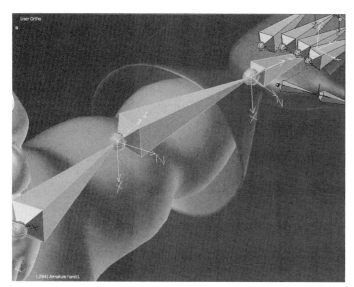

Figure 4.40

Bone rolls for elbows and wrists

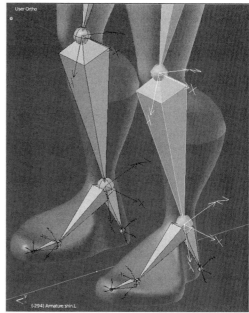

Figure 4.41

Bone rolls for legs

Generating the Rig with Rigify

Once you have the meta-rig set up, the next step is to use it as the basis for a full rig. To do this, select the meta-rig armature object, and find the Rigify Buttons settings in the Armature properties window, as shown in Figure 4.42. Click Generate. Your rig will appear as shown in Figure 4.43. The rig is a new armature object with the object name `rig`. The original meta-rig armature is no longer needed. You can put it on a different layer out of sight. It's best not to delete it, though, because you might want to go back and use it to regenerate a new rig.

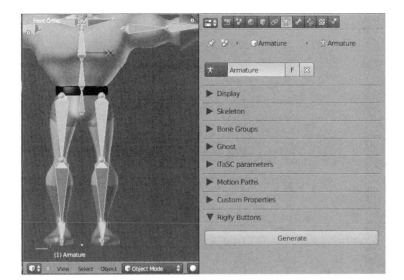

Figure 4.42
Rigify buttons

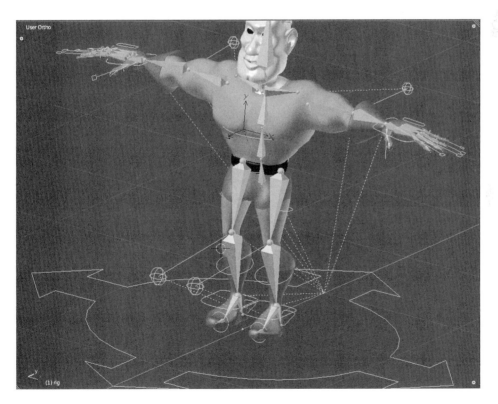

Figure 4.43
The generated rig

This new rig object has saved you a ton of work. As you'll soon see, it is already fully poseable and ready to skin, with IK/FK switching functionality and a load of other features that make it an incredibly flexible and easy-to-use character rig. However, there are still a few adjustments you should make to ensure that the rig is best suited to your model.

First, take a look at the display options on the Properties shelf shown in Figure 4.44. I find that it's not really necessary to constantly see the dotted lines indicating parent relationships, so I deselect Relationship Lines in the Display options. This is a personal preference, but it helps to clean up the viewport a bit.

Figure 4.44

Clearing relationship lines from the display

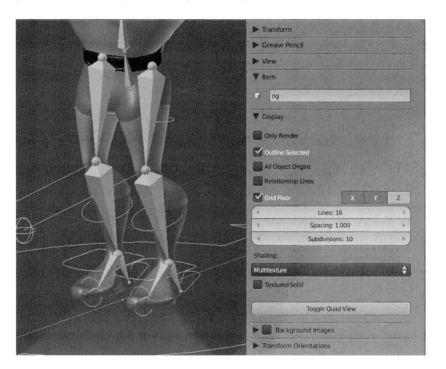

Next, you should make some adjustments to the custom bone shapes used for the control bones. As you learned at the beginning of this chapter, there are control bones, deform bones, and function bones in a rig. When you generate a rig, only the control bones are visible, and they have been set to display using specialized mesh shapes. The leg control bones, for example, display as blue rings around (or in this case penetrating) the legs, as shown in Figure 4.45. It's a good idea to edit these mesh shapes in a way that makes them more accessible when posing.

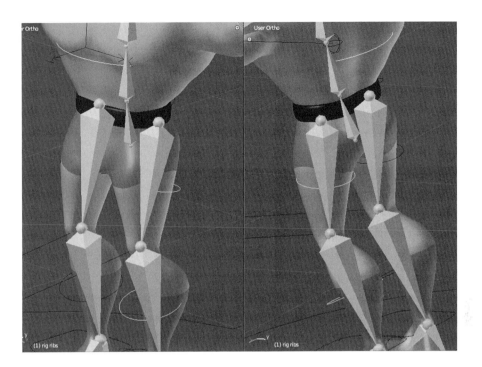

Figure 4.45

Circular custom bone shapes for leg control bones

You'll find the mesh shapes for the custom bones all collected together on layer 20, as shown in Figure 4.46. Select them all by pressing the A key, and suddenly you'll see them pop into position showing their actual placement in the rig, as shown in Figure 4.47.

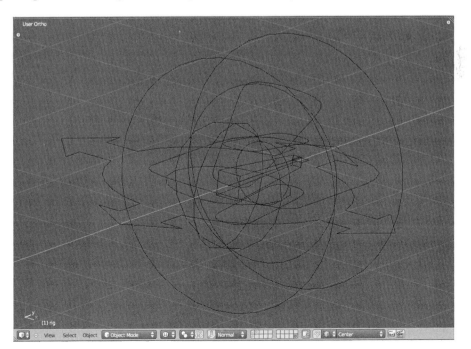

Figure 4.46

Mesh shapes for custom bones

Figure 4.47

Custom bone shapes correctly placed

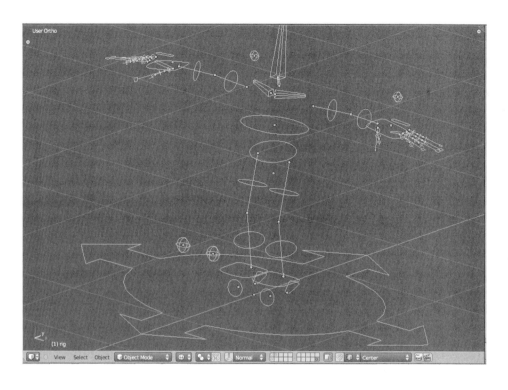

Figure 4.48

Custom bone Mesh objects

Make this layer and the layer your character model is on both visible. You can now select the custom bone Mesh objects in the ordinary way and tab into Edit mode to edit them,

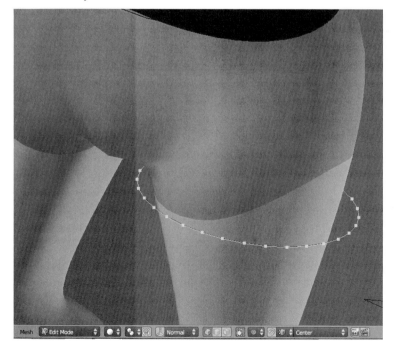

as shown in Figure 4.48. You'll need to scale some of the rings and control shapes and move them around a little bit to create a set of controls that visually suits your character. The upper arm control bone, for example, was entirely hidden by the mesh before I edited the control bone mesh. The resulting control armature should appear something like the one shown in Figure 4.49. Note that the armature is not displayed in X-Ray style. This helps to enhance the three-dimensionality of the control bones and make them more intuitive to use.

Figure 4.49

Control bones for Captain Blender

Attaching the Mesh

Your body armature rig is now finished. Next you need to associate the armature with the rig. This entails two tasks: creating an Armature modifier and creating a set of vertex groups representing the influence of each bone. As you saw previously in this chapter, both of these steps are handled automatically by Blender when you parent the mesh to the armature using automatic bone weights. You'll do that now. First enter Object mode. Then select the mesh followed by the armature (using Shift+right mouse button). Press Ctrl+P to bring up the parent menu shown in Figure 4.50, and choose Armature Deform With Automatic Bone Weights.

Figure 4.50

Parenting the body mesh to the armature

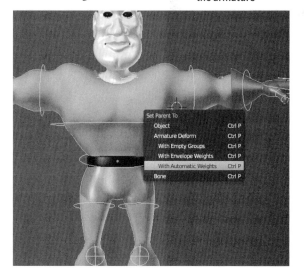

Figure 4.51

**Changing the order
of the modifiers**

Recall the importance of the order of modifiers on the Modifier stack. Move the Armature modifier up above the Subsurf modifier on the stack, as shown in Figure 4.51, to ensure the best deformations. You can see the effect of changing the modifier order on deforming the leg in Figure 4.52.

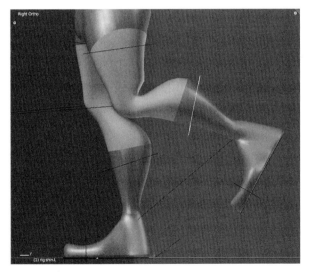
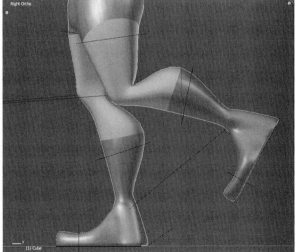

Figure 4.52

**Before and after
rearranging the
modifiers**

Weight Painting

Blender's automatic vertex weighting functionality is a great improvement over the way skinning used to be done. For simple character meshes, particularly skinny ones where the mesh stays fairly close to the bones that should control it, the automatic weighting may be all that's necessary. For most characters, however, you must adjust the weights by hand to get optimal effects.

Captain Blender's broad chest is an example of a place where the automatic weighting is likely to need some help. To see why, enter Pose mode, grab one of Captain Blender's bicep control bones, and rotate it downward, as shown in Figure 4.53. Notice that as you do this, the side of Captain Blender's torso is pushed inward with the motion of the arm. The arm deform bone is influencing the vertices of the body in a way that it shouldn't.

The solution to this is to manually set the weights (influence) of the bones on the vertices. This can be done in several ways, but the most intuitive and visual way to do it is to use *weight painting*.

Weight painting is a way to make bone influences visible and to edit them directly, similar to spray-painting. Blender's Weight Paint mode enables you to select deform bones to display their influences as colors on the surface of the mesh.

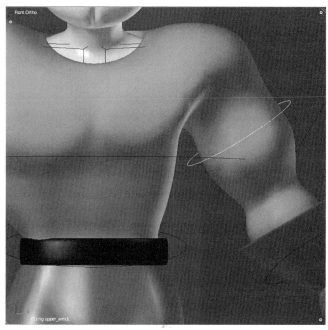

Figure 4.53

Incorrectly set weights

To do this, however, you need to make the rig's deform bones visible. So far, you have only seen the control bones of the mesh. The deform bones have been placed on a hidden bone layer. Bone layers are analogous to the view layers you've worked with in the 3D viewport. However, rather than controlling the visibility of objects in the 3D scene, bone layers control the visibility of bones in an armature. Each bone can be placed on a layer in the Bone properties window, and the armature's bone layer display is set on the Armature properties window.

In the rig you've just created, the deform bones are all located in the third layer from the right on the bottom row, shown highlighted in Figure 4.54. The top row layers contain the various control bones. Select layers to make visible by pressing Shift and clicking the layer's button. For weight painting, you will want the deform bones layer visible. You'll also want the control bones visible and set to X-Ray draw mode so that you can easily pose the rig during the process of weight painting.

Figure 4.54

**Selecting the bone
layer with the
deform bones**

The deform bones are shown selected in Figure 4.55. These are the bones that actually directly affect the deformation of the mesh. As you can see, the deform bones make up a shape that is structurally pretty similar to a human skeleton. These are the only bones you need to worry about for weight painting.

Figure 4.55

**Deform bones
selected**

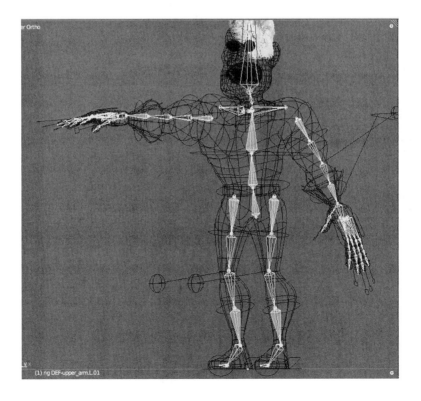

To enter Weight Paint mode, begin with the armature in Pose mode, and then right-click the mesh to select it. This part is important. If the armature is not in Pose mode before the mesh is selected, the bones will not be individually selectable in Weight Paint mode. When you select the mesh, the mode will automatically switch to Object mode. From there, you can enter Weight Paint mode using the menu in the 3D viewport header, as shown in Figure 4.56. If you did this correctly as described, the mesh will be displayed with weight paint, the armature will be displayed in Pose mode, and you can select and pose its bones. The mesh will mostly appear deep blue. Depending on which bone was selected last when you entered Weight Paint mode, there may be areas of other color on the mesh.

Figure 4.56

Entering Weight Paint mode

Weight paint is a visual representation of the weights of vertex groups on vertices. By default, the color range goes from blue (weight value 0.0) to yellow (weight value 0.5) to red (weight value 1.0). Here the term *weight* is used interchangeably with the term *influence*. For each bone, the corresponding distribution of colors over the surface of the mesh shows you where that bone does and doesn't have influence.

Selecting control bones will not show any vertex influence. This is because nondeform bones do not influence the mesh directly. Select the deform bone for the upper bicep, as shown in Figure 4.57. You can see that the main influence of that bone is where it belongs, on the upper part of the bone. However, if you look close, you will see a yellowish or greenish tint extending well up onto the torso and chest. There is also too much yellow around the underarm. These are the problem areas. In the grayscale representation of this book, the yellow appears as lighter gray, and the blue appears as darker gray.

Figure 4.57

Weights for the upper-arm deform bone

The settings for weight painting are accessible through the Tool Shelf in the 3D viewport (you can open the Tool Shelf with the T key), as shown in Figure 4.58.

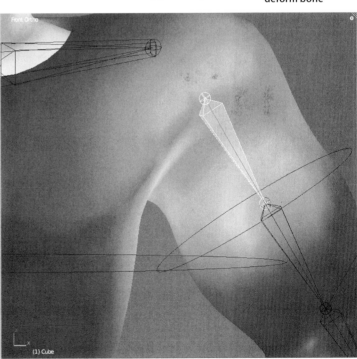

Figure 4.58

Weight paint settings

You can choose brush types by clicking the brush type icon and choosing the radius, strength, and jitter of the brush in the correspondingly named fields. The Weight field determines the weight (the weight paint color) that you'll be painting. The Strength value determines how strongly the new color overrides the current color. You can think of it something like opacity in traditional digital painting environments. For reducing the weight on the torso, you should set Weight to **0.0** and Strength to something like **0.5**, as shown in the figure.

You now begin the task of weight painting. As you paint 0 weight influence onto the mesh, you will see the mesh's deformation change in real time. The chest and torso will return to its undeformed state as the vertex weights are diminished. Eventually, after painting the chest, torso, and underarm, you'll arrive at a deformation that looks something like Figure 4.59.

Re-pose the arm a few times to see how the deformation looks in different poses. Also, keep in mind that the upper bicep may not be the only bone causing problematic deformations. The lower bicep bone may also be influencing the torso. Continue weight painting until all the deform bones in the model influence only the parts of the mesh that they should influence and all deformations are as smooth as you can get them.

Figure 4.59

Weight painting the shoulder, chest, and underarm

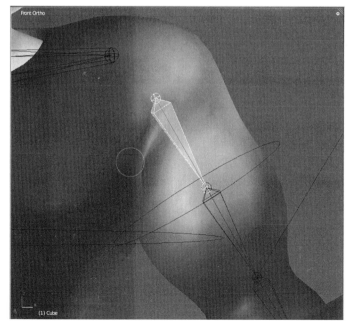

Be sure to experiment with fairly extreme poses. Of course, there is a limit to the range of poses you will use in actual animation, but the character should deform nicely in all of the possible poses, so make sure you go through a full range of motion. In Figure 4.60, the hand is posed at a sharp angle to emphasize the problems with the glove flare. The glove and arm need to be weight painted to fix this.

In Figure 4.61, you can see the effect of painting zero weights onto the glove flare with the hand posed downward. In Figure 4.62, you can see that posing the hand upward reveals other problems. These can also be solved by painting zero weights on the arm mesh.

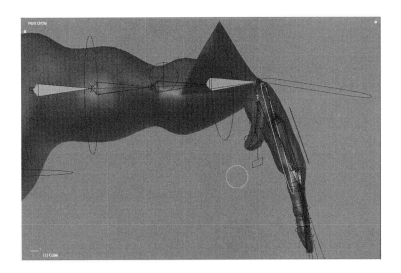

Figure 4.60

Problems with the glove weights

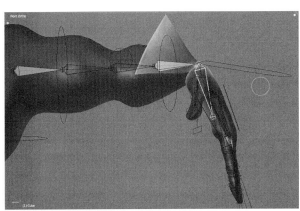

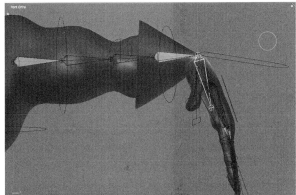

Figure 4.61

Weight painting the glove flare

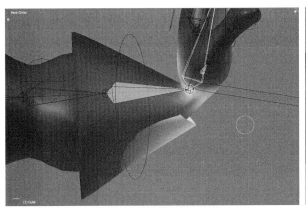

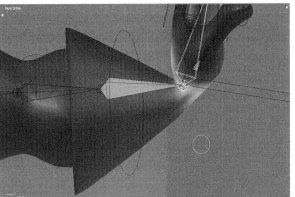

Figure 4.62

Weight painting the arm mesh

You can also set your weight paint options to do additive, subtractive, or multiplicative painting and also to restrict the painting to lighten and darken (light meaning higher or redder values; dark meaning lower or bluer values). There are circumstances in which these finer controls come in handy, but I do not think you need them for this model.

Effective weight painting requires patience and some skill, and experience and practice benefit you more than reading about it, but here are a few pointers you should keep in mind:

- Paint for posing. The whole reason for weight painting is to make sure your meshes deform nicely when posed, so you should pose your model frequently while weight painting, as you saw in the earlier figures. Areas that deform in unwanted ways will be easy to identify.

- Work with vertex groups directly when you can. There are often cases in which many more vertices belong to a particular vertex group than are necessary. An advantage of weight painting—that it lets you apply subtle weight changes to verts—is also a disadvantage because you can inadvertently give verts hard-to-see, near-zero weights that can add up and become problematic. For this reason, it is a good idea to occasionally go into Edit mode with a bone selected and select the vertex group for that bone in the Vertex Groups area of the Mesh Properties window.

- Be conscious of the possibility of overshooting. If you are painting the pinky red and you are not careful of the position of your mesh, you might inadvertently hit points on other parts of the mesh. You might wind up making the heel green, for example, which would result in messy deformations of the foot every time the hand moves. There are some useful tricks for avoiding this. In Weight Paint mode, you can click the icon to the right of the display mode drop-down menu in the header to enter Face Selection mode and select the faces that you want to paint. When you return to Weight Paint mode, only the selected faces receive the weight paint. You can hide faces with the H key in Face Selection mode, and they will remain hidden in Weight Paint mode, enabling you to weight paint hard-to-reach areas.

- Be aware of the effects of unwanted bone influence. If an area of mesh is fully red but it does not seem to be following the bone it is supposed to follow, it is probably also being influenced by another bone that is not moving. Posing the armature in a drastic way might help identify the direction that the unwanted deformation is pushing your mesh and can help narrow down where the offending bone is.

- Make sure your bones are deform bones. This should be obvious, but nondeform bones can have nonzero weights, even if they don't do anything with those weights. You might think you're painting a bone's influence, but if the deform button is not selected for that bone in the Bone properties, it doesn't move the mesh anywhere. If your mesh is not responding properly to a bone, even if it is properly weighted, this might be the problem.

Several Python scripts in the standard distribution of Blender can help clean up vertex weights and reduce problem areas. You can read more about how to use these scripts in Chapter 12.

Finishing Off

The head object needs to be armature-parented to the armature in the same way that the body was. Once again, you need to make sure the modifiers are in the correct order. In the case of the head, there's one more modifier to worry about: the Hair particle system.

Particles are also dealt with in the modifier stack. If the Hair particle modifier occurs above the Armature modifier in the stack, then deforming the mesh with the modifier will leave the hair in place. Clearly, the hair should follow the position and shape of the head, so be sure that the order of the modifiers is Armature first, then Subsurf, and then Hair, as shown in Figure 4.63.

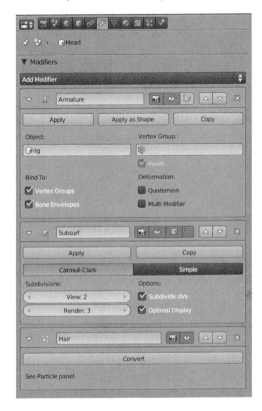

Figure 4.63

The modifier stack for the head

For the other objects in the head, the mouth and eyeballs, you won't use the Armature modifier right now. These will be rigged using different bones in the next chapter. For a quick, temporary way to make them simply follow the head bone, you can use bone parenting.

Begin with the armature in pose mode, and then select the objects you want to bone-parent (the eyeballs and mouth mesh). Shift+select the armature, which will be in Pose mode with individual bones selected. In the armature, select the head bone. You should wind up with the Mesh objects selected and the head bone selected in Pose mode, as shown in Figure 4.64. Press Ctrl+P to bring up the parent menu, as shown in Figure 4.65. Select the Bone option from this menu. If Bone is not listed, go back through this paragraph, and make sure you've selected everything in the correct order and mode. Bone parenting is very useful for mechanical rigging and other rigging where you want to control the movement of objects without needing to deform their meshes. In this case, it gives you a quick and dirty way to make the eyes and mouth follow the motion of the head until you can get around to rigging them properly.

Figure 4.64

Preparing to bone-parent objects

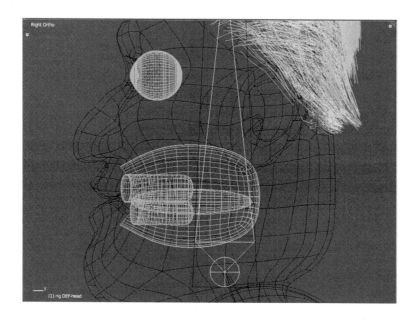

Figure 4.65

Bone parenting

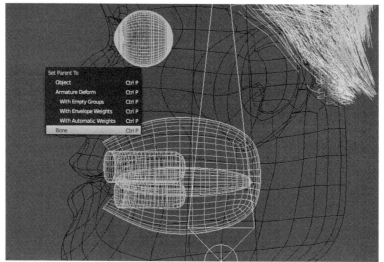

Posing

You'll get into the details of posing later, when you start into the character animation chapters of this book. For the time being, it's enough to know some basics so you can start to play around with your rig.

By default, this rig's IK constraints are set to zero influence, so the posing is FK. You've seen already how to do FK posing by grabbing bones in the limbs and rotating them. To do IK posing, you need to turn on IK influence for the limbs. This is done in the Rig Main Properties panel in the Properties shelf (N key) in the 3D viewport, as shown in

Figure 4.66. Notice that there are four FK/IK fields. The values in these fields determine whether FK or IK posing dominates. If the value is 0.0, the posing is FK; if it is 1.0, then posing will be IK. Values in between will result in both FK and IK controls having an influence, so the influence can be smoothly graduated.

To pose the left arm using IK posing, select the hand.L.ik control bone, and ensure that its FK/IK property is set to **1.0** under Rig Main Properties, as shown in Figure 4.67. Pose the arm by moving the hand.L.ik bone as shown. Note also that if you change the FK/IK value now, the arm will smoothly return to its original FK pose.

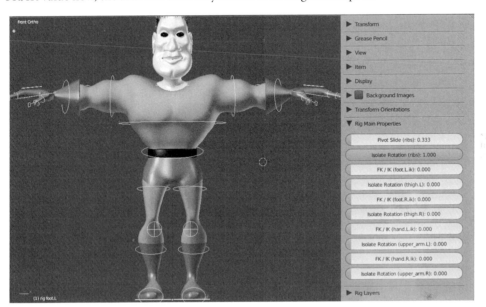

Figure 4.66

IK/FK switching controls

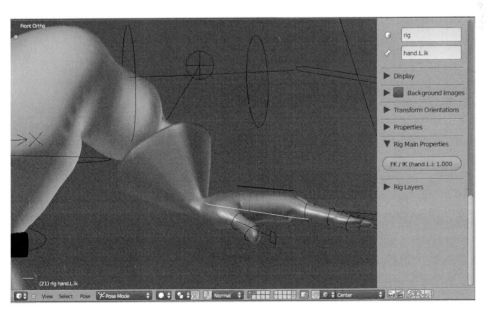

Figure 4.67

IK posing the arm

Figure 4.68

Curling the finger by scaling down the finger control bone

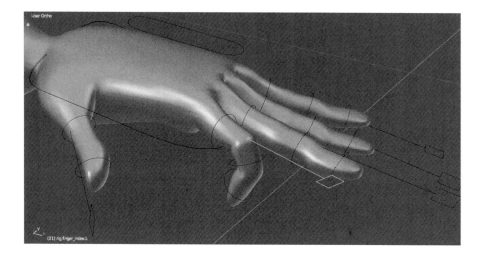

One more clever posing trick in this rig is the use of bone drivers for finger curl controls. You'll learn more about drivers in the next chapter, but their use here is some fairly advanced rigging. Fortunately, it's all done automatically for you, so you just get the benefit of very easy-to-control fingers. Figure 4.68 shows the finger curl controls. Scaling the finger curl control bone down (S key) will curl the finger, and scaling it up will bend the finger backward.

As you've seen, different control bones work differently. Some controls are rotated, some are grabbed (moved), and some are scaled. When you want to return the armature to its unposed state, you need to be sure to use Alt+R, Alt+G, and Alt+S as appropriate to remove rotation, translation, or scaling.

At this point, you're ready to start playing around with posing. In Figure 4.69, you can see that our hero has begun to come alive! You'll deal with the spaced-out expression on his face in the next chapter when you work on facial rigging. You'll also see how to fix other problem areas of the mesh that are hard to get right using weight painting only, such as the belt.

Figure 4.69

I've been rigified!

CHAPTER 5

Shape Keys and Facial Rigging

Now that you have rigged and skinned the body to an armature so that you can position the limbs, head, and trunk, you'll turn your attention to some important details of rigging characters. In particular, this chapter focuses mainly on setting up a face so that it can be easily posed to express emotion and to make the mouth movements that are necessary for lip syncing. (You'll learn how to animate facial expressions and lip sync in Chapter 8.)

There are many ways to go about facial rigging, and this book focuses on an approach that makes heavy use of Blender's powerful shape key system and driver curves to associate shapes with armature poses. After introducing shapes and drivers and learning about their use for facial rigging, you will also put them to another use: refining the body rig.

- Shape Key Basics

- Building a Shape Key Set for Captain Blender

- Facial Bones and Controls

- Improved Mesh Deformations Using Driven Shape Keys

Shape Key Basics

Blender enables you to create and animate various shapes for a single mesh using *shape keys*. Shape keys are similar to what other applications sometimes call *blend shapes* or *morph targets*. Shape keys have many uses, but in character animation one of the most important is to help create facial expressions. Blender's shape key system is simple to use,

Figure 5.1

The Shape Keys panel

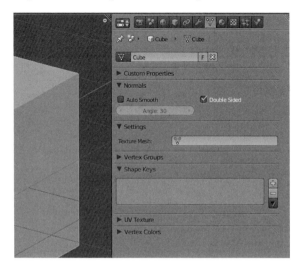

but (like many things in Blender) it takes a little getting used to.

You'll begin with a very simple example. Start an instance of Blender; with the default cube selected, look at the Shape Keys panel in the Properties window, shown in Figure 5.1. Click the plus symbol button to the right of the Shape Keys field to create your first shape key. You'll see a Basis shape key appear, as in Figure 5.2.

The Basis shape has some unique features, as you'll see shortly. It represents the shape of your mesh in its "rest" position, unaffected by any of the shape keys you will create. In this case, you made the Basis shape on the default cube, which means that now the vertex positions of that cube shape are represented by the Basis shape.

Figure 5.2

Basis shape key

Now that you have the Basis shape, you can use it to build a new shape. The process is simple:

1. In Object mode, click the plus button again. A shape key called Key 1 will appear, as shown in Figure 5.3.

Figure 5.3

Key 1 shape key

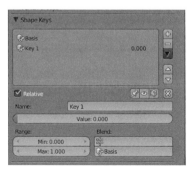

2. Enter Edit mode, and edit the shape as you want it by moving vertices. For this first example, select the top four vertices and scale the face, using S followed by Shift+Z to constrain the scaling to the x- and y-axes. Scale the top of the cube down, as in Figure 5.4.

3. Return to Object mode. Now add another key in the same way, Key 2, and edit it to look like the shape in Figure 5.5 by selecting the edge shown and translating it up along the z-axis.

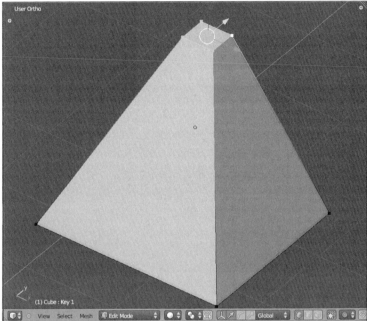

Figure 5.4

Editing the first shape

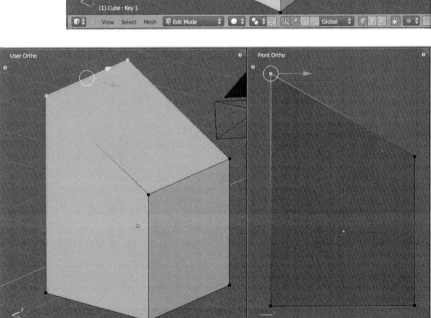

Figure 5.5

Editing the second shape

You now have three shapes: the Basis shape and two animatable shape keys called Key 1 and Key 2. Select each of the shapes in the field. You should notice a few things. The first Basis shape is special because it has no slider. Sliders on shape keys represent a gradation from a relative shape (typically the Basis shape) to the shape of the mesh as defined by the shape key. Because the Basis key represents the mesh in its default position, it makes sense for it to have no slider; there's no difference between it and itself.

By default, the slider ranges from 0.0 (no change from the basis mesh) to 1.0 (full effect of the shape key changes on the basis mesh). Position the slider for Key 1 somewhere between 0.0 and 1.0. You will see the mesh go from the Basis cube shape to the fully tapered shape you created in the Key 1 shape key. You can see how this shape affects the mesh at various levels of influence. But that's not all. What you are actually seeing when you move the slider back and forth is how *all* the shapes are simultaneously influencing the mesh. You are seeing the cumulative effect of all the shapes, depending on where *their* sliders are currently set.

To see how this works, set the slider for Key 1 to 1.0. Click Key 2, and make it the active shape key. If you now slide the Key 2 slider to some value greater than zero, you see the mesh as it is influenced both by Key 1 and Key 2 simultaneously, with both keys exerting influence over the shape of the mesh. You should be seeing something like the shape in Figure 5.6.

Figure 5.6

The mesh with both Key 1 and Key 2 influencing

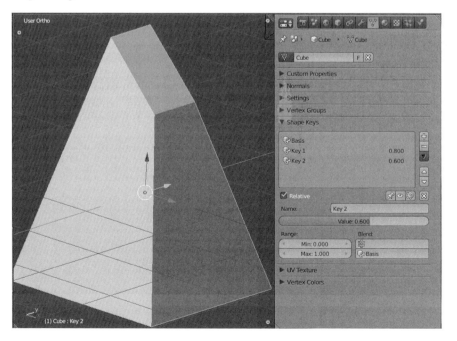

The fact that you can go from one shape key to another and set each one's sliders enables you to see how each key is mixing with any and all of the other keys in your shape key set. It also means you should usually keep your shapes' sliders set at zero while you are creating the shape key set when you are not specifically trying to view them mixed with other shapes to eliminate any possible confusion about what the Basis shape is or what the shape key you're currently looking at actually looks like. If you forget that one of your shapes is set at something other than zero, you might not see what you expect to see when viewing other shapes. You can reset all the sliders to zero by clicking the little X-shaped icon to the right of the visibility icons above the key's name field.

Blender can extrapolate the movement of vertices in shape keys beyond the range of 0 and 1 if you want. Zero is always the basis that the key was created on, and 1 is always the form of the shape that you see in Edit mode when you enter Edit mode with that key active. If you make the minimum value in the shape key's range less than 0, you can use the slider to go into the negation of the shape. To see an example, go to your Key 1 shape key, and set the Min: value to −1.0. Now the slider extends down past 0. Move the slider down to see what the shape looks like with the negation of Key 1 active. As you can see in Figure 5.7, the shape you see is the "reverse" of the pyramid shape you made for Key 1. Likewise, you can extend the positive change of the shape key by increasing the Max: value beyond 1. Before you continue with this section, put the Min value for Key 1 back to 0.

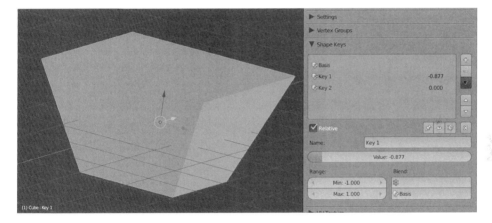

Figure 5.7

Key 1 shape at a negative slider value

Additivity

The shape keys you are using work by adding their relative coordinates. This is an important concept to get a handle on if you will use blended shapes.

To see an example of this in action, make sure that all your shape keys are currently set to zero; then select Key 1. Move the slider to 1.0. Click the plus symbol to create a new shape key, which will be called Key 3. Key 3's shape will now be a copy of *whatever shape was visible in the 3D viewport when you added the shape key*. In this case, that means Key 3 will be a copy of Key 1. If you set Key 1's slider to 0.0 and set Key 3's slider to 1.0, you will see this.

However, if both shape keys are set to nonzero values, the effect is cumulative. This may be what you want, but it may cause problems if you are not careful. For example, if you set Key 1 to 1.0 and set Key 3 to 0.7, you will see the undesirable effect shown in Figure 5.8.

Figure 5.8

**Additive effect of
Key 1 and Key 3**

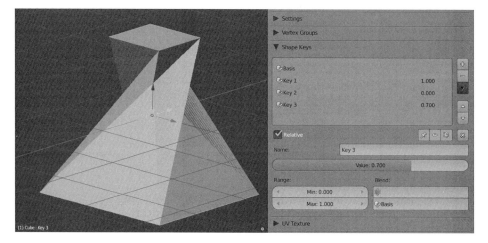

Although Key 1 and Key 3 are the same shape, their cumulative effect is not the same because of additivity. It's important to be careful of this when creating facial shapes that you intend to blend together. If two shapes have a redundant effect, you can wind up with some undesirable additive effects.

Adding and Deleting Vertices

Shapes record the positions of verts within a mesh. The verts and the edges that connect them are properties of the mesh itself, so they can be added or deleted in Edit mode. They are not specific to a particular shape, however. If you add verts in a shape, they will also exist in all the other shapes you have defined. In principle, their position should be unchanged from the position in which they were created; you will have to specify their location separately for each shape in that shape key's Edit mode. However, significant mesh edits that change the topology of the mesh will confuse Blender and can wreck your shape keys completely. In practice, you are better off planning not to do mesh edits involving creating or deleting verts after you have started creating shapes.

Basis Key

The Basis shape is special in some respects and not in others. It is not keyable, so it has no slider. However, in most other respects it is about the same as any other shape key. It can be deleted; if you delete the Basis, the next shape key down in the list of shapes (probably the first one you added on top of the basis) will pop up to the Basis shape key position, and its slider will disappear. In this case, your original base mesh shape will also be lost, and whatever you had in Key 1 will take its place. You can change the name of the Basis key, but you will probably never have a reason to do so. If you change the Basis shape by moving vertices around, these changes will be automatically reflected in other shape keys.

Finally, insofar as the Basis shape key is special at all, it is only special by grace of its being the first shape you create and therefore the first shape key in your set. In fact, the order of shape keys can be rearranged, and *any* shape key can be the first. In this case, the shape key named Basis will no longer be the true basis key, and it will have acquired a slider. However, because keys represent relative changes, the Basis key's slider will not change the shape of the mesh. I cannot imagine any circumstance for which this would be desirable, but because keys might become shuffled accidentally, you should know how to put them back in order. To reorder the shape keys, simply use the up and down arrow buttons to the right of the shape keys' names in the Shape Keys field, or use the keyboard up and down arrow keys while the mouse pointer is over the shape key area.

Shape Key Drivers

Shape key drivers are crucial to the way you will rig Captain Blender's face, so it's necessary to introduce them before continuing.

Drivers are related but distinct from the F-Curve animation curve system that you will read about more in Chapter 6. They are similar insofar as they represent mathematical functions and can be viewed in Blender's Graph Editor. Drivers are probably the most technically demanding aspect of Blender to work with that I will discuss in this book, in that they do require a little bit of math. If you passed your high-school math classes, you should be OK (and if you haven't, then getting your head around drivers should give you a good head start!).

A function curve, whether it be an animation F-Curve or a driver, is a representation of some value that changes depending on some other value. In the case of animation F-Curves, the value changes according to time, resulting in animation. In the case of drivers, you can set a value to change as a function of *any other changing value.* As one value changes (for example, the rotation of a specific bone), another value changes (such as the slider value of a shape key). In this case, you would say that the shape key is *driven* by the bone's rotation.

Figure 5.9

Adding an armature

Setting Up a Driver

You'll set up a very basic shape key driver now by using the shapes you have just created:

1. In Object mode, add an armature object to the side of the default cube by pressing Shift+A and selecting Armature → Single Bone, as shown in Figure 5.9. The resulting armature should look as shown in Figure 5.10.

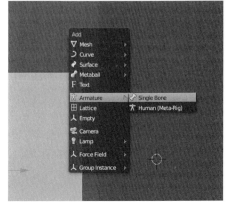

Figure 5.10

Default cube and a single bone armature, front view

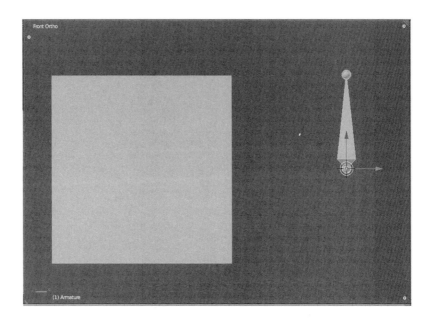

2. Select Key 1 in the Shape Keys field, move the cursor over the numerical value to the right of the shape key name, and right-click to bring up the menu shown in Figure 5.11. Choose Add Driver from this menu.

3. To see the driver, you will need to open a Graph Editor window using the Editor Type drop-down menu, as shown in Figure 5.12, and then choose Drivers from the Mode drop-down menu in the header in the Graph Editor window, as shown in Figure 5.13. The driver is displayed, as shown in Figure 5.14. In the left side of the window you can select available drivers. The middle area is the graph viewer proper, where the driver function curve is displayed, and the Properties Shelf in the right of the window (toggled with the N key) displays the driver properties in detail.

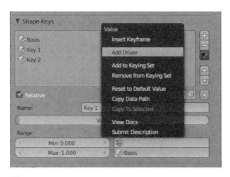

Figure 5.11

Choosing Add Driver from the Value menu

Figure 5.12

Opening a Graph Editor window

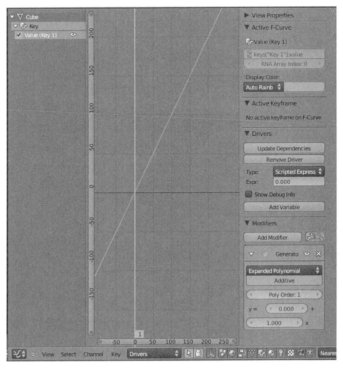

Figure 5.13

Entering Driver mode in the Graph Editor

Figure 5.14

The driver displayed in the Graph Editor

4. The driver you will create will depend on a variable representing the rotation of the bone. Any time a driver of any kind depends on a value, this value must be encoded as a variable for the driver. Set up the variable as shown in Figure 5.15. Choose Transform Channel for the variable type, Armature from the Object drop-down menu, and Bone in the Ob/Bone field that appears. Choose Z Rotation from the drop-down of transform channels, and select the Local Space check box.

Figure 5.15

Setting up the Transform Channel variable

5. Choose Averaged Value from the Type drop-down menu, as shown in Figure 5.16.

6. Test the driver by rotating the bone in pose mode, as shown in Figure 5.17. You should find that the bone

Figure 5.16

Selecting Average Value as the driver type

rotation corresponds to the activation of the shape as shown in the figure. You've now completed a very basic shape key driver.

Figure 5.17

The basic shape key

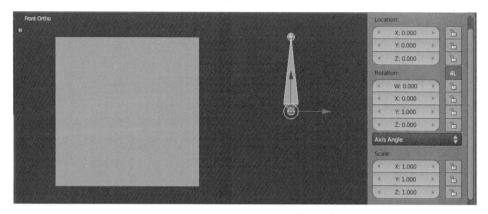

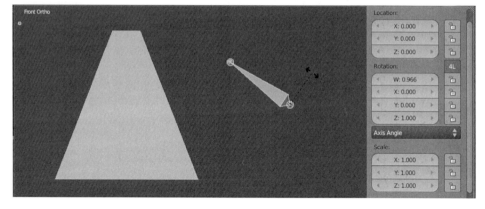

Tweaking the Driver

Although the driver you created in the previous section works, the relationship between the rotation and the shape key activation may appear arbitrary. In fact, it is a one-to-one relationship, by default, as defined by the polynomial equation in the Generator Modifier panel on the Properties Shelf of the driver, shown in Figure 5.18. But what are the units of this one-to-one relationship? The y-axis represents the shape key's activation, ranging from 0.0 to 1.0. The x-axis of the graph represents the

Figure 5.18

A Generator modifier describing a one-to-one relationship

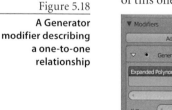

rotation of the bone around its own local z-axis *in radians*. This may be a bit unexpected, because in most places in the Blender interface, angles are expressed in degrees.

If it's been a while since you did trigonometry and you're not a programmer, you may be hazy on radians. Radians are simply a unit of measuring angles, just like degrees are. A full circle is 2 * pi radians. Pi is approximately 3.14, so one radian represents an angle a bit less than a sixth of the way around the circle. The angle of the bone in the earlier figure is about one radian in the counterclockwise direction. Radians have mathematical properties that make them very good for calculating functions relating to circles, so most programming languages express angles in radians under the hood. However, they are difficult for humans to work with for several reasons, a big one being that the number of radians in a circle isn't a nice integer. Degrees are much easier for people to work with because full circles, half circles, quarter circles, and eighths of a circle can all be expressed with integers.

If you want to make your driver a bit more intuitive and have it use right angles, then you'll need to do a bit of math and think a bit in radians. Since there are pi radians in a half circle, for a shape key driver with a y range of 0 to 1 over a half-circle rotation, you'll need the x to range from 0 to pi. So, the question to ask is, what number when multiplied by pi yields 1? The answer, of course, is 1/pi.

Let's say you want the bone to drive the shape key over a 90-degree rotation. In this case, the bone rotation needs to have twice the effect that it would in the case of a half-circle rotation, so the number to multiply x by is 2/pi. You can actually enter this directly into the x coefficient field in the polynomial panel verbatim as **2/pi**, and Blender will calculate the result, which is displayed as 0.637, as shown in Figure 5.19. When you rotate the bone 90 degrees counterclockwise, the shape will be at its maximum point, as shown in Figure 5.20.

Figure 5.19

The polynomial for a 90-degree driver

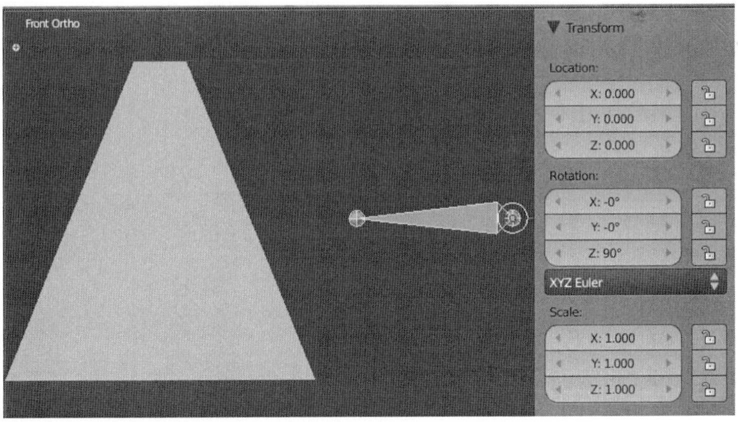

Figure 5.20

The shape key driver bone rotated 90 degrees

You've now created your first driven-shape driver. To make more drivers, you can follow the same steps or take a shortcut by copying and pasting drivers from one shape to another. To do this, right-click the numerical value of the key from which you want to copy the driver, and choose Copy Driver from the menu, as shown in Figure 5.21. Then right-click the numerical value on the key you want to copy the driver to, and choose Paste Driver.

Figure 5.21

Copying a driver

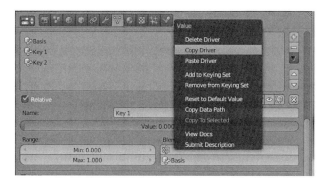

Do this to copy the driver of Key 1 to Key 2, and then edit the new driver as shown in Figure 5.22 so that the x coefficient is negative (−0.637) rather than positive. The resulting pair of drivers will control the two shape keys, as shown in Figure 5.23.

Figure 5.22

Editing the x coefficient for the new driver

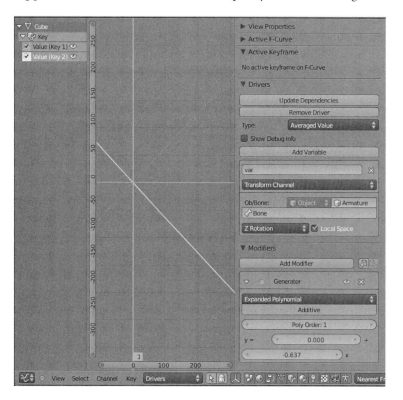

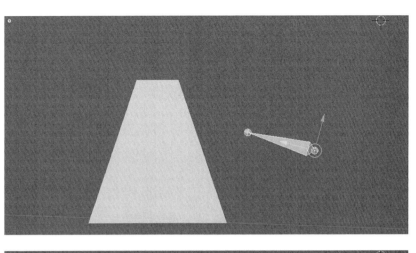

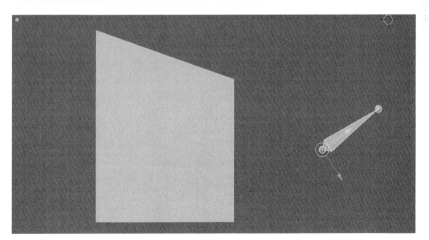

Figure 5.23

**The two drivers
in action**

The drivers can also be independent of each other, simply by associating them with independent values. Edit the Key 2 driver again, and change the Transform Channel value from Z Rotation to X Rotation. When you do this, you will be able to control the taper shape with the z rotation of the bone and the wedge shape with the x rotation of the bone. Rotating the bone in both directions at once will activate both shapes simultaneously, as shown in Figure 5.24. Experiment with double R key trackball rotation by pressing R twice to rotate the bone.

Figure 5.24

Two independent drivers

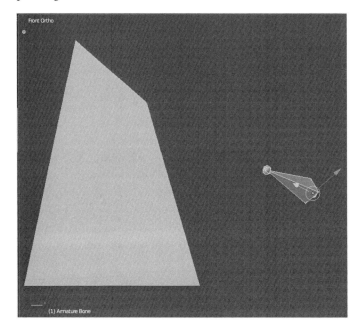

After you set up drivers for the shapes, the driven shapes can no longer be independently controlled with the shape sliders, but if you create a new shape on the basis of a driven shape, the new shape can be controlled independently with its own slider.

Building a Shape Key Set for Captain Blender

Now that you understand how shapes and drivers work, you'll turn to putting these tools to work on the character. First, you will use shapes for Captain Blender's facial movements. You will rig up the eyes and the tongue with bones in the next section, but aside from this, you will accomplish all the facial expressions and positions by blending various shapes together. This is a common way to create facial movement, but it is by no means the only way. Some people prefer to use bones for certain parts of the face, such as the jaw movement or eyebrows. Professional character rigs often use a combination of driven shapes, bone deformation, and other types of deformation to get the facial effects needed.

An argument in favor of a bone-oriented setup is that it allows more freedom of movement and posing for the facial expressions, and indeed this might make it more appropriate for heavily toon-styled rigs, in which a lot of exaggeration is the norm in facial expressions. On the other hand, for somewhat more realistic facial movements, individual muscle movements are usually quite simple, and you do not always need a large amount of freedom in the individual elements, so the control afforded by shape keys is more suitable. I chose to model the face movements with shape keys because they are comparatively simple to create. They also offer good examples for discussing the various distinct facial formations that combine to create expressions and lip movements. Regardless of what method of deforming the mesh you use, it is necessary to account for more or less the same set of basic facial shapes. It is worthwhile to experiment with other methods, such as the mouth rig mentioned previously. See Chapter 18 for more suggestions to broaden your understanding of facial animation.

Once you begin making shape keys in Blender, your options for further modeling become restricted. There are not too many "points of no return" in Blender, but creating a shape key set is one of them. You will not be able to apply some modifiers, such as the mirror modifier, once you have created shape keys (without deleting all your shape keys), and ideally you will not want to change the geometry of the model once you've started working with shape keys, although it is possible. So, try to finish your primary mesh modeling before moving on to shape keys.

A First Shape: Eyes Closed

If the most basic sign of awareness in the human face is open eyes, then certainly the most basic sign of responsiveness is the blinking of those eyes. Conveniently, closing the eyes is a simple example to start with for shapes, and it also affords you a good opportunity to look at the issue of asymmetry and how to incorporate it into Blender shape keys. So, you'll begin now by making Captain Blender blink.

First, you want to make your life a little easier by hiding the vertices you will not be using so you don't inadvertently select them in wireframe mode. You do this by selecting the vertices you want to hide (which includes most of the back and the sides of the head), as shown in Figure 5.25, and pressing H. The selected vertices should disappear, leaving you with the front of the face, as shown in Figure 5.26. (To unhide all vertices, simply press Alt+H.)

Figure 5.25

Selecting vertices to hide

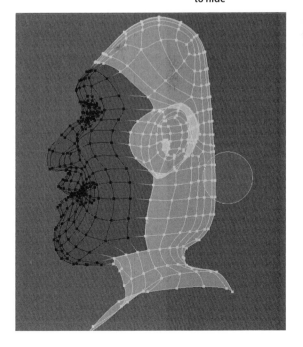

Figure 5.26

**The head with
vertices hidden**

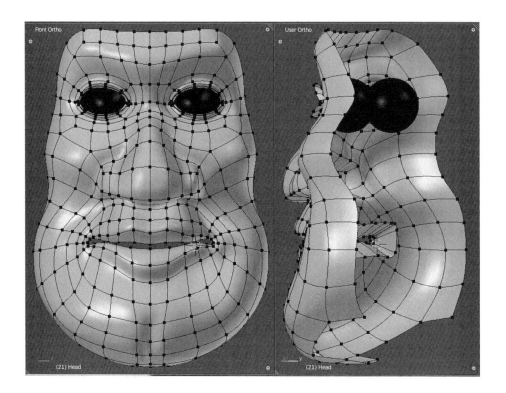

To create shape keys, click the plus icon to the right of the Shape Keys field in the
Properties window, just as you did in the previous section. First create a Basis key.

Click the plus icon again to create a new shape key. Change the name of the new shape
from Key 1 to **EyesClosed**. Now enter Edit mode. There is no longer a Mirror modifier
on this object, but it would be nice to have your edits mirrored. Fortunately, you can do
this with the X Mirror option under Mesh Options in the Tool Shelf on the left side of
the 3D viewport (see Figure 5.27). X Mirror will work as expected only if your mesh is

Figure 5.27

X Mirror editing

symmetrical to begin with. That is, it will work only on symmetrical parts of your mesh. It will also not mirror changes to
the topology of the mesh. You cannot mirror extrusions, cuts,
or deletions in this way.

With X Mirror active, select and edit the top eyelid, as shown in Figure 5.28, moving the necessary vertices downward along the z-axis. To select these vertices, use the
Circle Select tool (press C). To unselect vertices, use Circle Select while holding down
the Alt key. The middle vertices of each eyelid should move down farther than the others. The closed eyelids should extend just around two-thirds of the way down the eye.
Be sure that you have selected the verts of the eyelashes, too, to be sure that the eyelashes move along with the eyelids. You also need to make sure that the eyelids move

forward along the y-axis so that the eyeball does not poke through the eyelids. Adjust the eyelids along the y-axis in Solid mode so that you can see what's happening with the eyeball, as in Figure 5.29.

Figure 5.28

Selecting and editing vertices in the eyelid

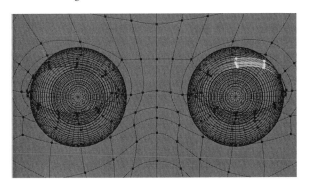 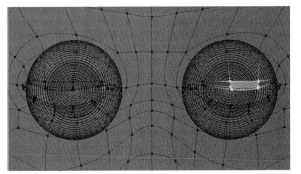

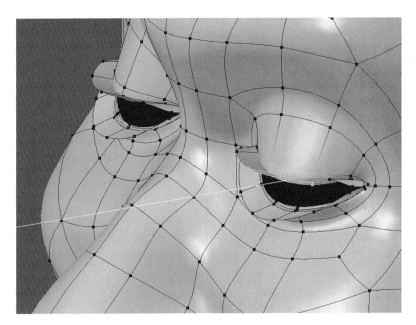

Figure 5.29

Fixing the eyelids along the y-axis

The process is the same for the bottom eyelid. Bring the pertinent vertices up to meet the top lid, being sure to also include the eyelash vertices.

When you're satisfied with your closed eyes shape, return to Object mode. You should be sure to check the shape at several different points between 0 and 1 to make sure that its full range of motion is clear of problems. In Figure 5.30, you see the EyesClosed shape as it appears with slider values set at 0.25, 0.5, 0.75, and 1. No problems appear. (Characters with protuberant eyes might require a slightly different set of shape keys to take their extreme curvature into account—for example, a basis with the eyes partially closed, one fully closed, and the final one fully open.)

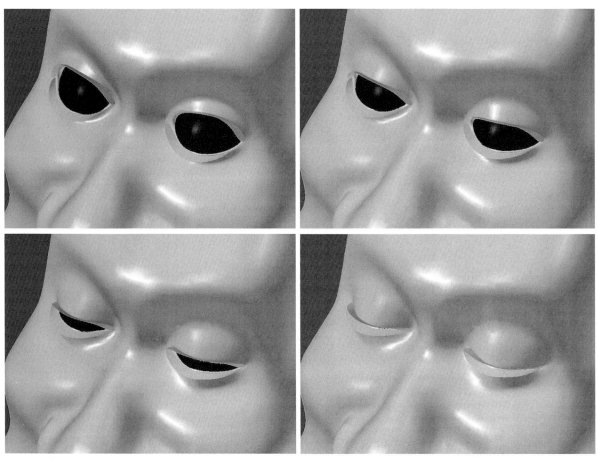

Figure 5.30

The EyesClosed shape key at four values

Finally, you'll make use of the shape key's range settings to get a little bit more from this shape. In Object mode, change the Min value of the EyesClosed shape from 0 to −.25. You now have a bit of room on the slider to move in a negative direction, which gives you the wide-eyed shape shown in Figure 5.31 for free.

Figure 5.31

Eyes wide open

Asymmetry

It can be convenient to model many shapes symmetrically using X Mirror editing. However, humans do not move symmetrically, either in body or in face. To be able to control different halves of the model separately, you must split the shapes into separate keys. Fortunately, it's not difficult to convert symmetrical shapes to asymmetrical shapes; you can use vertex groups. You create two vertex groups, one representing Captain Blender's left side and one representing his right side. You'll then make copies of the shape keys and apply them to each vertex group separately.

To create a new vertex group, click the plus icon to the right of the Vertex Groups field in the Properties window. Name the new group RightSide, as shown in Figure 5.32. Enter Weight Paint mode, and paint the head so that the right side of the head is solid red (1.0), the left side is solid blue (0.0), and a streak down the middle is green (0.5), as shown in Figure 5.33.

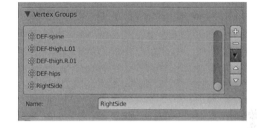

Figure 5.32

Adding the Right-Side vertex group

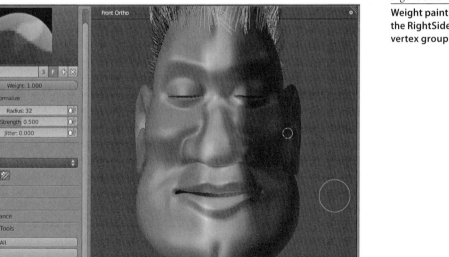

Figure 5.33

Weight painting the RightSide vertex group

Copy the RightSide vertex group by clicking the black triangle icon to the right of the Vertex Groups field to open the menu shown in Figure 5.34 and selecting Copy Vertex

Group. Rename the new vertex group **LeftSide**. Tab into Edit mode, and mirror the vertex group values using the same menu you used to copy the vertex group (for unclear reasons, the Mirror Vertex Group menu item is active only in Edit mode). The resulting mirrored vertex group will appear as shown in Figure 5.35 in Weight Paint mode.

Figure 5.34

Copying a vertex group

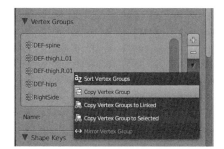

Figure 5.35

The LeftSide vertex group

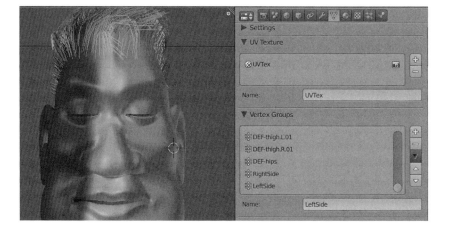

Now that you have the RightSide and LeftSide vertex groups defined, you can use them to create asymmetrical shape keys. To create asymmetrical keys for the EyesClosed shape, do the following:

1. In Object mode, with the mesh selected, go to the Shape Keys field, and select Eyes-Closed as the active shape. Set the slider value to 1.0. The shape in the 3D view should be displayed with the eyes fully closed.

2. Click the plus icon to the right of the Shape Keys field to create a new shape key. You have now created an identical copy of EyesClosed. Name this shape **EyesClosed.L**. In the VGroup field, enter **LeftSide**. The shape is now restricted to the LeftSide vert group. Return to the EyesClosed shape, and set the slider value back to 0.0.

3. Repeat steps 1 and 2 to create the EyesClosed.R shape key applied to the RightSide vertex group.

Adding a new key will always create a key the shape of whatever shape is active and visible in the 3D viewport. If you add a key while another key is active that has an associated vertex group, the new shape key will be a copy of the original key as applied to the vertex group, but the new key itself will not have a vertex group associated with it. For example, if you copy EyesClosed.L, the new key will affect only the left eye, just as with the original but without the need of a vertex group to limit it. You can use this fact to copy portions of shape keys by creating temporary vertex groups covering the area of the shape key you want to duplicate, applying the vertex group to the shape key you want to duplicate part of, and then copying the shape key with that vertex group applied. The new shape key will differ from the Basis key only in the places covered by the vertex group. This method is also useful for breaking a single facial expression into component shapes. For example, you can create a single "angry" face and then use this method to create separate shapes for different parts of the face, which can then be blended together as you saw in this chapter. It is also possible to use weight painting to see the different shapes blend in real time.

Shapes for Lip Syncing

The main references for lip syncing in animation are variations on Preston Blair's original phoneme set. In the excellent book *Stop Staring* (Sybex, 2003), Jason Osipa recommends breaking phoneme shapes (and all other expressions) down into more basic component parts, such as vertical stretching of the lips, which are designed specifically not to be used alone but to form lip positions in conjunction with other shapes. Because the main point here is to illustrate how this all works in Blender, I remain somewhat agnostic with regard to optimal shape key sets and cover a middle road between phoneme shapes and component shapes. Still, I cover the main lip positions, which I've described in Table 5.1.

PHONEME	POSITION
A, I	Formed with the mouth in a fairly relaxed and open position.
E	The lips are stretched wider than A and I, but the jaws are much more closed. Teeth are very visible.
O	The mouth is rounded and somewhat open.
U	The mouth is rounded and is less open than with O, and the lips protrude somewhat.
C, D, G, K, N, R, S, T, Th, Y, Z	These phonemes are mostly articulated inside the mouth, so the lips do not distinguish them much. The mouth is somewhat more open than with E, the lips are less wide, but the teeth are still quite visible.
F, V	The bottom lip folds in and connects with the top teeth.
L, D, T, Th	The mouth is almost as open as A and I, so the articulation of the tongue is visible. This is an option for phonemes that are articulated with the tongue.
M, B, P	The lips are shut tightly. For plosives such as B and P, they might also curve in slightly before opening suddenly.
W, Q	This is like U, only more tightly puckered.
Rest	This is a relaxed position that serves as a pause between phonemes and a transition point from certain phonemes to others.

Table 5.1

Lip positions

Because you are dealing with blend shapes that can be combined to create phoneme positions, you will not have a one-to-one correspondence between shapes and phonemes. But it should be clear how the shapes you build can be combined to create the phoneme positions listed.

The creation of these shapes itself is straightforward. You can follow the instructions in the previous section for creating, naming, and editing new shape keys. The modeling of these shapes should be limited to moving existing vertices around. Some suggestions for facial shape modeling include the following:

- Model symmetrically. Use x-axis mirroring when you can.

- X-axis modeling works only on meshes that are already symmetrical, and it can be sensitive to subtle asymmetries. It might work with some vertices in a mesh but not with others, if the vertices do not already perfectly mirror each other. So when using x-axis mirroring, keep a good eye on both sides to make sure that all the vertices that you want to move are actually moving.

- For vertices that you cannot edit with X Mirror editing, you can approximate mirrored editing by selecting both sides simultaneously and constraining all transforms to specific axes. You can approximate mirrored translating in the X direction by scaling along the x-axis to move the vertices apart or together.

- You will often select vertices in wireframe mode, and this is much easier to do if you have hidden vertices that are not relevant to the shape you're editing. Use the H key to hide vertices that you are not working on.

My set of lip shapes is illustrated and described as follows. Note that with lip sync shapes there is no need to make asymmetrical copies because speech is one of the few more or less symmetrical things that human beings actually do. You can always add whatever slight asymmetry you might want in the mouth by mixing in shapes from the next section. The set of shapes is as follows (Basis is not shown):

Jaw Down Create this shape by selecting the jaw and chin area of the main mesh; also select the tongue and the bottom row of teeth using the L key. In side view, locate the cursor slightly below the ear where the jawbone forms its hinge with the skull; then, using the cursor as the pivot point, rotate the jaw down into an open position.

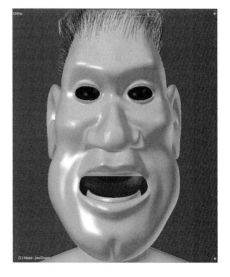

Lower Lip In Select verts on the outside and inside of the lower lip, raise slightly and move inward slightly on the y-axis, and also rotate slightly back around the x-axis. Verts below the lip should be moved out and upward slightly to indicate where the teeth would be pushing against the inside of the lip *(below left)*.

Upper Lip In Similar to lower lip in but with the vertices of the upper lip rotated downward around the x-axis *(below right)*.

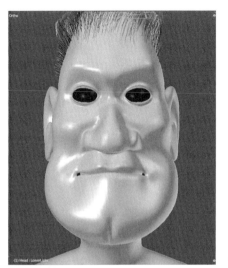

Lower Lip Out Select the same verts as lower lip in, but move them forward and curl the lip slightly downward *(below left)*.

Upper Lip Out Similar to the previous poses, but the upper lip protrudes and curls upward slightly *(below right)*.

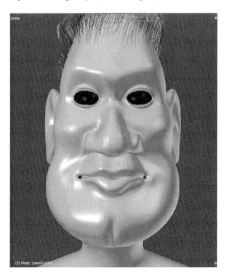
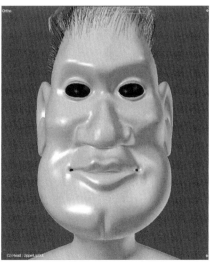

Lips Together Similar to the rest pose, but with the lips fully together. Blended with lower and upper lips in, this will give a tightly pursed position *(below left)*.

Lips Wide Teeth together and lips widely spread; at its maximal point, the teeth are fully bared. Simply select and move the verts of the lips to form the shape *(below center)*.

Round Lips are parted vertically and brought together horizontally to form an O shape. Pushed slightly past its maximum and blended with upper and lower lips out, this shape will form a tight pucker. Again, creating this shape is basically a matter of selecting and moving the lip verts until you are happy with the shape *(below right)*.

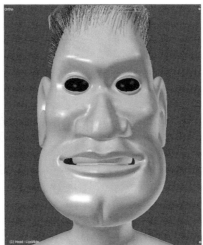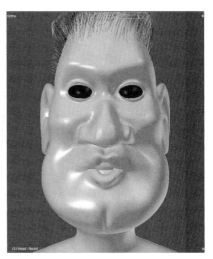

This collection of shapes and the various blended positions you can get with them, in conjunction with the tongue rigging you will see later in the chapter, provide you with all you need for basic lip syncing.

Shapes for Expressing Emotion

There is no hard and fast rule about what shapes are necessary to give a character a full range of emotional expressiveness. The most expressive parts of the face are the areas surrounding the eyes, so it is necessary to have a range of shapes to control eyelid movement, eyebrow movement, and some upper cheek movement. The mouth is, of course, important for smiling and frowning, but the sincerity of smiles and frowns has at least as much to do with the eye area as the mouth. Also, with mouth movement, the crease running down from the flap of the nose to the edge of the mouth is important to emphasize the smile. A smile that does not affect the cheek and the area around the nose appears unnatural.

The modeling suggestions for lips hold for these shapes, too. I modeled them all symmetrically first; I then made asymmetrical copies where necessary using the RightSide and LeftSide vertex groups.

It is certainly important to have separate discrete shapes for different parts of the face that you can blend together to create expressions. However, there is a lot of flexibility in how you create these shapes. One common approach is to model full expressions in advance and then isolate small component shapes using the vertex group technique referred to previously. This ensures that the component shapes work well together to create complete expressions and reduces the chance that their additive properties will conflict with each other. For the sake of expediency, I did not take the extra step of creating full expressions in advance; I modeled component facial movements directly.

The shapes are described here:

Brows Together This shape is actually formed less by the eyebrows coming together (although they do, slightly) than by the wrinkles forming between the brows. You form the wrinkles by bringing neighboring edges forward and back along the y-axis and emphasizing the depth of the wrinkles by moving the edges closer together. This shape is usually used in conjunction with other shapes to create a range of eyebrow movements, often indicating concentration, anger, or fear. It is not possible to knit only one brow, so there is no need to make right and left copies for this shape *(right)*.

Nose Crinkle (Left and Right) Raise the flap of the nostril while pushing the crease around the nostril deeper and bringing the cheek slightly forward, further emphasizing the crease. The wrinkle at the bridge of the nose can also be included in this shape. This shape occurs in a variety of expressions; it is very pronounced in expressions of disgust and some angry expressions, but it also will have an effect in a big smile *(below)*.

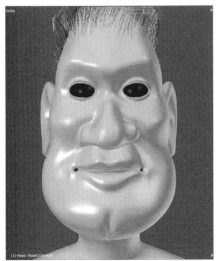
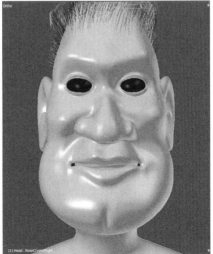

Smile (Left and Right) The edges of the mouth are raised and rotated slightly. The crease from the nose is deepened, and the cheek is brought forward slightly. This mouth shape is an important component of a smiling expression, but it is not the only one. It must be mixed with appropriate movements of the cheeks, the nose, and the area around the eyes to convey the desired emotion.

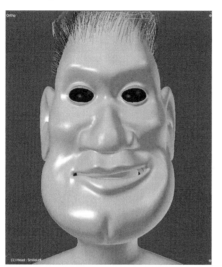 

Frown (Left and Right) Edges of the mouth are brought down and rotated slightly. This shape is often used with expressions of dismay, sadness, or anger.

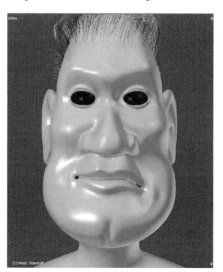 

Squint (Left and Right) The crease at the edge of the eye is emphasized, and the cheek is raised. In addition to being used to indicate concentration (or of course physical difficulty seeing something), a squint is also a component in a big smile.

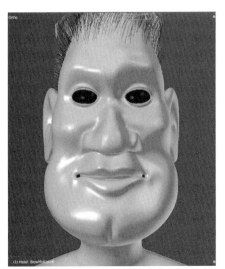 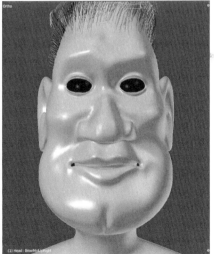

Brow Middle Up (Left and Right) The portion of the brow over the nose is raised, and forehead wrinkles are emphasized. This shape is often used in expressions of worry or fear.

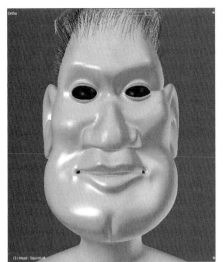 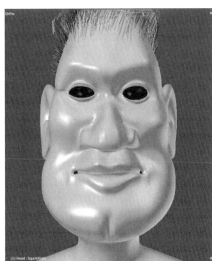

Brow Outside Up (Left and Right) The portion of the brow farthest from the nose is raised, and forehead wrinkles are emphasized. This shape is often used in expressions of delight, surprise, or disbelief.

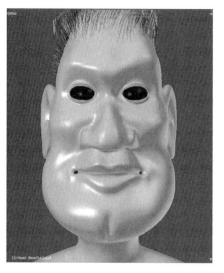 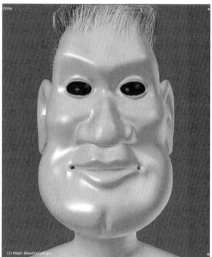

Brow Down (Left and Right) The entire brow is brought downward. This shape is often used in conjunction with the brows together shape and can indicate anger, concentration, and (when applied asymmetrically) suspicion.

 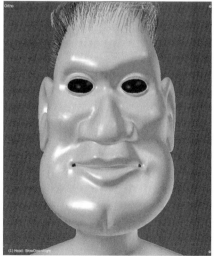

Jaw Left/Jaw Right The same jaw area that drops in jaw down is moved slightly from side to side. It is an emotionally very neutral shape that can be applied to add variation to a lot of different expressions and often is part of a thoughtful expression.

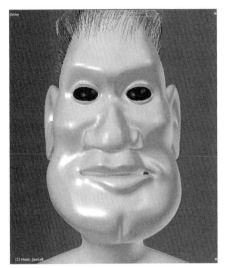 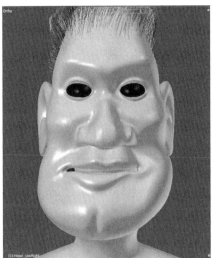

You now have a pretty complete set of facial poses to create facial animations with. In the next section, you will see how to associate these various shapes with driver bones so that when you get to animating, you can control everything by using a well-organized set of armature controls.

Facial Bones and Controls

As mentioned earlier, there are lots of possibilities for how to rig a face. Almost all of them make use of some combination of shapes and bones. Bone deformation-oriented methods usually incorporate some driven shapes to gain a little more control over certain deformations because facial movements can often be complex in subtle ways that are difficult to mimic using only bones. Likewise, the approach here—which leans heavily on shapes—uses bones for several things.

First, you will use bones to control the eyes because they are simply the most straightforward way to control eye rotations. You will also use bones to rig the tongue. Depending on your style of lip syncing and the degree of realism you are after, the tongue might be important for certain phonemes. However, its exact movement should usually be independent of other mouth shapes, which makes it difficult to do a good job of animating the tongue using only blend shapes. For example, if you want the tongue to tap the teeth, encoding it with a blend shape works only if you assume that all the other connected shapes are held to a particular position. The additive nature of shapes means that the position of the tongue depends on the degree of openness of the mouth, so tapping the teeth with the mouth open wide requires an entirely different shape than tapping the teeth with the mouth only slightly open. For this reason, you'll go with bones for the tongue for more control and freedom.

Finally, you will be using bones as drivers for all the facial shapes. This will simplify posing, enabling you to have complete control of the character through the single armature.

Rigging Eyes and Eyelids

The character's eyeballs are rotated by the use of bones. Furthermore, you will set up bones to raise and lower the bottom and top eyelids to follow the vertical motion of the iris, which will create a much more realistic eye-movement effect. To set these bones up, take the following steps:

1. In Object mode, select the left eyeball object. Press Shift+S, and select the option Snap Cursor To Selection.

2. Select the armature, and enter Edit mode. Press the 3 key to go into side view and add a bone with the spacebar. The bone should appear with the base at the center of the eyeball—where the cursor is. With the cursor selected as the pivot point, rotate the bone −90 degrees so that it is pointing straight forward with its base still in the center of the eyeball. Shift-select the head bone, and press Ctrl+P to parent the new bone to the head bone. Choose Keep Offset from the menu.

3. Repeat these steps for the right eyeball. The bone setup should be as in Figure 5.36. Name the bones **Eye.L** and **Eye.R**.

Figure 5.36

Eye bones

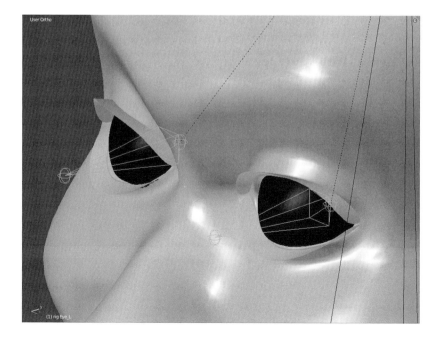

4. Extrude a bone from the head bone. Select this new bone, and press Alt+P to disconnect the bone from its parent. Move the new bone some distance out ahead of the face along the axis, as in Figure 5.37. Name this bone **Gaze**.

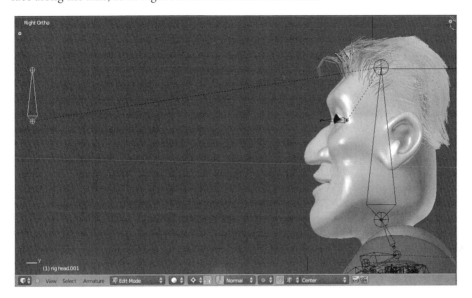

Figure 5.37

Gaze bone

5. With the armature still in Edit mode, snap the cursor to the base of the left eye bone. In side view, copy the bone by pressing Shift+D, and rotate the new bone up about 30 degrees (the cursor should still be selected as pivot point). Name this bone **UpperLid.L**. Copy the eye bone again, and rotate it downward about 30 degrees. Name this bone **LowerLid.L**. Now copy the eye bone one more time, and scale down to about 50 percent of the size of the eye bone without rotating or changing the location at all. This should be called **LidMove.L**. Parent UpperLid.L and LowerLid.L both to LidMove.L, making them both unconnected children of that bone. Parent LidMove.L to HeadDeform. You should now have a setup like the one in Figure 5.38. Do the same on the right side.

6. In Pose mode, you need to set up two types of constraints on each eye. First, set up an IK constraint on the Eye.L/R bones, with the target the Gaze bone. (You could use a Track-to constraint, but doing so might introduce some unwanted incidental rotations, so for this case I find IK the simpler option. The intention is the same.) Make sure to set the IK chain length to 1. Your eye bones should now follow the movement of the Gaze bone.

7. The second constraint you will set up is a copy rotation constraint on LidMove.L/R with the target as Eye.L/R, respectively. However, you do not want to copy the rotation on all axes. You want the eyelids to move up when the eye rolls upward, and you want the eyelids to move down when the eye rolls downward, but you do not want

the eyelids to move from side to side when the eyeball swivels to the side. So, you must make sure that the local x-axis button only is selected and toggle the other axis buttons off in the Copy Rotation constraint panel. You should now be able to move the Gaze bone around and have the Eye.L/R bones follow its movement, whereas the eyelid constructions go up and down in response to vertical movement of the Eye.L/R bones, as in Figure 5.39.

Figure 5.38

Eye bone, eyelid bones, and eyelid motion bone

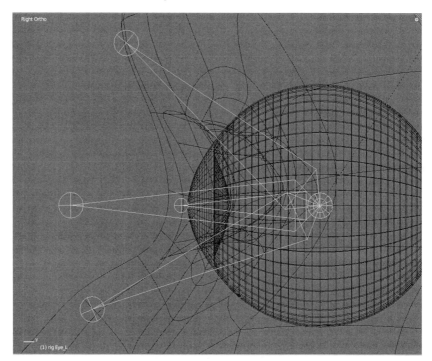

Figure 5.39

Eye armature setup in action

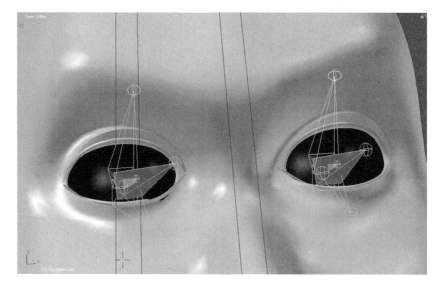

The eye armature is now complete; what remains is to rig the mesh to it. There are several things to keep in mind:

- Make LidMove.L/R nondeform.

- Attach the eyeballs to the eye bones by selecting an eyeball; then Shift+select the corresponding eye bone in Pose mode, press Ctrl+P for Parent, and select Bone from the pop-up menu. This process makes the eyeball object the child of the eye bone and only the eye bone. Generally speaking, it is the preferred method of attaching mechanical joints in Blender, of which ball-in-socket is an example.

- Weight paint the upper eyelids to UpperLid.L/R and the lower eyelids to LowerLid.L/R. As with any weight painting, test how this looks in several poses to make sure the weights are distributed as well as they can be.

Custom Bone Shapes

For bones that have special uses (especially facial bones, which are often clustered together and can be difficult to distinguish), it is a good idea to create recognizable shapes for them to take. You've already seen custom bone shapes in action in Chapter 4, but you haven't looked at how to set your own. To do this for the Gaze bone, create a new Mesh object in Object mode. It's a good idea to put this object on the same layer that all the other custom bone shapes are. I began with a 32-section circle and used some very simple modeling to create the form in Figure 5.40 to represent the Gaze bone. Give the object a recognizable name such as **WGT-Gaze**. The custom bone shape Mesh objects created by Rigify all begin with the WGT prefix, and it's a good idea to follow this convention to keep things organized.

Figure 5.40

A custom bone shape for Gaze

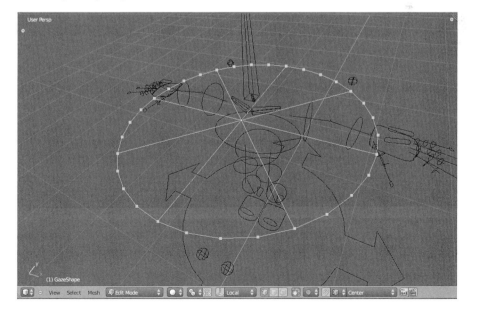

In Pose mode, select the Gaze bone, and find the Custom Shape field in the Bone properties window. Enter **WGT-Gaze** as the name of this object, as shown in Figure 5.41. You

Figure 5.41

Setting a custom bone shape

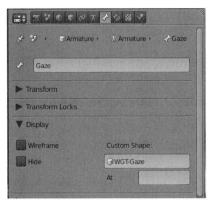

will now see the Gaze bone represented by this Mesh object, as in Figure 5.42. You can control the rest size, rotation, and location of this representation by adjusting the size, rotation, and location of the bone itself in Edit mode. You can move, rotate, or scale the object in Object mode to make it match the size and location of the bone representation. Changes made to the Mesh object in Object mode will not affect the appearance of the bone in the armature.

Figure 5.42

The Gaze bone with a custom shape

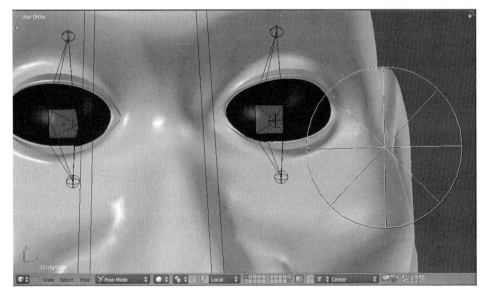

Rigging the Tongue

You'll rig the tongue as a three-bone-long IK chain with stretch constraints very much in the style in which you rigged the spine. First, extrude and disconnect a bone from the tip of the head bone. Place this bone at the root of the tongue, and extrude three bones forward in the Y direction, as shown in Figure 5.43. Name the bones (back to front) **Tongue1**, **Tongue2**, **Tongue3**, and **Tongue.IK**. Reparent Tongue.IK to the head bone. In Pose mode, set up a length 3 IK chain targeted to Tongue.IK, as shown in Figure 5.44. Make sure that the Rotation option is selected. Give each bone a Stretch value of 0.300.

Figure 5.43
Tongue bones

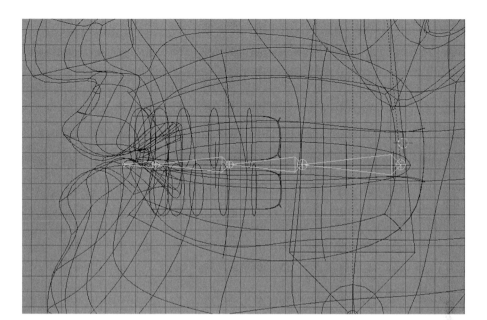

Figure 5.44
Tongue bones in Pose mode

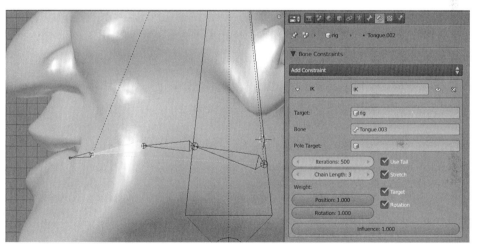

Now make copies of the three bones in the tongue armature, leaving them in place, so that they overlap with the currently existing bones, as you did with the spine. Name these bones **TongueStretch1**, **TongueStretch2**, and **TongueStretch3**.

Reparent each of these bones to HeadDeform. Set up copy location and copy rotation constraints on each of these bones, targeted at the corresponding tongue bone. TongueStretch1 should copy the location and rotation of Tongue1, and so on. Finally, add the stretch-to constraints to each bone. TongueStretch.1 should stretch to Tongue2.

TongueStretch2 should stretch to Tongue3. TongueStretch3 should stretch to Tongue.IK (see Figure 5.45).

Tongue1, Tongue2, Tongue3 and Tongue.IK should all be nondeform bones. The bones that should deform the tongue mesh are TongueStretch1, TongueStretch2, and TongueStretch3. You can add these bones to the vertex groups list by hand and assign the tongue verts to the appropriate bones by hand in Edit mode.

This setup will give you a flexible and poseable tongue rig, as shown in Figure 5.46.

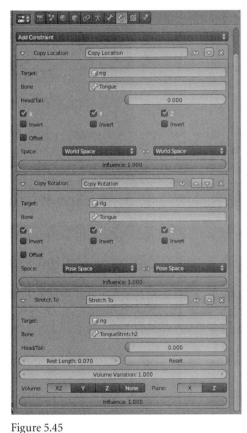

Figure 5.45
Constraints on the TongueStretch1 bone

Figure 5.46
Tongue armature in action

Shape Key Controls

At the beginning of this chapter, you saw that it's possible to use bones to drive shape keys. I'll now return to that topic. You're going to put this technique to use to make the face poseable with the armature.

A Controller for Lowering the Jaw

You'll start with the bone to control the movement of the jaw. This bone will drive both the jaw down shape and the jaw left and jaw right shapes, but you'll focus on jaw down first.

Extrude and disconnect a new bone from the head bone and place it in front of the face, as in Figure 5.47. Rotate it 90 degrees to make the bone's local y-axis point up and down. This bone will be called JawControl.

The facial controls all have custom forms associated with them, and you might as well design them as you go. For JawControl, I modeled a Mesh object to represent Captain Blender's chin. Putting the custom bone shape in place as you did with the Gaze bone gives you a JawControl, as in Figure 5.48.

Now you must set up the driver. The driver you will set up first will drive the jaw down shape. Because the bone's original position will correspond to zero on the shape, you already know that the x- and y-axis values on the driver curve will meet at zero. The maximal value of the shape will be 1. What bone value should this correspond to? To avoid a lot of guesswork, you can check on that in advance by pressing N in the 3D viewport to bring up the Transform Properties window.

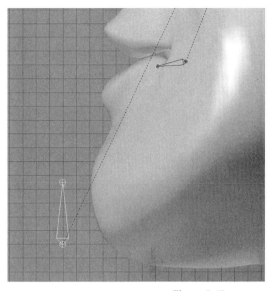

Figure 5.47

JawControl bone

Figure 5.48

Custom bone shape for JawControl

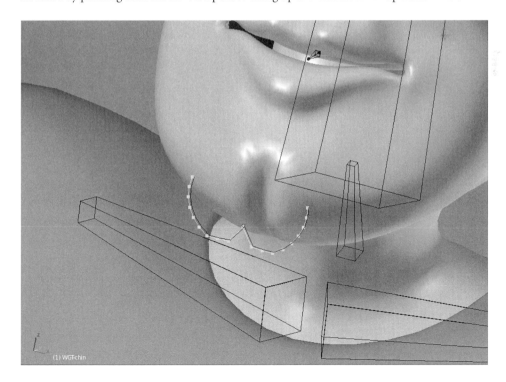

Move the JawControl bone downward in the local Y direction to the place you want to represent the fully open mouth. About −0.05 looks like a good location to have the mouth fully open in my model. Bear in mind, your model might be constructed at a different scale, so this value might be different. Set it in a way that makes sense to you, and if need be, refer to the fully rigged Captain Blender model on the accompanying DVD to see how the drivers should look in action. It does not need to be precise, but it's good to get an approximate idea of where the curve should go. In the case where the bone moves −0.05 units, the driver polynomial should be $y = -20x$. Set up a driver as you did in the previous section to control this shape, with the settings as shown in Figure 5.49.

Figure 5.49

A driver for the JawDown shape

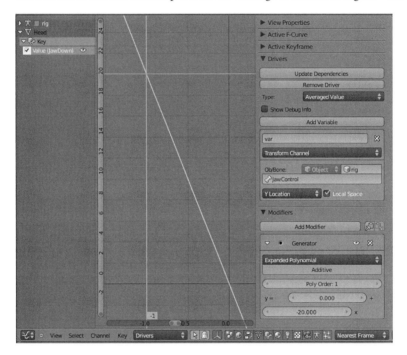

Smile and Frown Controls

To control the smile and frown shapes, you'll use two custom control bones, one for each edge of the mouth, as in Figure 5.50. Create these bones by copying the JawControl bone in Edit mode twice and using the mirror editing to place the bones in a symmetrical way. Create an appropriate mesh shape for each controller. Frown and smile are mutually exclusive, so you can control the smile by moving the controller bone up and can control the frown by moving the controller bone down, having both shapes' values at zero when the controller bone's Y location is zero. Again, you will be driving the shape keys with the local Y location value of the bones.

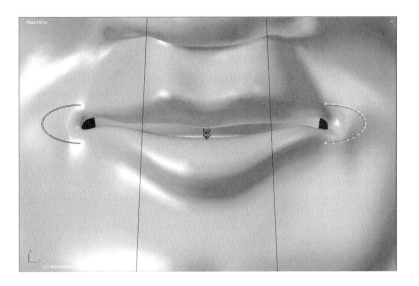

Figure 5.50

**Smile and
frown bones**

To create the four drivers necessary for the full smile and frown controls, begin with the smile-left driver. Set this driver up in the same way that you set the JawDown driver up in the previous section. In this case, you want the full smile shape to be in effect with the bone raised to about 0.025. Again, your distances might vary slightly, depending on the size of your object in relation to the background grid. In the example, the x coefficient is 40. For the frown value, copy the driver, and negate the x coefficient to −40. For the right smile and frown drivers, copy the left-side drivers, and change the drivers' target bones. Figure 5.51 shows the drivers (the values shown are for FrownRight).

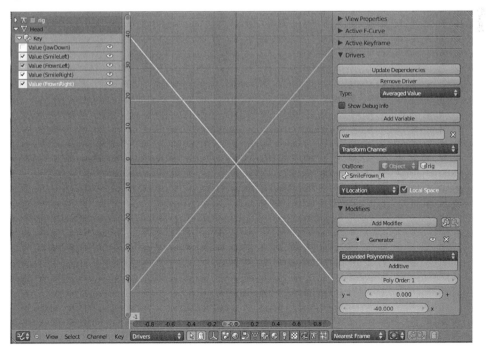

Figure 5.51

**Driver values for
FrownRight**

Restrict the movement of the control bones by locking their rotation and all location channels except for the y channel in the Properties Shelf to the right of the 3D viewport, and then add a Limit Location constraint to further restrict the bones' movement along the y-axis to a range from −0.025 to 0.025, as shown in Figure 5.52. You should do this for all your controls.

You should now be able to control the smile and the frown shapes by moving the controls up and down. Test this and make sure it's working, as in Figure 5.53.

Figure 5.52

Constraining the bones' movement

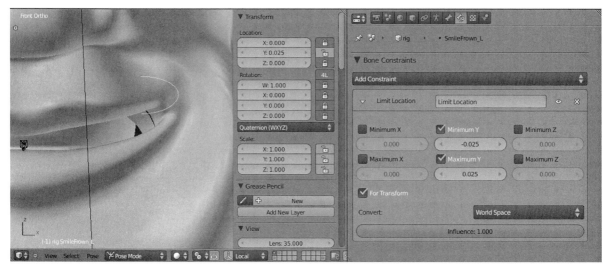

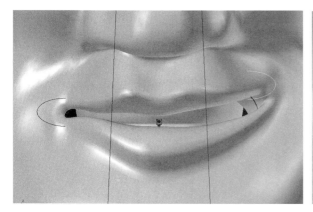
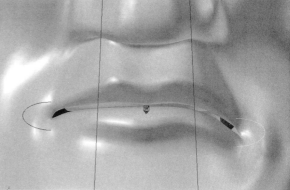

Figure 5.53

Controlling the smile and frown shapes

In Figure 5.54 you can see the custom bone shapes I've used for the other facial controls and the placement of these controls at rest in front of the character's face.

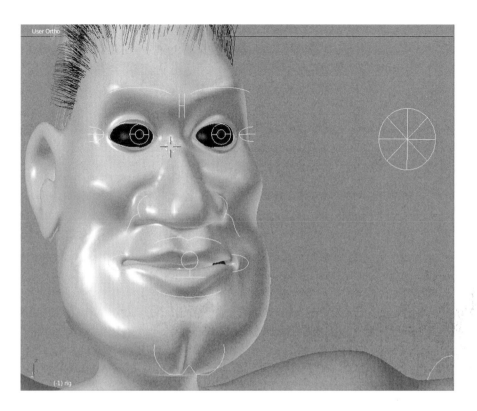

Figure 5.54

**Facial controls
in position**

The controls are as follows:

Eyebrow Controls Vertical motion (y-axis) controls the mid-brow raise for the respective eye. Rotation (z-axis) controls the outer brow raise. Locked to Y loc and Z rot transforms.

Squint Controls At the edge of the eyes, the squint controllers activate the squint for their respective eye by moving toward the eye along the x-axis. These are locked on all transforms except X loc.

Eyelid Controls The eye-shaped controls directly in front of the eyes close the eyes when lowered along the local y-axis and widen the eyes slightly when raised. Locked on all transforms except the Y loc.

Brow Knit Control The single control at the bridge of the nose knits the brow when lowered slightly. Locked on all transforms except Y loc.

Nose Crinkle Controls When raised along the local y-axis, these controls raise and crinkle their respective nostril flap and cheek. Locked on all transforms except Y loc.

Upper Lip Control When raised slightly, this control activates upper lip out. When lowered, it activates upper lip in. Locked on all transforms except Y loc.

Mouth Edge Control Smile and frown controls. Locked on all transforms except Y loc.

Lip Part Control Placed directly in front of the lips, this controller activates the round lip shape when raised and activates the wide lip shape when lowered. When rotated along the local z-axis, this control activates the lips-together shape, tightening the lips. Locked on all transforms except Y loc and Z rot.

Lower Lip Control When raised, this control activates lower lip in. When lowered, it activates lower lip out. Locked on all transforms except Y loc.

Jaw Control When lowered along the local y-axis, this control activates the jaw down shape, opening the mouth. When moved slightly to the right along the x-axis, it activates jaw right, which moves the jaw slightly to the right. When moved to the left, it activates jaw left, moving the jaw slightly to the left. This control is locked on all transforms except Y loc and X loc.

Improved Mesh Deformations Using Driven Shape Keys

You've seen how bones can be used as controls for facial shape keys. Shape keys can also be used to augment ordinary armature mesh deformations. If you have played around with posing the Captain Blender rig, you know that there are certain positions in which the rig, currently weight painted, does not deform very well. With Captain Blender as I have him weight painted, the belt area is causing problems when the legs are posed in certain ways, as shown in Figure 5.55.

Figure 5.55

Deformation problems with the belt

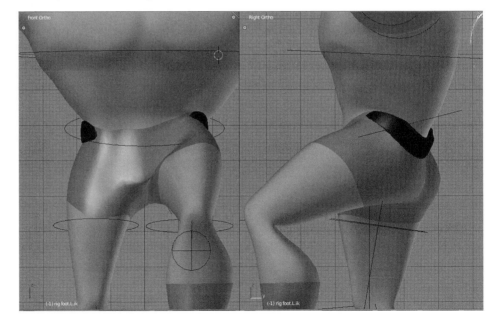

Sometimes this kind of problem can be solved by clever weight painting, but depending on the angles of the bones and the location of the vertices, this is not always the case. In cases such as this belt, there is no obvious way to paint the vertices that will result in a good-looking deformation here.

However, as you know now, armature deformation isn't the only way to get bones to influence the shape of the mesh. Driven shapes are a tool that you can use here. Basically, you want to create a shape that will force the vertices into a more natural-looking configuration when the leg is raised.

To do this, you first need to set the Armature modifier to display in Edit mode by pressing the toggle button highlighted in Figure 5.56. If this is not set, the armature deformation will not be applied in Edit mode.

In Object mode, create two new shape keys: the Basis shape key and a key called **BeltCorrect.L**. With BeltCorrect.L selected, pose the character in the pose that requires correcting. Enter Edit mode, and edit the mesh so that the belt looks good in that posed position, as shown in Figure 5.57.

A good way to drive corrective shapes is to use the rotational difference between a deform bone and a specially added target bone. Rotational difference calculates an absolute value difference between two three-dimensional rotations. The exact math behind this isn't important for you to know; the important thing is that when the two bones are exactly lined up, the value is zero. You can create a bone angled in the pose that should drive the corrective shape and then set the driver so that the shape is activated as the rotational difference between the bones approaches zero. Figure 5.58 shows this in action. The target bone has been added in Edit mode and extends forward from the character's hips. When the rotational difference of the thigh deform bone approaches zero, the corrective shape is activated.

Figure 5.56

Setting the Armature modifier to display in Edit mode

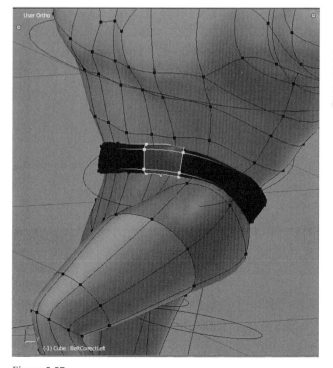

Figure 5.57

Correcting the posed mesh shape in Edit mode

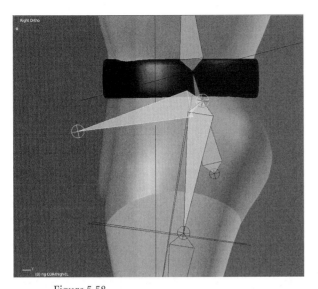
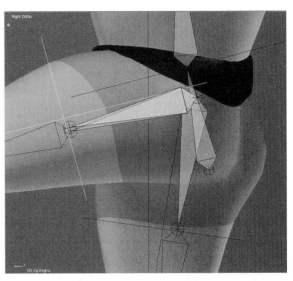

Figure 5.58

Driving the key with rotational difference between a deform bone and a driver target bone

To create this, you must first add the bone. Call the bone COR-thigh.f.L to indicate that it is a corrective shape key driver and that it is the forward correction for the left leg. Set up a driver as shown in Figure 5.59. Note that the driver angles downward for the left, so the shape key is driven by the decreasing value and hits its maximum at zero.

Figure 5.59

The driver for the corrective shape key

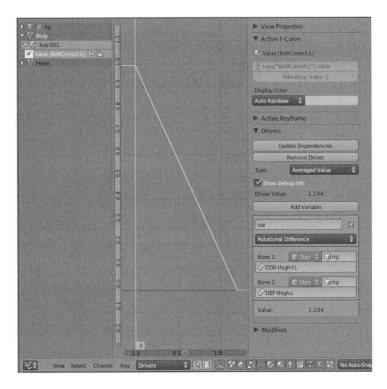

In this example, you will need corrective shape keys for both legs and for cases in which the leg is far forward and far to the rear. This will require setting up four drivers, each with its own appropriately positioned target bones. Figure 5.60 shows the complete set of target bones.

Now you know all you need to know to create a complete rig on your own. By tweaking the values and adapting these techniques as needed, you can rig any character you like. In the next part of the book, you will begin to learn how to make your characters come alive with animation.

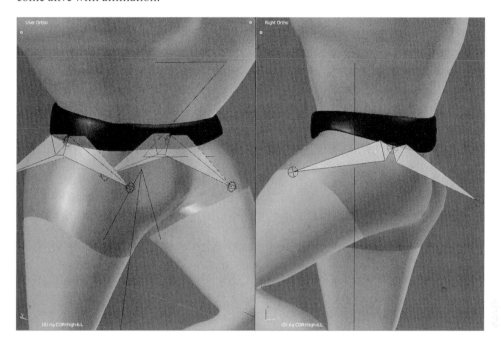

Figure 5.60

A set of driver target bones for front and back deform corrections for both legs

PART II

Bringing It to Life: Animation

In Part II, *you move into actual animation using the character created in Part I. In this part, you will be introduced to all the basic functionality of Blender as it relates to character animation. You will learn how to work with keyframes and function curves (F-Curves) and how to pose and animate with armatures. Nonlinear animation, lip syncing, interacting with props, and a variety of other issues will be covered. Ideas of general relevance to character animation are woven in among concrete descriptions of how to accomplish practical animation tasks.*

CHAPTER 6 ■ BASICS OF ANIMATION

CHAPTER 7 ■ ARMATURE ANIMATION

CHAPTER 8 ■ FACIAL ANIMATION AND LIP SYNC

CHAPTER 9 ■ ANIMATION FOR PRODUCTION

CHAPTER 10 ■ FURTHER ISSUES IN CHARACTER ANIMATION

CHAPTER 11 ■ LIGHTING, RENDERING, AND EDITING YOUR ANIMATION

CHAPTER 12 ■ PYTHON SCRIPTS AND ADD-ONS

Basics of Animation

In this chapter, you'll set aside your rig briefly to take a general look at how animation happens in Blender. I'll be introducing a few terms that anybody familiar with CG animation will know and presenting them in the context of Blender's animation system. If you are new to CG animation, you'll want to pay close attention because although the details are Blender-specific, the ideas are universal, and the functionality is essentially the same as you will find in any other 3D software.

- **Keyframes and Function Curves**

- **Using the Graph Editor: Bouncing a Ball**

- **Interpolation and Extrapolation**

Keyframes and Function Curves

Animation involves creating a series of slightly altered still pictures that, when viewed in rapid sequence, create the illusion of motion. In this respect, it hasn't changed since Winsor McCay essentially invented the art form by painstakingly drawing tens of thousands of individual frames for his early animated short films. In most other respects, it's gotten a heck of a lot easier.

In the so-called golden age of hand-drawn animation—after Walt Disney came up with a few improvements on McCay's workflow to speed up the process—an animator would draw a series of pictures, several frames apart, representing main points in the character's motion. These points would usually be the "extreme" poses, which were the ones most crucial to conveying the illusion of physical substance and motion. Although I'm slightly simplifying some of the jargon, generally speaking these drawings were termed *keyframes* (a term that's still in use).

After the animator finished the task of drawing the keyframes, an assistant would come around, empty the animator's ashtray, and draw the *in-betweens* (another term that survives as *tweening*). A skilled assistant would make the transitions between the animator's drawings as smooth and unobtrusive as possible. A tendency toward stricter workplace smoking laws has made the first part of the job of the animator's assistant redundant. The second part has been made redundant by *function curves*, which are the topic of this section and will be playing a major part through much of the rest of this book.

In Blender, as in other 3D software, the concept of keyframing survives in a different form. You set keys at specific frames for the values you want to animate from one extreme of a range to the other. Blender automatically calculates a curve between the keys over time by *interpolating* between the keyed values. In Blender, this curve is called an *F-Curve*, or function curve. Keyable values in Blender include angles and location coordinates. They also include a wide variety of other values, such as scale, color, parameter values for many effects and properties, influence values for constraints such as the IK constraint, display layers, and slider values for shapes. In short, any value that can change over time in an animation can be keyed, and Blender fills in the transitional values between the values you key.

Keys and automatically generated F-Curves aren't the end of the story, though. To paraphrase a comment I heard once by an experienced animator, you're responsible for what goes on between the keyframes, too. F-Curves are like a diligent and precise assistant but not a terribly bright one. Unless you want all your motion to look like a series of unbroken sine waves (or like CG animation from 1985), you need to work with F-Curves directly, making decisions about their modes of interpolation and editing the shapes of the curves themselves as appropriate. Blender gives you plenty of tools to do this, and you'll be looking at these tools in this chapter.

The Timeline

You'll use a couple of windows a lot when doing animation. One is the Timeline window (see Figure 6.1). This window does not require much vertical screen space, so in the default screen setup it runs along beneath the 3D viewport. You can also select the Animation screen configuration from the screen drop-down menu in the Information window header  (or by holding Ctrl and pressing the right or left arrow key to cycle through the configurations), which organizes your windows as shown in Figure 6.2. This screen configuration contains most of what you need already laid out.

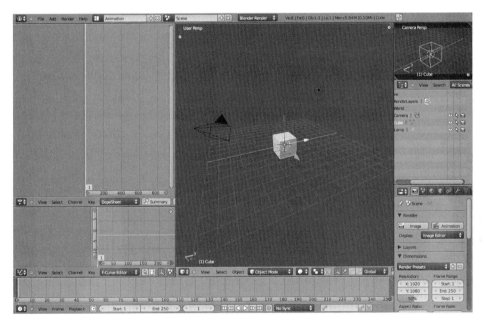

Figure 6.1
The Timeline

Figure 6.2
Default Animation screen

> HOTKEY: Pressing Ctrl+right arrow or Ctrl+left arrow cycles through desktop configuration possibilities.

The Timeline's basic functionality is self-explanatory. When you press the Play button ▷, the animation plays from the Start frame to the End frame on continuous repeat. The current frame is displayed in the field to the right of the Start and End fields, and you can input a desired frame number here directly. You can also use the left and right arrow keys on your keyboard to advance forward and backward by single frames, and you can use the up and down arrow keys to advance forward and backward by 10 frames at a time. Holding Shift and pressing the left or right arrow key will set the current frame to the start and end frame values, respectively.

HOTKEY: Pressing Shift+right arrow or Shift+left arrow sets the current frame to the Timeline Start and End frame values, respectively.

In addition to the play button in the Timeline, you can also play back animation by pressing Alt+A. Pressing Alt+Shift+A plays back the animation backward.

HOTKEY: Pressing Alt+A key plays the animation.

HOTKEY: Pressing Shift+Alt+A key plays the animation backward.

You'll also want to look at a Graph Editor, so open a Graph Editor in one of the windows on your desktop. If you have selected the Animation screen layout, your Graph Editor will be displayed to the left of the 3D window, beneath the DopeSheet window.

Using the Graph Editor: Bouncing a Ball

I'll introduce the basics with a classic piece of beginning animation: the bouncing ball. Start Blender, delete the default cube, and add two Mesh objects—a plane and a UV sphere with eight segments and eight rings. Put a subsurf modifier on the sphere, set the shading to smooth just to make it look nice, and set Object to Solid view in the Tool Shelf. Then go to the Object Properties panel, and select the Wire display option. Also, select the Optimal display option on the subsurf modifier. Figure 6.3 shows the sphere and the plane viewed from top view (7 on the numeric keypad).

Figure 6.3

Adding a plane and a ball

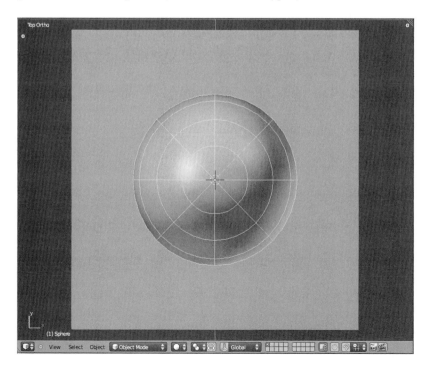

Move to front view (1 on the numeric keypad). Make sure the plane object is lined up with zero on the z-axis. Move the sphere to 10 Blender units (BUs) above zero along the z-axis.

The first thing you'll do is key the ball's vertical motion. In Blender, you use the I key to insert a key. You want to key the ball at frame 1 at the high point of its bounce. On the Timeline, make sure you are in frame 1 (this is also displayed in the lower left of the 3D viewport). With the mouse over the 3D viewport, press I to insert a key, and choose Location, as shown in Figure 6.4. You'll see some horizontal lines appear in the Graph Editor, which represent the x, y, and z coordinates of the ball. You may need to scale the Graph Editor view using the Home key on your keyboard or using the scroll wheel of your mouse to see things clearly. The x and y coordinates are both 0, so these two lines lie on top of each other at the zero point.

HOTKEY: Pressing I inserts an animation keyframe.

HOTKEY: Pressing Home scales a view so that its contents are all fully visible.

As in the Timeline, you can move back and forth one frame at a time in the Graph Editor using the left and right arrow keys, and you can move 10 frames at a time using the up and down arrow keys. Press the up arrow key twice to move 20 frames forward. The default frames per second setting is 24 fps (this setting can be changed in the Playback menu of the Timeline), so moving 20 frames forward moves you just less than a second forward in time. This is about right for the amount of time it will take for the ball to hit the ground, so move the ball down along the z-axis until it is touching the ground you created. Key this position in the same way you keyed the previous one. Note the curve shown in the Graph Editor in Figure 6.5. The Z Location curve displayed in blue now dips from 10 to about 1.

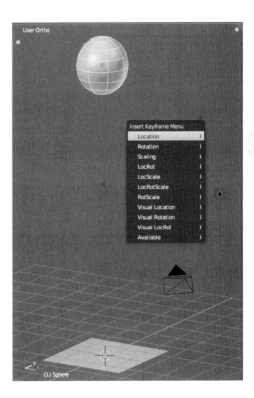

Figure 6.4

Keying the ball's location

Figure 6.5

Graph Editor

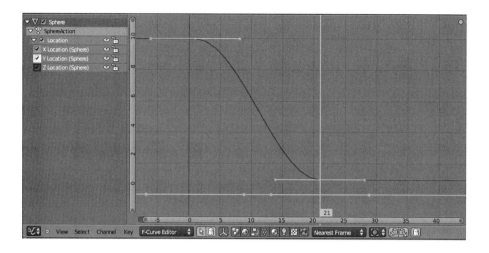

You have now added F-Curves to three *channels*, which are listed down the left-side shelf of the Graph Editor. The channels that are available for F-Curve creation depend upon the object selected and channels selected in this list. You can select or deselect objects and channels and make different channels visible or invisible using the eye icons next to the channel names.

Working with Control Points

By default, F-Curves are created as Bezier curves, with control point triples that enable you to adjust the shape of the curves manually. You can select control points by right-clicking the control point or using the B key's Box Select tool to select multiple control points. You can select all the control points that share a frame by holding Alt and right-clicking. The A key toggles selecting all points and deselecting all points.

To complete the down and up bounce movement for the bouncing ball animation, select the first control point on the Z Location curve, representing the high point of the ball's location. Duplicate this control point by pressing Shift+D, and move the copied control point to frame 41, as shown in Figure 6.6. Hold the Ctrl key while moving the control point to constrain it to frames. You can also constrain the direction you move the keys to an axis in the window by pressing the X or Y key.

> HOTKEY: Shift+D duplicates keyframes or key points on an F-Curve.

You now have a single up-down motion for the ball, which ends in the same place it begins. You can make a cycle out of it by setting the Start and End frames on the Timeline to 1 and 40. Note that the duplicate of the first key is actually at frame 41, so frames 1 and 41 are identical. This means that cycling from 1 to 40 gives you unbroken repetitions of up and down movement.

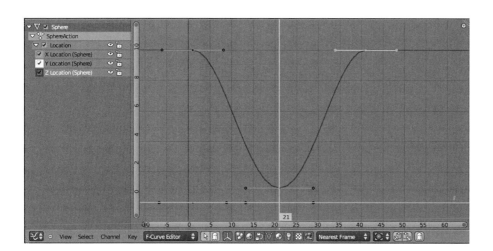

Figure 6.6

The full down and up cycle

Press Play on the Timeline to watch the ball move. You should see the ball rise and fall in smooth repetitions. (If there is any jerking movement, you need to check your keys and make sure they are the right values and placed correctly.) However, the motion is clearly not the motion of a bouncing ball. Bouncing balls do not drift smoothly up and down like this. You need to adjust the motion between keyframes. To do this, you need to edit the curves themselves.

Edit Mode

In the Graph Editor, you can edit curves that are in Bezier Interpolation mode as Bezier curves, using control points with handles you can manipulate. Selecting the center point of the control point enables you to move the entire control point, handles and all. Selecting either of the handles enables you to control the shape of the curve. With a control point selected, you can change the handle type under the Set Keyframe Handle Type menu, accessed with the V key. The options for handle type are as follows:

> HOTKEY: Pressing V in the Graph Editor opens a menu to change the control point handle type.

Auto Blender automatically calculates the length and direction of the handles to create the smoothest curve.

Auto Clamped This is the same as Auto, except that control points at extremes of the curve are clamped horizontally. With Auto Clamped, local maximum or minimum points on the curve always run through at least one control point. This is the default.

Aligned Blender maintains a straight line between the two handles, so if you move one handle, the other one is also moved.

Free Either handle's endpoint can be moved independently of the other handle.

Vector Both handles are adjusted to point directly to the previous and next control points.

The main problem with the bounce curve is that the low point of the bounce is slowing down gradually and then speeding up when the ball returns upward. In a real fall, the object would continue to accelerate because of the force of gravity, so the curve would get steeper and steeper on the way down, before the ball is suddenly stopped by the unyielding ground. The ball retains most of its kinetic energy after this collision, but its direction is reversed back upward, which means it starts back upward with almost the same velocity it had when it struck the ground.

For this example, you'll ignore the loss of energy and assume that the ball can keep bouncing forever, in which case the kinetic energy going upward out of the bounce is the same as that coming into the bounce. This energy, in countering the resistance of gravity, diminishes until the top of the cycle, when once again gravity takes over as the strongest force acting on the ball, and the ball comes down again.

In practice, this all means you want two parabolic curves angling downward to meet at a point. You need to adjust the lowest point on the Z Location curve. Select the control point by clicking the midpoint of the control point triple.

A quick way to create a sharp vertex is to use the V key and select the vector handle type to change the handle type to vectors. Try this, and you will see that the handles now point in the direction of the preceding and following control points. This is an improvement, as you can see if you run the animation now. But the curves straighten out too soon, and the acceleration of the ball is not maintained all the way down. To adjust this, you can bring these handles' controls closer together, making for a steeper curve. Editing a vector-type handle automatically changes it to a free type, so you can go ahead and select one of the handle points and press the **G** key, or you can right-click and drag the control point to move it slightly toward the middle of the curve, as shown in Figure 6.7. Play your animation and see the improvement in the bouncing motion.

Figure 6.7

Sharpening the F-Curve at the bounce

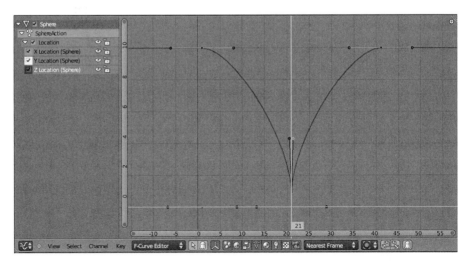

Color Gallery

Scrappy adventuress Sintel and the baby dragon Scales are the main characters of the Blender Open Movie Project's latest offering, *Sintel*.

Two scenes from *Sintel*. Scales the baby dragon cries out, and Sintel confronts a full-grown dragon in the climax of the movie.

Big Buck Bunny is the second short movie from the Blender Open Movie Project. It's a cute and furry tale of malice and revenge that represented a giant leap forward for Blender's particle hair functionality.

These scenes are from the open source movie *Elephants Dream*, the result of the Blender Foundation's Orange Project. It was intended to showcase Blender's power as an animation tool and also to spur the development of needed production functionality.

LEFT: *15 Minutes of Glory* by Kamil Kuklo (Mookie) takes advantage of particle fur and subsurface scattering to create a realistic mouse character.

RIGHT: Toudou+'s *Minotaur* uses particles and textures to create a fantasy beast.

TOP: An alligator relaxes in bed with a book in Julia Korbut's whimsical render.
BOTTOM: A still from Reynante Martinez's dreamlike short animation *Slumber*.

These characters, created by Zoltan Miklosi, demonstrate some of the incredible power and flexibility Blender provides for realistic character modeling.

TOP: Akira Hiki's images both show the unmistakable influence of the Japanese anime style. **BOTTOM LEFT:** By Yuichi Miura. **BOTTOM RIGHT:** By Akutsu Tomohiro. Two more examples of anime-styled character renders from Japanese Blender users. Akutsu's image here is an excellent example of toon-style shading.

This collection of characters is from the feature-length animated film *Plumiferos*.

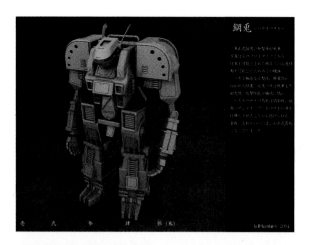

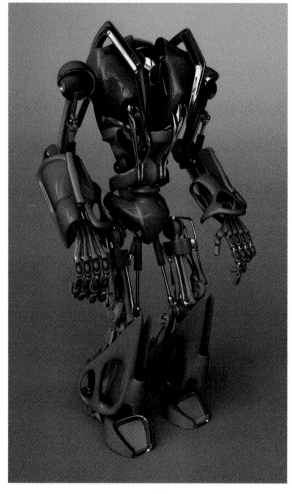

TOP: By Yuichi Miura. BOTTOM: By Eric Terrier.

TOP: By Mauro Bonecchi. **BOTTOM:** Super WuMan, from a concept and design by Sacha Goedegebure (Sago), was modeled and animated by Andy Dolphin (AndyD). These further demonstrate the variety of stylistic options available and how textures and materials can help make an image more realistic or cartoony.

By Sacha Goedegebure (Sago). Sacha went on to direct *Big Buck Bunny*.

Two examples of highly realistic portraiture. **TOP**: Lucas Falcão's Ruby. **BOTTOM**: Scott Wilkinson's Ex Nihilo.

Images from David Revoy's animated short *The Little Fairy*. David went on to be the concept artist for *Sintel* and to release his own Blender Open Movie Workshop training video on creating 2D artwork, called *Chaos and Evolutions*.

Robert J. Tiess's striking and varied images display a range of techniques and effects possible with Blender.

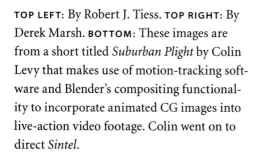

TOP LEFT: By Robert J. Tiess. **TOP RIGHT:** By Derek Marsh. **BOTTOM:** These images are from a short titled *Suburban Plight* by Colin Levy that makes use of motion-tracking software and Blender's compositing functionality to incorporate animated CG images into live-action video footage. Colin went on to direct *Sintel*.

Keying Scale: A Simple Squash/Stretch Effect

Now that the ball's bouncing motion looks more or less right, you'll add a little squash and stretch to add some more dynamism to the motion. The use of squash and stretch effects in this way dates back to early drawn animation, and the style at that time was inevitably cartoony.

Squash and stretch are real physical phenomena, but the exaggerated degree to which they are often used in animation is not realistic. Real squash and stretch depends upon the material of the object and the forces to which it is subjected. A steel ball and a water balloon, obviously, have different degrees of squash when bounced against a surface and different degrees of stretch when dropped from a height. Something like a baseball, for example, would have an imperceptibly slight squash and stretch in real life. Anyone who has seen photographs of a baseball contacting a bat knows that although the bat makes a deep instantaneous impression on the ball, the impression is quite local and does not alter the roundness of the ball very much. However, in a cartoon-styled animation, the squash and stretch for a baseball would be highly exaggerated to emphasize the dynamism of the ball.

You will take a very simple (and not very flexible) approach to animating squash and stretch here, simply keying values for scale. To do this, follow these steps:

1. Go to frame 1. With the ball selected in the 3D viewport, press I and select Scale. You should see keys appear in the Graph Editor and their corresponding channels appear in the list in the Graph Editor shelf, as in Figure 6.8. If the channels are collapsed, you can click the gray triangle to get the view shown in the figure.

Figure 6.8

The original scale

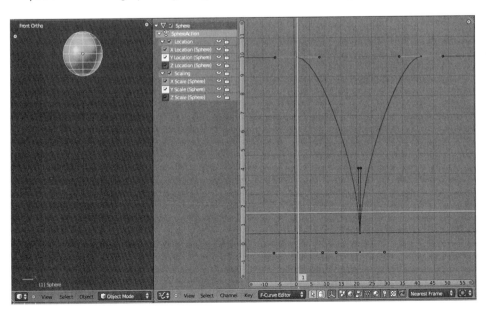

2. Select this first frame's control points by holding Alt and right-clicking a control point in the first frame. Duplicate these control points with Shift+D. Move the new keys 40 frames to the right, holding down the Ctrl key.

3. Skip forward 20 frames (press the up arrow key twice) to frame 21, and scale the ball to a squash shape. To do this, scale the ball down along the z-axis to .5. Then scale again; this time, use S followed by Shift+Z to scale up in the other two directions to 1.5. Be sure not to change frames without keying this new scaling, or you will lose it (it will go back to whatever is keyed for the frame you go to; in this case, the first keyed value). Key the new scaling, as shown in Figure 6.9.

HOTKEY: Pressing Shift+Z following a G, R, or S key transformation constrains the transformation to the plane defined by the x- and y-axes. Shift+Y and Shift+X behave similarly.

4. Because the ball is now scaled down vertically, you need to lower the low point on the Z Location curve so that the ball comes in contact with the ground instead of bouncing back just short of it. Do this by selecting the center control point on the Z Location F-Curve and lowering it with the G key and the down arrow button on your keyboard. Adjust it until your squashed ball is properly set on the ground. You do this by editing the curves directly; if you simply moved the ball onto the ground in the 3D view and then reset the key with I, you might lose your special edits to the handles of the F-Curve at that key.

5. The stretch effect is a result of gravity and should be at its maximal point at the same time that the gravitational acceleration is highest. This is, of course, the frame immediately before the ball makes contact with the ground. Go to this frame and press Alt+S on the ball to clear all scaling. Then scale up along the z-axis to 1.25, and scale down along the x,y plane to .75. Key the scaling.

Figure 6.9

Scaled to a squash shape

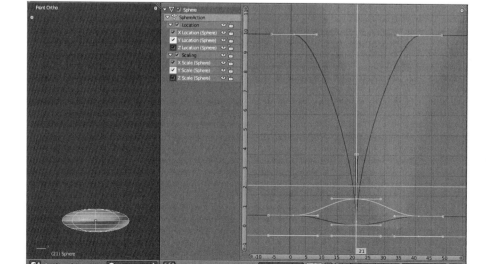

6. Because the kinetic energy of the ball is still high on the recoil, it should spring back into the stretched position quickly, but because it is not influenced by hitting a solid surface, it does not have to spring back within the space of a single frame. Duplicate the stretched key from frame 20 and place it a few frames after the actual contact frame. The squash scaling also should not begin early. The ball should squash on impact. Figure 6.10 shows the final key frame positions for the stretch scaling.

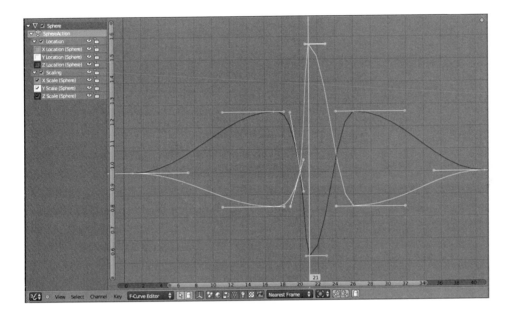

Figure 6.10

Placing the stretch keys

Interpolation and Extrapolation

Blender generates an F-Curve that passes through a set of keyed values. You can determine the kind of curve by selecting the Interpolation mode from the key menu and setting Extrapolation mode of the curve. *Interpolation* refers to the algorithm Blender uses to calculate the shape of the curve between keyed values. *Exrapolation* refers to the algorithms used to calculate the shape of the curve forward and backward in time beyond the first and last keyed values.

Interpolation

Three types of interpolation are available in Blender: Bezier, linear, and constant. Each of these types has a markedly different effect on the motion of the object it is applied to, and each offers different possibilities for editing. You can access these through the Interpolation mode submenu of the Key menu.

Bezier Interpolation

The default interpolation type is Bezier, which creates a smooth, rounded curve between the keyed values. The key points are Bezier control points with two handles, and the curve's shape can be edited manually, as you saw in the previous section. Taking two Z Location keys as an example, this default interpolation results in the curve shown in Figure 6.11.

Figure 6.11

Bezier interpolation

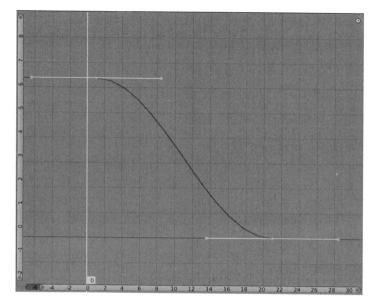

This curve type creates the most naturalistic movement of the three types, although this does not mean that unadjusted Bezier curves will always produce convincing movement. It is important to consider the physical forces being applied to the object, as discussed in the previous section.

An equally important quality of Bezier interpolation is that it is the only interpolation type that allows editing of the shape of the curve itself.

Linear Interpolation

Linear interpolation creates a straight line between keyed values. This can be useful for mechanical movements, but it is also useful for animating properties other than movement, which might change in a linear fashion. Linear interpolation is not a convincing way to model organic movement. Editing the shape of the curve is also highly restricted. In the Graph Editor, you can move key points around freely, but you cannot change anything else about the shape of the curve. Figure 6.12 shows a linear interpolation between points.

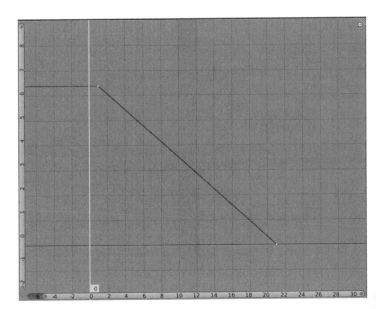

Figure 6.12

Linear interpolation

Constant Interpolation

Constant interpolation holds each keyed value constant until the next value is keyed, as in Figure 6.13. This does not model motion at all but rather sudden, discrete changes in position or value. This is the interpolation mode to use for instantaneous changes. In fact, when keying an object's layer, this is the only interpolation mode possible. For animation, the constant interpolation mode might seem useless to novices, but it can be very effective at blocking out the key poses of an animation sequence, making sure the gross timing is correct before going on to further refine the animation.

Figure 6.13

Constant interpolation

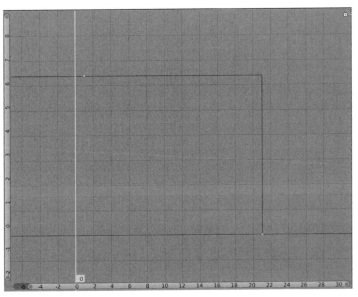

Extrapolation Types

There are two extrapolation types: constant and linear. You can use these types with any of the interpolation types. In the following examples, they are shown with a curve using Bezier interpolation. I have included two examples for each—one with two key values and one with three—to emphasize cases in which this makes a difference to the behavior of the curve. You can access these in the Extrapolation mode submenu of the Key menu.

Constant Extrapolation

Constant extrapolation holds the values of the first and last keyed values constant in the positive and negative directions on the Timeline. Figure 6.14 shows constant extended curves in cases with one and two key points. Constant is the default extend value.

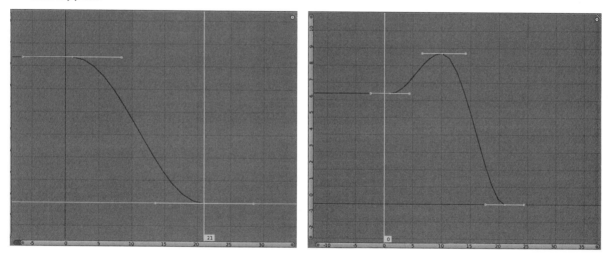

Linear Extrapolation

Whereas the constant extrapolation type holds the value constant, linear extrapolation holds the *angle* at which the curve passes through the first and last keyframes constant and calculates the continuation of the curve as an extension of the line at that angle, as shown in Figure 6.15. You can use two points to create a straight F-Curve at any angle. You can use linear extrapoloation, for example, to continue certain transforms indefinitely, such as rotation. A linear extrapolated curve with two defining values on the rotation curve is a good way to animate a spinning wheel.

In the case of three or more points, the extrapolation extend appears as in Figure 6.16. This is a much less common use of linear extrapolation.

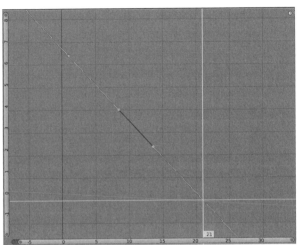

Figure 6.15

Linear extrapolation with two key points

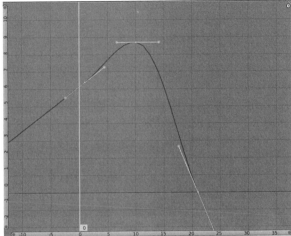

Figure 6.16

Linear extrapolation with three key points

F-Curves and F-Curve Modifiers

F-Curves are the basis of all animation in Blender. Any time a value changes, there is an F-Curve guiding its change. In the next few chapters, you will see a number of different ways and places in which you can create and manipulate keys; you can key some values in the Properties window by pressing the I key over a field, you can key some values by using sliders, and much of the armature-based work you will be doing will take place in the DopeSheet window and the Non-Linear Animation Editor. Nevertheless, all these contexts are fundamentally interfaces laid over the basis of F-Curves and key point values. It is important to remember that when problems arise in these other areas, you can always find the F-Curve that's giving you trouble in the Graph Editor and find out what's going on with it directly.

Figure 6.17

Noise F-Curve modifier

F-Curves can also be nondestructively modified by using F-Curve modifiers. You can access F-Curve modifiers in the Properties Shelf of the Graph Editor window with an F-Curve selected and editable. A variety of types of modifiers enable you to change the shape of the curve in many ways. Figure 6.17 shows a Noise-type F-Curve modifier that adds a random component to the curve. Figure 6.18 shows a simple F-Curve before and after the modifier is activated. Like Object modifiers, F-Curve modifiers can be deleted or deactivated.

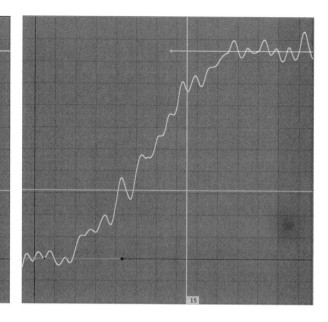

Figure 6.18

**Noise-modified
F-Curve**

You can use modifiers to create cycles, steps, or limits in your F-Curves, apply built-in functions to the curves, and even influence the F-Curve values using Python, giving you a huge amount of power over the shape of the curves.

In the next chapter, you'll step away from this low-level F-Curve view of animation and look at practical tools for animating fully rigged characters.

CHAPTER 7

Armature Animation

In this chapter, you finally get down to the business of full-fledged character animation in Blender. You rigged the character, took a look at the underlying mechanisms of how animation works, and probably have become pretty comfortable with the interface. It's time to see what you can make Captain Blender *do*.

Although this book is not intended as a substitute for in-depth study of the art of animation, this chapter touches on some basic principles of creating convincing motion that have stood the test of time from the early days of Disney. Animation is a descendent art form of cartooning, which used simple drawings to express a wide range of emotions and ideas, and as such exaggeration is a crucial aspect. Although CG can enable you to work with very realistic images, the exaggerated, cartoon-influenced aspect remains significant, as anybody familiar with such "live-action" films as *The Mask* or *The Matrix* is aware. In hyper-realistic CG, use of motion capture and related technologies can move out of the realm of proper animation and into something else entirely. In films such as *King Kong* and *The Lord of the Rings*, for example, the character models for Kong and Gollum essentially amount to digital costumes applied to a human actor.

This book is mainly concerned with animation in the traditional sense, which almost inevitably assumes a certain degree of exaggeration.

- Posing and Keyframing with the DopeSheet and the Action Editor
- Walk and Run Cycles
- Pose-to-Pose Animation

Posing and Keyframing with the DopeSheet and Action Editor

The starting point for armature animation is the DopeSheet, which you can access by selecting the diamond keyframes icon in the Window Type drop-down menu. The DopeSheet has three modes: the DopeSheet proper, the Action Editor, and the Shape Key Editor. You can select these with the drop-down menu in the DopeSheet window header.

Figure 7.1 shows two DopeSheet windows. The top one is set to DopeSheet mode, and the bottom one is set to Action Editor mode. They look similar, but how they function differs in important ways.

Figure 7.1

The DopeSheet and Action Editor

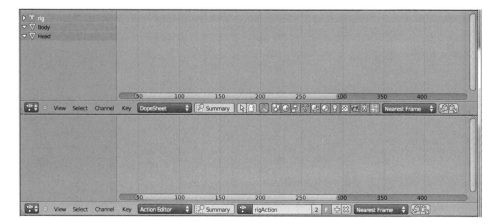

In this chapter, you're mainly going to work in the Action Editor. The Action Editor is essentially an interface for keying and organizing collections of keyframes associated with a specific object. The DopeSheet is an overview of actions for multiple objects. Keys you create or edit in the Action Editor or DopeSheet represent actual key points in the underlying F-Curves and can be edited as such, but the Action Editor and DopeSheet interfaces make it much easier to see the arrangement of keys for many bones in an armature (or in the case of the DopeSheet for many objects) at once, rather than having to deal with a huge number of F-Curves and key points. For example, locating and rotating a single bone at a particular point in time actually involves seven different F-Curves. You don't want to have to see all those curves just to know that the bone has been keyed for location and rotation. The Action Editor and DopeSheet show you pertinent information about where keys are without giving you too much information.

The Action Editor enables you to create and edit separate actions independently of each other. As you will see in the next few chapters, you can use and combine individual actions in several ways. This chapter will focus on creating and working with individual actions.

Bouncing Captain Blender

You'll begin by creating a basic jump action. Add a plane at the zero point, as shown in Figure 7.2, and scale it up along the x- and y-axes. This will be the ground.

Now you'll really start animating. You'll want a 3D viewport window and an Action Editor window open here, as well as a Timeline window. One option is to select the Animation screen from the Screen drop-down menu at the top of your work area to create a display like that shown in Figure 7.3. This gives you a setup that includes most of the necessary windows. There is only one DopeSheet window, however. For this chapter, split the DopeSheet horizontally, and set one of the DopeSheet windows to Action Editor mode. The default animation length is 250 frames, which corresponds to a 10-second animation.

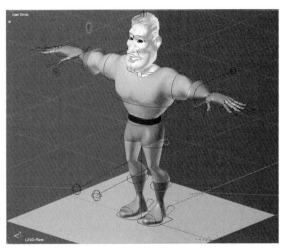

Figure 7.2

Positioning the character on the floor

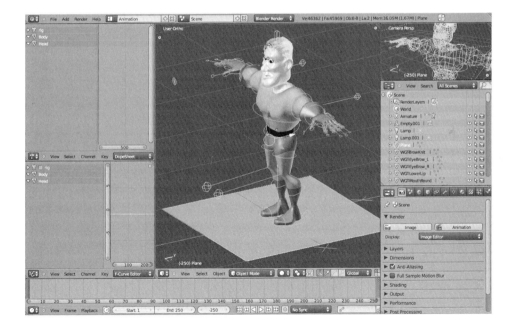

Figure 7.3

Animation screen

You can create new actions in several ways. First, you can click the New button in the Action Editor header. All currently existing actions can be found in the drop-down menu that occupies the same space as the New button in the header, as shown in Figure 7.4. The first action created when you click New will be named Action. Subsequent new actions will be called Action.001, Action.002, and so on, and you can rename them by typing a new name into the field. If an action is currently active in the Action Editor, several familiar buttons appear to the right of the action's name, as you can see in Figure 7.5. The number

immediately to the right of the Action name field shows how many datablock users of the action are currently in Blender. Clicking this button will create a copy of the action and make it a single-user datablock. The F button to the right of this toggles a fake user for the action. With this button toggled off, unused actions will be discarded when your current Blender session is shut down. The plus symbol button

Figure 7.4

The Action Editor drop-down menu

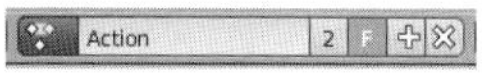

to the right of this creates a new empty action, just like the New button. Finally, the X symbol button to the right of this removes the current action from the Action Editor and disconnects it from the current animation. The action will still be available to select from the drop-down, and it will persist from session to session if the fake user is left in place, even if it is not used in the scene.

Figure 7.5

The Action field and buttons

When there is no active action, you can create a new action by simply keying. The newly created action will be automatically given a name that incorporates the object's name to which the action corresponds. For example, if you key the Cube object, the new action will be named CubeAction by default.

Make sure your Timeline says you are on frame 1, select the rig object in the 3D viewport, and enter Pose mode. Before you begin, make sure your IK and FK posing settings are the way they should be. For the jumping, walking, and running cycles you'll be looking at in this chapter, the legs will be posed using IK posing, and the arms will be posed using FK posing. This makes it easy to pose the legs to interact with the ground and to pose the arms in a way that creates nice arcs. You can see the IK and FK settings by selecting the bones in Pose mode (go ahead and select them all with the A key) and looking under Rig Main Properties in the Properties Shelf to the right of the 3D viewport (toggle the Properties Shelf visibility with the N key), as shown in Figure 7.6. Set the FK/IK values for the foot.ik.L and foot.ik.R bones to 1 by sliding the sliders all the way to the right, as shown in Figure 7.6.

Enter Right Ortho view by pressing 3 on the numeric keypad and toggling into orthographic view using 5 on the numeric keypad. In the 3D viewport, select the following bones: hips, ribs, head, foot.ik.R, and foot.ik.L. Press the I key over the 3D viewport, and choose LocRot from the keying options in the menu that appears. This will create location and rotation keyframes for each of the five bones. These will show up in the DopeSheet and Action Editor, as shown in Figure 7.7. As you can see in the DopeSheet, the objects in the scene are listed, and a single summary keyframe is shown for the rig object. In the action, each keyed bone is given its own horizontal channel, and the keyframes for that channel are displayed as white diamonds (yellow when selected). This keyframe display is actually a shorthand for several underlying F-Curve key points.

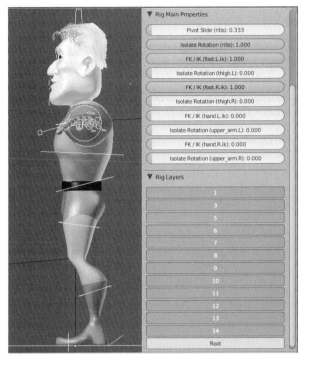

Figure 7.6

The FK/IK settings for bones

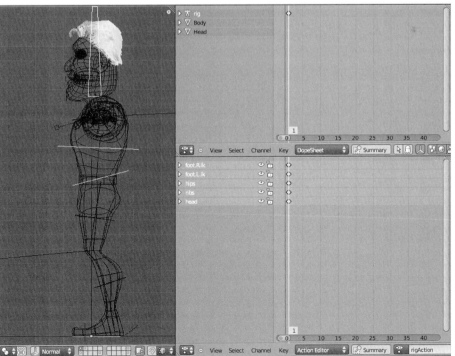

Figure 7.7

Keyframes for the first frame

The five bones you've keyed are the main bones you're concerned with for the jumping motion. Other bones will also be involved to enhance the effect, but the main motion will depend on these bones. You'll create a cycle that begins and ends with the armature's rest pose, so you'll key the relevant bones now.

You'll incorporate a little exaggeration right off the bat, in terms of the timing. Because you want to emphasize the motion and the height that Captain Blender is jumping to, you'll make the whole motion slightly slower than it would be in real life. The whole action will take 50 frames, or 2 seconds. This is not slow enough to appear to the viewer as actual slow motion, but it will highlight the sense of mass and energy in the motion.

This motion has three main parts, aside from the rest positions at the beginning and end. There is the initial crouch as the character gets ready to launch upward. Next is the apex of the jump, where the character is at his most extended point, and then is the recoil point after pressing the ground on the way down, which forces the character down into a position not much different from the initial crouch.

The timing of the up and down motion needs to be symmetrical because, like the ball bouncing, the rise and fall of an object with gravity create a parabolic shape. So, you want the figure's movement into and out of the crouching position at the beginning and the end of the jump to be considerably slower than the leap and landing, which you want to be explosive and jolting, respectively.

To complete the keyframing for the jump, follow these steps:

1. Ensure that the hips, ribs, head, and foot.ik.L/R bones are keyed in the rest position in frame 1, as described previously.

2. Go to frame 16 by entering the frame number in the Timeline field. Position and key the hips, ribs, head, and foot.ik.L/R bones at frame 16, as shown in Figure 7.8. This gives the figure a bit longer than one-half second to get down into the crouching position.

Figure 7.8

Crouch pose

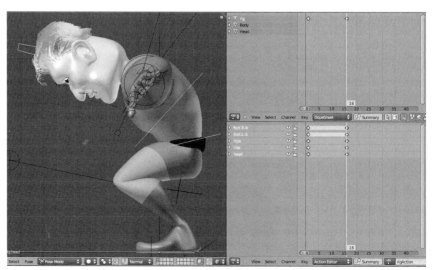

3. Go to frame 26, select all bones with the A key, and then press Alt+R and Alt+G to clear all location and rotation transformations on the bones. Pose the character as shown in Figure 7.9, which will be the apex of the leap. Notice that the chest is somewhat curved back, while the hips are pushed a little bit forward. Key these bone positions.

4. In the Action Editor, select all the keys in frame 16 with the Box Select tool (B key). Selected keys will be yellow. Selecting keys with the Box Select tool does not automatically unselect other keys, so double-check that only the keys in frame 16 are selected. Press Shift+D to duplicate the keys. Then while holding down Ctrl, move the copied keys to frame 36. Holding down Ctrl while moving keys constrains their placement to full frames. Do the same thing to duplicate the keys from frame 1 to frame 51. The result should look like Figure 7.10.

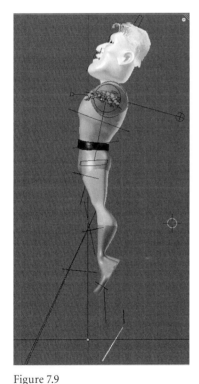

Figure 7.9

Apex of the leap

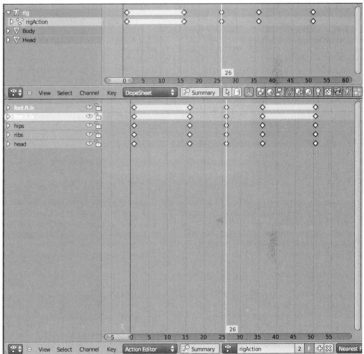

Figure 7.10

Duplicating keyframes in the Action Editor

5. You'll make a few small modifications here to improve the effect. One will be to key the rotation of the toe.L/R bones. They should be in rest position before and after the jump and rotated at the apex of the jump, as shown in Figure 7.11.

6. Position and key the arms as shown in Figure 7.12, Figure 7.13, and Figure 7.14 to complete the posing for the animation.

Figure 7.11

Modifications to improve the effect

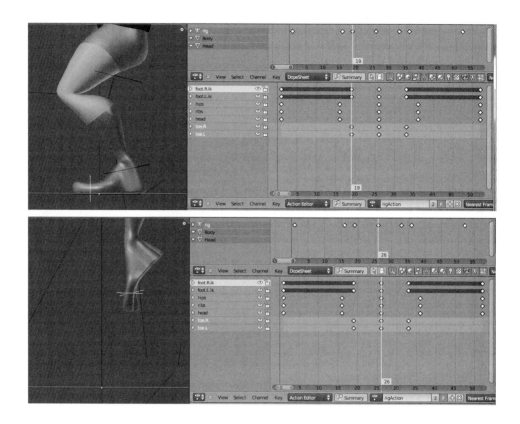

Figure 7.12

Rest arm position (frames 1 and 51)

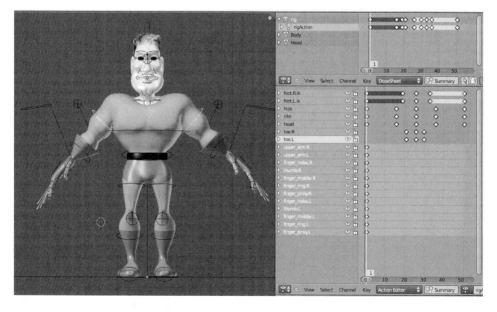

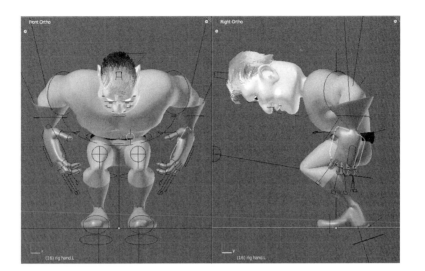

Figure 7.13
Crouched arm position (frames 16 and 36)

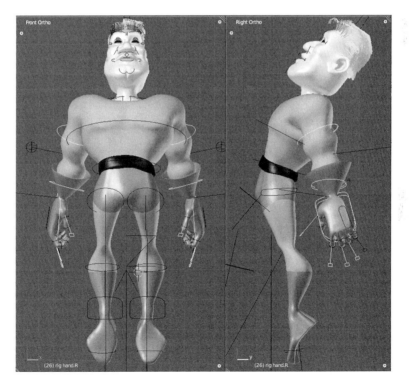

Figure 7.14
Apex arm position (frame 26)

Previewing Your Animation

Now that you have finished the basic keyframing of your jump action, you'll want to see how it looks. You can do this by pressing the Play button on the Timeline to activate the animation or by pressing Alt+A in the window where you want to activate the animation.

The problem with simply watching the animation in this way is that, depending on the speed of your computer's processor and the complexity of your character mesh, the delay caused by calculating the figure's position for each frame means that the animation might play back either much too quickly or much too slowly to give you an accurate portrayal of the motion. With a fairly high-poly mesh like Captain Blender, including particle hair, this calculation is likely to be unusually slow and certainly does not give you a realistic idea of what your animation looks like at the proper frame rate.

A quick-and-dirty solution is to select only the layer with your armature object and watch the animation run with only the armature. This will still be slowed down from the correct frame rate, but it will probably be watchable as movement. For certain trouble-shooting tasks, this is a useful method. However, it is still important to see the entire mesh figure deforming at full speed to see what your animation really looks like.

The other extreme is to properly render an animation, as you'll learn how to do in Chapter 11. However, this process is impractical at a project's early stage of development because it takes up large amounts of time and resources calculating light and surface effects for each frame that you do not need to see when you are only trying to evaluate the animation.

The most accurate way to play back an animation in real time without fully rendering the images is to use the 3D viewport's OpenGL render button, which you can find on the header of the 3D viewport (it is the rightmost button displaying a movie clapperboard icon). Clicking this button gives you an animated render of the 3D window as it is currently shown (the button to the right of this button, with a camera icon, gives you a still OpenGL render).

After you render the animation, you can play it back at full speed in the player of your choice. See Chapter 11 for suggestions on external video players and instructions on how to integrate them with Blender. Because your 3D viewport is getting rendered here, you can use 0 on the numeric keypad to go into camera view to get a render of the animation from the camera's point of view. So, you can render your animation from a few different perspectives and see how it looks. If you run into problems with this part, you might want to skip ahead to Chapter 11 to read up more fully on rendering animations.

Figure 7.15

Sync option for animation playback

There is still another option for playback, which is probably the most suitable for our purposes here. In the Playback menu of the Timeline window there is toggle button labeled AV-Sync (see Figure 7.15). Enabling AV-Sync tells Blender to attempt to play back animations triggered by the Play button or Alt+A in real time. If necessary, Blender skips frames to show you the proper timing of your animation. Before you go to the trouble of doing the OpenGL render, try using the AV-Sync option. It gives acceptable results, even under demanding circumstances. Also, one advantage of keeping your animation preview live (nonrendered) is that Blender enables you to transform the view, even while it is playing your animation in real time. Try using the scroll wheel, Shift+MMB-drag, and MMB-drag in a third window while your animation loops in real time.

Tweaking F-Curves

When I rendered the jumping animation, it turned out pretty well, but the jump was happening awfully quickly. Quick may be realistic for a jump like this, but to get the motion effect I was after, I wanted to exaggerate the length of time spent at the apex slightly. This would help emphasize the character's physical strain at the apex and give more of a sense of height, power, and mass.

To do this, you need to work directly on the curve responsible for holding Captain Blender in the air, namely, the Z Location F-Curve on the hip bone.

With your torso bone selected in the 3D viewport, switch your Action Editor to the Graph Editor, open the Hips channel by clicking the triangle icon to the left of the channel name, and select the Z Location channel. In Figure 7.16, you can see that the curve is too sharp right now. The character is returning to the ground too abruptly, so you'll want to round off this curve. You can do that by simply selecting the two Bezier handles of the topmost control point and scaling up with the S key. The result is the rounder curve shown in Figure 7.17.

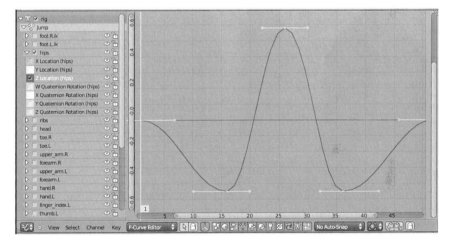

Figure 7.16

Z-axis F-Curve as calculated

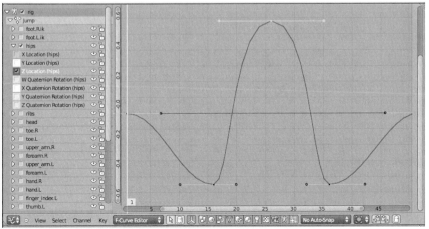

Figure 7.17

Rounded off to exaggerate

Check the new motion with Alt+A. Never mind whether it's more realistic; it's definitely better looking and more evocative.

You can see an overview of each keyframe and its poses and keys for the complete action in Figure 7.18. The fully rendered video of the action is in the file jump.avi on the accompanying DVD.

F-Curves make the task of animation much easier by automating a lot of the most painstaking work. However, remember that you must strike a balance between doing things by hand and using automated tools. Getting a sense of how much to tinker with F-Curves requires experience and skill. Overkeying and overediting curves can result in choppy, erratic movement, whereas simply letting the F-Curves do all the work yields unconvincingly smooth motions.

Figure 7.18

Jump action

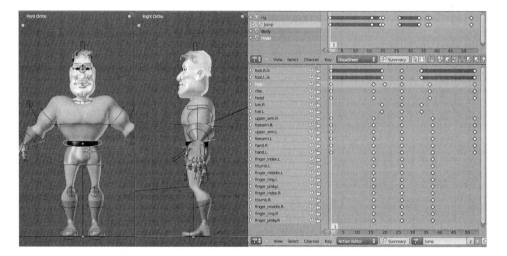

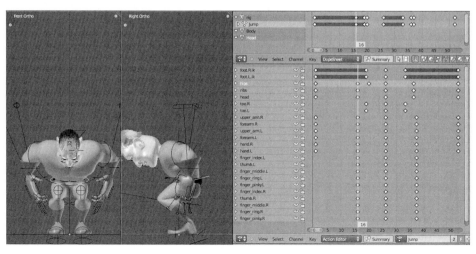

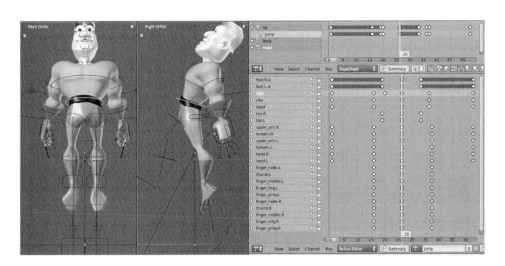

Figure 7.18

(continued)

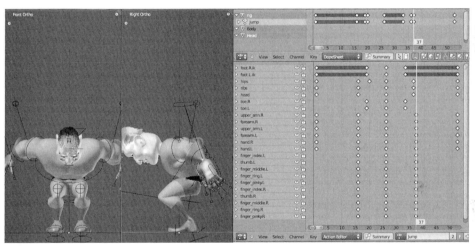

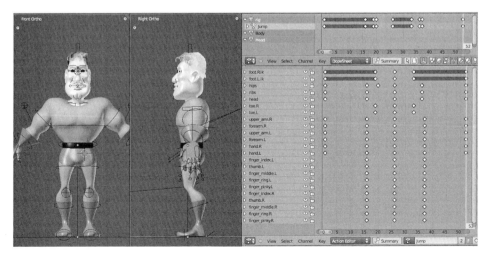

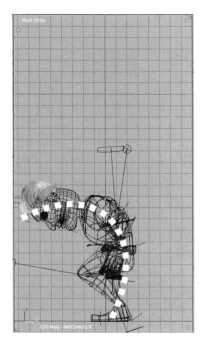

Figure 7.19
Line of action for the crouch pose

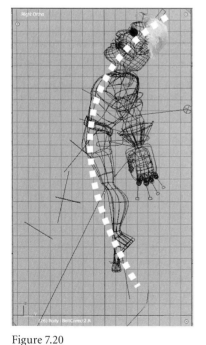

Figure 7.20
Line of action for the apex pose

Line of Action

"In animation, the line of action is the basis for rhythm, simplicity, and directness!"

—Preston Blair

An important aspect of animation, as with cartooning, is boiling down complex visual information to its simplest, most basic elements. This is related to the exaggeration discussed earlier. You know that you need to exaggerate certain aspects of form and pose to get the motion effects you want. The question is, what to exaggerate? A big nose, for example, is a form of exaggeration, but enlarging Captain Blender's nose at the apex of his jump obviously does not contribute to the effectiveness of the animation. The answer to how to use exaggeration effectively can be found in an awareness of *lines of action*.

The line of action for a pose is a single smooth line that you can draw through the pose, which conforms to the pose in terms of energy and direction. It is more basic to the pose than any specific portion of the figure or armature's position. Effective animation is an interplay between lines of action, and one important trait of a good animator is some intuitive feeling for these lines. Lines of action do not have any explicit manifestation in your software, but you should try to cultivate an awareness of them in your mind.

I drew lines of action through the extreme poses in the jump animation in Figure 7.19 and Figure 7.20. As you can see, these lines capture the curled, hunched quality of the crouch position and the stretched, arcing quality of the apex pose. They also give you insight into what you need to exaggerate to make the pose more effective. Squash and stretch effects should agree with the line of action of the movement.

Not all poses have such immediately obvious lines of action, but it is a good idea to think in these terms when creating your poses. If you can envision a single line that expresses the energy and motion of each pose and work to make your exaggerations and secondary movements complement and support this line, your animation will be much more effective.

Manual vs. Auto Keyframing

Keying a value such as a bone position fixes that value for subsequent frames in the animation. You can pose a bone in a particular frame, and it will hold that pose (pressing Alt+G and Alt+R to clear position and rotation is the same as posing to the rest position) as long as you are on that frame. However, if you do not key the positions, they will jump back to their previously keyed positions as soon as you move to another frame.

You can set Blender to use automatic keyframing in the user preferences by selecting the Auto Keyframing button shown in Figure 7.21. You can also activate Auto Keyframing using the similar button on the Timeline. Selecting this option inserts a keyframe every time you change the pose of your armature or transform an object, eliminating the need to use the I key.

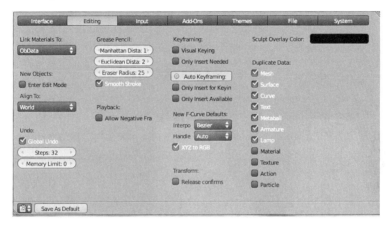

Figure 7.21

User preference for auto keying

Using Auto Keyframing is entirely a matter of personal preference. Some people find that it speeds their workflow, whereas other people prefer to set up their pose first and then key the positions when they have them as they like them. In both cases, it is important to make sure you are on the correct frame before you begin keying so that you don't delete any keys unintentionally. The danger of doing this is slightly higher when using auto keying.

One interesting use of Auto Keyframing is to turn it on and move an object in real time while playing the animation in the 3D viewport. By doing this, you can record the movements of an object as you make them in real time.

Walk and Run Cycles

Walking and running are two of the most basic actions for most characters. Because these movements are by nature repetitive, you want to create each action so it can be easily repeated. In this section, you'll set up simple bipedal walk and run cycles for your character.

Setting Up a Basic Walk Cycle

With actions that are designed to repeat cyclically, it is necessary to consider the best pose to use as start and end points. In the previous example, each jump was entirely self-contained, beginning and ending with the rest pose. In the case of walking, however, the action is cyclical and does not break and return to the rest pose at any point. A good place to start in such cases is at an *extreme* pose. The term sounds a bit more exciting than it actually is. An extreme pose simply means the point at which the action has hit its limit in some respect. The rest of the motion typically consists of moving from one extreme pose to another.

In the case of walking, the extreme poses are the ones in which each foot is extended the farthest, one with the right foot forward and the left foot back, and the other with the feet reversed. You'll start with the left foot's forward extreme. The foot movements and the up and down movement of the hips are the most basic parts of a walk cycle. You'll start with the bones relevant to these movements—namely, the foot.ik.L/R bones, the foot.roll.L/R bones, and the hips bone. Pose the left leg forward, the right leg back, and the hips bone lowered slightly so that the feet maintain contact with the ground. Key the four of them in frame 1, as shown in Figure 7.22.

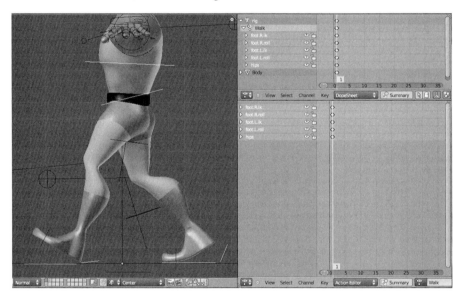

A single step in a leisurely walk can be expected to take about a second, so you will put the right foot forward extreme 25 frames later, at frame 26. To place this second extreme keyframe, follow these steps:

1. With the current frame at 1, select these five keyed bones: foot.ik.L, foot.ik.R, foot. roll.L, foot.roll.R, and hips. Make sure that these bones have had their positions correctly keyed as described previously.

2. Copy the pose of the bones to the Clipboard using the [icon] button in the 3D viewport header.

3. Go to frame 26, either by moving the green frame marker line with the arrow keys or by typing **26** into the current frame field on the Timeline.

4. Paste the mirror image of the copied pose in reverse using the 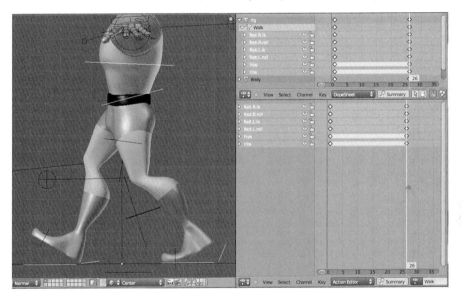 button. This function requires that the bones all be named correctly, with matching bones on the left and right having the same base name followed by .R and .L. If you have problems with this working, go back and double-check that your bones are properly named.

5. In this case, the four bones you're concerned with should already be selected. However, in cases in which the mirrored pose uses different bones than the original pose, the relevant bones are *not* automatically selected. The original bone selection remains unchanged. So before keying the new pose, be sure that all the bones you want to key are selected. Then key the pose as shown in Figure 7.23.

To complete the walk cycle, in the Action Editor window, select the four keys in frame 1. Make sure that only these keys are selected. Press Shift+D to duplicate the keys and move them to frame 51, as shown in Figure 7.24. Set the end frame in the Timeline to 50. Preview the animation. You should have a smooth (albeit very slidey) start to a walk cycle.

Figure 7.23

Keying the mirrored extreme pose

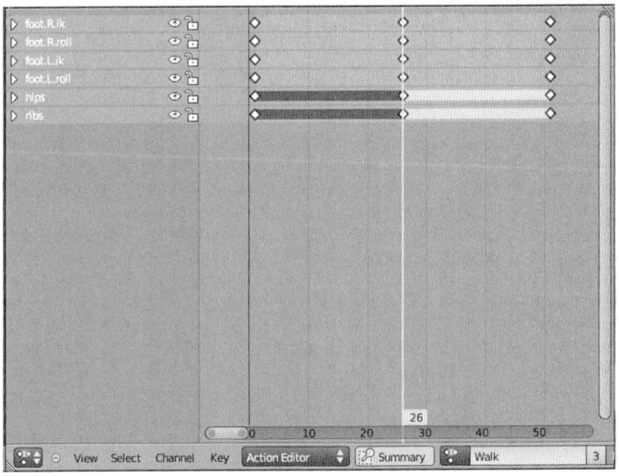

Figure 7.24

Duplicating the pose from frame 1

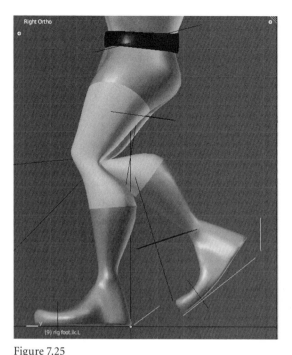

Figure 7.25
Keying the first in-between pose for the feet

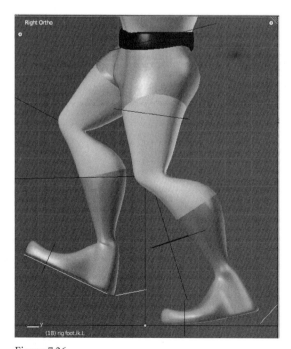

Figure 7.26
Keying the second in-between pose

When people walk, their feet come off the ground during the forward motion, and you need to animate that. Following the same steps as the extreme poses, key the foot positions for the pose in Figure 7.25 at frame 9, and key its mirror image (using Copy and Paste Mirrored) at frame 34. Then key the pose shown in Figure 7.26 at frame 18, and key its mirror image at frame 42. Don't key the hips this time. Again, preview the animation. It should look more like an actual walk.

The last thing you need to do with the lower body is key the vertical motion of the hips bone. You've already keyed the hips bone to be lower at the extremes. At frames 14 and 38, where the height of the walk hits its apex, key the torso at its rest position (select the bone and hit Alt+G to make sure it is in its rest position). Preview the animation again to make sure it looks natural.

Why Start with the Extremes?

Traditionally, you create the extreme poses first because they hold most of the interesting information about the form and mood of the movement. The in-between poses, although very important, can be thought of as functioning largely to fill in the space between extreme poses.

In CG, you want to think about how you place extremes, particularly if you want to create a cycling action. In this case, the curves leading out of the action must match up seamlessly with the curves leading into the action, both in value and in angle; otherwise, the repetition will be jumpy. The easiest place to make curves match is at the point where they are both at zero angles. The apex of a curve whose value is reversing is a very good spot for this. As mentioned earlier, the pose extremes tend to be the places where values are reversing, which make them good candidates for cycle points.

Upper Body Movement in the Walk Cycle

You now have the lower body moving the way you want it. But the human walk involves more than just the legs and feet. The whole body is involved in walking, and this section looks at the movements of the head, shoulders, and arms.

A basic principle of character animation is that the character's movements say as much or more about the character as the visual aspects of the character. Most animators practice their skills on extremely simple models to focus their energies on expressing emotion through motion. At all points of creating actions, you should be considering what the pose says about the character's mood and personality.

Captain Blender's walk is a confident, deliberate walk that befits a superhero of his stature. You'll give him a pronounced swing to the shoulders to emphasize this. This is a simple, smooth motion that needs to be keyed only on the extremes. The upper body moves in opposition to the legs in a normal walk, so in frame 1, rotate the ribs bone around the z-axis to bring the right shoulder forward, as shown in Figure 7.27. Use the Clipboard copy pose mirroring to put the reverse pose at frame 26, as shown in Figure 7.28. Of course, the key from frame 1 should also be copied to frame 51.

Figure 7.27
Keying the mirrored shoulder position

Figure 7.28
Reversing the pose

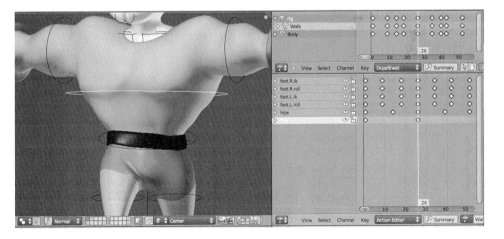

He is now swiveling a lot, but this is not quite enough to give you the confident, determined aspect you're looking for because his head is moving back and forth as well. To fix this problem, you should key the head to be in a forward position at frame 1 and frame 26, as shown in Figure 7.29. I recommend doing the poses for both frames by hand, without

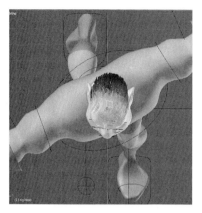

using the copy function or being overly precise, to enable a slight amount of variation into the movement. So far, you've been using a lot of copying and mirroring tools, which can lead to robotic movements. Of course, frame 51 needs to be identical to frame 1 to keep the cycle smooth, so it needs to be copied directly.

Arms and Hands

The arms are currently set to use FK posing, so you can pose the bicep, forearm, and hand to swing naturally along with the walk. It is enough to pose the arms to coincide with the extreme frames.

First, pose the left arm for frames 1 and 26, as shown in Figure 7.30, and then use the Clipboard and pose mirroring to duplicate the motion on the right side, as in Figure 7.31. Making some very slight modifications in the right- and left-side arm and hand movements can help loosen things up, but do not make them too uneven, or else the walk will look strange.

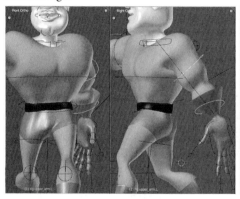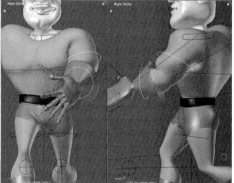

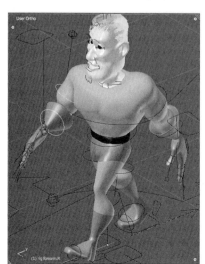

Figure 7.32 gives a complete overview of keys and poses for the walk cycle. You can find the video file, which is called `walk.avi`, among the downloadable files for this book.

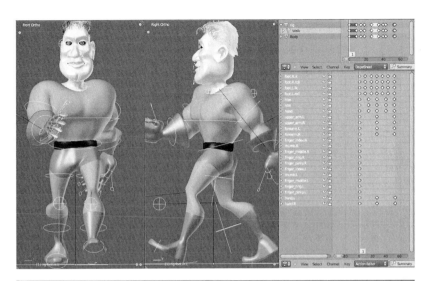

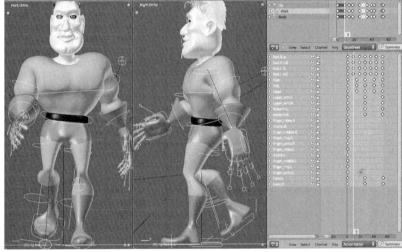

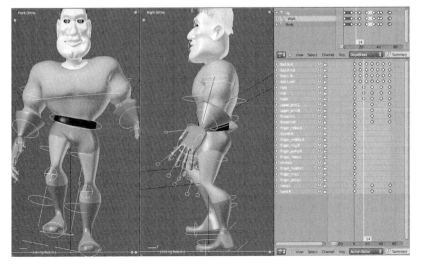

Figure 7.32

**Walk cycle keys
and poses**

Figure 7.32

(continued)

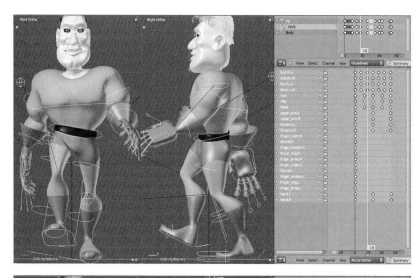

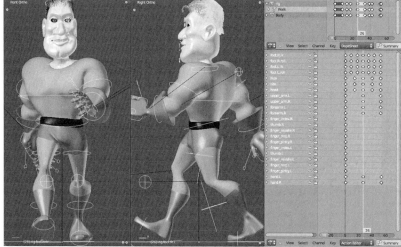

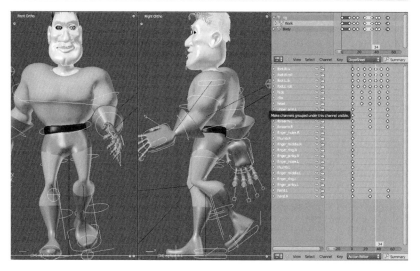

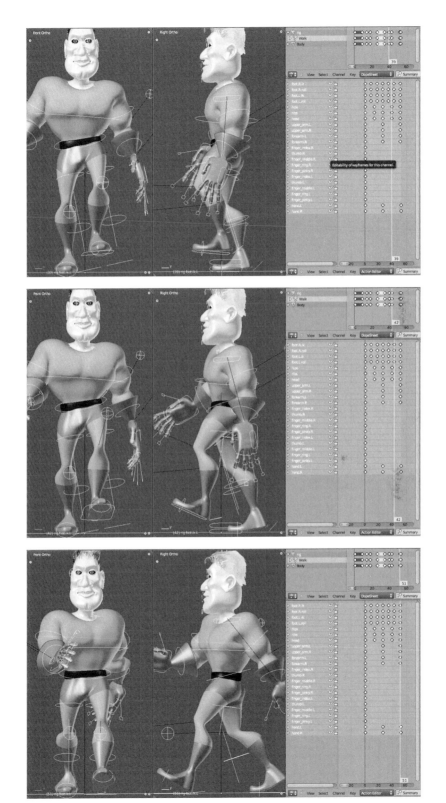

Figure 7.32
(continued)

IK vs. FK Posing

You now have used both IK posing and FK posing, and you understand the difference. But it's worth giving some thought to when exactly you should use each kind of posing. You know why you used IK posing for the feet: IK posing for the feet during a walk or jump cycle enables you to simulate the way real feet are fixed on the ground during these cycles. But why FK posing for the arms?

You can see the answer to this by comparing Figure 7.33 to Figure 7.34. Both figures use two keys with identical start and end poses. However, Figure 7.33 uses IK posing, whereas Figure 7.34 uses FK posing. The pose for Figure 7.33 is created by moving the hand.ik bone, and the pose for Figure 7.34 is created by rotating the upper arm bone. In Figure 7.33, the movement of the hand.ik bone is interpolated, resulting in the hand traveling from one pose to the next in a straight line. In Figure 7.34, the rotation of the upper arm is interpolated, resulting in an arcing motion.

Ordinarily, people's arms swing freely in arcing movements. It is very unnatural for a person's hand to move in a perfectly straight line through space unless it is in some way physically restrained. This is the key to deciding when to use IK or FK posing. When the end of a limb is held by something or constrained to move with some other object, IK posing is a good option. When a limb, be it arm, leg, head, or tail, is swinging freely, you will get the best results with FK posing.

Figure 7.33

IK posing (IK influence set to 1)

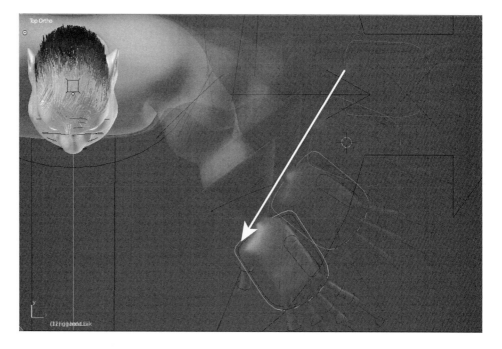

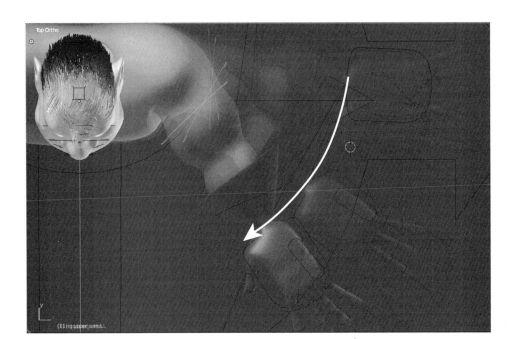

Figure 7.34

FK posing (IK influence set to 0)

A Run Cycle

This book doesn't walk you through the run cycle because the process of creating the run cycle is more or less identical to the walk cycle. The main difference between running and walking is that in a walk, at least one foot is always in contact with the ground, whereas in a run, the body spends a fair amount of time completely aloft. The extreme poses, in particular, feature both feet fully off the ground. The other difference, of course, is that running tends to be faster on a strides-per-second basis. Instead of a 50-frame cycle, the present run cycle is 30 frames long.

Figure 7.35 is an overview of the run cycle poses' keyframes. You should be able to figure out the details of their placement yourself. Pay special attention to the posing of the upper body; notice that the figure strains forward on the extremes. Also, because there is a considerable amount of up and down movement, make sure you key the head to point approximately in the same direction throughout the action. Use the gaze bone's position to gauge this as you pose the head bone. Do this by hand, and not too precisely, because it will not be realistic if the head's direction is robotically fixed while the character is running at full speed.

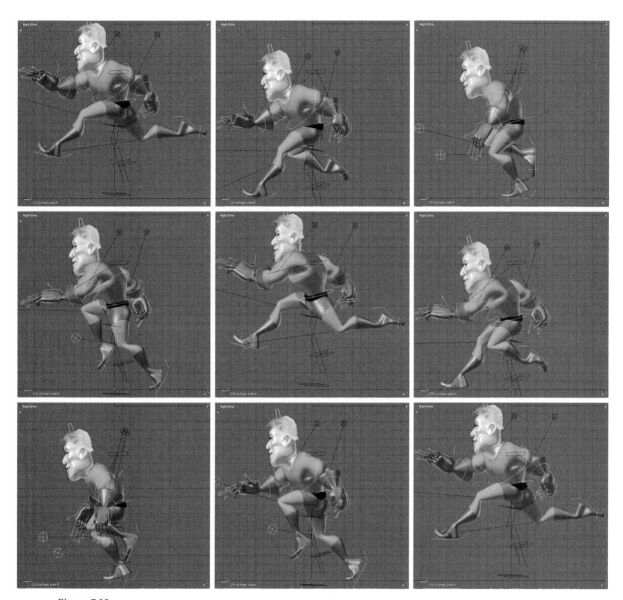

Figure 7.35

**Keyed poses for a
run cycle**

You can see the animated run cycle in the file run.avi on the DVD.

To speed up or slow down the cycle, you can select all the keys and scale them by pressing the S key. This process scales them toward or away from the vertical green line, so it's a good idea to put this at frame 1 to keep all the values positive. Also be sure to adjust your animation's end frame accordingly. If you choose to scale your action to adjust the timing, you can, after you're done, snap the keys onto whole-numbered frames by pressing Shift+S and replying OK to the prompt.

Expressing Weight

Certain points in a run cycle can exhibit evidence of mass that is not visible at the slower speeds of the walk cycle. Specifically, with a fairly massive character such as Captain Blender, you should emphasize the force of his impact. You can see this illustrated in Figure 7.36, in which the head and rib bones are keyed just before the impact frame and keyed in a more crunched position just after the impact. This pose relaxes again over the course of the next several frames.

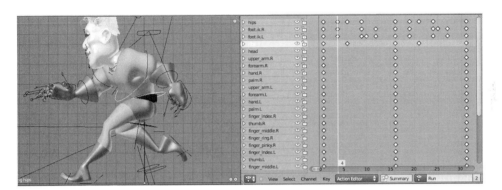

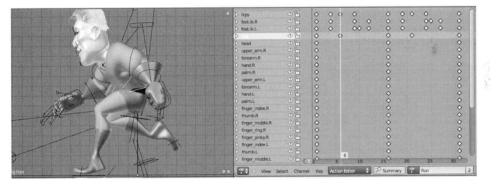

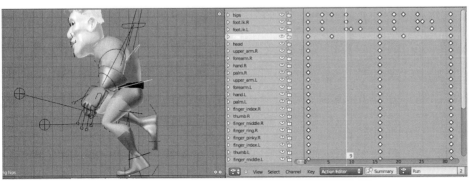

Figure 7.36

The ribs and head crunch slightly just after impact.

Remember that with character animation, perfect stillness is the kiss of death. Living things are never perfectly still. A single perfectly motionless limb on a character can be enough to remind viewers that they are not truly seeing a living being and jerk them out of the animation experience. The key is to combine a variety of smooth movements with complementary directions and timing to create an overall feeling of movement that is irregular but not choppy or inconsistent. Whenever you work with armatures, keep all these things in mind so that you can work toward convincing, natural-looking movement for your characters.

Pose-to-Pose Animation

In traditional animation, two methods of animation are often distinguished: *straight-ahead* animation and *pose-to-pose* animation. Straight-ahead animation, in its purest sense, consists of starting at the beginning of an animation and progressing forward, creating each new frame as the motion unfolds. Pose-to-pose animation, on the other hand, consists of placing specific desired poses at carefully considered places along the Timeline and then filling in the spaces between with intermediate poses.

The straight-ahead approach is typically thought of as being freer and potentially yielding more flowing and spontaneous animation. Pose-to-pose animation, on the other hand, enables much more control over precise timing and positioning. In fact, even in traditional animation, it is generally recognized that the best way to work is with some combination of the two of these approaches. This hybrid approach blocks out complex motion with the pose-to-pose approach, but it fills the intermediary positions with the straight-ahead method.

In CG, the medium is much more forgiving than traditional animation, so the distinction is blurred even more. It is perfectly possible to key certain body parts, for example, in a pose-to-pose manner, whereas you can pose other body parts completely straight ahead in the same animation, allowing for the best of both worlds. Furthermore, with the amount of control over key positions and F-Curves that CG allows, you can finesse the timing of straight-ahead animation and loosen up the feel of pose-to-pose animation, making the distinction more a matter of how the animator chooses to think about a task than an actual practical choice. Nevertheless, it can be helpful to bear the difference in mind and to think in terms of taking advantage of both straight-ahead and pose-to-pose approaches.

Changing Location

Walk and run cycles are good for practice and demonstration purposes, but the real reason why characters walk and run is to get someplace. Past versions of Blender had several methods for making characters follow paths while repeating a walk cycle. These methods were more complex than simply making an object follow a path (as you might do in the case of a bird flight) because of the need for calculations to enable the feet to stay fixed to the ground. However, these tools have been (at least temporarily) abandoned because of lack of demand. Automatic path-following approaches can be useful if you need to make a character walk a long distance in a single shot with very little variation in movement, but this situation doesn't arise often.

In general, the control you give up using automatic cycling approaches is not worth the benefits. The best way to animate a character walking forward is to position the feet manually. The approach I take here is an example of the hybrid pose-to-pose/straight-ahead method. The basic walk cycle is the same pose-to-pose walk cycle you looked at earlier, whereas the forward movement is accomplished in a straight-ahead way.

To change the in-place walk cycle to a forward walk, make sure the right and left feet stay in place when they should stay in place (when the rest of the body is moving

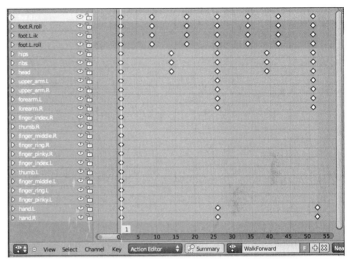

Figure 7.37

The WalkForward action to begin with

forward) and that the feet and hips move forward appropriately the correct distances. In other words, you need to replace the backward foot motion of the in-place case with forward motion of the other foot and hips bone (the hips bone will carry the rest of the body forward).

Figure 7.38

Selecting the foot.ik.L bone

1. First, create a new action by duplicating the Walk action. In Pose mode, select the Walk action from the drop-down menu in the Action Editor header. Click the button labeled with the number 2 (this may show a different number if you have used the Walk action in any other ways than described so far in this book). When you have clicked this button, a new single-user copy of the action will be created, automatically named Walk.001. Change the name to **WalkForward** to create the action shown in Figure 7.37.

2. Select the foot.ik.L bone as shown in Figure 7.38. This foot is extended forward and should not move until it is time for it to move forward again on the next stride. In the Action Editor, delete all of the keys for this foot right of the first key, as shown in Figure 7.39.

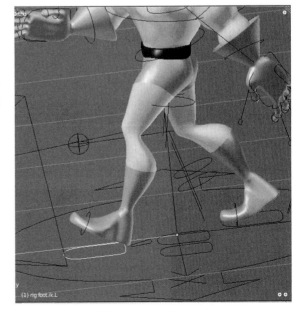

Figure 7.39

Deleting the keys

3. Advance to frame 26, the other extreme. Captain Blender will assume an awkward position like the one shown in Figure 7.40. To fix this, select both the hips bone and the foot.ik.R bone simultaneously and move them forward by pressing the G key followed by the Y key. Move them forward until they look right, as shown in Figure 7.41. Don't worry about being precise. Slight variations in stride length add to naturalness.

Figure 7.40

Advancing to frame 26

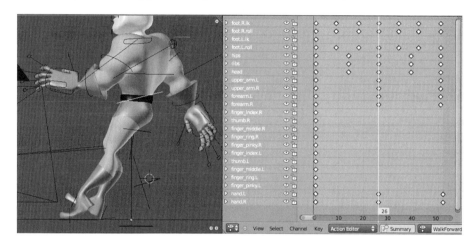

Figure 7.41

Bringing the right foot and the hips forward

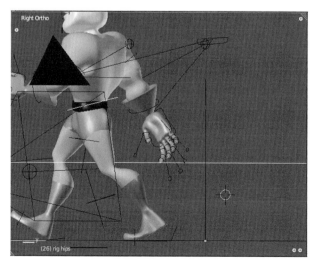

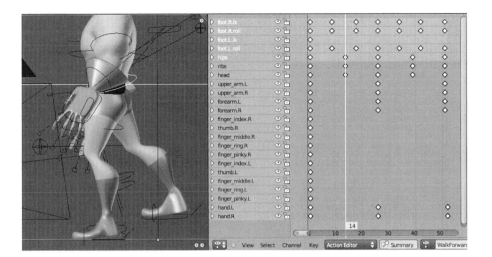

Figure 7.42

Bringing the hips forward in mid-stride

4. Move back to frame 14, where the hips are keyed. The hips need to be brought forward as shown in Figure 7.42.

5. Frames 9 and 18 are where you key the in-between poses for the right foot. In each of these frames, you simply need to bring the foot.ik.R bone forward along the y-axis. Figure 7.43 shows the pose for frame 9. Do the same thing for frame 18.

6. From frame 26 on, the right foot should stay planted on the ground. Select the keyframes for this bone subsequent to frame 26, as shown in Figure 7.44, and delete them.

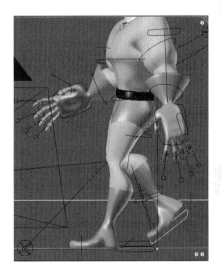

Figure 7.43

The first in-between pose for the right foot

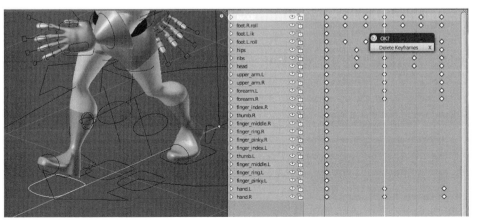

Figure 7.44

Deleting keyframes for the right foot

7. Advance to frame 51. You'll need to bring the hips bone and the left foot all the way forward from their original frame 1 positions, as shown in Figure 7.45. Key these bones in the new positions.

Figure 7.45

Bringing the hips and left foot forward from the first frame position to the 51st frame position

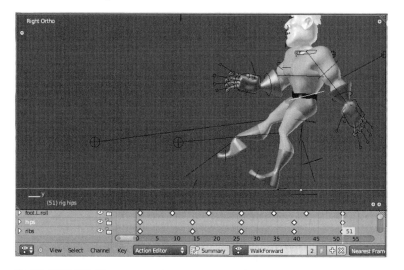

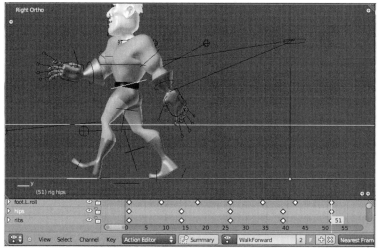

8. Bring the hips forward for frame 38 and key their position. For frames 34 and 38, you will use the pose clipboard copy and mirrored paste to reverse the opposite foot's poses from frames 8 and 18, respectively. Paste these poses in reverse onto the left foot, and then move the foot forward appropriately before keying the new position. Figure 7.46 shows the resulting poses.

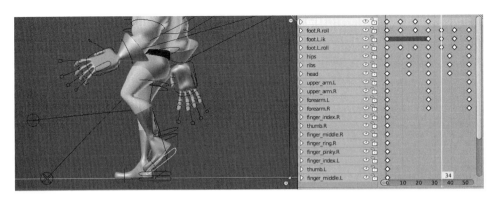

Figure 7.46

**Moving both Torso
and FootRoot.L**

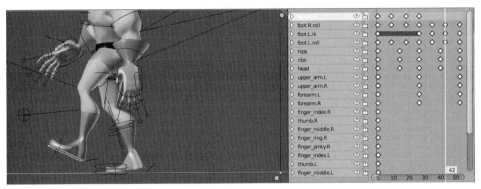

9. Create further strides by first pasting the extreme pose and then moving the hips and noncontact foot forward and keying the noncontact foot and hips. In-between poses should also be created in the same manner, by pasting the pose and then moving the necessary bones forward. Of course, if you continue this walk beyond 51 frames, you will also need to copy the poses of the other bones. You will only ever need to adjust the locations of the hips and the two foot IK bones.

Weighty Words from Captain Blender

Timing movements to coincide with sounds is a good example of a situation that might call for a more pose-to-pose–oriented approach. In this example, you will look at animating Captain Blender's basic movements while uttering a very simple pronouncement. In the next chapter, you'll combine these movements with lip sync and facial movements; in Chapter 9, you'll look at combining the action you have created with the walk cycle by using the Non-Linear Animation Editor.

To get started, you must first load and position the sound file you'll be using for syncing. Find the sound file among this book's accompanying downloadable files; it is called `every-era-has-its.wav`. Place this file in a convenient location on your hard drive. You can listen to the `.wav` file in the sound editor of your choice. Audacity is an excellent open source option. The sentence is "It has been said that every era has its visionary."

Sound and the Sequence Editor

Blender handles sound through the built-in Video Sequence Editor (VSE). The VSE is actually a full-fledged nonlinear video and audio editor, and in Chapter 11 you will learn more about these aspects of its functionality. In this chapter, you will be using it only to load and position the sound file to sync with your animation.

Figure 7.47

Opening a Video Sequence Editor window

Open a Video Sequence Editor window by choosing the icon shown in Figure 7.47 from the Window Type drop-down menu.

Importing files into the Video Sequence Editor is simple. Simply press Shift+A in the window to add a sequence strip. Choose Sound from the menu that opens. In the File Browser, find the every-era-has-its.wav file. You should see a strip appear in the main Video Sequence Editor area. Place this strip so that it starts at frame 1. Open the Properties Shelf of the Video Sequence Editor by pressing the N key. Select the Caching box, as shown in Figure 7.48.

Figure 7.48

The sound file imported into the Video Sequence Editor

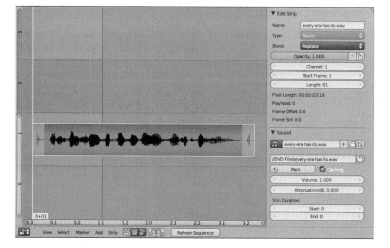

Posing with Speech

Figure 7.49

Enabling Audio Scrubbing

To enable audio playback when you manually change frames, you must enable Audio Scrubbing in the Playback menu of the Timeline, as shown in Figure 7.49.

Now, when you move from one frame to another, you hear the snippet of sound that corresponds to the .wav file at that specific frame. Likewise, dragging the frame indicator within the Video Sequence Editor plays the audio as the indicator passes over it. This technique is called *scrubbing*.

For Captain Blender's gesticulations, you can do a very simple pose-to-pose animation. As he utters "It has been said that every era has its visionary," you have him raise
one hand grandly to coincide with "said" and then gesture widely with both hands as he
says "every era." And then, as he says "visionary," you have him bring his hands inward in
a slight clutching motion while lifting his head hopefully.

The start frame is 1, and the end frame you use is 85. You should determine the placement of the poses based upon listening to the sounds at each frame. You can key the three
poses described and also a more naturalistic "rest" pose than the actual rest pose (which,
of course, has the character's arms out at a strange and not very restful angle).

You can see the poses and their associated keys in Figure 7.50.

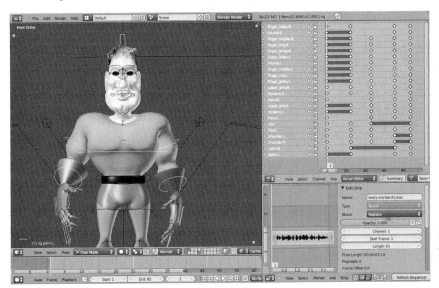

Figure 7.50

**Poses to accompany
the phrase "It has
been said that every
era has its visionary"**

Figure 7.50

(continued)

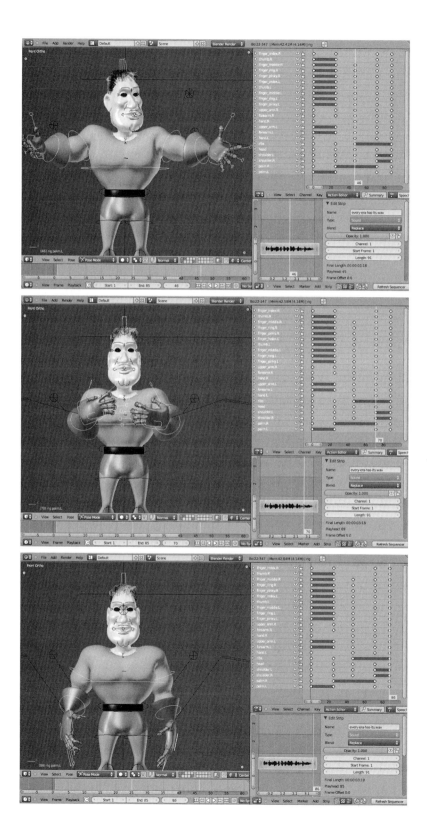

This is all you need for the time being. Name the action **speech**. You can see a rendered still from the action in Figure 7.51. You can now move on to adding facial animation to sync up with the sound. In the next chapter, you will use the facial rig you created in Chapter 5 to add lip sync and expressions to go with the movement you have created here.

Figure 7.51

A rendered still from the animation

CHAPTER 8

Facial Animation and Lip Sync

This chapter builds on the pose-to-pose example from the previous chapter, adding facial movements and lip sync to go with the gesticulations you have already put into place.

Lip syncing and facial animation are sophisticated arts that can take years to become proficient in. The goal here is just to get you started with this kind of work in Blender, so be prepared to spend time practicing before your results are exactly how you want them. Furthermore, as with almost everything in Blender, there are a variety of ways to go about doing lip sync and facial animation. As I mentioned in Chapter 5, I have chosen to use shape keys driven by bones. I find this to be an easy way to work, and it is a good fit with nonlinear animation, as you will see in more detail in the next chapter.

In Chapter 18, I suggest several tutorials to look at for different approaches, including one approach based entirely on shape keys, without bone drivers, and another approach based almost entirely on using a sophisticated facial armature to do mesh deformations. Your own work will certainly benefit from trying a variety of approaches to see which suits your personal animation style best.

- **Facial Posing**

- **Lip Sync**

- **Playback**

Facial Posing

The approach I'm taking to facial posing will use the controller bones to pose the face. Aside from the tongue, none of the deformations is directly due to bone influence; the bones all act as drivers for shape keys. This driver setup enables you to treat facial posing as if it were armature posing (more or less the same as the armature posing you did in Chapter 7). The bones are keyed in the same way they were keyed previously, and you have to keep many of the same issues with the F-Curves and key placement in mind to avoid facial movements becoming robotic.

One difference is that you won't be using much mirroring here. For one thing, it's not necessary. Unlike something like a walk cycle, facial posing doesn't involve a lot of repetitive movements that need to be nearly identical on right and left. In fact, even in cases in which you have fairly symmetrical facial expressions, such as a smile, your facial posing will benefit from some asymmetry. Whereas asymmetry in a walk can wind up looking like a limp, properly used asymmetry in facial animation creates more convincingly human expressions.

The trick in facial animation is to understand the way shapes combine to form expressions. In Figure 8.1, you see several full facial expressions for Captain Blender. Compare these expressions with the sequence of face shapes described in Chapter 5. A few fairly simple shapes can yield a broad palette of emotional expression when combined properly. In the figure, you can see how the bones controllers are positioned to yield each facial expression. Note that the gaze bone is not shown, and other armature bone positions other than the shape drivers (for example, the head bone) are not shown.

The first expression (a) is a happy, optimistic expression, featuring a slight (and slightly asymmetrical) curl of the nose to emphasize the smile. The smile itself is not simply the smile shape, either, but also involves widening the lips and lowering the jaw slightly. The eyes are slightly squinted, and the eyebrows are raised; in particular, the left outer brow is raised.

The second expression (b) is a fearful expression. The mouth gets its shape from a combination of rounding and frown to bring the edges down slightly. The brows are knit and raised in the middle.

The third expression (c) shows nervous anticipation. The brows are raised very slightly. The mouth is closed, with the bottom lip curled in and one edge of the mouth raised in a hesitant half-smile.

The fourth expression (d) is an angry, menacing expression. The eyebrows are down with the outer portion slightly raised, angling them downward even more sharply. The mouth is closed with a hint of frown, and the lips are pursed inward slightly. The nose is crinkled asymmetrically. Perhaps the most important thing to note about this expression is the angle of the head. Head, neck, and even shoulder positioning is easy to overlook, but they are a crucial aspect of facial posing.

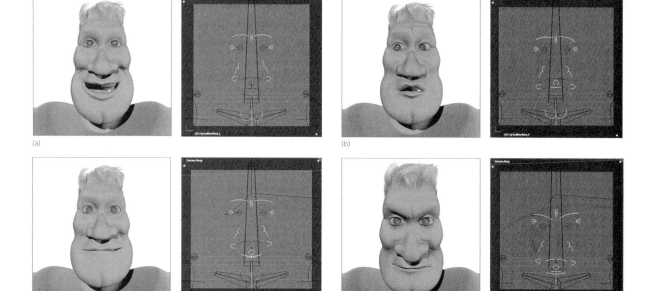

Figure 8.1

Facial expressions composed of multiple shapes

To get started posing the face, go into the Action Editor as you did previously to pose the body. Select all face bones in the rest position, and key their location and rotation in frame 1 with the I key in the 3D viewport, as you did with other bones. Once keyed, channels will be created for the bones in the Action Editor, as shown in Figure 8.2.

Figure 8.2

Keying face bone rest positions

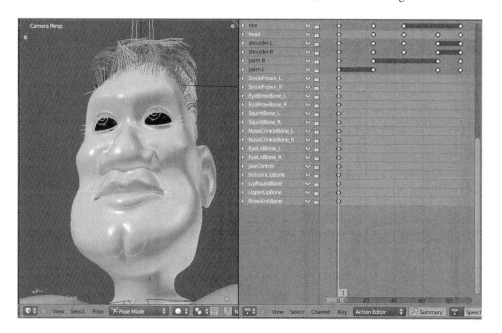

Pose-to-Pose vs. Straight-Ahead Revisited

Facial animation presents a special case where you must choose between a pose-to-pose approach and a straight-ahead approach, introduced in Chapter 7. The importance of timing might suggest that a pose-to-pose approach would be appropriate, but flow is equally important. Simply moving from one face shape to another does not yield convincing facial animations. Another challenge here is that the timing is particularly demanding in the case of lip sync. If timing is slightly off, it can be quite noticeable; getting the timing precisely right the first time is difficult without seeing a real-time playback of the animation.

When you don't have to worry about lip sync, facial posing for expressiveness is much less demanding. You can do something like the pose-to-pose animation you did at the end of the previous chapter for that here. You don't touch the mouth or the lower face right now; simply pose the eyes in a way that makes sense with the utterance. You can always go back and adjust it if there are problems with the timing or the interaction with the lip sync.

To time your animation to a specific sound file, you need to load the sound file and position it where you want it on the Timeline. For this, you'll use the file `every-era-has-its`.`wav`, which you can find in the downloadable files that accompany this book.

To place the sample where you want it on the Timeline, you will need to use Blender's Sequence Editor. Open up a Sequence Editor window now. In the Sequence Editor, press Shift+A to load media, and select Sound from the available options. Find the sound file on your hard drive, and select it. The file now appears as a block in the Video Sequence Editor. Place this block so that it is flush against the first frame in the sequence display.

Look now at the Properties Shelf to the right of the sequence display in the Video Sequence Editor. If you can't see it, press the N key to toggle its visibility. The sound file you loaded in the Sequence Editor is listed as a sound datablock. Select Caching under the Sound properties, as shown in Figure 8.3. Finally, select Audio Scrubbing in the Playback menu in the Timeline, just as you did in Chapter 7 to ensure that the audio plays back in time with the animation when you scrub forward and backward manually along the Timeline.

In Figure 8.4, you can see a selection of the main key points in the animation. Note the frame number parentheses at the bottom of each screenshot. The first frame is the rest position. Frame 25 occurs just before the end of "It has been said," which marks the beginning of the pronouncement. The expression is dispassionate here. In frames 46 and 70, while the main portion of the utterance is being spoken, the character emotes more strongly. The last two screenshots show the expression going back to approximately the rest pose. Note that you will not be making this action cyclic, so there is no need for it to end as it began. It is no problem that Captain Blender's brows remain slightly knitted.

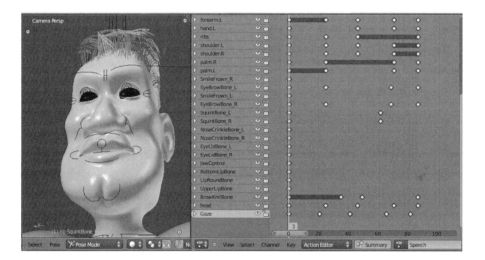

Figure 8.3

The sound file as it appears in the Video Sequence Editor

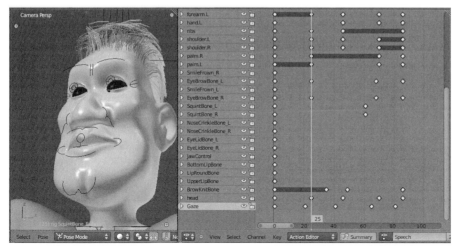

Figure 8.4

Animating the expressions of the eyes

Figure 8.4

(continued)

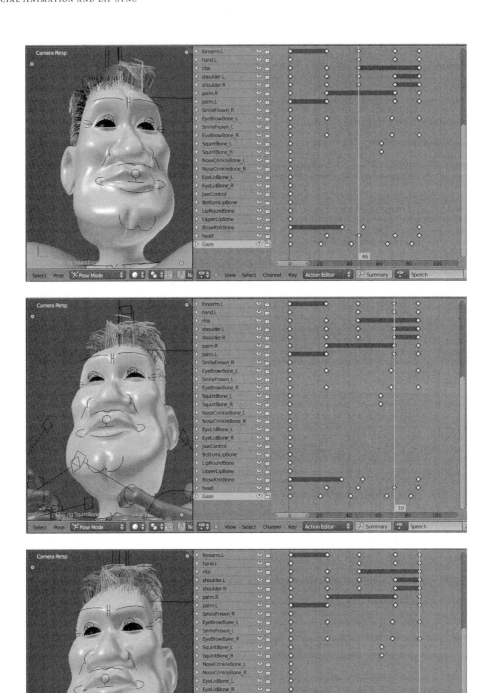

The second-to-last screenshot catches the character in mid-blink. Be sure not to forget to make your characters blink. People ordinarily blink more than once every 10 seconds or so, and it will become noticeable if your character does not blink occasionally. A total of six frames—three frames to shut and three frames to open—is a good length for a blink. If you can place a blink for dramatic effect, it is a bonus, but you should have blinks in any case. It makes for a nice realistic effect to have a character blink when changing the direction of its gaze, but do not do this all the time.

One hard-and-fast rule about the placement of blinks, which holds for any film medium, is that shots should not be cut on blinks. No shot should begin or end with the character's eyes closed, no matter how briefly. For this reason, don't place blinks too close to the beginning or the end of an animation because it could restrict your options for editing the shot later.

I mentioned the importance of not having facial movements coincide too much with one another. As you can see by looking at the keys in Figure 8.5, even in this simple series of movements around the eyes, I tried to mix things up. The eyebrows do not move in sync with the squint movements, and the knitting of the brow is also not in sync with either of them. The head movement and the gaze bone movement are also keyed slightly out of sync, with the gaze bone slightly ahead of the head movements. Several movements beginning and ending in an overlapping manner help conceal the essentially linear nature of shape keys.

Figure 8.5

Key placement for head and face movements

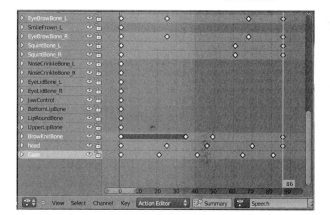

Lip Sync

My approach to lip syncing is really neither pose-to-pose nor straight ahead, although it probably has more in common with straight ahead. I go from one segment of speech to another, and in each local segment I key in a straight-ahead fashion while scrubbing through the sound frame by frame. It might seem painstaking, but there is really no easy way to do lip syncing, and this is really not too bad. I do a rough run-through first and then modify the placement of my keys and controllers based upon how things look. It's better to do a rough run-through of the whole animation, or at least a reasonably long chunk of it, because real-time playback requires a few steps and isn't something you want to be doing every time you key a frame.

The best way to get a sense of lip syncing using shapes and drivers is to do it, and the best reference for what kind of mouth pose is best suited to a specific sound is your own face. Have a mirror on hand while you do lip syncing, and check it as you go.

Figure 8.6 shows the poses and keys for several frames throughout the utterance. Jaw movement is, unsurprisingly, important. The movement of the jaw makes a difference to the roundness of the mouth, which enables you to express the difference between sounds such as "ee," located high in the mouth and spoken with a wide mouth, and "ah," located lower in the mouth and spoken with a less-wide mouth.

The first four images cover the portion of the utterance "It has been." The focus here is simply on the shape of the open mouth until you hit the "b," which requires a closed, slightly pursed mouth that will open in a rapid burst, after which the jaw remains high and the lips round slightly.

Figure 8.6

Animating the first part of the utterance "It has been said that every era has its visionary."

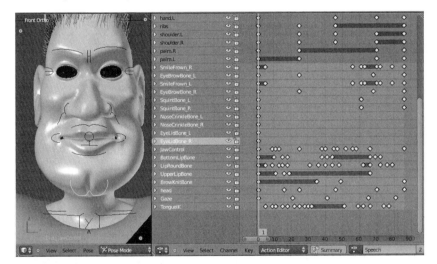

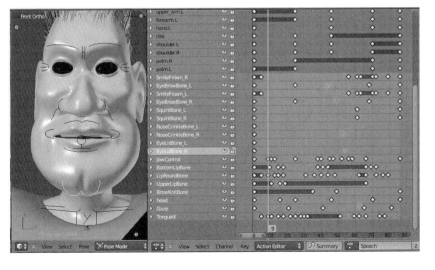

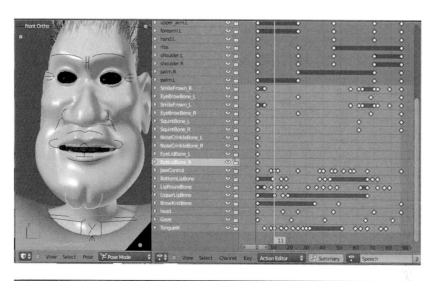

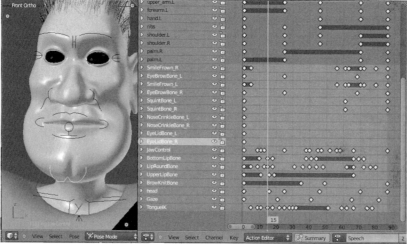

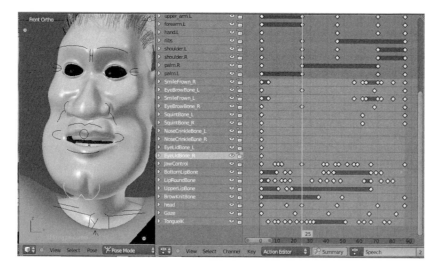

Figure 8.6
(continued)

In the previous image, the portion of the utterance in frame 25 between the words "said that" seemed to call for some tongue movement. Not all sounds that use the tongue necessarily demand that the tongue be animated. If you can't see it, don't animate it. But between the "d" and the "th," it seemed conspicuous when I omitted tongue movement on my first pass through this animation.

In Figure 8.7, the focus is on "visionary." The frames shown represent every other frame for the lip sync of that word. The "v" is created by putting the lips together, mainly by raising the jaw and rolling the lower lip in by raising its control bone. This shape releases and moves into a widening of the mouth as the LipRound bone is lowered. The jaw remains fairly high. The rest of the movements are fairly subtle. The "zh" sound in "visionary" is enunciated entirely within the mouth, out of view, so you don't deal with this. Also, although "visionary" ends with an "ee" sound, the actual pronunciation in the recording is sufficiently deemphasized that an exaggeratedly wide "ee" position would not fit the sound well.

Another approach that works more quickly is to create shapes for each of the phoneme sets mentioned in Chapter 5. Instead of manipulating a number of individual controls to form the long "e" sound, you simply activate the single "e" shape controller. Depending on what system you choose to use, you can make anywhere from 10 different shapes that will pretty much cover all human speech, down to just a few. Of course, the fewer shapes you create and use, the less convincing your lip sync will be.

Figure 8.7

A closer look at "visionary"

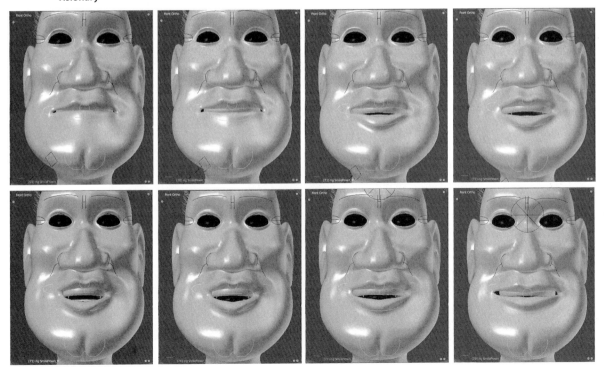

The advantage of creating shapes is that you can name each shape by its associated sound (for example, "ee"), making it easy to identify the proper controller and set keys while scrubbing through the audio. You can combine and refine this quicker approach by using the individual controllers mentioned previously, really tweaking the facial shapes as each case demands. If you don't need camera close-up hero animation, a shortcut like this can save a lot of time. Obviously, the level of detail and nuance you need in your shape set also depends a lot on the degree of realism you're going for in your animation.

Keying Shapes Directly

You can also use the DopeSheet to key shape values directly by using its shape sliders in the Shape Key Editor. You enter Shape Key Editor mode using the same drop-down menu you used to enter the Action Editor. Figure 8.8 shows a simple example of this. When a mesh is selected in Object mode, the channels displayed in the Shape Key Editor correspond to available shape keys.

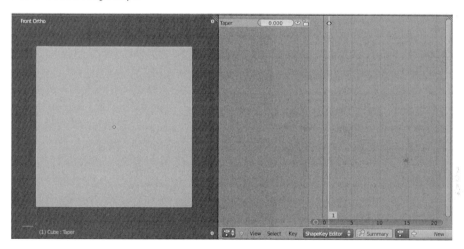

Figure 8.8

A shape key keyed directly in the Action Editor

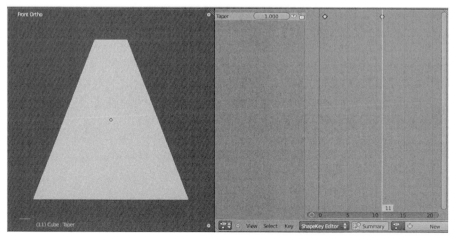

In this simple example, there is a single shape key, Taper, defined for the cube, with no drivers associated with it. The single channel in the Shape Key Editor corresponds to this shape. To the right of the channels is an area for shape sliders.

New keyframes can be placed by clicking the slider. If you click the slider only, a key with the current slider value is created; if you slide the slider, a key with the new value is created, as in the lower image. This keying is automatic and does not require the I key.

Direct keying of shape sliders becomes more complicated (and less advisable) when the shapes are also driven by bones. The key points from the drivers themselves are displayed as keys in the Action Editor, as you can see in Figure 8.9, which shows the Shape Key Editor display of the shapes you have been working with in this chapter (note that the mesh, not the armature, is selected). This way of displaying keys might be slightly confusing, but it can be useful if you want to see the exact value of any given shape key at any point in the animation. You can edit driven shape keys directly in the Shape Key Editor, but the values will be overridden by keyed driver values, so there's usually not much point doing this.

It is sometimes simpler to work with direct keying. However, with a complex rig that uses multiple shape keys together, an intuitive rig using drivers is the best way to go.

The bone-posing approach is intuitive and direct in terms of working with visual representations of the shapes. Furthermore, posing bones enables you to incorporate facial movements into the same action as other bone movements, as you have done in the example in this chapter.

Figure 8.9

The Action Editor display of driven keys

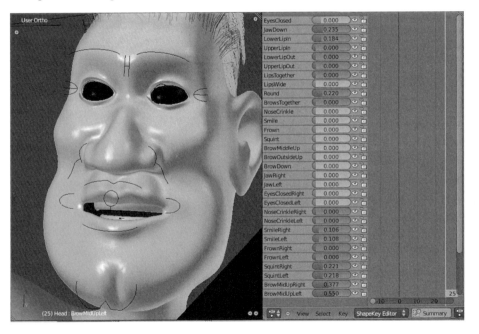

Regardless of how you choose to key your shapes, the task of creating lip-synced animation remains essentially the same. It involves working with a few basic shapes, frequently referencing a mirror, and using a healthy dose of trial and error. To find out how your keys are looking, you need to know how to play back your animation at full speed with your sound synced.

Playback

Depending on your hardware, Blender may well be able to display your animation with sound for an acceptable real-time preview without rendering. Make sure that AV-Sync is enabled in the Audio buttons and that the audio file is positioned properly in the Sequence Editor Timeline. This will keep the video timed with the audio, dropping frames when necessary if Blender cannot draw the video fast enough to keep up with the audio. With this selected, pressing Alt+A in the 3D window plays back your animation with sound.

With slower computers, there may be a considerable delay with this mode of playback. As you saw in Chapter 7, simply playing back the animation in the 3D viewport might not be adequate to get a good idea of the timing. This is doubly true if you are dealing with sound sync. As the need for precision is greater, so is the delay in playback. So, you have to render out a rough of the animation to see it played back at full speed. There's an added complication here, though: Blender's render playback simply plays back rendered animations. There is no facility for it to play back sound simultaneously when dealing directly with rendered images.

To get the sync sound playback you want, you have to turn once again to the Sequence Editor. You also need to look a little bit more closely at what actually happens when you render your animation.

Sequencing Rendered Frames

Chapter 11 deals in considerably more depth with rendering animation, so I will not send much time on this here. If you run into any trouble following the steps here, you might want to skip ahead and read that chapter to get a clearer understanding of what's going on. For now, I will stick to the necessary points and assume that everything is set to defaults. To prepare the render output, read the renders into the Sequence Editor, and view your real-time playback, follow these steps:

1. The frames you output when you render an animation are, by default, stored in the /tmp/ directory. If you render a variety of different animations, their frames will all be stored in the same directory, which can lead to confusion in managing and playing back the files. For this reason, you'll add a subdirectory in which to store this particular animation.

You can edit the new subdirectory in the top field in the Output tab in the Render Buttons area. You can type a name into the field directly, as shown in Figure 8.10. Note that in these fields, Blender considers both a slash and a backslash to indicate a directory. So, the slash at the end of speech has the same meaning as the backslash at the end of renders and means that lipsync is a subdirectory of renders. The double slash at the beginning of the path indicates that the output directory is a subdirectory of the current working directory, that is, the directory that the .blend file is in.

Figure 8.10

Setting the output path for the rendered images

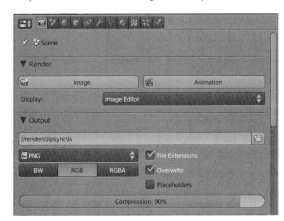

2. Now, when you render, your frames appear, by default, as a collection of numbered PNG files in this directory. Render the contents of the 3D viewport now by clicking the Render button on the header of the 3D viewport while holding down Ctrl. Remember to go into camera view to get the best idea of how your animation is looking. You can zoom the whole 3D view forward and backward for better framing in your 3D viewport by using the + and – keys or by rolling your mouse wheel, if you have one. This does not affect the rendered result, only the way it appears in the viewport.

3. After your animation has fully rendered, open a Sequence Editor window. You actually want two Sequence Editors open, so split this window. In one of the two Sequence Editor windows, select Image Preview by clicking the middle of the three header buttons shown here.

4. In the Sequence View window, you should already see the audio strip that you imported previously. You want to bring in the images now, so press Shift+A to add a sequence strip, and select Images from the available options. In the File Browser, go to the /renders/lipsync/ directory where the frames are. Select the entire contents of this directory with the A key, and click Add Image Strip. You will be returned to the Sequence Editor.

5. You can move Sequence Editor strips around using the G key in much the same way that you move other things in Blender. Place the new strip so that the first frame of the strip is at frame 1.

6. Play back the sequence using Alt+A or by pressing the Play button in the Timeline. This process ensures that the animation is played back in all windows, as shown in Figure 8.11. After maybe one or two slow run-throughs, your animation should play back at full speed with the sound. If the sound is not synced with the video, first try to adjust the relative placement of the audio strip in the Sequence Editor to get the best possible match.

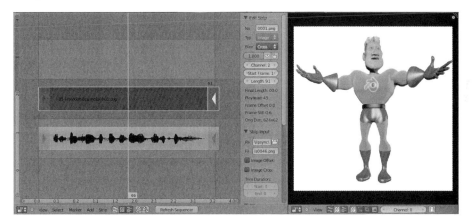

Figure 8.11

Playing back the animation in the Sequence Editor

Take note of the places where the facial and mouth movements are unconvincing or seem out of sync. Then go back to the Action Editor and fix the positions and timing. When you have this working to your satisfaction, it is time to move on to see what else you can do with the actions you've created so far.

In this chapter and in previous chapters, you have worked a fair amount with actions. You have seen how the Action Editor works as a convenient front end for the more complicated and involved F-Curves and how you can create multiple separate actions to serve a number of purposes: to keep movements grouped together in meaningful ways or to put together combinations of movements that can be controlled by simple bone movements in action constraints. But this is not all you can do with actions. The next chapter discusses the Non-Linear Animation (NLA) Editor, and you will see the rest of the story on actions.

CHAPTER 9

Animation for Production

So far, you've learned most of the basics for making your character move and express himself. Producing an animated movie requires that simple elements of animation be combined with each other and integrated into a scene. Furthermore, even a simple animated production can benefit from keeping processes such as modeling and texturing separated from animation and setting up a well-integrated production pipeline.

Blender has a number of tools to enable you to create animation for a production environment. The armature proxy system and the Non-Linear Animation (NLA) Editor are two of the most significant. The armature proxy system enables you to link rigged characters from external files in a nondestructive way so that the model can continue to be updated even while animation is progressing. The NLA Editor provides a layer of abstraction to work with the actions you created in previous chapters so that you can control looping and speed of actions and combine multiple actions.

- ▪ **Working with Proxies**
- ▪ **Using the NLA Editor**
- ▪ **NLA in Action**

Working with Proxies

In a production environment with multiple artists working on different parts of an animated movie at the same time, it's important that as much of the pipeline as possible is modular and nonlinear. Being able to work on different parts of an animation in parallel saves time in general and makes it possible to make corrections or revisions on one part of the project without throwing away work done on another part. Even when little parallel work is being done, as in the case of a single-person production, it's important to be able to go back and make adjustments, for example to a texture or a mesh model, without having to completely redo animation.

In addition, you want to be able to quickly and easily reuse assets in multiple scenes and to automatically apply any updates to the assets in all the places where those assets are used. In a typical short movie, there may easily be dozens of different shots that all use the same character. If you change the texture of a character's jacket when half the scenes have been animated, you want that to be reflected in all the animated scenes automatically.

Linking and Appending

In general, you accomplish this kind of asset reuse in Blender using the linking functionality. You can link an object or other datablock from one .blend file to another by selecting Link from the File menu, as shown in Figure 9.1. When you do this, a file browser window opens, and you can navigate into another .blend file to select the datablock you want to link (Blender's file browser treats other .blend files identically to directories).

Figure 9.1

Linking

When you link a datablock in this way, the instance in the receiving .blend file cannot be edited. You can only edit the object in the original file, which is now referred to as a *library*. When you make changes to the object in the library file, the changes will also be applied to the linked instance. When you link datablocks, the relationship on the disk between the library .blend and the linking .blend file becomes important. If the .blend files are moved with respect to one another or if the library .blend is renamed, then the linking .blend file will be broken.

A useful cousin to linking is appending. Append is also found in the File menu and carried out identically to linking. However, when you append a datablock, the appended datablock is a complete and independent copy. The appended object or datablock is no longer dependent in any way on the original file and may be edited. Changes in the original file will have no effect on objects or datablocks appended from that file.

Linking Rigged Characters with Proxies

In the case of props or other things that do not need to be animated or can be animated at the object level, ordinary linking is sufficient. However, rigged characters are more complicated. In particular, the armature needs to be poseable, which is not possible using ordinary linking. For this reason, proxy rigs are used.To link and proxy a rig for animation, it's necessary to first prepare the library by ensuring that the entire character rig—meshes, armatures, and all—are grouped together in a single group. If you haven't done that already, do it now.

Using the file from the previous chapter, select all the objects in your Captain Blender rig: the body, the eyeballs, the Empty object that controls the logo mapping, and the rig, as shown in Figure 9.2. Press Ctrl+G to group the objects. Grouped objects are displayed with a green wireframe, and in the Properties window under Groups, a group called Group will be displayed for objects in that group, as shown in Figure 9.3. Change the name of that group to CB-Rig, as shown in Figure 9.4. Now that these objects are grouped, you can append or link them to another .blend file in one step. Save the file with a name that identifies it as a library or resource for the character.

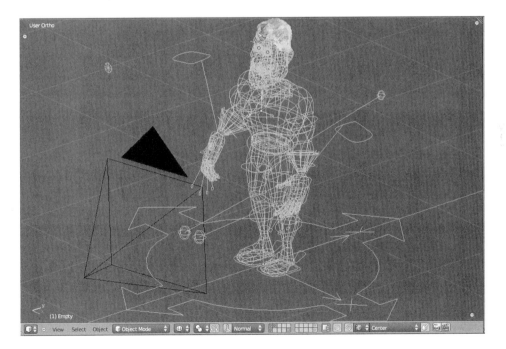

Figure 9.2

Selecting all the objects in the character rig for grouping

Figure 9.3

**Grouping the
objects**

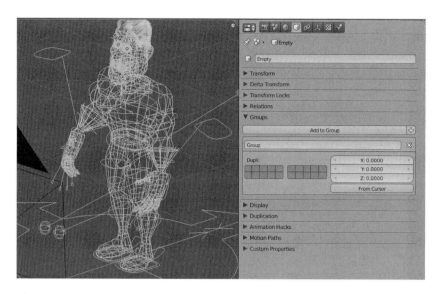

Figure 9.4

**Changing the
group name**

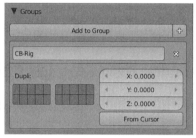

To create a proxied rig from the rigged character in your library, follow these steps:

1. Open a new Blender session. Save the session immediately, as shown in Figure 9.5, giving it a meaningful name. Saving is necessary for linking, because the linking process depends on creating a relationship between two relative locations on the hard drive. When you've saved the file, delete the default cube.

Figure 9.5

**Saving the fresh
session**

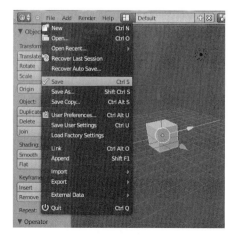

2. Choose Link from the File drop-down menu. In the file browser, navigate to the library `.blend` file on your hard disk. Click the `.blend` filename to navigate into the `.blend` file, and then click Groups to navigate into the Groups virtual directory. You

Figure 9.6

Linking the CB-Rig group datablock

should find a datablock there called CB-Rig (or whatever the name of the group was that you created when you prepared the library), as shown in Figure 9.6. Select this datablock, and click the Link/Append From Library button in the upper right of the file browser. The grouped rig will appear in your 3D viewport, as shown in

Figure 9.7. If necessary, press Alt+G to return it to the center of the space. Notice that this group instance can be selected only as a unit. You cannot select individual objects within the group.

Figure 9.7

The linked group

Figure 9.8

The Make Proxy menu

3. Press Ctrl+Alt+P to create a proxy object. When you do this, a menu will open, as shown in Figure 9.8, to enable you to choose which object you want to make a proxy for. Choose the rig object. This will make a proxy for the armature. This new object will be named CB-Rig_proxy. If you select it and enter Pose mode, you will be able to pose the character, as shown in Figure 9.9.

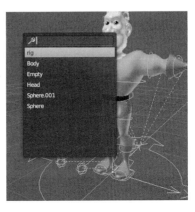

Figure 9.9

Posing the proxy armature

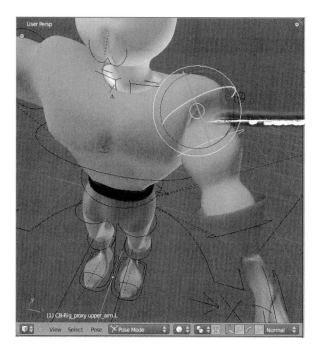

Figure 9.9

Posing the proxy armature

4. This step is not strictly necessary, but it's a good idea to help avoid accidentally selecting the group instance when you want to select the proxy object. Open an Outliner window, and choose Current Scene in the display drop-down menu in the header. To the right of the CB-Rig entry, click the little arrow icon to toggle selectability of the CB-Rig group instance (see Figure 9.10). When this is toggled off, the group instance will not be selectable in the 3D viewport. This will make it easier to select the proxy rig every time. You will never need to select the group instance when animating.

Figure 9.10

Toggling the CB-Rig group instance to be unselectable

You've now created a proxy rig to do your animating. The Mesh objects are all traditionally linked to their library sources, so if the meshes change in the library, they will change in this scene without affecting the animation. You can now animate exactly as you would ordinarily animate.

From here on, you should do any posing or positioning of the character in Pose mode. This includes simple positioning of your character in space. Do not move the rig proxy object or the group instance in Object mode. If you want to relocate your character in the 3D space, enter Pose mode and do so by moving the root bone, as shown in Figure 9.11. Notice that the object center remains at the origin of the space.

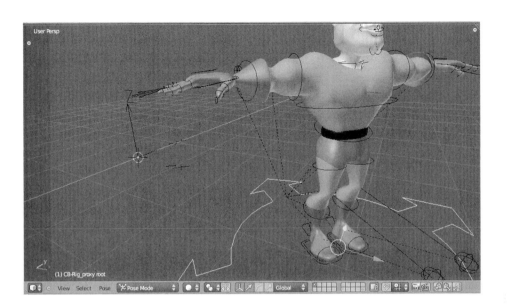

Figure 9.11

Moving the root bone in Pose mode

Using the NLA Editor

At first glance, the NLA Editor appears very similar to the DopeSheet, as you can see in Figure 9.12. It shows a representation of the Timeline, and the area at the left displays its channels. Both editor views serve the similar functions of arranging or modifying a set of underlying F-Curves to output an animation. Although the DopeSheet displays a simplification of many F-Curve views, with each key representing one or more F-Curve keys, the NLA Editor enables the combination of actions.

The main type of element in the NLA Editor is called a *strip*, and each strip represents one of your already-created actions. In this way, you can use the NLA Editor to place many different actions on the Timeline as strips, layering them, repeating them, and applying other parameters to them to generate a final animation.

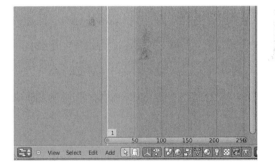

Figure 9.12

NLA Editor

Linking Actions to the NLA

To understand the relationship between individual actions and the animation created by the NLA Editor, you'll take a look at a very simple example. Start a new blend, delete the default cube, and add an armature object with a single bone. Make sure you have your workspace set up so you can see a 3D viewport, an Action Editor, and an NLA Editor simultaneously, as shown in Figure 9.13. (You will probably also want a Timeline visible.)

Figure 9.13

3D viewport, Action Editor, and NLA Editor

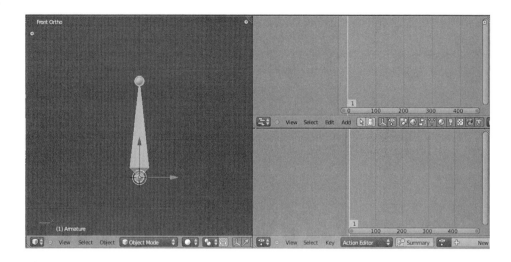

You'll create two actions. The first action will have the bone swing gently from side to side. Rotate the bone slightly to the right, and key the rotation at frame 1, as shown in Figure 9.14. The key will appear in the Action Editor as you expect. In the NLA Editor, a channel will be automatically created for the armature object. Under this channel, slightly indented, is a channel representing the current action, as you can see in Figure 9.15.

Press the up arrow key on your keyboard to advance 10 frames to frame 11. Rotate the bone to the left extreme, and key the pose, as shown in Figure 9.16. Copy the key from frame 1, and move the duplicate to frame 21. Rename the action SideToSide, as shown in Figure 9.17, and notice that the name of the action channel has changed to reflect this in the NLA Editor. Also, set the end frame in your Timeline to 20 to make this animation repeat smoothly.

Figure 9.14

Keying a first bone pose

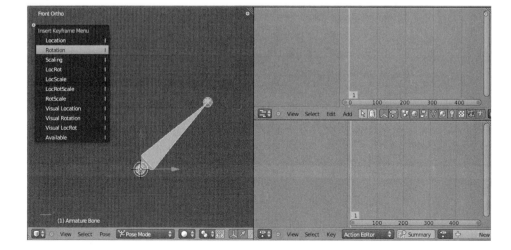

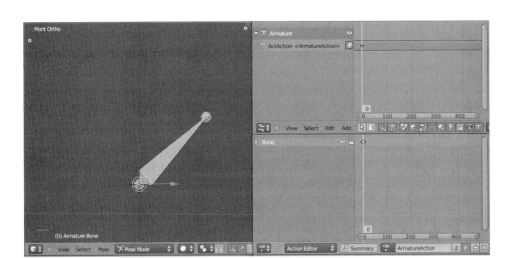

Figure 9.15

The keyed pose

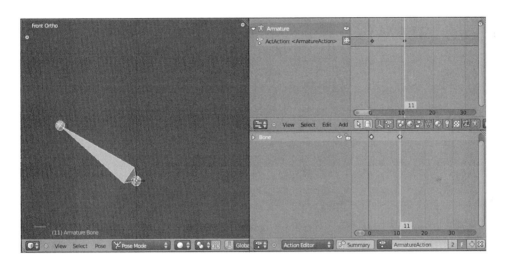

Figure 9.16

Second bone pose

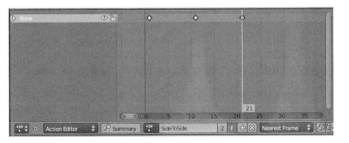

Figure 9.17

SideToSide action

Now that you've finished creating the SideToSide action, you'll create a new action called FrontToBack. To do this, you *could* simply select Add New from the Actions drop-down menu, which would duplicate the SideToSide action and give you a new action called SideToSide.001. In this case, however, start fresh with a new, blank action. To do this, click the X to the right of the Actions drop-down menu, which unlinks the SideToSide action from the armature. Note that this does *not* delete the action from your .blend file.

> When you create actions, Blender gives them a fake user by default. For this reason, actions remain part of your .blend file, even when they are not in use by any object. (Recall the discussion of fake users in Chapter 1.) To fully delete a created action from your .blend file, deselect the F icon in the Action Editor. After you do this, assuming that no objects are using the action, the action will not be persisted the next time the file is closed.

For now, rest assured that you're not likely to accidentally delete actions. All this does is remove the action's association with the armature and thus remove it from the NLA Editor. Select the bone, and press Alt+R to clear any rotations on the bone so you can truly start fresh with the new action, as shown in Figure 9.18. Although you have

unlinked the action from the armature and removed it from the NLA Editor, notice that the bone stays in whatever position it was in when you unlinked the action. If you want to start from a completely clean slate, be sure to select the bone and press Alt+G and Alt+R to clear any translations or rotations.

Figure 9.18

Starting fresh with a clear Action Editor

To create the second action, simply rotate the bone forward a bit around the x-axis and key the pose in frame 1. Again, this will automatically create an action called ArmatureAction, which you will rename to FrontToBack. As you can see in Figure 9.19, FrontToBack is now the active action; as such, it is represented in the NLA Editor under the Armature channel.

Figure 9.19

Creating FrontToBack

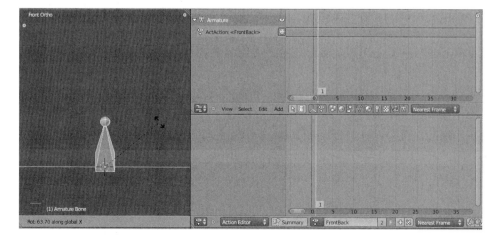

Finish creating a back-and-forth swinging motion around the x-axis by keying a back frame and duplicating frame 1 to frame 21.

You now have two actions created. You can select the active action using the drop-down menu in the DopeSheet header, as shown in Figure 9.20. Currently, the active action is FrontToBack because that is the last action you worked on. The active action is also the one represented in the NLA Editor.

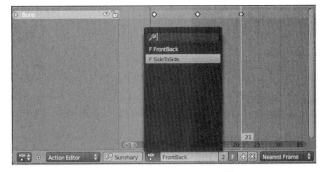

Figure 9.20

Selecting the active action

Working with NLA Strips

The NLA Editor wouldn't be much use if all it did was display the currently active action; as you can guess, it does considerably more than this. To insert an action into the NLA Editor so that you can incorporate it into the final animation, you need to create an *NLA strip* from the action. The NLA strip for an action is separate from the action itself; it is a representation of an action that the NLA Editor can process in various ways.

Figure 9.21

Creating an NLA strip

To create an NLA strip for an action, click the snowflake icon to the right of the action's name in the action channel. When you do this, the action will be converted to an NLA channel and be made inactive as an action, as shown in Figure 9.21. The name of the created strip is the same as the name of its corresponding action.

Now, in the Action Editor, select the SideToSide action from the drop-down menu and make it the active action. Note what happens (see Figure 9.22): the active action channel in the NLA Editor now contains SideToSide, but the FrontToBack NLA strip

remains in place. After an NLA strip has been created for an action, the strip remains in the NLA Editor regardless of what happens in the Action Editor. NLA strips can be deleted like anything else in Blender with the X key, but don't do that now. Instead, click

Figure 9.22

SideToSide as active action

the snowflake icon to create a strip for SideToSide, which will appear as shown in Figure 9.23. You can select strips in the same way as you select other objects in Blender—by right-clicking or by selecting all strips and keys with the A key.

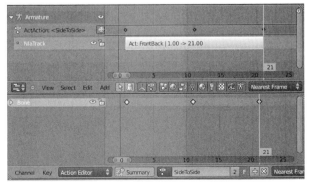

Figure 9.23

NLA strip for
SideToSide

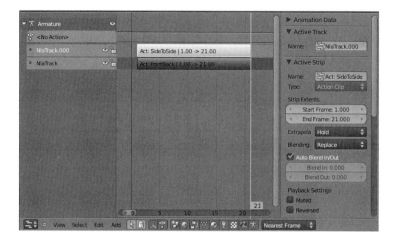

Action Output and NLA Output

Animation generated from the NLA Editor is based upon the interaction of NLA channels. The NLA channels are organized by precedence from top to bottom; by default, you
will see the animation for the topmost channel in the 3D viewport.

When you select an action in the Action Editor, the action appears as a red channel
across the top of the NLA Editor, as you have seen. In this state, the active action is the
animation that plays in the 3D viewport, overriding whatever other animation has been
created in the NLA Editor. While this action is in this raw action state, there's not much
you can do with it in the NLA Editor. If you want to integrate it in some way with other
channels in the NLA Editor, you must convert it to a strip as described previously.

Once the actions have been converted to strips, they can be combined in several ways,
determined by the Blending value of the uppermost strip. The default Blending value
is Replace, meaning that the uppermost strip will override the strips below it. So, for
example, if you play the animation that you just created, you will only see the SideToSide
movement. However, if you change the Blending value to Add in the Properties Shelf
(toggled visible with N key), then the F-Curve values of the two action strips add to one
another, resulting in a diagonal swinging movement that is the sum of SideToSide and
FrontToBack, as shown in Figure 9.24.

Multiplicative blending and subtractive blending are also available. However, these
blending options are less frequently used, and their results are less intuitive than additive blending. For most armature animation, you will use either replacement or additive
blending.

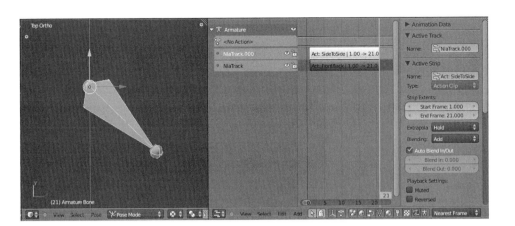

Figure 9.24

The two strips playing with additive blending

More Fun with NLA Strips

NLA strips are more than simply instances of actions. They also have a number of properties of their own that determine their behavior and how the action they contain interacts with the whole animation. You can see the properties of the selected strip in the Properties Shelf in the right side of the window. As always, the Properties Shelf is hidden and shown with the N key.

Among other things, the strip's transform properties determine the starting and ending points of the strip and the number of repetitions of the action the strip represents. When first created, the number of repetitions is 1, and the length of the strip is identical to the length of the action itself. Select the topmost strip, SideToSide, and set the Repeat value to be 3 while keeping the End Frame value at 21, as shown in Figure 9.25.

Figure 9.25

Changing the repeat value of the strip

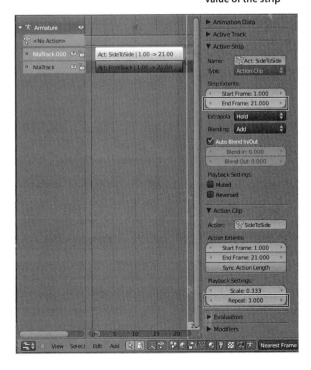

You can now see the difference between playback modes very clearly. The bone swings back and forth at triple speed, per the repeating strip, three times for every one forward-backward swing.

You can isolate individual strips by clicking the little dot to the left of the strip's name. This will show you only the selected strip's animation result in the 3D viewport.

NLA in Action

This section takes a look at a few basic uses of nonlinear animation. In the first example, you'll see how to use an NLA strip to sync two unrelated cyclical motions to cycle nicely together. In the second example, you'll see how to use the NLA Editor to enable a walking figure to follow a path using a stride bone to prevent foot slippage.

Syncing Cyclical Motions: A Walk Cycle with Camera Rotation

If you looked at the walk cycle video in the walk.avi file on the DVD, you probably noticed that it wasn't exactly what you were rendering at the end of Chapter 7. To present the animation in a more appealing way, I gave it some nice lighting, a background color, and a material for the ground he walks on. Furthermore, I added a slow rotation on the camera to show the walk cycle from all angles. If you play the video file with autorepeat turned on in your media player, you'll see that the walk cycle and the camera rotation are timed to repeat at the same point, creating a fluid cycling of both movements as the video repeats.

This is simple to do using NLA strips. In this section, you'll first set up the camera motion in the scene file you created in the first section of this chapter, and then you'll append the walk action from the library file you created. You'll apply the action to the proxy rig and then set up the looping using the NLA.

Setting Up the Camera Motion

Before you deal with the walk cycle itself, you'll create a smoothly rotating camera motion. Applying a TrackTo constraint to a camera targeted at an Empty object is a very useful and general-purpose method of aiming the camera. Set up the camera rotation by following these steps:

1. In top view, add an empty on the same layer that the camera is on. It is a good idea to have these two objects on their own layer so that you can access them independently of the other objects in the scene.

2. Place the empty at the center of the subject of the shot (in this case, the Captain Blender figure). In this case, because you haven't moved the Captain Blender figure from the origin point, you should be able to place the empty directly at the origin point for the x- and y-axes, as shown in Figure 9.26.

3. Raise the Empty object up along the z-axis so that it is somewhere around the middle of Captain Blender's body, as shown in Figure 9.27. This is the point at which the camera will aim.

Figure 9.26

Initial camera and empty positions

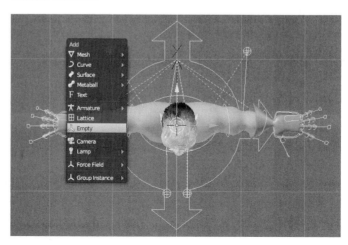

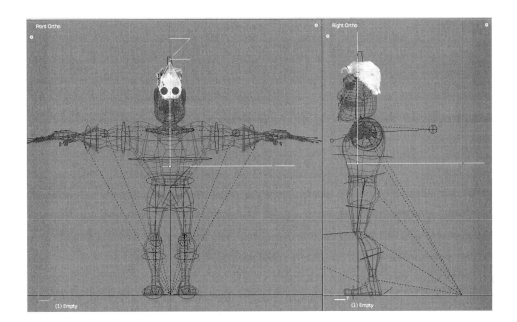

Figure 9.27

Adjusting the location of the Empty object

4. Position the camera directly in front of the Empty object, some distance away, as shown in Figure 9.28.

5. Select the camera first, and then choose the Empty object second (making sure no other objects are selected). Having them on their own layer should be helpful for this. Press Ctrl+T, and select the TrackTo constraint, which causes the camera to point directly at the Empty object at all times.

6. Next, with the same objects selected in the same way, press Ctrl+P to create a parent relationship. This parents the camera to the Empty object so that when the empty moves, the camera also moves.

7. Press 0 on the numeric keypad to go into camera view. In this mode, you can select the camera object by clicking the rectangular line around your view. Move both the camera and the Empty object to create a nicely framed view of your subject.

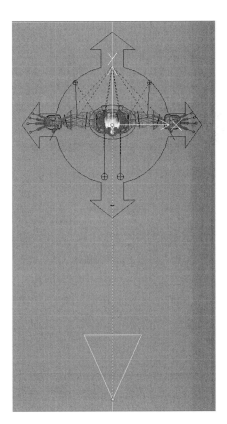

Figure 9.28

Initial camera position

Remember that to move the Empty object or the camera up or down, you can select the object and translate along the global z-axis. To zoom the camera in and out, select the camera and translate along the local z-axis. Press G and then press Z twice. Your shot should wind up looking something like the example in Figure 9.29.

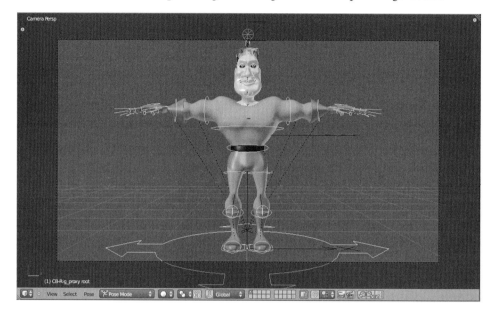

8. Press 7 on the numeric keypad to get back into top view, and select the Empty object. Key its rotation. Move forward 10 frames; rotate the empty slightly counterclockwise, constraining the rotation to the z-axis; and key its rotation again.

9. With the empty selected, open an F-Curve editor window. Select the first point, and place it manually at x position 1 and y position 0 by inputting the values directly in the Key X and Key Y fields. You want the Empty object to complete a 360-degree rotation in 101 frames. So, set the second point to Key X value 101. For the Key Y value of the second point, remember that you must express angles in radians. There are 2π radians in a complete circle, but you don't need to calculate this yourself. Simply enter **2*pi** in the field, and Blender will automatically calculate the value to 6.283, as shown in Figure 9.30. Make sure that the handle types are set to Vector for both points and that the extrapolation type is linear.

You should now have a smooth camera rotation that cycles after 100 frames. Set your Timeline end frame to 100, go into camera view by pressing 0 on the numeric keypad, and click Play to watch the rotation from the camera's point of view.

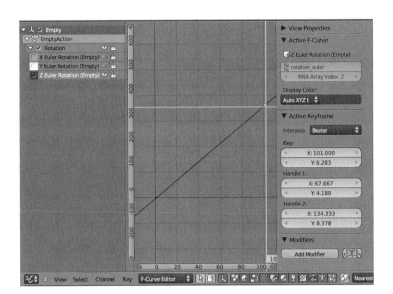

Figure 9.30

Setting the F-Curve point values

Using NLA Strips to Sync Walk Cycle Repetitions

To make your character walk, you first need access to the Walk action that you created previously. You can append the Walk action datablock from the library file in the same way you append any other datablock. Choose Append from the File menu, and use the file browser to navigate into the CB-CharacterResource.blend virtual directory. There,

Figure 9.31

Appending the Walk action

you will navigate into the Action virtual subdirectory, as shown in Figure 9.31, and select Walk. Click the Link/Append From Library button.

Now Walk will appear in the Action Editor drop-down menu. Select the CB-Rig_proxy object, enter Pose mode, and select Walk from the menu, as shown in Figure 9.32.

Convert the Walk action to a NLA strip as you learned to do in the previous section. Set the repetitions to 2, and set the End Frame value to 101, as shown in Figure 9.33. When you've done this, you're finished. Your character's walk cycle will play twice for each complete rotation of the camera, and both movements will repeat smoothly after 100 frames.

For a quick preview, play the animation with only the armature layer and the camera layer visible, which plays back much faster than including the mesh in the view and shows how smoothly the cycle point turned out.

Figure 9.32

Selecting the Walk action

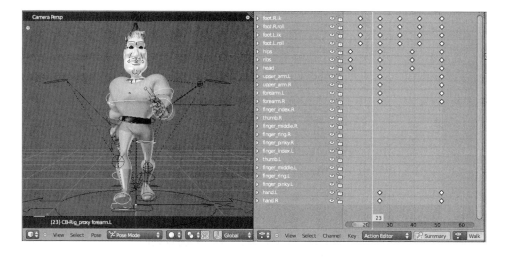

Figure 9.33

Settings for the NLA Walk strip

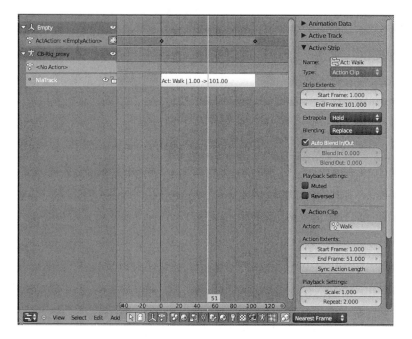

Mixing Actions: Walking and Talking

The real power of the NLA Editor is in its capability to combine multiple actions into a single animation. When several animations overlap, Blender decides whether there are any F-Curves that overlap each other (that is, curves that influence the same values), and if so, it assigns a precedence to the curves (or, if you chose additivity, it adds them). In cases where curves do not conflict, such as when separate F-Curve channels are involved or when the F-Curves belong to different bones or objects, the motion from all F-Curves is played simultaneously.

For this example, you can continue working on the same scene that you worked with for the previous example, but you will need to append the Speech action, just as you appended the Walk action in the previous section.

To set up a nonlinear animation using the two actions Walk and Speech, follow these steps:

1. Select CB-Rig_proxy, and enter Pose mode. In the DopeSheet, in Action Editor mode, select the Speech action (you need to have appended this action from the library already, or it will not show up in the drop-down menu). When you've done this, the action should display in the Action Editor and the NLA Editor, as shown in Figure 9.34. Notice that the Walk strip is already present.

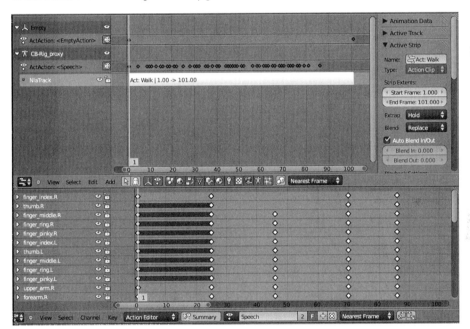

Figure 9.34

The Speech action

2. Create an NLA strip from the Speech action by clicking the snowflake icon. You need to decide whether Blending for this should be additive or replacement. They are both possibilities to consider here. With additive blending, the swinging of the arms will be incorporated into Captain Blender's gesticulations, which makes it look like he's talking while hurrying or doing some kind of cardio exercise. Be careful, though; in this case, the additive effect on the fingers causes them to crunch up unnaturally. For this example, use Replace blending. The NLA strips will look as shown in Figure 9.35.

Figure 9.35

The two action strips in the NLA Editor

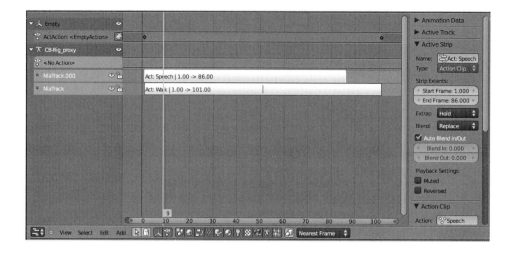

3. Place your Speech action strip along the Timeline where you want it by selecting it and moving it with the G key. Set the Blend In and Blend Out values to 20 to create a very smooth transition between the Walk poses and the Speech poses. This particularly affects the arms. A shorter Blend In value will make the transition from the lower action strip pose to the higher action strip pose more sudden. The Blend Out value corresponds to the end of the higher action strip. The results look like Figure 9.36.

Preview your animation, and watch Captain Blender walking and talking at the same time while the camera rotates.

Figure 9.36

The combined action strips in motion

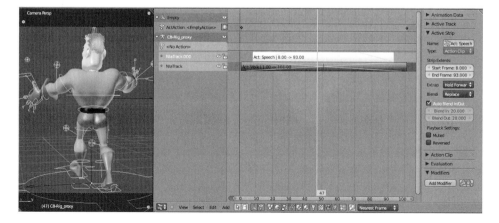

Actions for Nonarmature Animations

Actions were originally developed as a way to organize armature movements. However, in Blender 2.5, they have been expanded to work for all kinds of animation. In Figure 9.37, you can see location, rotation, and scale keys on the default cube object displayed in the F-Curve editor, the Action Editor, and the NLA Editor. This action can be converted to an NLA strip in the same way as any other action.

Figure 9.37

An action on the default cube object

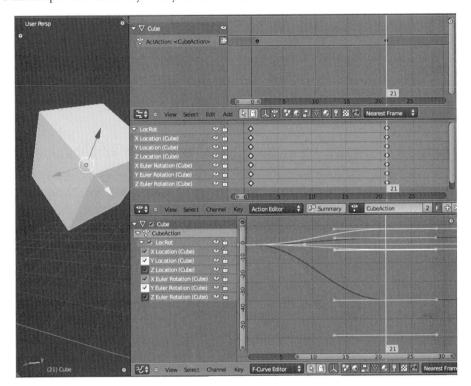

You've covered quite a bit of ground at this point, and by now you should have a pretty solid basic understanding of how to do character animation in Blender. You know how to build and animate a character using armature deformations and shape keys, and you know how to combine basic animations to create more sophisticated ones in the form of actions in the NLA Editor. There are still a few topics left to cover, though, before you'll be ready to produce your own animated shorts to completion. In the next chapter, I'll go over a few more tips and techniques related to character animation that I haven't had the chance to discuss so far.

CHAPTER 10

Further Issues in Character Animation

Before going on to the issues of lighting, rendering, and editing, there are a few more topics I'll cover here. In the first part of this chapter, I'll give you an idea of how you can use constraints to incorporate props smoothly into your character animations. The rest of the chapter is concerned with various ways to represent particular physical effects. For example, with lattices and mesh deformers, you can deform your meshes in ways that would not be easy or even possible using only bones. The softbody system simulates realistic soft object behavior, and with metaballs, you can create interesting effects that are not possible with meshes.

- ▪ **Interacting with Props**
- ▪ **Lattices and Mesh Deformers**
- ▪ **Softbodies and Metaballs**

Interacting with Props

Almost all character animation involves props at some point. The challenge with props is that they influence or are influenced by the character's movement but are not part of the character itself.

In some cases, the interaction between the character and the prop is too complex to allow automatic solutions, and the best approach is to key the action by hand. In other cases, tools exist to make the job much easier than it would be if you needed to key everything directly.

Furniture

With props such as chairs and tables, the interaction typically involves the character's whole body and might even involve other props. It is more often than not simplest to do most animation by hand in this case. If the armature is sufficiently versatile, then interactions with furniture should not be difficult to key manually. For example, you can seat the character on a chair by simply keying the location of the torso bone.

In a case such as that shown in Figure 10.1, you want the figure's hands to stay fixed to the table, in spite of the other motion of the rest of the body. The character should be able to stand and sit or lean forward or to the side, without the hands moving from their position on the surface of the table. You can do this by setting the hands' FK/IK value to 1 in Rig Main Properties in the Properties Shelf, as shown in Figure 10.2. If you want to animate this value, you simply press the I key over the value. Once you have the arms set to IK posing, you pose the hand.IK bones first, and then you can animate the body while keeping the hands fixed, as shown in Figure 10.3.

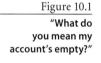

Figure 10.1

"What do you mean my account's empty?"

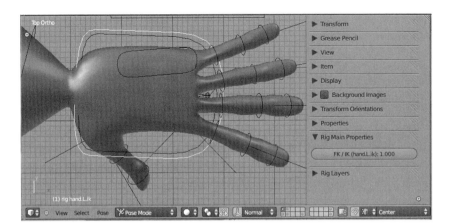

Figure 10.2

Setting IK posing

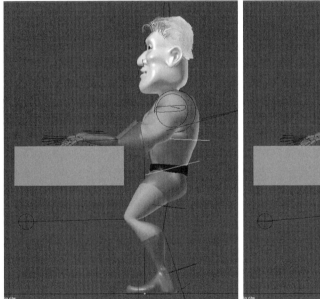
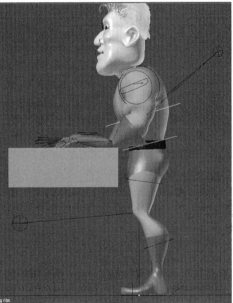

Figure 10.3

Moving the body with the hands planted

Grabbing and Holding Objects

Many props, however, are more than just obstacles, so they require a different approach. In many cases, the character needs to hold and manipulate the prop. This is not as simple as the case of furniture because in this case you want the prop to behave as an extension of the character itself when being held but to behave as an independent entity when not being held.

With a sword or a stick, for example, you want the prop to be poseable in the same way that the character is poseable if the character is using the weapon to fight. It would be far too complicated and inflexible to key the object entirely independently. Nevertheless, if the character drops or throws the prop, it should no longer depend on the character's movements.

You can do this by using copy location constraints (and in some cases copy rotation constraints), as you will see in the simple example of Captain Blender picking up and throwing a ball.

Picking Up and Throwing a Ball

This example focuses on using constraints to enable good prop interaction. I'm not going to go into the various bone poses that compose the action. Figure 10.4 gives an overview of the full animation.

Figure 10.4

Overview of the pick-up-and-throw action

The animation shows Captain Blender crouching forward, grasping the ball, pulling back for a pitch, and throwing the ball. The main concern in this section is the motion of the ball when Captain Blender is holding it in his hand. Of course, with an object F-Curve, you can control the movement of the ball for every frame in the animation if you want. You could simply key the ball's position to follow Captain Blender's hand.

But an object F-Curve is not a good solution. If you do this, you might need a large number of keys to make the ball follow the motion of the hand, even if the motion itself is determined by only a few bone movements. Furthermore, if you edit the throwing action at all, which is very likely with a movement like this, you have to adjust or even rekey many location keys for the ball. Clearly, what you want to do is to have the ball follow the hand's motion automatically.

To make this possible, you will create a new bone by extruding and detaching a new bone from hand.L/R, called Hold.L/R, as shown in Figure 10.5. Extrude with the E key (the edits should all still be mirrored, so you can do this on either hand) and then detach the bone by pressing Alt+P and selecting Disconnect Bone. This bone is located in the middle of the space just below the palm of the hand, in approximately the spot where you would like a held object to be, as you can see in Figure 10.6. It is not connected to any other bone, but, as mentioned, it is parented to the hand bone.

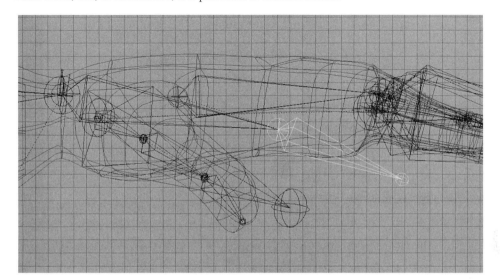

Figure 10.5

Extruding the hold bone

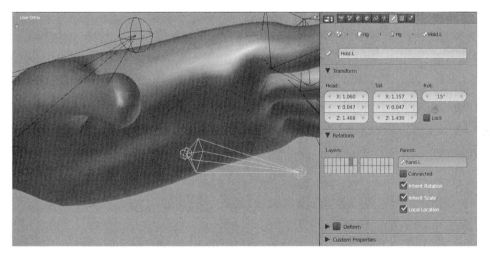

Figure 10.6

Placing the hold bone

After you create and place the ball (a subsurfed icosphere), set up a copy location constraint on the ball, as shown in Figure 10.7. In the OB field, type the armature's name, in this case simply **rig**. When you enter an armature's name in this field, a second field appears for the bone name. Name it **Hold.R bone** here. Use the slider to set the influence to 0.

The influence slider determines to what extent the ball's location is determined by the constraint. If the slider is set to 1, the ball is fixed to the hold.R bone's location. If the slider is set to 0, the ball will return to its original position or the position that it is keyed to as an object and be completely independent of the bone or armature's movement. Intuitively, a value of .5 places the ball halfway between its own original (or keyed) location and the location of the hold.R bone.

Figure 10.7

The copy location constraint

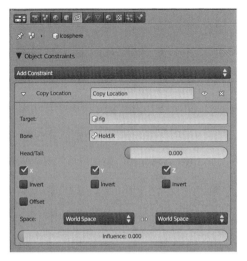

Most importantly, you can key the influence of the constraint to an F-Curve by pressing the I key over the influence slider. In this way, you can animate smooth transitions in the influence of the constraint. You begin by keying the constraint influence to 0 and keying the ball's location to the place you want it to be at the beginning of the animation.

You can see constraint influence F-Curves by looking in the Graph Editor. Figure 10.8 follows the copy location constraint's influence curve from 0 to 1 as Captain Blender picks up the ball.

Figure 10.9 follows the more sudden release of the ball when he throws it. Note that the Graph Editor is scaled slightly differently in Figure 10.9, so it is important to pay attention to the values themselves.

Figure 10.8

The shift in constraint influence as the character picks up the ball

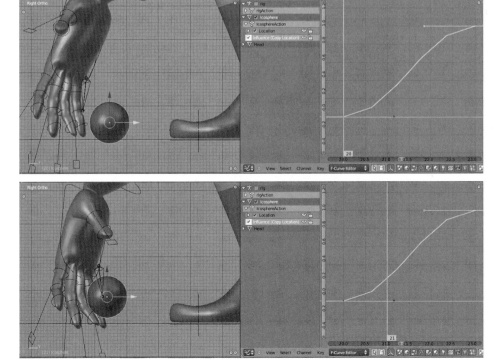

Figure 10.8
(continued)

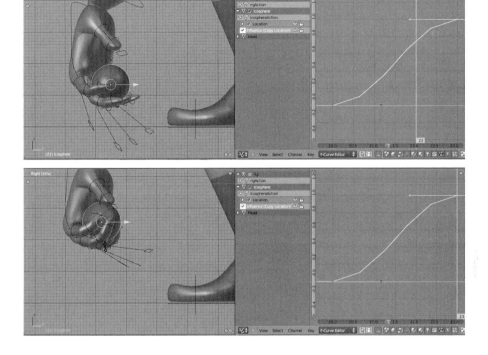

Figure 10.9
Releasing the ball

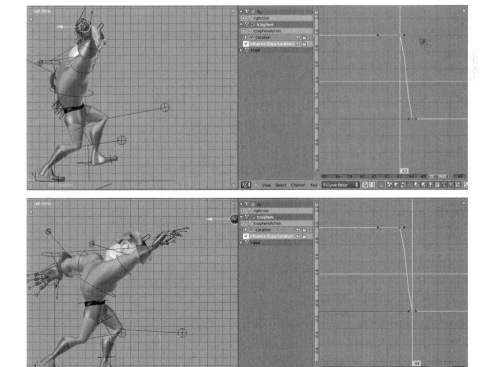

The ball's location needs to be keyed so that when the constraint influence is turned off, it will spring to the appropriate location. You need to take the actual location F-Curves of the ball into account, even when the constraint is active.

For example, if you keyed the ball's location to the ground in frame 1 and made no more location keys until the point after the ball is thrown, you would see the ball begin to float toward that destination even before the character picked it up. For this reason, you will need at least one duplicate key of the ground position, located after the ball has been picked up, to keep the F-Curve flat up until that point.

Lattices and Mesh Deformers

Lattices create certain kinds of uniform deformations on meshes that would be much more difficult to do by editing the mesh directly or by using bones.

Lattice Modifier

A lattice is a three-dimensional, right-angled grid of vertices. Like an armature, it is intended solely as a modifier of other object types. And like an armature, it never shows up at render time.

The default form of a lattice is a simple eight-vertex cube, but it can be subdivided into more compartments by changing its width (in vertices) along each dimension. When a lattice modifies a mesh, moving the vertices of the lattice results in a proportional distortion of the shape of the mesh. For example, if you modify a figure with a rectangular lattice and then edit the lattice to fatten the middle, the figure is fattened around the middle.

As an example, you will create a lattice to animate a deformation of Captain Blender's eyeball. The classic cartoon bugging eye is a good example of a deformation that is comparatively easy to do with lattices, although you can also use shape keys. (Unfortunately, currently you cannot use lattice deformations to create shape keys, so a combination approach is not an option.)

To deform the left eyeball with a lattice, follow these steps:

1. Select the left eyeball object. Snap the cursor to the object using Shift+S. In front view, press Shift+A to add a lattice object, as shown in Figure 10.10. Resize the object to fit around the eyeball, as shown in Figure 10.11. Make sure you do not do this resize in Edit mode; otherwise, your eyeball will shrink as soon as you apply the lattice.

2. In the lattice properties panel (see Figure 10.12), set the lattice resolution to 3 along the dimensions U, V, and W, resulting in the lattice shown in Figure 10.13.

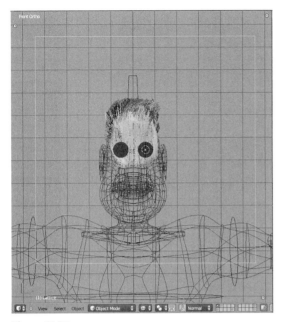

Figure 10.10
Adding a lattice

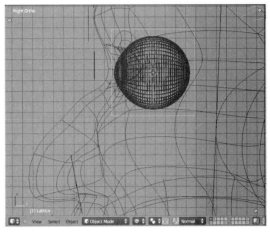

Figure 10.11
Resizing the lattice to fit the eyeball

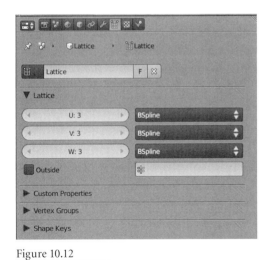

Figure 10.12
Lattice parameters

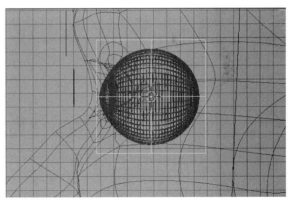

Figure 10.13
A 3×3 lattice on the eyeball

3. Select the left eyeball object, and add a Lattice modifier on the Modifiers tab. In the Object field, enter the name of the lattice, **Lattice**, as shown in Figure 10.14. Take care to select the correct eyeball, which might require reorienting the view slightly to double-check.

Figure 10.14

Adding the Lattice modifier

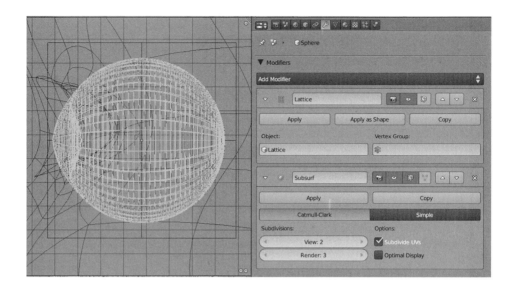

4. With the lattice selected, find the Shape Keys panel in the Lattice Properties window, as shown in Figure 10.15, and add a Basis shape key by clicking the plus icon just as you did with meshes in Chapter 5.

5. Still in Object mode, add another shape key by clicking the plus icon. With this shape key (Key 1) active, enter Edit mode, and edit the shape of the lattice, as shown in Figure 10.16. Notice that when you move lattice vertices, the mesh is also deformed in a corresponding way. Edit the lattice so that the eye bugs out of its socket.

Figure 10.15

Keying the Basis lattice shape key

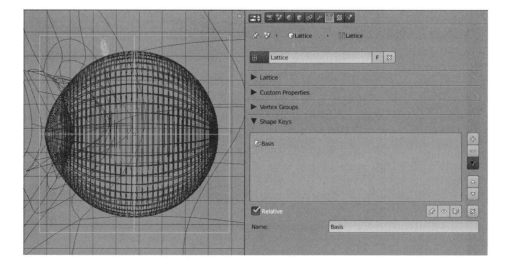

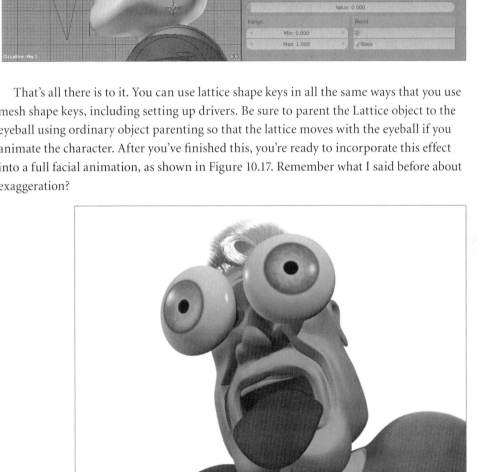

Figure 10.16

Creating a lattice shape key

That's all there is to it. You can use lattice shape keys in all the same ways that you use mesh shape keys, including setting up drivers. Be sure to parent the Lattice object to the eyeball using ordinary object parenting so that the lattice moves with the eyeball if you animate the character. After you've finished this, you're ready to incorporate this effect into a full facial animation, as shown in Figure 10.17. Remember what I said before about exaggeration?

Figure 10.17

Example of the kind of subtle and nuanced performance you can get with lattice deformations

Mesh Deform Modifier

A Mesh Deform modifier behaves similarly to a lattice but is more flexible in that its initial shape is based on a mesh that you model yourself. Like a lattice, it can deform a mesh using shape keys or in real time in Edit mode. However, unlike lattices, the mesh deformer can also be rigged directly with an armature and weight painted, just like any other mesh. (It is possible to control a lattice with an armature, but you must do this in a somewhat roundabout way, using hooks. This is touched on briefly in Chapter 15.)

In this section, you'll see an example of an alternate way of rigging Captain Blender's legs using a Mesh Deform modifier instead of using an armature directly. In this example, the Armature modifier has been deleted from the Captain Blender body mesh, so the rig does not have any direct influence on the character mesh.

To deform the legs using a Mesh Deform modifier, you must first model the deform mesh, as shown in Figure 10.18. This is an ordinary Mesh object, modeled from the default cube. It must fully cover the area that you intend to be deformed by it. Parts of the character mesh that are not fully contained in this mesh will not be deformed by it.

Be careful if your character mesh is subsurfaced, as in this example, because this may cause the mesh to appear smaller than it really is. The unsubsurfaced "true" edit cage of the character model must be completely enclosed by the deform mesh. Furthermore, the deform mesh must be a fully closed simple manifold mesh. There can be no missing or unconnected faces, and the mesh should have a well-defined inside and outside. In Figure 10.19, you can see that the leg deformer mesh used in this example conforms to this requirement.

Figure 10.18

A deform mesh for Captain Blender's legs

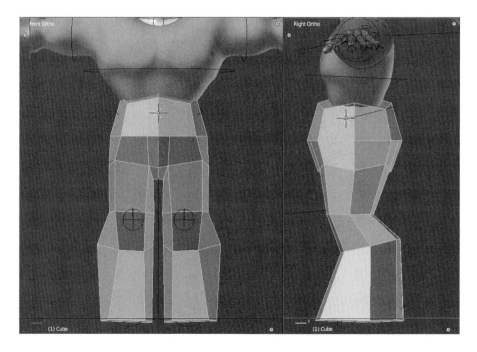

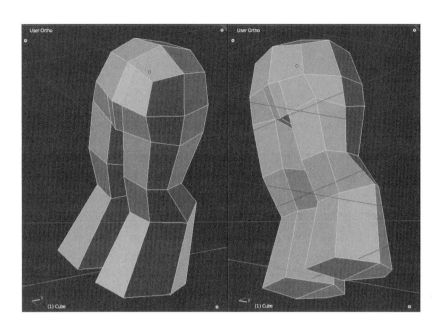

Figure 10.19
**The deform mesh
is a fully closed
manifold mesh.**

Obviously, the deform mesh is no different from any other mesh, so you can rig it to the armature in the same way you would rig any other mesh, using Ctrl+P and selecting an Armature deform with automatic weights. Having done this, you can pose the deformation mesh with the armature as in Figure 10.20. Note that the Captain Blender character mesh is *not* rigged to the armature.

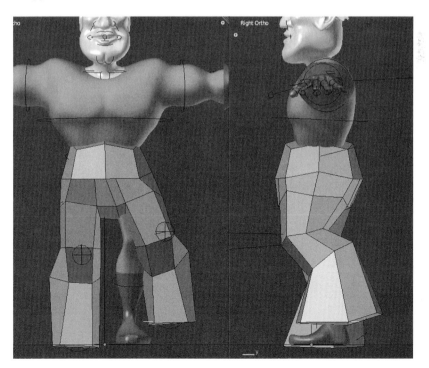

Figure 10.20
**Posing the deform
mesh with the
armature**

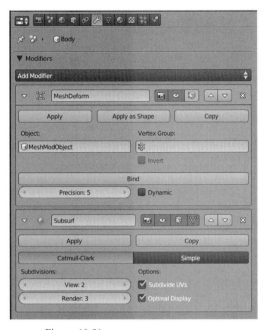

Figure 10.21

The Mesh Deform modifier

Figure 10.22

Displaying the deform mesh with the Wire display type

Now you can add a Mesh Deform modifier to the Captain Blender body Mesh object, as shown in Figure 10.21. As with the Armature modifier, the Mesh Deform modifier should be above the subsurf modifier so that the deformed mesh is sub-surfed. You must enter the name of the deform Mesh object, in this case **MeshModObject**, in the Object field.

Before the Mesh Deform modifier will work, you need to click the Bind button to bind the character mesh to the deform mesh. When you do this, any change to the deform mesh will deform the character mesh. If you want to edit the deform mesh after this point without changing the character mesh, you must unbind the modifier and then rebind it again when you are ready to use it again. Be aware that binding the mesh can take time. If you have a complex deform mesh, binding can slow things down considerably for a while. Don't worry, though, your computer (probably) hasn't crashed.

For visualization purposes, I have set the deform modifier to display with the Wire display type, as shown in Figure 10.22. Of course, in practical rigging situations, you would probably make the deform mesh invisible to animators, but wireframe view is a good way to see what's going on with the deform and character meshes.

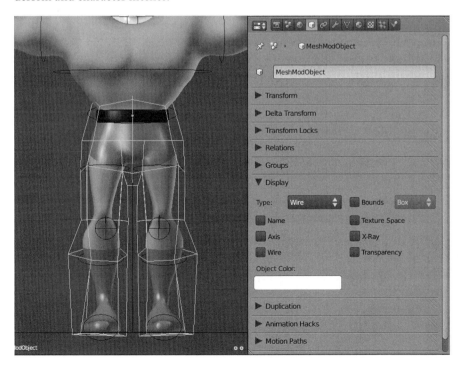

Now, when you pose the armature, you get the results shown in Figure 10.23. Note what's happening here. The armature is influencing the deform mesh, and the deform mesh is deforming the character's leg. This results in a considerably different pattern of influence on the surface of the char-

acter mesh and can yield smoother deformations than direct armature influence.

Certain character shapes can benefit greatly from this kind of deformation. For example, a round character with rolls of fat or some other complex aspect to its shape might not be handled well by the automatic bone weighting algorithm and might be much easier to rig using a simple mesh deformer.

As you can see in Figure 10.24,

Figure 10.23

The mesh deformer in action

a bound deform mesh deforms the character mesh when it is edited in Edit mode. You can use this for shape key animation in a similar way to the lattice example that you saw previously.

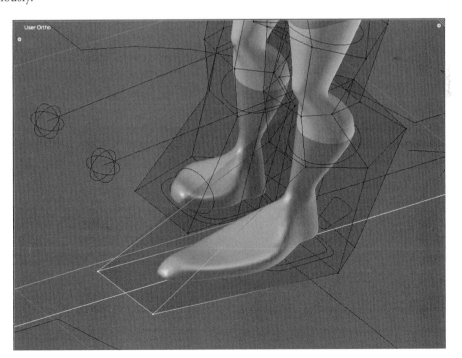

Figure 10.24

Deforming in Edit mode

Softbodies and Metaballs

If lattices enable you to deform your meshes like Silly Putty, softbodies and metaballs enable you to create Jell-O and Slime, respectively. So, moving along in order of liquefaction, you'll look at those two tools in this section.

In fact, the two tools play very different roles in character animation. As you'll see, I included metaballs more as an amusing side note than as any crucial character animation tool. Softbodies, on the other hand, can be very useful for adding realism to a variety of character types.

Using Softbodies

The softbody simulation system is one of several impressive physics simulation systems built into Blender, but it is the only one you will be looking at in this book. As its name implies, it is a way of simulating softness, bounce, and elasticity in objects. There are a number of ways to use the softbody simulator, but you usually use it to create a bouncy, gelatinous effect for the softer portions of solid objects.

Captain Blender Puts on Some Pounds

Figure 10.25

Captain Blender's spare tire

For an ideal showcase of softbodies, you'll return to the jump action you created in Chapter 7—but with a slight modification. It seems that during a recent vacation from do-gooding, Captain Blender gained a little bit of weight, and typical for guys his age, it all went straight to the belly. In fact, he gained so much weight he couldn't even fit into his trusty utility belt, as you can see in Figure 10.25.

I'm not going to go into any depth on the modeling of Captain Blender's new physique, because it was simply a matter of pushing a few verts around and adding a few edge loops, as you can see in Figure 10.26. (When you make this modification to the model, be sure to use Save As so as not to ruin to your original file.) What you're concerned with is how to apply a softbody simulator to Captain Blender's new belly to give it some real jiggle as he strives to get back into shape with a grueling regimen of jumping in place.

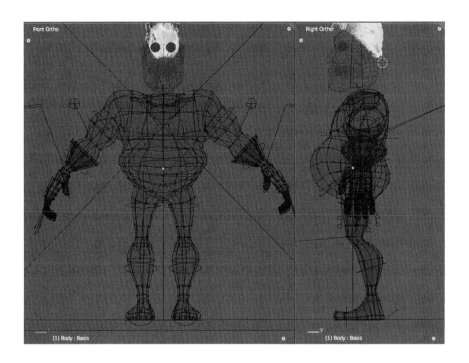

Figure 10.26

Captain Blender's weight gain in Edit mode

To apply softbody behavior to Captain Blender's belly, follow these steps:

1. Because you want part of the mesh to be soft and part of the mesh to retain its form completely, you need to use a vertex group. With the Captain Blender mesh selected, tab into Edit mode, and on the Links and Materials tab, under Vertex Groups, click New. Name the new vertex group **Softbody**, as shown in Figure 10.27. Select all vertices in the mesh, and assign them all to the vertex group, making sure that the weight is set to 1.

   Figure 10.27

   Softbody vertex group

   You don't really want all the weights set to 1. In fact, for the portion of the mesh that you want soft, namely, the belly, you want the weights set to around 0.25.

2. Enter Weight Paint mode, and select the Softbody vertex group from the Vertex Groups drop-down menu. Using the Weight Paint tool with Weight set to 0.25 and Opacity set to

0.5, paint the belly as shown in Figure 10.28. It will work best to use X-Axis Mirror. Around the edges of the 0.25 area, paint at 0.5 weight. The whole mesh should be

red in Weight Paint mode, except for the belly, which should be green. The area just below the sternum should be yellow. When you finish weight painting, switch back into Object mode.

3. In the Physics Properties area, click Add in the Soft Body panel, as shown in Figure 10.29. Set the settings for Soft Body and Soft Body Goal as shown in Figure 10.30.

These are general parameters for the soft body simulator and parameters to control how much the simulation adheres to the "goal." In this case, the goal will be your Softbody vertex group, so enter that into the Vertex Group field as shown.

Figure 10.28

Weight painting the soft belly

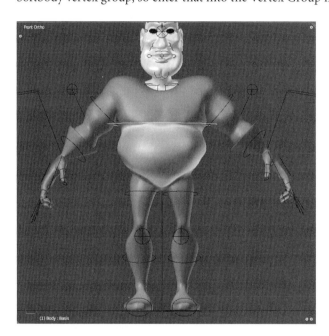

Figure 10.29

The Soft Body panel

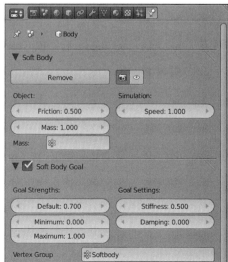

Figure 10.30

Settings for Soft Body and Soft Body Goal

4. Set the values for for Soft Body Edges and Soft Body Self Collision as shown in Figure 10.31. These determine how flexible or bouncy the edges of the mesh are during the simulation and whether and how accurately the mesh collides with itself.

5. Figure 10.32 shows the settings for Soft Body Cache. These are parameters that control caching and baking of soft body simulations.

   For information on what the various individual fields actually do, hover your mouse over the field and read the tool tip that pops up. However, even with this information, finding the correct settings for a specific use often involves some trial and error, and you should expect to do a lot of experimenting before you have an innate sense of how these parameters affect the outcome. Unfortunately, it's beyond the scope of this book to go into all of these parameters in more detail.

6. Now you have the softbody simulator set up. Check on your modifier stack. You'll see that a modifier has appeared called Softbody. However, you want the Softbody modifier to be sensitive to the movement of the character's body. To have that information, it must have access to the movements created by the Armature modifier. If you think back to Chapter 2, recall that the ordering of mesh modifiers is closely bound up with what kind of information is available to each one. In this case, the Softbody does not react to Armature motion as is. You need to bump the Softbody modifier down a notch using the down arrow button on the modifier itself so that the Softbody modifier *follows* the Armature modifier (see Figure 10.33).

After you do this, you're good to go. Preview your animation to see the effect of the Softbody simulator. Figure 10.34 shows a side view wireframe representation of several frames from this simulation.

Figure 10.31

Settings for Soft Body Edges and Soft Body Self Collision

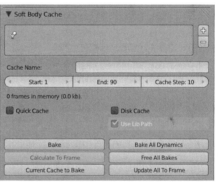

Figure 10.32

Settings for Soft Body Cache

Figure 10.33

The modifier stack

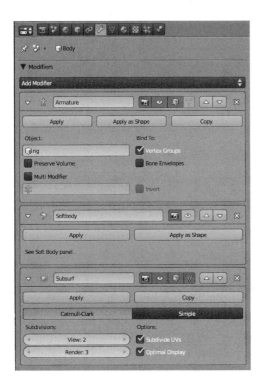

Figure 10.34

Stills from the soft-body animation

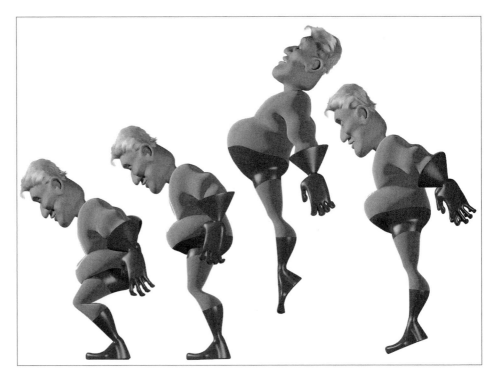

Metaballs

Metaballs are spherical mathematical constructs that merge or cling together when placed within a set proximity of each other, as shown in Figure 10.35. They are a very limited tool for modeling, but their liquid-like properties are very difficult to mimic in any other way.

Figure 10.35

Behavior of metaballs

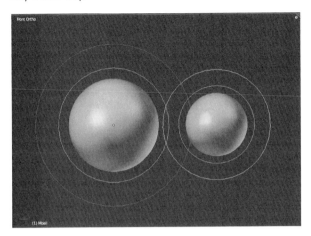 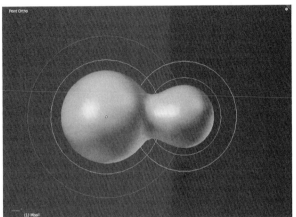

Perhaps the best-known Hollywood examples of what metaballs can be used for are the liquid metal character in Terminator 2 and the animated green goop from Flubber. Metaballs are the basis for the Meta Object type in Blender, and the various meta-objects are all essentially built from the basic metaball.

Although metaballs cannot take an Armature modifier, you can use bone parenting to control the movements of metaballs with an armature if the metaball model is built of separate metaball objects that can be parented independently, as shown in Figure 10.36.

To parent a metaball to a bone, make sure that the armature is in Pose mode, select the metaball object (Blender reverts to Object mode automatically), select the armature again (Blender reverts to Pose mode), and, with the desired bone selected, press Ctrl+P. Select the option to parent to a bone.

In this way, you can create a poseable character with metaballs that also retains the liquid qualities special to metaballs, as you can see in Figure 10.37.

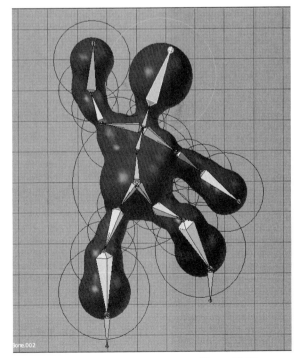

Figure 10.36

Applying an armature to a metaball figure using bone parenting

Figure 10.37

**Animated grape
jelly man**

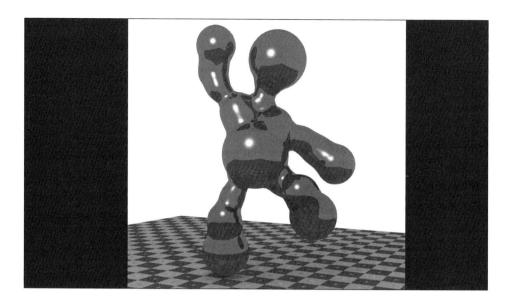

In this chapter, I tried to give you a hint of some of the possibilities for animation in Blender. Unfortunately, there are many useful and interesting tools and tricks that I do not have space to cover. Using dupliverts, duplipaths, and dupligroups; using curve deform; and using modifiers such as array, build, and wave—these are all topics that warrant extensive discussion but are outside the scope of this book. In Chapter 18, I point out where to find out more about these and other useful functions.

Indeed, there is really no end to the possibilities for both modeling and animation by using Blender's various tools. I hope that what you have read so far has begun to whet your appetite. It is far from the end of the story. In Chapter 11, you'll look at the basics of how to light and render your scenes to create good-looking, fully realized images. You'll also see how to use the Blender Sequence Editor to combine sequences of rendered images to create completed animations.

Lighting, Rendering, and Editing Your Animation

At this point, you've learned the basics of creating and animating characters in Blender. However, before you can see your animations the way you envision them, I need to go over some fundamentals of presenting and outputting your work. In this chapter, I'll give you a brief overview of Blender's lamps and lighting system and then explain how to light your scenes and characters. I'll also describe the process of rendering and talk about your options there. Finally, I'll give you a bit more information about the Sequence Editor and tell you how to output finished animated sequences in the format you want.

Lighting, rendering, and editing are all topics that deserve a great deal more attention than what I'll give you here. This chapter will scratch the surface of what there is to know about these aspects of CG animation and of Blender's capabilities in particular. See Chapter 18 for references and further information on these topics.

- ■ **Lighting Basics**

- ■ **Rendering Your Animation**

- ■ **Editing in the Sequence Editor**

Lighting Basics

Perhaps the area in which CG animation is most similar to traditional cinematography is in lighting. The methods used in CG lighting mirror the methods used in traditional film very closely. Lighting is a matter of selecting and placing lights and adjusting their values.

You can preview lighting setups in a number of ways, short of a full render. You can select view modes with the drop-down menu to the right of the Mode Select drop-down menu in the 3D viewport header, with the cube-like icon. In Solid view, as shown in Figure 11.1, although the object appears "shaded," this shading is specific to the Blender 3D viewport and does not reflect the lighting setup you will use to render (you can adjust the viewport shading setup in the user preferences, specifically, in the Solid OpenGL Lights area in the System panel). This is the default view mode, and on most ordinary computers it is much faster to work with than any other view (except, of course, wireframe).

To get a better sense of the shading based on the actual lighting of the scene, you can activate GLSL viewport rendering by selecting GLSL in the drop-down menu under Shading in the Display panel of the 3D viewport Properties Shelf. GLSL viewport rendering enables high-quality real-time rendering of textured objects if you choose Textured Viewport Shading from the drop-down menu in the 3D viewport header, as shown in Figure 11.2.

Figure 11.1

Solid view

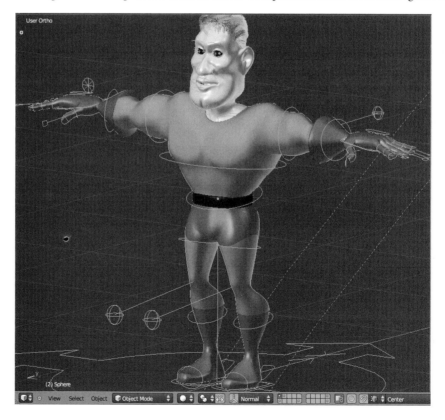

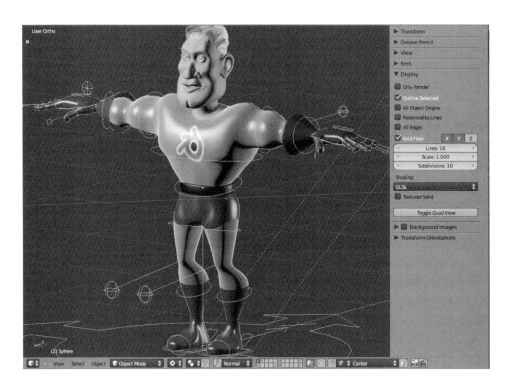

Figure 11.2

GLSL textured view mode

This view will update in real time as you move the lamp, but it is computationally expensive, so many processors will experience a significant lag. Some older video cards do not support GLSL, so this option may not be available.

These various tools can be useful in placing lights, but I find that for assessing lighting, nothing beats a proper render.

Cheats

A *cheat* in film lighting terms is an unnatural or unlikely use of light to give a desired effect. Because a film audience views a scene with fixed borders and from limited angles, it is possible to take many liberties even with real lights (adding light sources that would not exist in nature, moving light sources from their "true" positions, and so on).

Cheats are the norm in traditional lighting and even more so in CG lighting, in which moving lights costs nothing and adding lights costs only additional render time. Nevertheless, it is a good idea to have a sense of when you are using cheats and to consider the ultimate effect of your lighting on the viewer. Always have an idea of what the actual lighting situation in the 3D scene *should* be and where the viewer should perceive the light as coming from. Because they are by definition unnatural, cheats should never be obvious to the viewer.

Lamps

Lights are represented by the object type Lamp, which has the following subtypes:

- Point
- Spot
- Hemi
- Area
- Sun

The Lamp properties, shown in Figure 11.3, are accessible in the Properties window when a Lamp object is selected. The figure shows a typical example of the buttons and parameter values for a spotlight.

You select the lamp type from the buttons along the top of the Lamp panel. Below that, you access parameters such as the lamp's Distance, Energy, and RGB color values. In the Shadow panel, you access the parameters that govern the way the lamp casts shadows. In the case of spotlights, you can adjust the size and shape of the spotlight cone in the Spot Shape panel.

Figure 11.3

Lamp properties

Control over shadow properties is one of the areas in which CG lighting differs most drastically from traditional cinematographic lighting. Unlike reality, you can switch the shadows cast by a lamp on and off completely independently of the lamp itself. Furthermore, you have a choice between several different methods of calculating the shadows. You can use either buffer shadows, which are relatively quick to calculate and approximate, or ray shadows, which more accurately reflect the shapes and properties of the objects casting the shadows.

The graphic representation of the light in the 3D viewport tells you what shadow options are active on the light. In Figure 11.4, you can see the three options active for a spotlight, in order of appearance: no shadow, buffer shadow, and ray shadow.

Each of the different lamp types has specific properties and options that can be associated with it, and each has its own uses in practice. In this section, you'll look briefly at the different lamps and their effects.

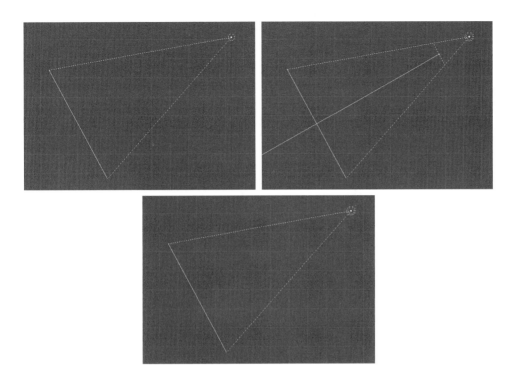

Figure 11.4
**No shadow,
buffer shadow,
and ray shadow
options for lights**

Point Lamp

The default lamp is a Point lamp (also known as an omnidirectional light) that can cast ray shadows or have shadows completely disabled but does not have an option for buff-

Figure 11.5

**Lighting by a
single lamp**

ered shadows. The Point lamp offers no control over the direction and throw of the light beam. Figure 11.5 shows an example of the light provided by the default lamp. (This render used the ray shadow option for cast shadows.)

Although something approximately like omnidirectional lights is common for household lamps and streetlights, there are not a lot of omnidirectional lights on movie sets and theatrical stages. But there *are* a lot of spotlights. The reason is simple: lighting requires control over where the light goes. Spotlights give this control; omnidirectional lamps don't.

In the present example, with a single lamp illuminating a single subject, the difference is negligible. However, when you have more than one subject and are concerned with lighting various parts of a scene convincingly with

shadows, highlighting, and fill lights, you very quickly run into situations in which you cannot do without the control you get with spotlights. Furthermore, because the default lamp casts light from a single point, it is inappropriate to use on its own for ambient light and is not especially suited for soft fill light. So, in spite of its apparent generality, the default lamp is actually quite limited in its practical applicability. It is useful as a prop light, for example when you have a lamp in your scene that needs to cast omnidirectional shadows. But for actual lighting, I rarely use the default lamp.

Spot Lamp

The spotlight is the most frequently used type of light in most lighting situations. The light has the same qualities as that of the default lamp, but you can control the beam. The direction, distance, width, and sharpness of the beam are all parameters you can set in the lamp buttons area.

Figure 11.6 shows the spotlight setup for the renders that you'll see in upcoming figures. Notice that the throw of the spotlight is clearly represented in the 3D viewport.

Unlike the default lamp, spot lamps have three options for shadows. These options have different applications, and there are some potential quirks to be aware of.

Figure 11.6

Spotlight setup in the 3D viewport

NO SHADOW

Using lamps with the shadow turned off is a classic CG cheat. In Figure 11.7, you see a render with shadow off. Note that the render still has places that are *in shadow*. They are simply the places where the light does not reach. In CG (although not in the physical world), the shading of objects is a completely separate phenomenon from cast shadows. Shadows thrown from one object onto another are calculated separately from the increase in energy on surfaces that are facing the light source.

Being able to turn off cast shadows can be very convenient; unwanted shadows are the bane of complex lighting setups in traditional lighting. However, there are issues to be aware of. Like any cheat, it is noticeable if used in an obvious way.

If your character is walking through the desert under a hot sun, turning off cast shadows is unnatural and distracting. In general, the light source that your audience perceives as the main light source (which might or might not truly be the main light source) should appear to cast shadows. Nonshadow lights are very good for fill lights, however, because they eliminate the real-world problem of double shadows that occurs when using fill lights that cast shadows.

When cast shadows are turned off, direct light affects surfaces naturally, but the shadows that shapes cast onto other surfaces are not calculated. In effect, objects and parts of objects become transparent in relation to each other. In some cases, the result can be problematic, causing the appearance of glowing nostrils or hair that appears to be lit from within.

BUFFER SHADOW

Buffer shadows work by making a grayscale render of the occluding objects from the light's point of view and then mapping that image onto surfaces behind the object. The shadow cast by the character's head onto his left shoulder in Figure 11.8 is a buffer shadow. Contrast this with the unnatural highlight in the previous figure, in which no shadows are cast.

Figure 11.7

Spotlight with no shadows

Figure 11.8

Spotlight with buffer shadows

Buffer shadows can be relatively quick to compute and are often very efficient to use. However, in certain cases the limitations of buffer shadows become apparent. Buffer shadows are cast at a fixed resolution, which must be set in advance. If the resolution is insufficient, the shadow can become pixelated. Only the Deep option for buffer shadows supports transparency, at the expense of greater computing time.

RAY SHADOW

Ray shadows are calculated by tracing the light beams emitted from the lamp, in a way most closely approximating the way that actual shadows fall in nature. This yields the most accurate shadows; the qualities of the shadows are entirely dependent on the lighting conditions.

Figure 11.9

Spotlight with ray shadows

The shadows in Figure 11.9 were generated using ray shadows. Because there is only one light source, they are dark and sharply defined, as would be the case in nature. They convey somewhat more definition of the shape of the character and handle the transparency of the eyes better than the Deep buffer shadows in the previous example. However, the cost is considerably longer render time with more complex scenes, so buffer shadows are often the better alternative.

Hemi Lights

Hemi lights provide a very diffuse light source, meaning that the rays of light are scattered and moving in many different directions. This is typical of light in many real-world conditions, in which much of the light you see is reflected. In this respect, hemi lights are both more "naturalistic" than spots and much less naturalistic because no lamp exists in nature that is capable of producing the kind of illumination that hemi lights produce.

In Figure 11.10, you can see the figure lit by a single hemi lamp, positioned in the same place as the spot from the previous renders. Note that although there is a tendency for the highlights to be on the right side of the figure and the shadows to be on the left side, there are actually no completely unlit areas anywhere on the figure.

Hemis are sometimes useful for nondescript, utilitarian lighting purposes. Putting a Hemi into a file with a model results in inoffensive and fully visible renders of your model, and it is a good choice for a default light for a model when the model itself is the emphasis of the render. It is not a very good choice for serious lighting, however, because it will result in a flat and lifeless appearance, as in the render in Figure 11.10.

The hemi light is not generally very good for showcasing objects or for lighting complex scenes. When working with animation, however, in which you try to reduce your render times per frame as much as possible, a hemi light can be useful as a fast, though not very accurate, outdoor fill light. When kept at low intensities and paired with a good key light for the sun, it can help you produce passable renders faster than with other methods. A hemi placed in the 3D space illuminates the whole rendered area. It does not matter where the hemi lamp actually is. The hemi is sensitive only to the angle at which it is placed. All the subjects of the scene will be lit from exactly the same angle, regardless of their position with respect to the hemi.

Figure 11.10

Hemi lamp

Sun Lamp

The sun lamp has the same uniform directional properties as the hemi lamp. Like the hemi, it will result in a uniform angle of lighting for all subjects in a scene, regardless of the lamp's position in the 3D space. All that matters is the angle of the lamp. This resembles the sun in that sunlight, because of the distance of its origin, behaves as a uniformly directed light source. The differences between sun and hemi lamps are that the sun lights only from a single direction, and that you can enable ray shadows with a sun lamp. As you can see in Figure 11.11, the lighting is much starker than that of the hemi.

In spite of its name, the sun lamp doesn't really produce what you typically think of as sunshine. You will need more than a single sun lamp to light a sunny outdoor scene convincingly. The main thing the sun lamp provides is a way to light multiple objects from a uniform direction, for example casting parallel shadows with only one light source.

Figure 11.11

Sun lamp

Area Lamp

Area lamps represent light that emanates from a large area and can be used in certain circumstances to represent the kind of light that comes from the sun, the moon, or an explosion. These lights are also often used in architectural rendering to show light from windows or banks of fluorescent lights and in product shots or any situation in which a real-life photographer or cinematographer would use diffusers.

Figure 11.12

Area light

As you can see in Figure 11.12, an area light produces a broad bath of light and can be useful to illuminate somebody peering into a fridge or being abducted by aliens, but it is unlikely to become your first-choice lamp for lighting characters in most situations.

Lighting Setups

In most cases, you should use more than one lamp for lighting subjects. With more complex scenes, it is almost a necessity. For the simplest lighting possible, a hemi lamp is tough to beat, but it will not result in the most attractive render. Another option is to use ambient occlusion, as you'll see later in this section.

Three-Point Lighting

Three-point lighting involves using three lamps, typically Spots, with the main illumination provided by the *key* light, shadows softened by a low-energy *fill* light, and highlights provided around the shaded portions of the form by backlighting, as shown in Figure 11.13.

Figure 11.13

Three-point lighting setup

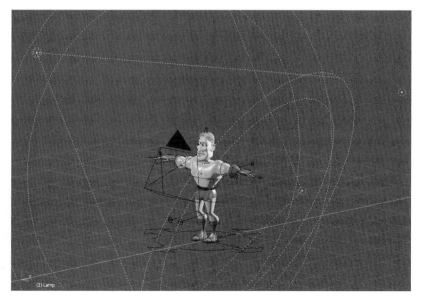

(2) Lamp

Any introductory textbook on lighting for film, photography, or CG will inevitably cover three-point lighting. It is such a ubiquitous and widely recognized approach to lighting that it has become almost a cliché. This, combined with the fact that it almost never occurs in nature and has fallen out of favor with filmmakers working in naturalistic styles, has led to something of a backlash against it among some CG practitioners.

Three-point lighting isn't naturalistic. But then, neither are bugging eyes, slow-motion bullets, or stretchy human heads. They are all cases of artistic license taken with realism to achieve a visual effect. As such, three-point lighting can have very effective uses.

Three-point lighting was developed as a means to use light to highlight and define shape, which was a basic goal in early cinema and remains a basic goal in most 3D animation. It should be regarded as an important tool, but you should also keep in mind that using stark three-point lighting can give a "studio portraiture" look to your work, so it should be used judiciously.

Figure 11.14
A render with three-point lighting

The render shown in Figure 11.14 uses the three-point lighting setup from the previous figure. In Figure 11.15, you can see the effect of each light. In the first render, only the key light is on. This mostly illuminates the subject but leaves the far side of the subject completely in the dark and undefined.

The second image shows the effect of only the low-energy fill light to the character's left side. This light serves to reduce the intensity of the shadows and brings the rest of the face into view. Note that even with two spots, the contrast is considerably starker than with a single hemi lamp, as you saw previously. Also, note that the fill light is set not to cast shadows. You don't want double shadows.

Figure 11.15
Breaking down the three-point setup: key light, fill light, and backlight

The third render shows the backlight only, which helps bring out the definition of areas that are in relative shadow and adds a dramatic aspect to the scene that is lacking with only the key and fill light.

Incidentally, showing you each light individually is an important thing to be able to do

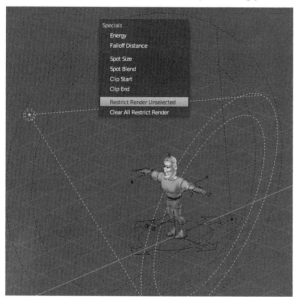

and involves a very handy but not too obvious feature. With complex lighting setups, you often want to see the exact effect of each light in isolation or of some subset of lights in isolation. To do this, you use the lighting Specials menu that you access with the W key in the 3D viewport in Object mode.

When you bring up the Specials menu, you will be presented with at least two options (more, if you happen to have a light selected): Restrict Render Unselected and Clear All Restrict Render. Choosing Restrict Render Unselected as shown in Figure 11.16 will suppress the effect of all lights that are not selected at the time. In this case, the rendered scene will be illuminated only by the key light. Choosing the Clear All Restrict Render option will set the scene to be illuminated normally by all active lights.

Figure 11.16

The Restrict Render Unselected option

Using Layers and Light Groups

Cheating lights is a very important part of creating good CG scenes, and for this reason there are a variety of ways to do it. Two of the most important are layers and light groups. On the Lamp properties panel for each light there is a This Layer Only check box. If this is selected, the light will only illuminate objects that it shares a layer with.

For even more control, you can assign a light group to individual materials. In the Material Properties window, in the Options panel, there is a field labeled Light Group. First, group the lights in the ordinary way that you want to affect that material. When you enter the group name in the Light Group field for that material, only the lights in that group will have an effect on that material.

Ambient Occlusion

Although it does not directly involve lights, ambient occlusion (AO) is worth mentioning in a discussion of lighting. AO is an approach to lighting or shading a scene in which illumination is calculated entirely based upon the geometry of the scene. It makes the assumption that the scene is lit with perfectly diffuse (randomly scattered) light and that the amount of occlusion (darkness) of a surface can be estimated based upon the surface's proximity to other surfaces.

If you look around the room you're in now, you will probably notice that wide-open areas such as walls are more brightly lit than the corners of the room and that the nooks and crannies between objects, such as the spaces between books on a bookshelf, are darker than other places. This is likely to be true for almost any ordinary lighting setup, and for this reason, it is possible to simulate without regard to the lights in a scene.

AO can be activated in the World Properties window, by selecting the box on the Ambient Occlusion tab. Figure 11.17 shows three cases that illustrate the effect of AO. The first image shows the three-point light setup from the previous section only, with no AO effect. Because of the backlighting, the shadow from the key light is very faint. In the second image, AO is used with the Multiply option to darken some surfaces based on their proximity to other geometry. Notice that the edges of the feet are shaded slightly where they meet the ground, resulting in a more anchored appearance. This is a main benefit of AO. In the third image, additive AO is used on its own to illuminate the scene, with all three lights disabled. This produces a perfectly diffuse illumination with no highlights and with shading based entirely on the geometry of the scene.

AO on its own can provide a very appealing source of illumination, particularly for displaying models with an emphasis on their shape. The main downside of AO is that it can add considerable render time.

Figure 11.17

Three-point lighting without ambient occlusion, three-point lighting with ambient occlusion (multiplicative), and ambient occlusion only (additive)

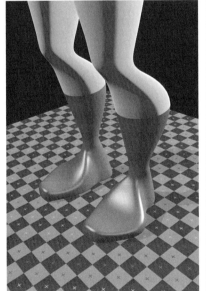  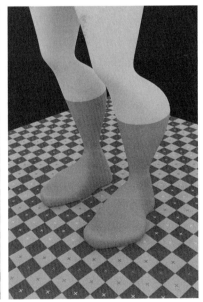

Rendering Your Animation

Rendering involves calculating all the various information Blender knows about the lighting and materials of a scene and producing a fully realized, detailed visual representation, that is, an image, of the scene. Rendering is analogous to taking a photograph of the scene.

When you are working in the 3D viewport, the scene is necessarily very much simplified. Rendering gives you the real deal, with reflections, transparency, strand effects, diffraction, and all of the other things that you don't ordinarily see while you're working on your scene.

Depending on the complexity of the scene, the vertex count, and the light effects you want to emulate, the process of rendering can take a long time and use a lot of computing resources. With moderately complex scenes, you will soon find that a major consideration in how you go about creating the scene is to ensure that it can be rendered in a reasonable amount of time on the hardware available to you. This is especially true for animation, which requires many frames to be rendered.

Render Properties

The Render properties window enables you to set the various parameters and options for rendering your scene. This window is shown in Figure 11.18.

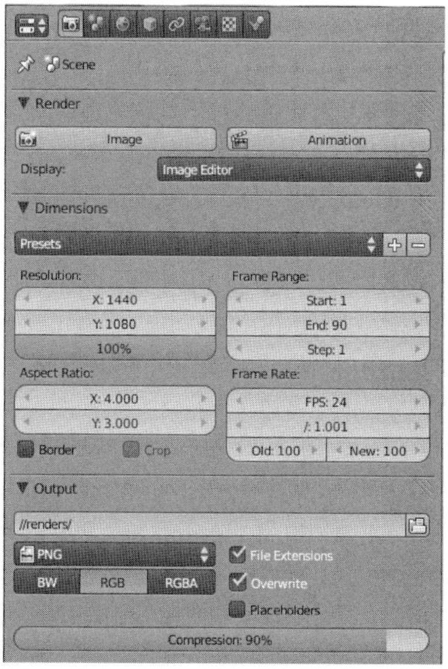

Figure 11.18

Render properties window

The Render panel simply contains the buttons for rendering a still image and a full animation and enables you to select how the resulting render will be displayed. The default is for it to be displayed in an Image Editor window.

The Dimensions tab gives options for the size and aspect ratio of the render. On the Output panel, you identify the location on your hard drive in which the finished animation renders will be sent and the file format in which they will be saved. The default for this is the /tmp/ directory, which is created automatically if it does not already exist. This is fine for very casual renders, but if you are rendering work that you want to do more with, for example, rendering a sequence of stills with the intention of later sequencing them in the Sequence Editor, it is a good idea to set a specific directory for the project (also, Mac OS X takes the temporary aspect seriously and deletes the content on /tmp/startup).

You can set a specific directory by simply putting the name of the desired output directory in the top field on the Output tab. Note that the directory's name must end with either a slash or a backslash (Blender considers both the same here) to specify that is a directory, as you can see in Figure 11.18. Without this, the name will be treated as a simple filename prefix, and the files will be placed in the directory above. The double slash you see in Figure 11.18 is shorthand for the same directory that the `.blend` file is saved to.

Output Formats

The Output tab also offers choices for the type of file to which you output your rendered animation. The type can make a big difference, so make sure to select the appropriate output format for what you're trying to do.

Movies and Stills

The first choice you need to make is whether to output the file to a movie or a still format. Most people eventually want their animation to be in some kind of movie format, but this does not necessarily mean you should select a movie format here when rendering your animation.

Rendering to a sequence of separate still images has the advantage of making it easy to stop and start rendering in the middle for whatever reason (you simply pick back up rendering the next still from the last still you rendered), which cannot be done with most movie formats. If, for whatever reason, you must kill a render midway, you will probably lose the whole output if it was a movie file.

Remember also that rendering animation is likely to take hours, even days (actually, the sky's the limit), on an ordinary computer. If you have a power outage three days into a weeklong render, you might want to have those three days worth of stills. Working with still sequences is very easy in the Blender Sequence Editor. You can do your initial renders to still frames and then render the sequence to a movie file in the Sequence Editor. For quick playback of still image sequences, the open source video player DJV Imaging can't be beat.

When you do finally render to a movie format, select a format with the appropriate degree of compression. Uncompressed file formats such as AVI Raw will create extremely large files. Unless you know for sure that you want an AVI Raw file, I do not recommend selecting this option. If you are rendering a movie for display on the Internet, a good option is AVI Codec, with an appropriate codec selected. MPEG4 is a compact and common codec for this kind of file.

Alpha Channel

One advantage that certain formats have over others is the presence of alpha channel information. In addition to RGB values, certain formats, such as Targa and PNG (but not JPEG or TIFF), allow a value to determine the transparency of portions of the image. By default, the background, which appears blue in renders, has a zero alpha value when rendered to these formats using the RGBA option on the Format tab of the render buttons. As you will see in the next section, this is often necessary for compositing tasks.

Off-Site Rendering

As mentioned previously, the rendering process is very demanding of computer resources. Although you can do a lot on an ordinary personal computer, certain things greatly increase the memory and time required to render your scenes. High vertex counts, large numbers of particles, lighting effects such as ambient occlusion or indirect lighting, antialiasing, some motion blur effects, and other factors can create a scene that takes ages to render and brings most personal computers to their knees. Even fairly simple scenes can easily become computationally expensive if these kinds of effects are present.

Rendering remains one of the prohibitive areas of animation; however, the available options are increasing. ResPower offers rendering services for Blender users, currently with options as low as $25 per month, with the option to quit at any time. This price is exclusive to Blender users, and the $20-per-month package for Blender users limits renders to a maximum of 15 minutes per frame, but their compute nodes are powerful enough that the service is very useful even given this restriction. Other inexpensive options are also available to Blender users who require more render time per frame, up to 90 minutes per frame for $125 a month. Check the website at www.respower.com for up-to-date pricing and offers.

Another promising possibility for off-site rendering is a project just getting underway to create distributed rendering networks, which make use of many different users' idle processor time. The Big and Ugly Rendering Project (BURP) is based upon the Berkeley Open Infrastructure for Network Computing (BOINC), which is software that enables computation-intensive tasks to be shared across a large network of computers, using the free processor time of many different machines to complete the tasks more efficiently than if a single machine were working on it. Members of the BURP project allow network rendering to be done on their computers at a low priority when the computers are not being used and collect points toward rendering their own work at a higher priority on the network. Membership and use of BURP are free. Currently, BURP is in Beta development, so there are some limitations to using it. Still, it is worth keeping an eye on. You can see the project at http://burp.boinc.dk/.

Editing in the Sequence Editor

It is often desirable to render animation frames to individual image files and to concatenate them into sequences in a separate step by using the Sequence Editor. You may want to break things down even further than single frames, rendering certain portions of a single image separately from other portions and putting them together later, before doing a final sequence render. This is called *compositing*, and Blender has a very powerful node-based compositing system that can be used for advanced compositing tasks. The node system is beyond the scope of this book, but you can accomplish simple compositing tasks without using nodes, and I will show one such simple example here to give you an example of how the Sequence Editor works.

Before beginning the Sequence Editor, I rendered the run cycle from Chapter 7 and sent its output files to the directory //renders/run/, as described in the previous section. I also rendered a second simple background animation to the directory //renders/background/. I rendered both to PNG files, and for the walk animation I used the RGBA option to make sure that the foreground image had alpha information encoded. You can find the rendered stills in the downloaded files accompanying the book, which will save you from having to do these renders yourself.

Adding Media

To use the Sequence Editor, you will want two instances of the Sequence Editor window open in your workspace. One of the windows should be set to Sequence view, and the other should be set to the Image Preview window. You select Sequence view with the leftmost of the three view buttons in the header. Image Preview is selected with the middle button.

In the Sequence view, press Shift+A to add a sequence strip. As you can see from the options here, there are a number of possibilities for the kind of media you can add. Select Images from the Add Sequence Strip menu, and go to the //renders/run/ directory in the File Browser window (or wherever the rendered frames of your foreground are located). Select all the files in the directory with the A key, and press Enter. This will take you back to the Sequence view, with a new sequence strip in tow representing the files you just selected, in order. Drag them so that the first frame lines up with frame 1 on the Timeline. With the arrow keys, you can now move through the Timeline and see the animation in the Image Preview window, as shown in Figure 11.19.

Figure 11.19

Running the animation sequence in the Sequence Editor

This is all you need to do to prepare to render to a movie file. You can now go to the render buttons and select your output format just as you would for an ordinary render. Select the start and end frames and the size of the picture, and click Animation in the

Render panel of the Render properties window. By default, Blender will render the contents of the Sequence Editor if there are any. If you want to render content from the 3D space while there are video strips in the Sequence Editor, you must deselect the Sequence check box in the Post-Production panel of the Render properties window.

Basic Compositing

You can now use a simple compositing feature of the Sequence Editor to drop a new background into the animation. As I mentioned, the background was created and rendered in advance to //renders/background/.

> This background animation was created with a very simple use of the array modifier, by the way, which you can find out more about in the references listed in Chapter 18.

Add the background animation images as you added the foreground images: press Shift+A and select all the images in the appropriate directory. Drag this strip to be flush with the previous strip. The channels are displayed bottom to top, and alpha information is not calculated by default. So when you put the new strip in channel 2, you do not see any difference in the display. Channel 1, our Captain Blender animation, is still displayed. You can try moving the strips around to see how this changes when the strips are positioned differently. Placing the foreground animation above the background animation will display only the background animation.

What you want to do is to create an effect strip that combines the two strips in certain ways. Select the foreground strip; then, holding Shift, select the background strip (the order matters here). To add the effect strip, press Shift+A as you would to add any other media. Select Alpha Under from the Effect Strip menu.

The resulting effect strip replaces its component strips in the display and causes the background to show through the zero alpha areas of the foreground. Blender's default background has an alpha value of zero, regardless of what its RGB values are. The resulting composite looks like the image previewed in Figure 11.20.

You can now render the sequence exactly as it appears in the Image Preview window.

Figure 11.20

A simple composite using Alpha Under

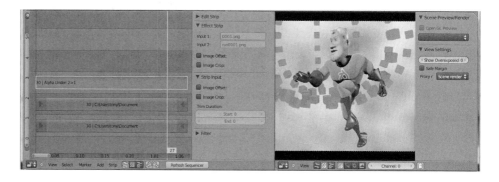

Sound

As you saw in Chapter 8, you can add sound files to the Sequence Editor for syncing. You can create a mixdown from sound files in the Sequence Editor and output this as a single sound file.

In the next chapter, you will take a brief look at Blender's powerful Python scripting capability and learn how to use currently existing Python scripts to make your job as an animator easier.

COMPOSITE NODES

In addition to enabling you to create node-based materials, Blender's Nodes system allows you to apply advanced image-compositing techniques that are tightly integrated with the render pipeline. One of the basic sources of input for the Composite nodes is Render Layers. On the Layers tab in the render buttons area, you can separate elements of your image so that they render to different render layers and in that way can be used as separate inputs into the composite nodes. When you select Composite in the render buttons and start a render, the output will be the final result of the network of composite nodes.

To use nodes for compositing, open a Nodes Editor window, toggle the Composite Nodes icon button (the Materials icon button is on by default), and select Use Nodes. When you do this, a render layer input node for render layer 1 and a composite node will appear. You can add new nodes by pressing Shift+A and selecting the node you want from the menu. Here is a very simple nodes setup with two render layers.

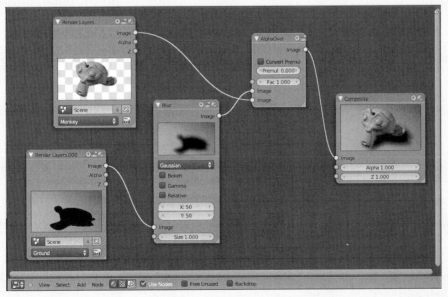

continues

COMPOSITE NODES *(continued)*

Render layer 1 includes the foreground with the monkey, and render layer 2 includes a plane upon which the monkey rests. These are rendered separately. The output from layer 2 is then used as input for a blur filter node, and the blurred output of this node is used as the backdrop in an Alpha Over node, which lays the monkey render over the background. The output of this node is sent to the composite node, which becomes the final output. The viewer node can be attached at any point to allow a better look at the composite at that point. Both the viewer's output and the composite image can also be viewed in the UV/Image Editor window.

More detail on using composite nodes is beyond the scope of this book. Check Chapter 18 for pointers on where to go to learn more.

CHAPTER 12

Python Scripts and Add-Ons

Python is a high-level, object-oriented scripting language. Powerful and relatively easy to learn, it is an obvious choice as a standard scripting language for an open source 3D application such as Blender. With Python scripts, you can automate a great deal of interaction with your 3D objects and scenes and add functionality without needing to touch actual Blender code. It is also a good way to try new functionality that can later be incorporated into Blender's C/C++ source.

With the changes in Blender 2.5, the Python API for developers has been completely overhauled, and a new interface for extending functionality in a totally seamless way through add-ons has been added. In this chapter, you'll take a look at the add-ons system and see some of the available add-ons. The rest of this chapter will give a brief overview of how Python works in Blender and point you at resources to learn more. People with some programming experience will find Python scripting for Blender relatively easy to pick up.

- **Using Add-Ons**

- **The Blender Python API**

- **Learning More about Blender Python Scripting**

Using Add-Ons

The Blender add-ons system enables anyone to extend Blender's functionality in a completely seamless way. Before the 2.5 release, integrating Python scripts into the interface was more difficult, with limitations on how they could be integrated. With add-ons, you simply activate the desired add-on in user preferences, and the functionality becomes available in a seamless and intuitive way in the interface. You don't have to think about loading or executing scripts, and you never have to even see any code if you don't want. Under the hood, this was made possible by major changes to both the Blender interface and the Python API that have resulted in nearly every value in Blender being made available for use in Python scripts. This has created a very powerful system for extending and prototyping functionality.

It's worth noting that Blender 2.5 and the revamped Python API are relatively new. All of Blender's previous script functionality has been rewritten from scratch. Some of the old scripts (such as sculpting) have already been made redundant by advances in Blender's core functionality, and most of the other important scripts have been ported already. However, scripts and add-ons are still under very active development, and there may be areas of functionality from previous scripts that have not yet been updated. This is particularly true of third-party scripts.

Activating Add-Ons

You can activate add-ons through the Add-Ons panel in the User Preferences window (Ctrl+Alt+U), as shown in Figure 12.1. Along the left of this panel is a list of add-on categories. Clicking one of these buttons will limit the listing to that category. In the figure, All is selected, giving a scrollable list of all the available add-ons.

Figure 12.1

The Add-Ons panel in User Preferences window

You can expand each entry of the list by clicking the arrow icon at the left of the entry to see a description of the add-on's functionality. You activate the add-on by clicking the check box at the right of the entry. When you do this, the add-on functionality is immediately added to Blender.

If that's all you do, the add-on functionality will disappear the next time you restart Blender. If you want the functionality to persist for future sessions, click the Save As Default button at the bottom of the User Preferences window.

The Install Add-On button enables you to use third-party add-ons that you download from other sites or create yourself.

Some Useful Add-Ons

The best overview of the add-on functionality available is the Add-Ons panel. The add-ons are clearly organized into meaningful categories and are named in a way that gives strong clues to their functionality. Expanding the description should give you all the information you need to find out what the add-on does. I strongly suggest browsing this list on your own to see the many interesting and useful features available.

The 3D View category includes various functionality connected to viewing the 3D space and organizing objects within the space. Alignment, navigation, and visualization tools can be accessed here, as well as some legacy menus used in previous Blender versions that have been discontinued or reorganized in the 2.5 interface. Figure 12.2 shows the functionality of the Measure Panel add-on, which enables the display of the exact distance between objects for precision placement.

Figure 12.2

The Measure add-on

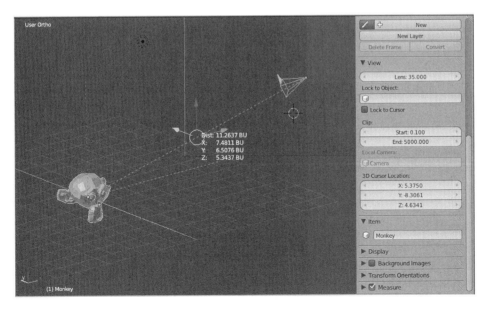

The Add Curve and Add Mesh categories provide additional object primitives for Curve and Mesh objects. The Curvaceous Galore add-on shown in Figure 12.3, for example, enables you to add ready-made parametric curve primitives of stars, cogwheels, flowers, splatter patterns, and other shapes. The ANT Landscape add-on for meshes enables you to add automatically generated landscape models, as shown in Figure 12.4.

Figure 12.3

The Curvaceous Galore add-on

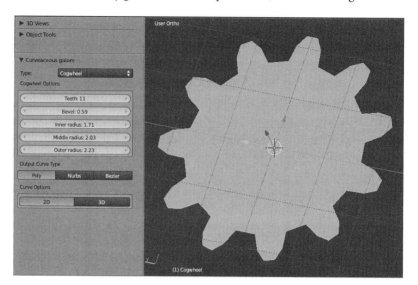

Figure 12.4

The ANT Landscape add-on

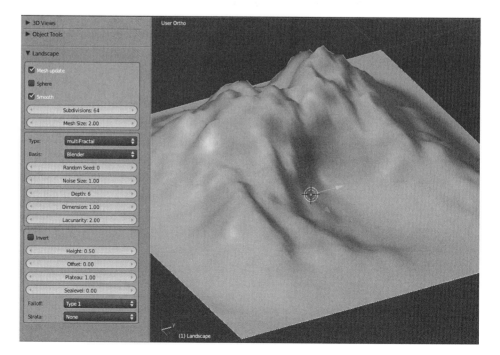

The Animation category includes an alternate method to create corrective shape keys and the Rotobezier add-on, which enables easy animation of curve shapes (this is particularly useful when rotoscoping for compositing but has many other possible uses as well).

The Import/Export category extends Blender's standard import and export functionality, enabling a wider variety of file types to be read from and written to.

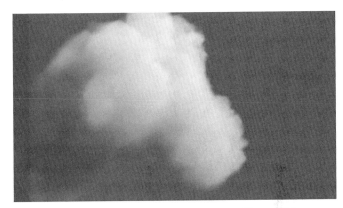

The Mesh category extends mesh datablock-related and mesh modeling–related functionality.

The Object category includes miscellaneous functionality that deals in some way with 3D objects at the object level. This category includes the Cloud Generator add-on for creating clouds like the one shown in Figure 12.5.

Figure 12.5

A cloud created with the Cloud Generator add-on

The other categories include Render, Rigging, System, and Text, all of which currently contain only one or two add-ons each. The Rigify add-on in the Rigging category should be familiar to you. You learned about it in Chapter 4.

The Blender Python API

The best introduction to scripting with the Blender API is on the official Blender website at `http://wiki.blender.org/index.php/Dev:2.5/Py/API/Introhttp://blenderartists.org/forum/showthread.php?t=164765&page=21`. There is also an excellent thread in the Blender Artists forum at `http://blenderartists.org/forum/showthread.php?t=164765`. At the time of this writing, the API remains somewhat subject to change, and it is beyond the scope of this book to give an in-depth introduction to Python scripting. The official web documentation is an excellent start if you want to try your hand at scripting.

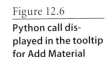

Figure 12.6

Python call displayed in the tooltip for Add Material

An even closer-to-home reference for the Blender Python API is Blender. You may already have noticed that the mouseover tooltips display a line of Blender code for most interface elements in Blender, as shown in Figure 12.6. Also, if you pull down the

Info bar window at the top of the default screen configuration to display its contents, you will see that it prints the Python call for every operation you do on the screen, as shown in Figure 12.7. If you want to know the Python call to rotate an object, simply rotate the object and watch what gets output to that window.

Figure 12.7

Python calls displayed in the Info window

```
bpy.ops.object.editmode_toggle()
bpy.ops.object.editmode_toggle()
bpy.ops.transform.translate(value=(0.296208, 2.66082, 1.61467), constraint_axis=(False, False, False), constraint_orientation='GLOBAL', mirror=False, pro
portional='DISABLED', proportional_edit_falloff='SMOOTH', proportional_size=1, snap=False, snap_target='CLOSEST', snap_point=(0, 0, 0), snap_align=False,
 snap_normal=(0, 0, 0), release_confirm=False)
bpy.ops.object.material_slot_add()
bpy.ops.transform.translate(value=(0.46104, -1.96282, 0.266106), constraint_axis=(False, False, False), constraint_orientation='GLOBAL', mirror=False, pr
oportional='DISABLED', proportional_edit_falloff='SMOOTH', proportional_size=1, snap=False, snap_target='CLOSEST', snap_point=(0, 0, 0), snap_align=False
, snap_normal=(0, 0, 0), release_confirm=False)
bpy.ops.transform.rotate(value=(0.657678,), axis=(-0.758124, -0.259199, -0.598384), constraint_axis=(False, False, False), constraint_orientation='GLOBAL
', mirror=False, proportional='DISABLED', proportional_edit_falloff='SMOOTH', proportional_size=1, snap=False, snap_target='CLOSEST', snap_point=(0, 0, 0
), snap_align=False, snap_normal=(0, 0, 0), release_confirm=False)
```

Learning More about Blender Python Scripting

To use these handy Blender Python references, you will need to know at least the basics of Python programming. You can find plenty of online tutorials on Python syntax. Chapter 6, "Python for the Impatient," of my book *Mastering Blender* gives a quick and easy introduction to the basics of Python. Although the Blender Python API described in other chapters of that book is now obsolete, the general introduction to Python contained in Chapter 6 remains an option for getting your feet wet with Python. You can find a much more thorough alternative in the official documentation on the Python web page at `http://docs.python.org/py3k/tutorial/index.html`.

However you decide to get started, you won't need anything other than Blender 2.5 to do so. A great new development in Blender 2.5 is the addition of a fully functional built-in Python interactive command-line interface, shown in Figure 12.8. Many introductory Python tutorials assume that you are working in such a command-line environment. In the past, you would have needed a separate development environment outside of Blender to work in this way. Now all you need is right there.

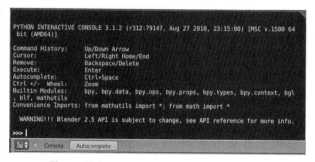

Figure 12.8

Blender's built-in Python command line

Once you have a handle on Python, you will be able to create your own extended functionality for Blender. The possibilities really are endless, so I hope that this very brief overview has piqued your interest.

Part III of this book takes a look at how Blender has been used in large-scale projects, requiring the reuse and sharing of 3D data. Looking at how the *Sintel* and *Plumiferos* teams handled these tasks will yield even more insight into how to use Blender's tools to create first-rate animation projects.

Blender in Production

Blender is still *an underdog in the world of professional-quality CG animation, but a growing number of major animation projects have used Blender as their primary tool. In this part, you'll learn about the Blender Open Movie Project and the movies it has produced, and you'll take a peek behind the scenes of the world's first Blender-made feature-length commercial film* Plumiferos. *There is a lot to learn from each of these productions, both in how Blender was incorporated into the workflow and in the details of how the animators used Blender to rig and animate expressive and engaging characters. The rigs you'll look at from those productions will provide you with a lot of interesting ideas and approaches to add to what you learned in Parts I and II about creating and animating characters. Seeing how Blender can be used in this environment might even inspire you to think bigger when planning your own projects.*

CHAPTER 13 ■ THE FRUITS OF FREEDOM: OPEN MOVIES AND OPEN CONTENT

CHAPTER 14 ■ A LOOK INSIDE THE BLENDER OPEN MOVIES

CHAPTER 15 ■ BEHIND THE SCENES WITH *SINTEL*

CHAPTER 16 ■ FEIFI THE CANARY—*PLUMIFEROS* TAKES WING

The Fruits of Freedom: Open Movies and Open Content

Software such as Blender cannot be developed in a vacuum. It is imperative that developers work hand in hand with highly skilled, dedicated artists to improve the software in the ways that really matter to creators. The developers of Blender, led by Ton Roosendaal, have taken this fact to heart. It was for this reason that the Blender Institute was established as an entity to put Blender to use in actual, fully realized productions. In the past five years, the Blender Open Movie Project has produced three stunning short movies, a game, and a growing series of training DVDs by some of the finest professional Blender users in the world, all released as open content under licenses that allow you to freely copy and reuse the material as you want. This chapter will introduce these projects and their backgrounds.

You'll also take a brief look at some of the questions related to using free software in professional production. There are sometimes misunderstandings about the implications of using open source software on for-profit projects, and discussions about releasing content under a Creative Commons license can sometimes obscure the issue even further. This chapter ends by clarifying what these various licenses are and what they might mean to you and your project.

- The Blender Institute
- The Blender Open Movie Project
- Free and Open Licenses for Software and Content

The Blender Institute

A danger of developer-driven programming projects is that they can lose sight of the needs of ordinary users. This can be more or less of a problem depending on the nature of the software. If the software is primarily used by highly skilled developers themselves, then it's not likely to be a problem. If the software is a broadly used application such as a browser, then the development team must take ordinary users' needs into consideration. In the case of 3D software, the target user base is narrower and more highly skilled than browser users, but their primary skill set is not programming; it's 3D content creation. This presents a special challenge. 3D software created without the constant input of active and highly skilled users would stand little chance of staying relevant to the user community.

For this reason, ensuring that Blender is used in actual productions has been part of the Blender development model for years. With the creation of *Elephants Dream* in 2006, Blender development and Blender-based animated movie production have had a symbiotic relationship, with highly skilled artists and highly skilled software developers (and in a few cases, individuals who are very highly skilled as both) working side by side to improve the software.

In 2007 the Blender Institute was established as a related but separate entity from the nonprofit Blender Foundation. The Blender Foundation is now solely concerned with the software development side of the equation, while the Blender Institute deals with more commercial and potentially risky concerns such as open content production, training, and merchandising. The most exciting work that the Blender Institute does is the Blender Open Movie Project movie productions and the associated Blender Open Movie Workshop training DVD series.

The Blender Open Movie Project

The Blender Open Movie Project has several goals. The first is to give talented Blender artists an opportunity to create their best work with as much freedom as possible in a well-supported professional setting. The second is to improve Blender itself by providing intensive, high-quality user feedback, bug reporting, and financial support for developers. The third is to produce high-quality open content to showcase Blender's technical capabilities and to serve as learning material for the Blender user community. To meet these goals, it made sense to release the artwork created with the project as open content under the Creative Commons license.

Although the Creative Commons license and the GPL are unrelated legally, they are closely aligned in spirit. Both of them acknowledge the importance of sharing ideas and building upon previous work as essential aspects of the creative process, while protecting the right of creators to receive credit for their work and to maintain some control over potential uses.

Elephants Dream

The first project to create an open movie was named Orange, and the resulting movie was *Elephants Dream* (see Figure 13.1). This movie was produced directly by the Blender Foundation, and its success was the motivating factor for establishing the Blender Institute. *Elephants Dream* was produced by Ton Roosendaal, founder of the Blender Foundation and chief developer of Blender. The film was directed by Bassam Kurdali.

Figure 13.1

Proog in *Elephants Dream*

The film was intended as a vehicle to demonstrate the potential of Blender in a large-scale production and also to spur the development of Blender in areas in which weaknesses became apparent. Production of the film was further constrained to using only open source software for all visual aspects of the film (the music was not subject to this constraint), which meant that functionality that could not be adequately found in other open source software, such as professional-quality video compositing, had to be built in to Blender.

The film itself is a dark and enigmatic piece of surrealist art. The story follows the journey of two strange men through the bowels of a bizarre and dangerous mechanical world, exploring the drastically (and eventually fatal) ways in which the two men perceive their surroundings. To be sure, the story is not everyone's cup of tea. The creators of *Elephants Dream* took the freedom afforded by the software and the Creative Commons release very much to heart, eschewing any pretense of trying to make the film marketable or broadly accessible. Instead, they gave themselves complete creative freedom and created a short film that is both visually stunning and thematically provocative. In spite of the abstruseness of its subject matter, the film garnered a considerable amount of press attention for the way it was created and released, including a feature article in the *Wall Street Journal*.

As a demonstration of Blender's capabilities, *Elephants Dream* holds up very well. Using advanced character modeling and animation tools and specially developed compositing functionality, *Elephants Dream* more than demonstrates that Blender is ready for prime time, visually speaking. Given the time and budgetary restrictions on the production and considering that many members of the team were relatively inexperienced in working in a production environment, the results are impressive. It's also apparent from the freely available "making of" interviews that the team produced progressively better work as members became accustomed to working together.

The film is freely available in multiple formats—both as ordinary downloads and as BitTorrent files on the film's official website (`www.elephantsdream.org`). You can also find the "making of" interviews and all the source `.blend` files at that website. You can also purchase the DVD, which has all these features as well as both NTSC and PAL versions of the film. The DVD that accompanies this book includes a high-resolution video of the film as well as all the source `.blend` files.

The Orange project also yielded a training video, Bassam Kurdali's *Mancandy FAQ*, which gives a detailed overview of the rigging and animation techniques at the heart of *Elephants Dream*.

Big Buck Bunny

The second project was planned from the outset to be a bit sweeter and a lot furrier than *Elephants Dream* and so it received the project name Peach. The Peach team, headed by director Sacha Goedegebure, wanted to add a level of Disney-esque appeal not present in *Elephants Dream* and to take a more conventional approach to storytelling. These goals meshed perfectly with the development-related goal of putting the new hair particle functionality to rigorous use to make it more stable and usable. The Peach project resulted in the open movie *Big Buck Bunny* (see Figure 13.2), an irreverent send-up of all that is cute and furry.

In addition to advancements in particle hair, *Big Buck Bunny* took advantage of improvements in many other areas of Blender, notably in the armatures and rigging system.

Just as in the case of *Elephants Dream*, the movie was funded through a combination of outside grants and advance sales of the DVD. Also, like the previous movie, all digital assets, textures, and `.blend` files for *Big Buck Bunny* were released as open content along with the movie. DVD extras included tutorials and over-the-shoulder artist sessions.

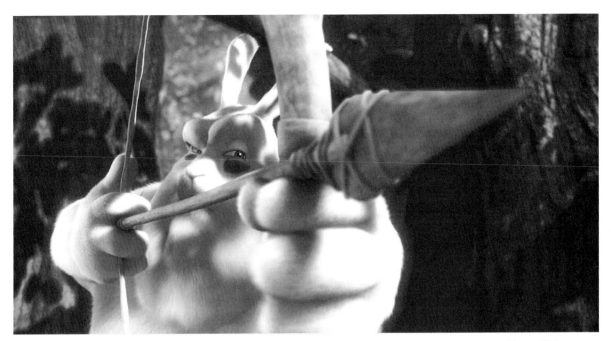

Figure 13.2

The eponymous hero of *Big Buck Bunny*

Stills and clips from *Big Buck Bunny* made their way into a variety of unexpected places. As open content, it was ideal for use as sample video in showrooms or online. The *Big Buck Bunny* website is located at www.bigbuckbunny.org.

The Peach project also contributed to the Open Movie Workshop series of training videos with two-time open-movie veteran Andy Goralczyk's *Creature Factory* training DVD on scene creation and animator William Reynish's *Learning Character Animation with Blender* training DVD.

Yo Frankie!

Enthusiasm from Blender Game Engine users had built up to the point that it made sense for the next open project to be a game, rather than a movie. Assets and designs from *Big Buck Bunny* were used to get the project started on the right foot. The flying squirrel character from *Big Buck Bunny* was promoted to the leading role for Project Apricot, which ultimately resulted in the game Yo Frankie! (see Figure 13.3). As usual, the content was released as open content. You can find out more about Yo Frankie! at www.yofrankie.org.

Project Apricot's contribution to the Open Movie Workshop came in the form of Pablo Vasquez's outstanding *Venom's Lab* training video, which deals with a wide variety of techniques in modeling, texturing, lighting, and other areas.

Figure 13.3

Frankie the Flying Squirrel kicks a rat in Yo Frankie!

Sintel

The most recent open movie was the result of the long-awaited Durian project, carried out side by side with the development of the recoded Blender 2.5. The focus for Durian was on action, physics simulation, and engaging storytelling. For the first time, the team brought on an outside screenwriter to ensure that the story was as solid as it could be. The team adopted a more realistic style for this project than in the previous movies, inspired by such films as *Final Fantasy: Advent's Children*. The Durian project was bigger in every respect than the previous projects; more people worked on the project and for a longer time. The result, the epic *Sintel*, directed by Colin Levy, did not disappoint. It is an action-packed short fantasy film about a young adventuress and the baby dragon she adopts (Figure 13.4). It is making the rounds at film festivals at the time of this writing. Check out its website at `www.sintel.org`.

Sintel was released as a four-DVD box set packed full of extras, including hours worth of in-depth tutorial videos from members of the creative team. In addition, concept artist David Revoy released the *Chaos and Evolutions* training DVD on creating 2D artwork with open source software as the latest installation of the Open Movie Workshop series.

Figure 13.4

Sintel and her baby dragon friend

Looking Forward to Mango and Gooseberry

As you read this, the Blender Institute is as active as ever preparing for the upcoming Project Mango, which will focus on integrating Blender-created CG content with live-action footage.

Beyond Mango lies Project Gooseberry, which is currently planned to be the Blender Institute's first-ever feature-length movie. At the time of this writing, no further decisions about that project have been made public, but it will surely be an exciting step in the history of Blender and the Blender Open Movie Project.

Free and Open Licenses for Software and Content

Just as it's worth understanding the similarities in spirit between open source software licenses and open content licenses, it's also important to have a sense of how they differ. Open content is central to how the Blender Institute views its creative mission, but this is not necessarily the case for Blender-made projects. The fact that Blender is open source has no implications for the licensing of content made with Blender in general (I'm excluding the case of stand-alone games created with the Blender Game Engine because, to be honest, the back-and-forth on this topic makes my head spin, and at the time of this writing I'm not entirely clear on what the options are for games). In this section, I hope to give a brief overview of what some relevant licenses apply to and what their implications are.

Any discussion I attempt of licenses or copyright-related topics needs to be prefaced with the standard disclaimer: I am not a lawyer, and if you have any questions about how you should proceed with licensing or handling of copyrights, you should seek qualified legal advice. Anything I say on the subject is accurate to the best of my knowledge, but I might be insufficiently informed, out-of-date, or just plain wrong about details. I'll include links to refer to the source documents where pertinent, but nevertheless, if you have legal questions, you should not rely on this book solely for your answers.

The license under which you release your work codifies the permissions that you are granting the public with regard to your work. Regardless of which license you choose to release the work under, you are the owner of the copyright for what you create. Individuals, companies, and organizations can feel fully at ease using open source software in their creative pipelines, knowing that their own rights with regard to their work will not be affected.

With that said, let's take a look at these licenses.

GNU Public License

The GNU Public License (GPL) is one of the best known and most widely used licenses for what is referred to as free software or open source software. Blender's code is released under the GPL. You can read the full text of the GPL at `www.gnu.org/copyleft/gpl.html`. The license was created by Richard Stallman, who is known for his advocacy of freely distributable, freely modifiable code. The GPL states, in essence, that the licensed code can be copied, modified, and redistributed by anybody without restriction, provided that modifications are clearly identified as such and that the subsequent derived code is also released under the GPL and according to the guidelines set out in the GPL.

The GPL is fairly strict in its insistence that free code interact primarily with other free code, although explicit exceptions are made for operating systems. Issues can arise with the use of nonopen libraries or APIs, so proprietary plug-ins for GPL software or GPL-derived plug-ins written for proprietary software can potentially infringe on the GPL. Other licenses exist, such as the Limited GPL and the Berkeley Software Distribution (BSD) license, which allow more freedom of interaction between free and proprietary code. You can learn more about the BSD license at `http://en.wikipedia.org/wiki/BSD_license`.

The writer of the code always retains the copyright to the code, and although that person can release non-GPL copies of their code at any time, any code already released under the GPL will remain so. Furthermore, with a code base as broad as Blender's, there are numerous contributing coders and therefore many copyright holders, all of whom would have to agree to change the GPL status of future releases of their code if such a thing were to be considered (it isn't).

The GPL deals with software. Specifically, it deals with publicly distributed software. You can do whatever you want with GPL code within the confines of your own project, and licensing of derived code need never become an issue until you decide to release your code to the world. In-house plug-ins or alterations are not a problem and do not need to follow any special criteria. Furthermore, the GPL bears *no relation at all* to content created with the software. Content you create with Blender or any other GPL software is copyrighted to you in the same way as content created in any other kind of software.

Creative Commons License

The Creative Commons license covers content and is an option for licensing your artistic creations. The decision to license your work under the Creative Commons license is entirely unrelated to the tools you used to create the work. Using open source software does not obligate you to release your work under a Creative Commons license.

There are several alternatives for Creative Commons licenses. You can license your work to be freely copied but require that the work be attributed to you and that copies of your work be restricted to noncommercial uses. You can allow commercial uses but require attribution, or you can relax the requirement for attribution.

If you want people to be able to freely copy, show, and distribute your work on the Web without fear of copyright repercussions, releasing your work under a noncommercial Creative Commons license might be a good choice. You remain the copyright holder, and you can revoke the license at any time. Your own use of the work (for example, if you sell it or license it for broadcast) might have an impact on whether you can continue to release it under the Creative Commons license if the buyer or broadcaster objects.

Blender Artistic License

The Blender Artistic license is a variation on the Creative Commons license and applies to images, .blend files, and animations. It allows copying and modification of files with some restrictions to ensure attribution. Material hosted on the www.blender.org website is required to be released under this license or the more permissive Open Content license. As in the case of the Creative Commons license, releasing work under this license is voluntary on the part of the creator and is not implied by using Blender to make the work.

CHAPTER 14

A Look Inside the Blender Open Movies

It's hard to overstate the benefits to Blender and the Blender community that have arisen from the Blender Foundation's Open Movie Project and its resulting movies, *Elephants Dream*, *Big Buck Bunny*, and *Sintel*. Not the least of these benefits are the opportunities to learn about animated filmmaking in Blender afforded by the free release of the original "source" files—the .blend files used to produce the movie—to the public. Online blogs for the projects are also a wonderful way to keep up with the developments as the projects progress. In this chapter, you'll take a peek into the process and look at some of the techniques behind the scenes.

- ■ **Learning from *Elephants Dream***
- ■ **Nonhuman Rigs in *Big Buck Bunny* and *Sintel***
- ■ **The Production Pipeline**

Learning from *Elephants Dream*

The two protagonists of *Elephants Dream* (see Figure 14.1) are anything but your typical cuddly animated film stars. The characters are unsettling and off-putting; Proog is an irritable, domineering, and very likely insane old man, whereas Emo is a sniveling, somewhat diseased-looking man-child. Both of them are awkward, edgy, incongruous people, and these characteristics are expressed in the way the characters are modeled. The production files are available as `.torrent` downloads from the official web page of the project at `www.elephantsdream.org`.

Figure 14.1

Proog and Emo in *Elephants Dream*

As you can see in the wireframe depictions of the two characters shown in Figure 14.2, the mesh structure of each character's body is deliberately jagged and shaky-looking. The mesh structure of the character's clothing, in particular, stretches and bunches and tugs in a way that suggests the material is about to break apart. Proog's trousers are tired and slack, bunching up slightly around his ankles and shins, whereas Emo's jacket appears to be so ill-fitting and constricting as to call to mind a straightjacket.

The circles you see all over these `.blend` files indicate forces. In particular, you see many curve guides used to guide the character's hair. With the Captain Blender rig, you only scratched the surface of what can be done with particle hair and curve guides, using a few guides to create a very simple hairstyle. Curve guides are a powerful but painstaking tool. When you need slightly more complicated or realistic hair effects, such as in these blends, you will quickly find that you need a large number of curve guides. To learn about how the *Elephants Dream* hair effects are accomplished, I suggest you spend some time with these files, editing and adjusting the various curve guides.

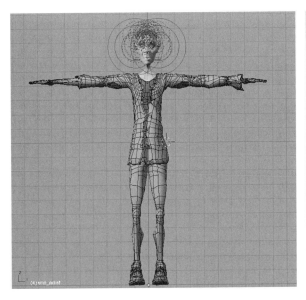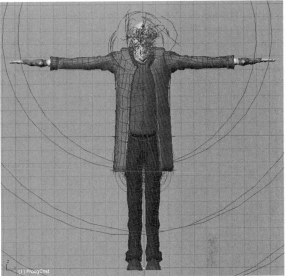

Figure 14.2
**Emo and Proog
meshes**

Figure 14.3 shows a few examples of shape keys on Emo. (It also provides a very clear view of the curve guides influencing Emo's hairstyle in the bad old days before the hair particle system was updated for *Big Buck Bunny*. As you can see, at the time, even fairly rudimentary hair effects were extremely difficult to obtain.) The approach to facial animation taken by the *Elephants Dream* character modelers is analogous to the approach I described in Chapter 8, using driven shape keys to get most of the expressions.

Figure 14.3
**Some facial shape
keys on Emo**

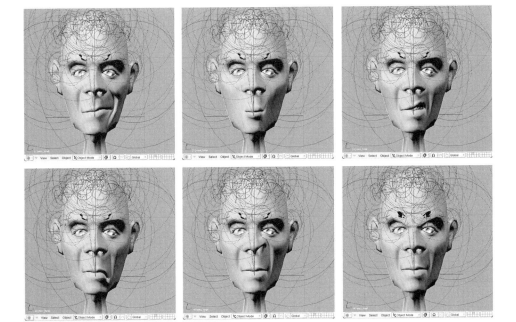

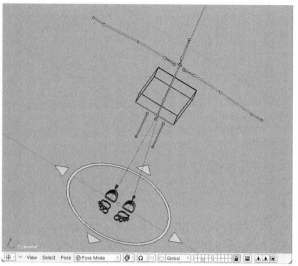 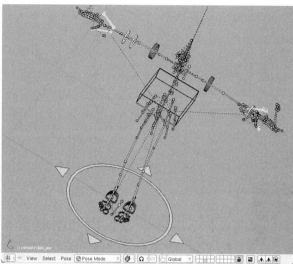

Figure 14.4

Emo's armature

Even though the armature and rigging system in Blender has been much improved and commonly used rigging techniques have been refined in subsequent open movies, it's instructive to look at the rigging techniques used in *Elephants Dream* for insight into how to solve more advanced rigging problems.

Figure 14.4 shows Emo's armature. The first image shows only the bones needed to do basic full-body posing; the second image shows the full armature with all bone layers displayed. An animator never needs to touch or see many of these bones. They are used for a variety of functions. Some of them are used as "fan bones," which move based on the movements of other bones to help give more control over joint deformations; other bones are used for other functional purposes within the armature.

Note the use of custom bone shapes here. The bone to control the swivel of Emo's hips, for example, is shaped like a flattened box around his hips. The root bone of the armature appears as a compass-like circular base to the character, and the foot controls are shaped like the parts of the feet that they control.

Another Approach to Hand and Foot Rigging

For the Captain Blender rig, you created the rig automatically using the Rigify add-on. That functionality wasn't available to the creators of *Elephants Dream*, and they approached the challenge of hand and foot rigging in a different way from the way they are done in Rigify. The hand and foot rigs in *Elephants Dream* are very simple and afford a high degree of control and ease of posing. For ordinary biped character rigging, I still recommend Rigify, but understanding the rigs described here will be very useful to you when you need to solve a rigging problem that is not dealt with automatically by Rigify.

Hands

In Figure 14.5, you can see the basic deform bones of the fingers. The three bones of each finger make up an inverse kinematic (IK) chain, with the fingertip bone as the IK solver (indicated by the dotted line extending from the high-lighted bone to the base of the index finger—in Figure 14.5, the IK targets are not shown). Note that the smaller bones you see branching off at the knuckles are fan bones used to correct mesh deformations. I'll talk about fan bones shortly, but for now you can disregard them.

Using IK chains for fingers is not a bad idea, but it can make it difficult to get the fingers to bend consistently in the correct manner. What makes the *Elephants Dream* hand rig interesting is how the IK target is used. In Figure 14.6, you see the IK target. The fingertip IK solver is IK con-strained to the finger-length highlighted bone, which in turn is connected/parented to the same hand bone to which the root of the finger IK chain is parented. With this setup in place, it is possible to simply rotate this fin-ger controller to have the entire finger follow the rotation. What's more, *scaling* this bone in pose mode with the S key results in bending or extending the finger, as you can see in Figure 14.7. Figure 14.8 shows a hand pose with the deform-ing bones hidden—only the bones that are necessary to pose the hand are shown. This is a very nice solution to finger posing.

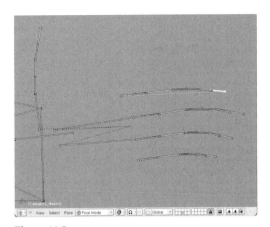

Figure 14.5

Finger deform bones form an IK chain.

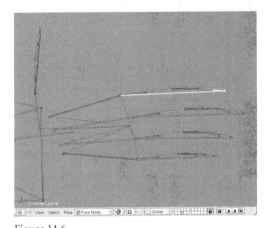

Figure 14.6

IK target bones are connected to the base of the fingers.

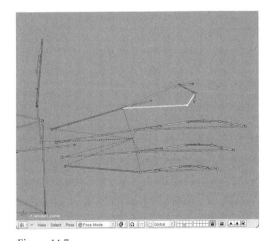

Figure 14.7

Scaling the IK target bends the finger.

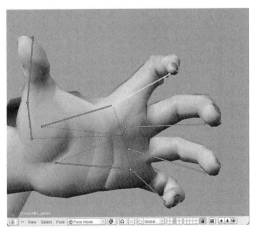

Figure 14.8

Posing is simple with this IK setup.

Feet

As with the hand rig, the foot rig for the *Elephants Dream* characters accomplishes a lot with a relatively simple setup—without using Action constraints. Figure 14.9 shows the full bone structure of the feet in B-bones view. The most immediately notable aspect of the feet is the use of custom bone shapes to identify the toes bone, the foot bones represented by the heel portion, and the ankle bones represented by the small, roundish custom bones to the rear of the ankle joint. (I am dropping the preceding L_ and R_ from the names of the bones here.) These custom bones are the only bones that the animator needs to touch.

Figure 14.9

Foot rigs for Proog

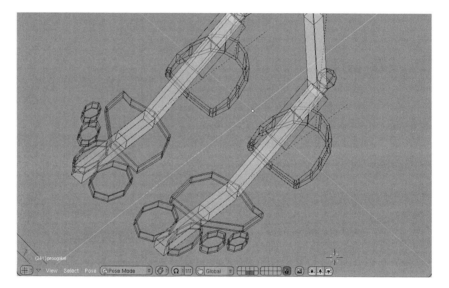

In Figure 14.10, you can see a view of the foot rig from the side and in octahedron view. In the figure, Figure 14.10a shows the foot rig as it actually is, and Figure 14.10b shows it exploded and labeled to clarify the placement and relationships of the bones. Dotted lines indicate nonconnected parenting. Connected bones are shown in their correct positions, attached by joints to their parent bones. The principal parent relationships here are between the foot bone and its nonconnected children. These include the toes bone and the ankle bone. Note the placement and position of the ankle bone. Its actual location is somewhat different from where the custom bone shape appears. Parenting the toes bone to the foot bone enables the tip of the foot to follow the overall movement of the foot and also enables the tip of the foot to be raised and lowered by rotating the foot bone. The ankle bone controls the angle of the foottop bone through a Copy Rotation constraint on the foottop bone, targeted to ankle. The foottop bone is also constrained to point to the ankle by an IK constraint. The ankle bone is also the connected parent of the legIK bone; in this way, raising or lowering the foot bone controls the position of the IK target for the leg, enabling the foot to be moved around.

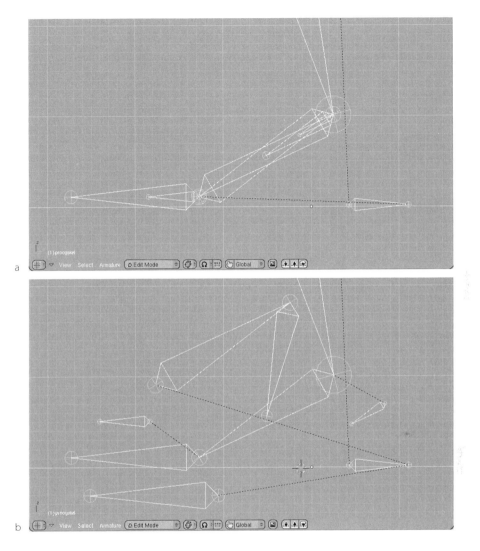

Figure 14.10

Bones of the foot

The ankle bone, being a child of foot, can also be rotated independently, as you can see in Figure 14.11. In Figure 14.11a and b you can see the rest pose and the heel-up pose of this bone; Figure 14.11c shows the actual position of the bone (because custom bones can be arbitrary shapes, it is not always possible to see where the pivot and influence of a bone are without looking at the bone in its original shape). Note that in the Transform Properties window all transforms are locked on this bone except for X rotation. Rotating this bone has two main effects: it raises the upper end of the bone, thus raising legIK and bending the leg to accommodate the raised ankle, and it rotates the foot top, which is constrained to follow the ankle's rotation. In Figure 14.11, you can also see the behavior of the fan bones of the foot, which I'll discuss shortly.

Figure 14.11

**Ankle rotation:
a) no rotation,
b) in a heel-up pose,
c) displayed without
custom bone shape**

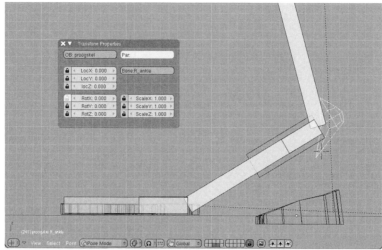

a

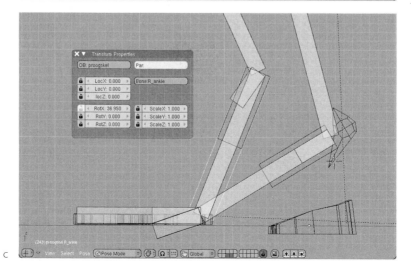

b

c

Figure 14.12 shows a few simple leg poses that involve moving the foot with the foot bone, raising the heel with the ankle bone, and raising the toe by rotating the foot bone. Recall that these last two are the same motions for which you used Action constraints in the Captain Blender rig created in Chapter 4.

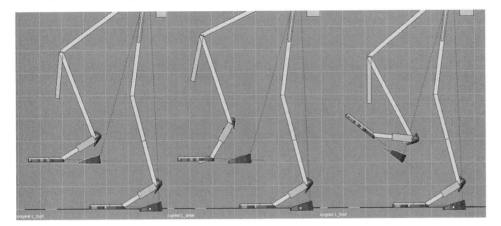

Figure 14.12

Leg poses involving the foot bone

Fan Bones

Fan bones are bones used to improve deformations by mitigating the localized effect of a sharply angled joint in an armature. In some cases, they can be used in place of or in addition to the bone-driven shape key approach in order to improve joint deformations, as discussed in Chapter 5.

In the leg poses shown in Figure 14.13, visible fan bones are indicated with arrows. The fan bone in the right (rearmost in the figure) ankle is not visible because the bone it

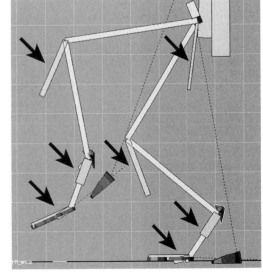

Figure 14.13

Fan bones

is constrained to is not rotated. The most obvious fan bones in this image are the ones extending down from the knees; fan bones are also visible at the left (raised) ankle and slightly visible at the balls of the feet where the toe bends. The two fan bones of the foot are named *footmid* and *anklerot*. Although these bones are constrained to copy the rotation of footbot and foottop, respectively, the influence of the Copy Rotation constraint is set at 0.5 instead of 1.0. The same is true of the fan bone extending from the knee, which is aligned to the lower leg bone in rest pose and set to copy the lower leg's rotation with a 0.5 influence. This provides an intermediate level of rotation, as you can see in the figure. These bones must be deform bones, of course, because their purpose is to soften the effect of the joint on the mesh.

Proog's Jacket

Living characters aren't the only things that often need armatures. In *Elephants Dream*, Proog's jacket has something of a life of its own. In addition to being modified by the Proog armature to follow the movements of Proog's body, the jacket has its own armature to govern the way the cloth hangs and responds to movement, as you can see in Figure 14.14.

One of the most interesting things about this setup is how the jacket incorporates a softbody modifier to assist in its cloth simulation. In Blender, cloth simulation is not yet fully implemented (although the work is underway). Ordinary Blender softbodies currently lack the capability to calculate for self-collision and are furthermore slow to compute with large numbers of vertices.

Figure 14.14

Proog's jacket in action

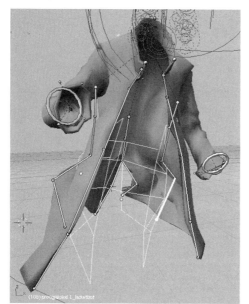

Proog's jacket's rig works around these problems by doing the softbody calculations on an invisible, low-poly "lining" for the jacket, which is shown selected in Figure 14.15. It has very few vertices to compute, so you can do softbody calculations very quickly with it, but it is placed in relation to the coat so that it mimics the way the actual jacket should hang if it were soft.

Figure 14.15

Low-poly softbody "lining" for the jacket

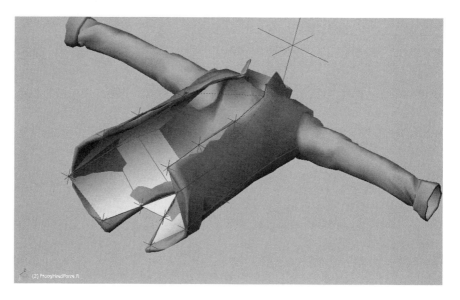

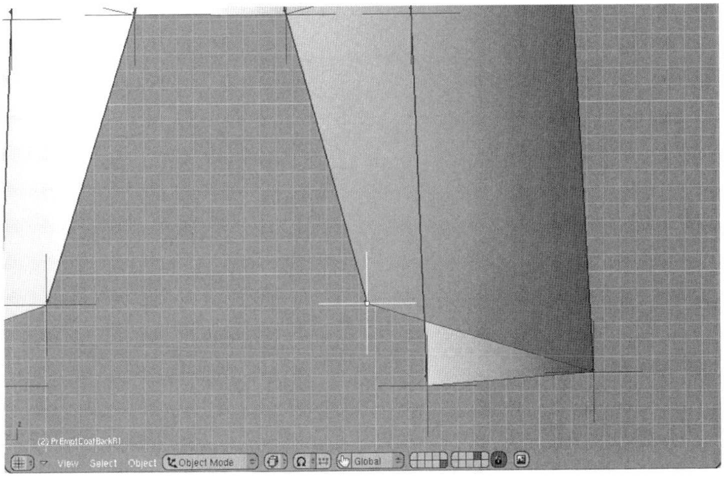

To allow the drape of this low-poly lining to control the drape of the actual jacket, empties are vertex-parented to verts in the lining, as shown in Figure 14.16. The highlighted empty is vertex-parented to the coattail vertex. Finally, this empty is assigned as an IK target for the highlighted IK solver bone shown in Figure 14.17. This armature controls the movement of the actual jacket mesh. By using this method of vert-parenting IK target empties to the softbody jacket liner in several key places, a softbody effect can be approximated for the jacket without dealing with the various problems that would come with putting a softbody modifier onto the jacket directly.

In future versions of Blender, it is likely that the roundabout approach of parenting IK solvers to empties to vertices will no longer be necessary to achieve a similar effect because the coders are currently working on a system that will allow one mesh, such as the low-poly liner, to directly deform another mesh, such as the high-poly coat in this example. This would be a practical improvement and make this approach even more attractive.

Figure 14.16

An empty is vertex-parented to the tail of the lining.

Figure 14.17

The empty is then made the IK target for the tailbone of the jacket.

Texturing Proog

Without a doubt, one of the most striking and distinguishing features of *Elephants Dream* is the almost obsessive attention to textures. Well-done texturing adds an entirely new dimension of realism to any 3D scene, and it's clear that the creators of *Elephants Dream* were keenly aware of the increase in production value that can be attained by texturing.

In terms of the characters, Emo's texturing is probably the most immediately obvious because of its strange discoloration and incongruous wrinkling, which is striking on such a young-looking face shape, but it is the more subtle and natural texturing of the Proog character that I find particularly interesting.

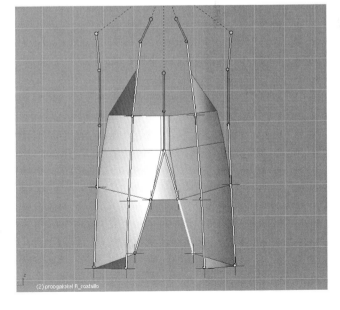

In Figure 14.18, you see the three main texture images for Proog's head: the color texture (unfortunately reproduced here in black and white), the bump map texture, and the specularity texture. In the color texture, various pinks, reds, and blues lie over a layer of pinkish skin tone. Veins are drawn lightly in blue, and light and dark areas represent variations in skin stress.

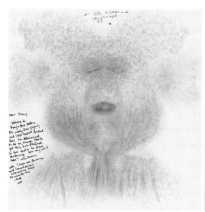 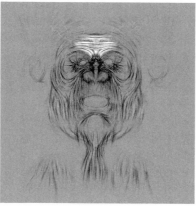 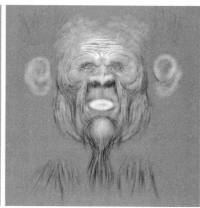

Figure 14.18

Texture images for Proog's head: color, bump mapping, specularity

The bump map texture shows areas of depression and elevation on the face, creating wrinkles, bumps, and indentations. The light veins in the forehead coincide with the blue-tinted veins in the color map to raise them slightly from the surface. Neutral gray has no effect on the normal value of the base mesh.

The light areas on the specularity map appear in the final render as shinier than the dark areas. When creating this texture, the artist took into account factors such as oiliness of skin, tautness of skin, and closeness of skin to bone. This texture follows the other two but is less highly contrasted than the bump map. Also, attention is given to areas such as the rims of the ears, which will have a slightly higher specularity than other areas but are not of particular interest for bump mapping.

Nonhuman Rigs in *Big Buck Bunny* and *Sintel*

Although the characters in *Elephants Dream* were ordinary humans (at least in shape), subsequent open movies had a wider variety of character forms. *Big Buck Bunny* notably had cartoony animals like the ones shown in Figure 14.19. The proportions of these characters were nonhuman, and rigging involved special considerations such as dealing with the movement of ears and fat. In addition, winged characters began to make an appearance, such as the bird shown in Figure 14.20. *Sintel* took things a step further by featuring fantasy dragon characters (the adult dragon shown in Figure 14.21 and the baby dragon shown in Figure 14.22) that were without precedent in nature in major, highly active roles.

Figure 14.19

Big Buck Bunny and the chinchilla

Figure 14.20

The bird from *Big Buck Bunny*

Figure 14.21

Sintel and the dragon

Figure 14.22

The bird rig for *Big Buck Bunny* actually had a Blender-based predecessor from the Argentine feature film *Plumiferos*, which you'll read about in Chapter 16. The bird rig here was inspired in large part by the rig you'll read about in that chapter. As you can see, the animator controls shown in Figure 14.23 are simple, but the wing deformation is more complex, as shown in Figure 14.24. See Chapter 16 for a more in-depth look at rigging birds.

Some other rigs worth looking at from *Big Buck Bunny* are the butterfly rig shown in Figure 14.25 and the Frankie the Flying Squirrel rig. You can download both of these rigs (like all *Big Buck Bunny* rigs) individually at www.bigbuckbunny.org in the downloads section. The butterfly rig is notable for its extensive use of B-bones, a type of bone that unfortunately is not discussed in this book. B-bones enable you to segment individual bones in a way that makes them bendable. This can create more flexible, bouncy rigs.

Figure 14.23

Animator controls for the bird

Figure 14.24

Wing bones for the bird

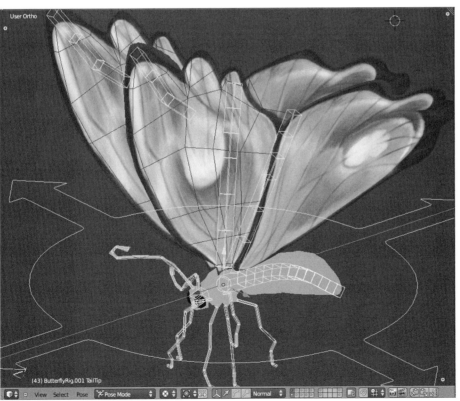

Figure 14.25

Butterfly rig

The flying squirrel rig is notable because it enables easy switching between different character shapes for when the squirrel is behaving as a biped walking on the ground and for when he's behaving as a flying animal; the rig also enables you to alter the pivot point

Figure 14.26

Animator controls for the flying squirrel

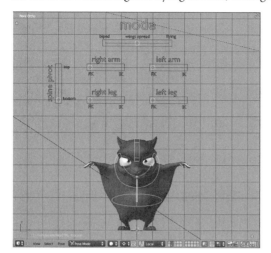

of the spine in order to animate a full range of motion as it does things like swing from trees, flip around, fly, and walk. Figure 14.26 shows the rig with the IK controls for all four limbs, the spine pivot control, and the mode control. Figure 14.27 shows the different positions for the mode control, from fully biped to fully flying.

Figure 14.27

Switching modes for the flying squirrel

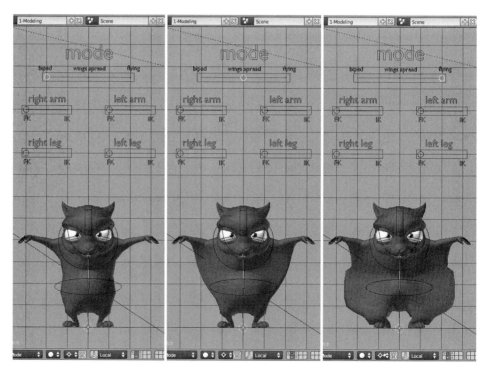

The Production Pipeline

The core Orange team consisted of eight individuals, including the soundtrack composer/sound designer. The other seven on the team all worked with Blender as producer, director, art director, technical director, and three lead artists. In addition to these production team members, several other people are credited with contributing smaller amounts of artwork, animation, and assistance in texture creation. The subsequent Open Movie Project ventures have been successively more ambitious with growing numbers of participants and spanning incrementally longer time periods for production. All of the production teams also relied heavily on the Blender developer community at large.

In any production, the process begins with a concept. The various projects have taken different approaches in this regard. In the case of the Orange Project, the creative team arrived at the concept for *Elephants Dream* in a very collaborative way after the project already began. With *Big Buck Bunny*, the storyline was an overall concept originated mostly with director Sacha Goedegebure and was then refined with input from the team. In the case of *Sintel*, an original story concept was proposed by the famous Dutch cartoonist Martin Lodewijk, which served as a starting point for screenwriter Esther Wouda to create a script with input from director Colin Levy and other members of the team. *Sintel* was also the first open movie to use a dedicated 2D concept artist, David Revoy (David is also a Blender artist whose Blender work appears in the gallery of this book, but for *Sintel* he focused exclusively on 2D artwork). In this sense, each open movie has represented a development not only in the 3D technology used but in the process of conceptualizing the movie from the very beginning.

In all cases, the preproduction phase is an important period, in which artists and technical workers must get together and decide on many aspects of how the film will be made and what it will look like. 2D artists are important at this point for drawing initial conceptions of characters, props, and locations. Figures 14.28 and Figure 14.29 show concept art for *Sintel* by David Revoy.

The open source 2D software Gimp played an important role at this stage in all of the productions. For *Sintel*, David also used MyPaint and Alchemy, two more open source 2D art applications. Clay was used in *Elephants Dream* to create 3D models of their main characters in advance of

Figure 14.28

Early character and concept artwork for *Sintel* by David Revoy

modeling them on the computer (see Figure 14.30). Figure 14.31 shows a 2D concept for the dragon in *Sintel*.

Figure 14.29

Sintel character art by David Revoy

Figure 14.30

Proog in clay

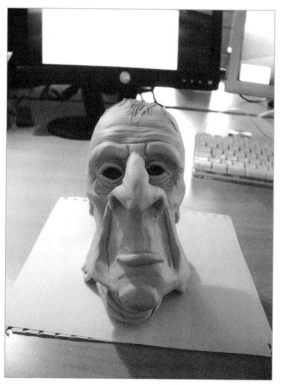

Figure 14.31

**Dragon concept art
by David Revoy**

Most medium- and large-scale productions map out their sequence of shots graphi-
cally with a storyboard, which is the best way for the director to communicate ideas and
intentions visually to the animators. Artists achieve this process by using 2D drawing
software such as Gimp or simply drawing storyboards on paper, which they often do to
post the storyboards on a wall so that many can be seen sequentially at once. After storyboarding, the team creates a 2D animatic, which is a very rough animated version of
a storyboard, to help visualize how the on-screen elements will move in relation to each
other. *Elephants Dream* did not use a 2D animatic, partly because of time constraints on
the preproduction phase, but the other two movies did.

After the team sketches the movement in the film in a 2D animatic, they begin the
process of creating the 3D world. By this time, modelers are working on creating the
rigged models and sets that will be used in the final film. By using Blender's capability
to append and link datablocks between files, a team can work on different aspects of the
film in parallel and bring them together later in the process. At this stage, they decide on
camera positions and movement, work out blocking in detail, and create a 3D animatic.

The open movie source files on the DVDs have several examples of 3D animatics among them. 3D animatics incorporate simplified rigs and movements but give
a much more detailed view of the relations between objects and the camera than is
possible in the 2D animatic. 3D animatics are of course created in Blender, as are
all sets, props, and character models. Blender's usefulness in creating 3D animatics has been recognized even in Hollywood. 3D animatics artist Anthony Zierhut
has written about how he used Blender to aid with visualization on the production

Spider-Man 2. (You can find his article on the Blender website at www.blender.org/cms/ Animatics_for_Motion_P.393.0.html.)

Eventually, the team begins the final animation work by using fully rigged characters, although modeling work might still be progressing with the final rigs. Texturing, in particular, must be done in conjunction with lighting because the appearance of textures depends closely upon the lighting of a scene. It is very important to plan the workflow so that multiple threads of production can be carried out simultaneously.

The final steps of production involve compositing, adding various visual effects, and finally rendering. Blender's compositing system is used to do the compositing and can be used in conjunction with other software to create effects. In *Elephants Dream*, the team rendered with Blender's internal renderer, which is optimized for speed, especially for use in animations.

Animation productions of even fairly small scales are likely to need render farm support, and midsize or large productions cannot be carried out without significant computing resources. Typically, this means a Linux cluster with a large number of parallel compute nodes. *Elephants Dream* used the DrQueue open source render farm manager to distribute rendering tasks across the machines on the cluster.

When shots have all been rendered, it is time to do postprocessing and editing. Blender has developed over the years to become a complete solution for these needs, and the post-production for the open movies has all been done using Blender.

Using Libraries

In any production large enough to require extensive reuse of models, animation curves, or other datablocks, using libraries is a must. A character, for example, might feature in numerous shots. It is important that changes made to the character model at any stage in the production be reproduced for all instances of the model throughout the film. Doing this by hand in a large production is out of the question, so the typical solution is to use libraries of models and other datablocks that can then be appended or linked to whatever scene they are needed in.

Appending, linking, and proxies are all crucial to medium-sized or large animation projects. You've already seen how to do all of these things in this book. This will help you understand what's going on if you decide to explore the scene files available for the open movies.

Collaboration with Subversion

Although creating an animated film is not the same as developing a piece of software, many aspects of the digital production pipeline bear similarities to a software development environment. For this reason, tools originally designed to assist collaborative software development can be useful and even necessary for digital productions, where a number of people must access and modify common files.

Subversion is an open source version management system for collaboration between programmers. It keeps a central copy of all files and enables users to maintain their own local copy of the files that they need to work with and to make changes independently of other users. When users make changes that they want to apply to the central copy of the file, they commit changes that are logged by Subversion and applied to the central file. Other users' copies are then updated to reflect the change. If two users commit changes at the same time, Subversion can identify where the changes are made and integrate them into the same new file. If the two changes affect the same part of the file, Subversion requires clarification about how to proceed, and the users have to make their changes agree with each other. Also, Subversion maintains a complete history of all commits, allowing access to any previous version.

The *Elephants Dream* team used Subversion to manage its digital assets for the production. The team opted for this for several reasons. First, Subversion is free/open source software and so fit with the mission of the Orange Project. Second, several of the creators are programmers, so they were comfortable with this way of working. For non-programmers, using a software version control system to manage digital assets might be confusing. There are, of course, a variety of commercial digital asset management tools available.

Back Into Blender

From the standpoint of a Blender user, the best thing about the Open Movie Project movies is that all of the features that are developed and refined during the process of making the movies are eventually released in future versions of Blender. Currently, the upcoming 2.5 release will boast features developed during all of the movie projects, including the complete node-based compositor developed for *Elephants Dream*, the hair particle and strand rendering functionality used for *Big Buck Bunny*, the fire and smoke simulation features used for *Sintel*, and the hundreds of other advances in rigging, texturing, lighting, animating, rendering, compositing, and editing. At this point, the number of features and fixes that Blender has enjoyed as a direct result of the Open Movie Project is almost impossible to quantify.

For this reason, I personally encourage you to consider buying DVDs of the already released open movies and keeping an eye on future projects. The Open Movie Project, like Blender itself, survives on community support. It's a great thing to be part of!

CHAPTER 15

Behind the Scenes with *Sintel*

The third installment in the Blender Open Movie Project, the short movie *Sintel*, premiered in September 2010 after a year of production and more than a year of planning. *Sintel* is by far the most ambitious and fully realized project the Blender Foundation has carried out to date. In this chapter, you'll learn about what the project entailed and hear directly from some of the creators of the movie.

- **From Durian to *Sintel***

- **The *Sintel* Open Content**

- ***Sintel* Artists in Their Own Words**

From Durian to *Sintel*

Even the project code name Durian suggested that this project was destined to be a big deal. The Asian durian is a gigantic, spiky fruit known for its overpowering (some would say repulsive) odor. If there is a king of fruits, few would dispute that the durian is a likely candidate. Following the Blender Foundation's tradition of code-naming projects for fruits, there couldn't have been a better choice to represent the ambitions of this project. The resulting short movie about a scrappy adventuress and her relationship with a baby dragon (see Figure 15.1) is without a doubt a major milestone in the evolution of Blender and the Blender community.

Figure 15.1

Scales the dragon from *Sintel*

From the beginning, the intention was to have a movie that was heavy on action, that featured fire and smoke, and that had a broad appeal. The recently coded volumetric smoke and flame effects figured into the early decision to move in this direction. At the same time, the previous Blender Foundation projects *Elephants Dream* and *Big Buck Bunny* had demonstrated the importance of planning and a solidly written story by an experienced screenwriter.

The project began in May 2009 when producer Ton Roosendaal brought together the core creative team of director Colin Levy, concept artist David Revoy, writer/cartoonist Martin Lodewijk, and composer and open movie veteran Jan Morgenstern. Soon after, screenwriter Esther Wouda took over the development of the screenplay. She worked from Lodewijk's original concept to create the final story for the movie. The remainder of the creative team was mostly established by the end of the summer of 2009, with a few more artists coming in at later points in the production.

The other members of the core team included Nathan Vegdahl, character rigger; Angela Guenette, modeler; Ben Dansie, 3D artist; Soenke Maeter, 3D artist; Lee

Salvemini, character animator; Brecht van Lommel, software developer; Campbell Barton, technical director; Pablo Vazquez, 3D artist; Beorn Leonard, character animator; William Reynish, character animator; Jeremy Davidson, character animator; and Dolf Veenliet, 3D artist. Contributions and assistance also came in from outside sources, including the Argentine team at Licuadora Studio in Buenos Aires and the Hand Turkey studios in the United States, among others.

All in all, the core budgeted project involved ten artists working for ten months, two full-time developers working for approximately twelve months, and a full-time producer working for twelve months. In contrast, the previous Blender Foundation open movie, *Big Buck Bunny*, took seven months with five artists and two developers, with twelve months of a producer working half-time and seven months of a production assistant.

In terms of computational resources, *Sintel* was also more intensive than *Big Buck Bunny*. Render time for *Sintel* averaged 20 minutes per frame over 888 seconds of screen time, while *Big Buck Bunny* averaged 10 minutes of rendering per frame over 600 seconds.

Other aspects of the production such as the script, music composition, studio rental, computer system maintenance, and DVD production also were more demanding on *Sintel* than previous projects.

The *Sintel* Open Content

As with previous Blender Foundation open projects, the resulting movie and digital assets of *Sintel* were all released under a Creative Commons open license. They can be freely reused, displayed, or distributed with proper attribution. The entire content is available for purchase as a four-DVD set from the Blender Foundation's e-shop. Buying this package helps support future Blender development and projects, and it's also the easiest way to get your hands on that huge quantity of content!

By this time, if you haven't seen *Sintel* already, you should check it out on Vimeo or YouTube. When it was released online, it generated a huge amount of buzz and received mostly very positive reviews as a short movie. But as a Blender user and animator, it's likely that the movie itself will be the least of the treasures you'll find in the DVD set.

Production Files

The third DVD contains all the assets you would need, in principle, to rerender the whole movie yourself. You probably won't want to do this, but diving into those assets is a great way to learn. Figure 15.2 shows the `.blend` file for the Sintel rig, the main character of the movie.

You can study the `.blend` files directly to learn about creating complex environments like the breathtaking city of Ishtar with its central ziggurat shown in Figure 15.3 or the intimately modeled and lit bedroom shown in Figure 15.4.

Figure 15.2

The Sintel rig

Figure 15.3

The main city set

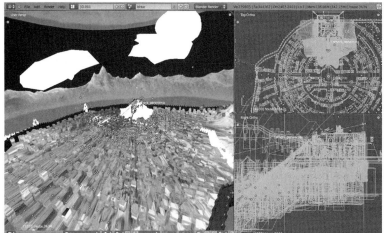

Figure 15.4

Sintel's bedroom

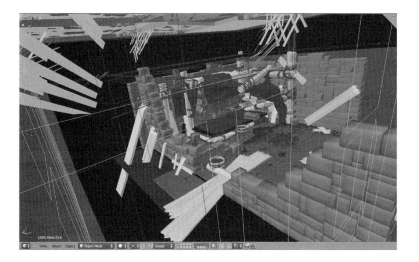

Background matte paintings like the one shown in Figure 15.5 are an important part of creating 3D environments, and studying these images and the `.blend` files they appear in is a terrific way to learn about how they are incorporated into a scene. Textures and matte paintings are also great resources to reuse in your own work.

Several alternate poster scenes are also included on the DVD, such as the one shown in Figure 15.6. Using the render branch of Blender included in the *Sintel* package, you can experiment with rendering your own *Sintel* posters.

Figure 15.5

A matte painting for the city of Ishtar

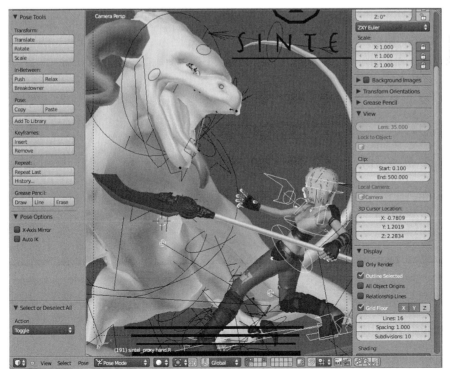

Figure 15.6

An alternate scene for a movie poster

3D assets and textures aren't the only interesting things included. The screenplay and shot-by-shot outline is also included. Study the shot breakdown spreadsheet shown in Figure 15.7 to learn how to plan your own projects down to seconds of screen time before diving into production. You can even find out exactly how the team used its time by looking at the included production schedules (Figure 15.8). If you're planning a slightly larger-scale or multiperson project, these are great references to learn exactly what you're getting into.

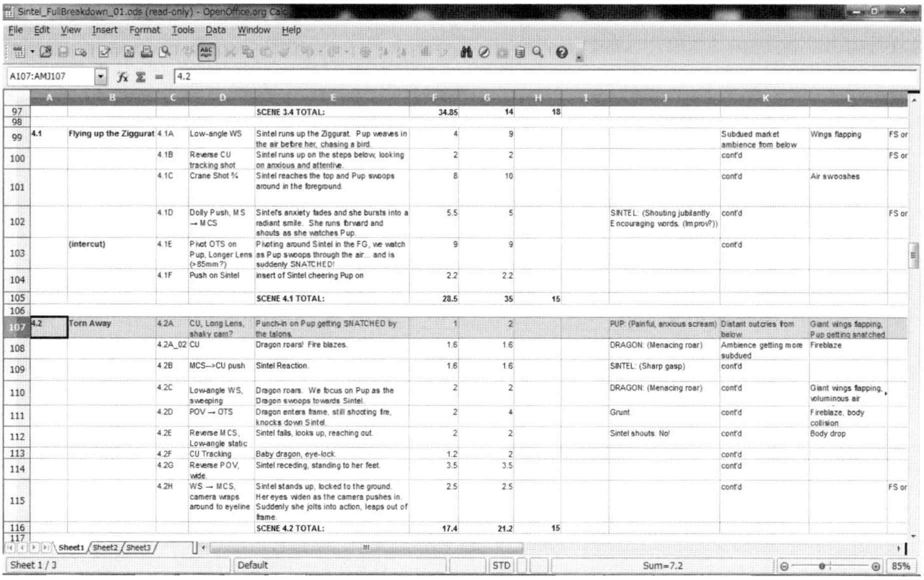

Figure 15.7

Shot-by-shot outline

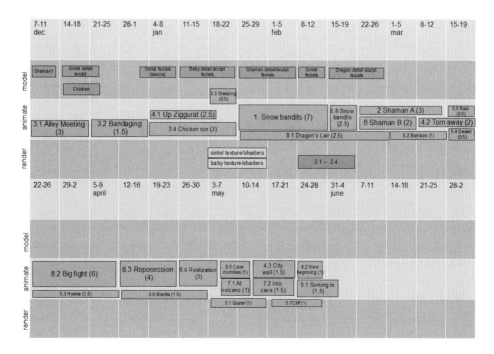

Figure 15.8

A production schedule

Tutorials

In addition to the production files, the DVD set includes dozens of video tutorials and specifically created tutorial .blend files, created by members of the Durian team such as Angela Guenette's series of modeling videos about how the Sintel rig's facial topology created an expressive and lively character (Figure 15.9). All aspects of the production of *Sintel* and crucial information about the new features of Blender 2.5 are presented here by the artists who know them best. You'll learn about environment creation, texturing, sculpting, rigging, character animating, compositing, planning shots, and more.

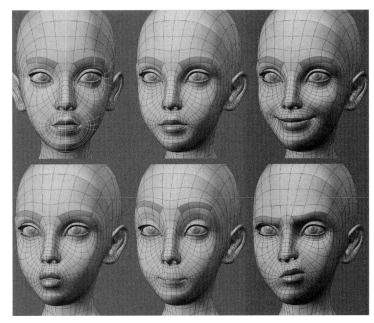

Figure 15.9

Facial topology for the Sintel rig

Sintel Artists in Their Own Words

Nobody knows more about the ins and outs of using Blender to create a movie in a professional production environment than the people who work on the Blender Foundation's official open movies. In this section, you'll hear from the creators directly.

Beorn Leonard (Character Animator)

Tell me a little bit about your previous work before Sintel. *Were you trained in traditional animation? Did you start out with other software tools, or did you develop your animation skills and Blender knowledge side by side?*

I have been working as a graphic artist for about 15 years. I started out at a small corporate video company in Melbourne, Australia, using 3d Studio 4 (that's the DOS version, for those old enough to remember) to produce graphics for their various productions. Ten years of freelancing followed until I got full-time work at the top commercial TV station in Australia, Channel Nine. It was during my five years at Nine that I became interested in Blender and started using it for my work there, as well as working on Blender projects in my spare time. One of these projects, *A Sad Sad Song*, was nominated for a Suzanne award in 2008. While I was largely happy with the results, I felt the character animation was considerably lacking and decided further study was required.

I then saved up some money and in 2009 enrolled in a course at Animation Mentor. After finishing class 1 at Animation Mentor, I left my job at Nine and moved from Australia to the Netherlands.

I had originally applied to be on the Durian team but was one of the many who didn't make the cut. However, while I was in Amsterdam, I took the opportunity to drop in on the Durian team to see how the production was progressing. When I found out that they needed more animators, I immediately submitted a revised demo reel and was lucky enough to make it onto the team.

A lot of your work on Sintel *dealt with animating action shots with the dragons and Sintel. (note: see the dragon rig in Figure 15.10). Is this kind of animation much different from other animation you've done in the past? Is it much different to animate a fantasy creature like a dragon than it is to animate humans or real animals?*

The dragons were especially a challenge as most of my training at Animation Mentor had been based on biped animation. I had rigged and animated a lizard for a previous job on a TV ad, but the thing about dragons is that there is nothing in nature quite like them. In fact, after doing research, I found out that no animal that big has *ever* flown.

The reference we ended up using for the baby dragon's flight was various fruit bats and slow-motion footage of finches and sparrows. When on the ground, the baby dragon behaved more like a puppy. For the flight of the adult dragon, I looked at birds of prey such as eagles and slowed down the action to give it a sense of weight. It was interesting that even though something like this has never existed, people seem to "know" how a dragon should move.

Figure 15.10

The dragon rig

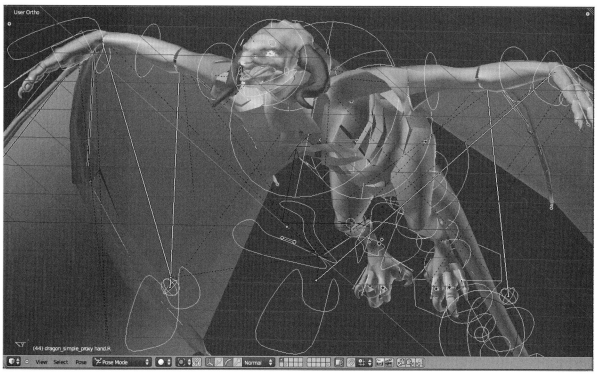

From the perspective of a character animator, what are Blender's biggest strengths and weaknesses? Are there any developments you are particularly looking forward to?

Much like its modeling tools, Blender's biggest strength is its speed. This is especially the case with the 2.5*x* series we used for Durian. I have done extensive character animation in both 3D max and Maya, but neither come close the ease of use of Blender. Also, a lot of the tools that are standard in Blender—for example, the motion paths tool for refining arcs, the Push and Relax Pose tools, and the Mirror Pose tool—are available in other programs only through plug-ins and custom scripts. All of these tools I find essential to a fast character animation workflow, and they are there in Blender as standard.

It's hard to discuss Blender's weaknesses in the context of *Sintel*, as it was constantly being developed the whole time we were working on the movie. I will say, however, that I've never been a big fan of the NLA and its use in good character animation. I used it sparingly, mainly to block out the flight animations of the birds and dragons, but I find the NLA to be one of the weakest parts of the animation tool set. NLA animations are very hard to refine, are difficult to append into other scenes, and in general should be avoided unless you really have to use them.

Also, the fact that you can't use more than one instance of a linked character is quite frustrating and defeats half the purpose of having a proxy system in my opinion. When animating the flock of birds in *Sintel*, we actually made many duplicates of the bird model to be linked into the scenes. This was inefficient and was basically a workaround for a bigger problem in the proxy system. I really hope it can be fixed in future releases.

Are there any particular features of Blender or techniques that you think are underused or not widely enough known about?

The Push and Relax Pose tools (Ctrl+E and Alt+E) are very useful and were unknown even to some of the Durian animators at the start of the project. They can be very useful when you are blocking out a shot to get breakdowns and extremes. But remember, you must always tweak; never let the computer do the art for you!

What are your tips for improving as a character animator?

1. Start simple: If you are starting out at character animation, start simple. There is a reason most animation courses start you off on a bouncing ball. When dealing with a full rig with facial controls, it's easy to get lost in the many details. The best thing you could do is start on a really basic task and master that before moving on to a more complex setup.

2. Open yourself to critique: Animation is an intrinsically collaborative process. It is always beneficial to have someone else check out your work at every stage of its

development. Don't wait until you have finished your animation to get comments from others, and don't be offended when people point out the problems they see. Use their critique to improve your skills. I cannot stress this enough. Even the top animators at Pixar, Dreamworks, and so on, ask their colleagues for critiques on a daily basis.

3. Observe life, not just other animation: If you draw inspiration only from other animation, your work will start to look derivative. Character animation is essentially acting, and the best actors draw their inspiration from real life and don't just copy other actors.

4. Focus on technique, not technology: As much as I love using Blender, it is essentially just another tool. It is possible to do brilliant animation with a pencil and a stack of paper, so don't be too focused on the software. Software changes over time, but good animation is timeless. The essence of good animation is good observation, not good software.

If you could dream up some plausible new Blender feature for a version 10 years in the future, what would it be?

Well, 10 years in software development pretty much puts us in the realms of science fiction, but off the top of my head...I have been dreaming of an extremely flexible multipurpose biped rig. This would be a blank character that you could mold into almost any human shape and change clothes and hair at any time through a layer of special controllers within the rig. This is a similar idea to Animation Mentor's recently released Bishop 2.0 rig but would be even more flexible. Basically, I envisage having the entire appearance of the character being able to be saved as a set of keyframes in an action. In production it could be really useful in crowd scenes. It would also be a great tool for animation students who don't want to have make their own rigs or use the same old existing ones.

I guess this isn't really a Blender feature; in fact, it can largely be done with the existing tools. It would be cool, though.

Apart from that, most of the new features I'm looking forward to are in the area of compositing, which I understand is the main goal for Project Mango.

Campbell Barton (Technical Director)

You're a longtime Blender developer and were technical director for both Big Buck Bunny *and* Sintel. *What exactly does a technical director do in an animation project? Specifically, in a Blender Foundation open movie environment, can you describe the relationship between yourself and the artists who are using the software?*

These open projects show up lots of challenges for the team on a technical level. This means someone needs to investigate how to approach a problem, what we can expect of Blender, what we have to work around, and how much time some feature might take to add into Blender.

Just because we have software developers on the project doesn't mean artists get all the features they like. Sometimes after discussions with artists we'd find what they wanted wasn't reasonable; other times I could write a script to automate it for them.

I also had to manage day-to-day studio problems so the artists could stay productive, do some server admin work, and set up render farms.

Blender's development team is spread out throughout the world. Nevertheless, for the open movies there is always a core team of artists and developers who work together in Amsterdam. How important is physical proximity in projects like Sintel *or* Big Buck Bunny?

Working together is really important; as a developer, you can get caught up in hypothetical problems, spending time in areas that aren't so useful. Having artists around using the software means you really know about it when things don't work right! It's very motivating and helps with prioritizing what's important.

Part of it is very practical too, though. The artists manage to have problems with large file sets that take time to bundle and upload. Sometimes the problem happens only on their system.

So, being in the same studio is just very convenient; we don't have to download gigs of files for something that may be a user error. We can start working on it quickly and look over the artist's shoulder if it was hard to re-create.

What is your own background as a developer? What advice would you give to people starting out who would like to develop their own features in Blender or to become serious Blender developers?

As an artist I used Blender for automating tasks for military simulations, but I became increasingly interested in the technical aspect and eventually got into Blender development after using Blender for some years. Blender has a history of users becoming developers, so starting with no background in software development isn't as unusual as you might expect.

As for becoming a Blender developer, firstly, Blender is a big application with many different areas, so the skills you need depend a lot on what area you want to work on; don't assume specific skills are needed before doing any Blender development. Pick a general area you'd like to investigate, and try making small changes, reading the source, and generally learning how it works; this way, you don't get bogged down by the fact Blender has thousands of files or all this code you don't understand!

I recommend you start on the easier tasks so at least you learn the process of making a change and submitting a patch and don't feel like you wasted a lot of time if your patch is rejected for some reason. In most cases, I suggest starting with Python. Even if you end up using C/C++ ultimately, Python is great for prototyping and learning how Blender works.

Blender 2.5 is the result of a massive overhaul of the software. The completely rewritten user interface is well-known and making a lot of waves among users of other applications who have been reluctant to make the change to Blender. Another major change that isn't quite as high profile is the rewriting of the Python API. What motivated this rewrite, and how do you think the user experience will be improved by the new Python API?

The primary reason for the Python API rewrite was data access. In 2.4*x* we basically had to write three different ways to access the same data: buttons, animation, and Python. Our Python API ended up being more than 100,000 lines mostly for access to settings; it was hard to maintain, and bugs would inevitably slip through. We also have unified tool system operators, which gives Python access to the same tools the users have. This allows users to create their own macros.

From our API rewrite, we also decided to have our user interface written in Python; for the user, this means it's a lot easier to extend the interface for their own workflow and integrate tools into Blender.

Are there any particular features that you think are especially underused? What are some of your favorite features that you think intermediate users might not know about?

View Port: Local view, view locking, fly mode, and preferences such as autodepth with mouse position zoom.

Mesh Editing: Automerge editing, rotating around the active vert/edge/face with normal orientation.

Transform: Numeric input, Shift+clicking the manipulator for two-axis constraint.

As a Blender developer, what do you find are the most frustrating and the most gratifying parts of the job?

Improving Blender without upsetting existing users is a balancing act, and we can't keep everybody happy. Each developer maintains their own areas, so mostly it runs smoothly, but from time to time controversial topics come up where the conservative decision is usually wins. Although I can't say this is always a bad thing, I worry we lose opportunities to innovate because of this tendency.

But I do this because it's fun, right? Improving Blender for different workflows I find very satisfying, especially when a clever solution can meet the needs of different users.

Sometimes users submit bug reports, and it's nice to be able to fix it the same day, occasionally adding important features users request. Of course, it can't always work like this, but this is one of the things that originally attracted me to open source.

Thinking about the future, are there any interesting graphics techniques or technologies out there that you'd like to see incorporated into Blender some day (even if there are no plans to do so at the moment)? In what ways do you think the Blender of 10 years from now might look different?

There are of course very cool technologies out there that would be great to have—GPU-based rendering/compositing is probably the main one, and camera tracking is another; however, these are not areas I'm involved with.

Personally I'd like to see Blender's modeling tools improve, with ngons and a new mesh structure as well as rewritten Decimator and Boolean modifiers.

Since I work on Python integration, I'm interested in the possibility of compiling RPython (restricted Python) to achieve close to C speed, which could allow Python to be used for plug-ins such as modifiers, textures, compositor nodes, and possibly shaders.

I think Blender development will move away from open projects to having development funded by companies and universities, with the Blender Foundation employing only a few developers to manage contributions and keep Blender stable.

Esther Wouda (Screenwriter)

As the script writer, you had a special role to play in the making of Sintel. *Although it's only tangentially related to the type of 3D software used, a quality screenplay is crucial to the quality of the resulting movie.* Sintel *was the first Blender Foundation open movie to use a script writer outside the core Blender user team, and it clearly benefitted a lot from that decision. In your view, what do you think is the most important contribution of an experienced, dedicated script writer?*

Well, my personal opinion set aside, I'd like to think that the value proves itself in the audience response—the number of views and downloads in little time and the numerous positive reactions and requests for "more of *Sintel*." I guess people sense the quality poured into the work, in both visuals and story. As writer and script consultant, I of course have to believe that story is the very backbone of a film. It is stories that ultimately touch people's hearts. So, the script is the basis on which all other elements of the film will be built. If that basis isn't strong, the whole structure can easily start to wobble. However skillfully actors play a scene, if it doesn't interest you, move you, or make sense to you, you will lose interest quickly. But everybody, whatever age or culture, likes to be told a story. I really believe and value this, and I love the whole storytelling process and the magic it can do. For *Sintel* I just tried to tell the best possible story within the boundaries and aims Blender had at the start, for that specific audience, within that limited time. It was a challenge, but I think a lot of it worked because of, as you say, dedication and experience in this area. Quite apart from the "magic" of that creative process, screenwriting is a craft, like carpentry (or rigging or animating!). So, you could build a chair with three legs or with four legs. The three-legged chair will still be a chair, but the four-legged one will probably "sit better." So, I guess I tried to build a very compact sofa.

On Sintel, *you worked within some pretty rigid constraints. Some story ideas were offered by Martin Lodewijk, the famous cartoonist, and your task was to assess these and create a story and fully fleshed out screenplay. On the other hand, there were budgetary constraints limiting how long the film could be and how many characters, effects, and scenes it could contain. How did all these constraints influence your work?*

It would go a bit far to call it a blessing and a curse, but it does paint the picture: with the goal that Blender had set for this "showcase," within that limited time (not just the minutes of screen time but also their planning schedule), it seemed near impossible. So much to achieve in so little time! But mostly, I quite enjoyed that. I quite like production and time constraints, as I feel there is more space for creativity if boundaries are clear. I just talked and worked with Ton and Colin, listened to what seemed possible and what would be too expensive or time-consuming (things like glow-worms in the dragon cave, the variety of landscapes in the traveling scenes, the number of man-to-man combats), and kept that in mind. Then I would go back to the drawing table and think of another way to show the same thing yet keeping the essence and emotion of the scene.

Also, when I was asked on board, it was pretty crystal what the limits were: the length was to be eight minutes, the Blender aims were clear, and the script had to be finished yesterday. This was because a lot of time had already passed trying to make a strong, rounded script out of that variety of fun yet loose ideas that were on the table. It was my initial task to bring clarity to this, assess the possibilities, and find the red thread. So, with Ton and Colin, I went through all the snippets of ideas and different suggestions for characters and arena and "simply" chose that very basic idea of "girl befriends baby dragon."

When I set out to write the new screenplay, with just that starting point, it was still our intention to use as much of the other original ideas too and incorporate them into the script somehow, but in practice this proved hard to do. More importantly, it did not serve the story. I had to make clear decisions—and defend them too. But I was certain it's better to take one very strong and simple core and grow the story from there, "inward out," rather than straining to make a coherent story out of all kinds of different (not necessarily compatible) story snippets. You can't really make it coherent, put in a "heart," in retrospect. We had to avoid that horse-behind-the-cart situation. So if you ask about constraints, I would say this for me was a tricky one: there were high goals and so many voices, and the team was used to a (sometimes overly) demo-cratic process of decision making. But we did need a compact and coherent script, one rounded story, and so on. And it needed to be well told. So, however interesting other variations and perceptions were, we had to tell one story, not 12, and I had to make that happen on the page. Luckily, Colin and I were very much in sync and worked well together to choose one central theme and take it from there. That made it possible to assess feedback and old and new ideas so I could make well-informed decisions on what would and what would not make it into the script. But in short, it was a process of sticking (sometimes quite fiercely) to that core story, which in the beginning took quite a bit of time and energy.

After creating the basic story structure and building it out into a first-draft script, all I did was condense, condense, and condense—without losing sight of our goal to tell an epic, three-act, structured hero's tale packed with action and emotion. Of course, this proved impossible in eight minutes, and there were several anxious moments in which we considered cutting (and sometimes did cut), for example, friendship/bonding scenes between Sintel and Scales, fight scenes, the whole shaman scene in the middle, and even a complete story act!

Thankfully, with Ton bringing more people on the team, this last bit of ruthlessness was not needed, and we gained a few more minutes to tell the full tale.

What kind of working relationship did you have, if any, with the animators and other Blender artists during the production of the movie? Was it simply a matter of them interpreting what you'd written, or was there any kind of feedback loop where parts of the script would be rewritten to reflect their work?

While writing the screenplay, I worked closely together with Colin, especially in the first development phase. At the start we had several brainstorming sessions; later when I was structuring and writing everything out, I would first send him a draft and dis-cuss, soon enough also with Ton, and essentially talk at length about the essence of the story and therefore also about the smallest of details and whether they fit that essence. Both Colin and I proved rather perfectionist in that regard. (I had the same experience with Jan, the composer, for whom I wrote the lyrics for the theme song. He is very particular about his work, as am I). So we had very long discussions, sent each other revisions, and had many nightly Skype chats, for example, when one of us would be "stuck" or had a sudden stroke of inspiration. They all fed into the story, and I feel it enhanced it a lot. In the beginning I would also take time to come to the Blender office for a few hours, present my ideas, see the animation progress, and listen to the ideas of the team. I would then go back and try to incorporate these, if they enhanced and fit the story.

I believe every scene and every element of the story should be meaningful and in this case even more so because we had to tell everything in only a few minutes. If we chose to show a certain part of Sintel's character or of her life, it had to be essential to the understanding and the experience of the story. We considered all of these choices quite carefully.

After the script was final, there were a few more late script polishes done, but I believe a lot of those were eventually "condensed out" again because we needed to keep the story compact. It was more about cutting even more. And I consciously wrote in very little dialogue, because I wanted to keep the film as accessible and international as possible and tell the story in images rather than words. Extra dialogue was written when recording the voices with the actors, but a lot of that was quite naturally cut again in the final edit. We just didn't need or want anything superfluous, having hammered out that core of the story so clearly.

Later in the process I viewed a couple of edits and spoke with Colin on how to convey certain emotions (for example, on Sintel's face or in movements) best and how to save time while still staying true to the story. Those discussions were very helpful as well, I believe, and we both would have liked to do those reviews even more regularly. In any case, I didn't find it too hard to "kill darlings," because we both very much agreed on that core theme. It remained a good horizon—both during writing and later in the process.

Do you feel that there are differences between writing for CG animation and live action? Would you have approached writing a similar fantasy story differently if it were going to be filmed in live action?

For animation, I believe it is best if you (not just the director but also the writer) know quite clearly and specifically what you want to show, in detail. If you write a story for live action, at a certain moment the actors will come in and interpret that story for you, which means they will exclude and include things, sometimes giving you "gifts"—unexpected extras. In animation, this is of course not possible. You have to have decided beforehand what story you want to tell and how exactly it is conveyed best. These are endless choices: facial expression, gestures, movement of the characters, movement of the camera, close or long shot, and cross fade or cut to—mostly directorial (or acting) choices but also art direction, editing, and lighting choices. The bottom line is, when writing for animation, it is useful to be aware that all these choices are or need to be made before you even start visualizing things. Especially when the animation process is expensive, you'd rather decide on a certain shot or scene a long way ahead, before you unnecessarily lose money creating it and then having to weed it out later in the edit. Preferably, the animation writer realizes this. And it can be helpful if the writer writes his script as detailed as possible, because every shot is considered beforehand—not decided or stumbled upon on set. Depending on the type of animation and format, this will be expected of the writer.

I think this is the most important difference. Of course, it very much depends on the director's preference, whether he or she wants to interpret for him/herself the scenes the writer has written or whether he or she wants to see each shot prepared as much as possible already in the script. In that case, the writer is well off with knowledge of camera and editing techniques. In the case of *Sintel*, I had not written the script much more detailed than I usually would, only the first few drafts so as to draw out the arena of, for example, the city of Ishtar. And Colin made excellent choices in conveying the emotion of the scenes in the characters, even the dragon(s), in the way he used camera movement in the action scenes but also the smallest moments of relative "peace and quiet" in the film. Those really carry the emotion and make the atmosphere.

Another difference for me (from writing for live action) was that I had a lot of freedom in my writing, maybe more because of the genre than specifically because of it being for animation. The epic fantasy genre meant I could come up with all kinds of less realistic, more symbolic, and fantastical details for the arena as well as for the characters. I had to get used to that in the beginning, but once that opened up, it was quite interesting. And the stunning art direction did the rest, of course.

What determines whether a short film will work well? For readers who are interested in making their own short movies, what tips do you have for how to make the story effective? What are some common pitfalls?

Especially after *Sintel*, where time was of the essence and I had so much to tell, I would advise this: know what your story is really about. In one word, no more. And then work outward from there, but stick to that core, because you will need it to keep focus while writing (and filming). For a short film, it is especially important to know that everything you show needs to have *meaning*. Otherwise, why show it? And for the audience, why watch it? This works the other way around too: everything that you do decide to show *becomes* meaningful simply because you have chosen to show it to the viewers. Therefore, they will take it as meaningful. So if that then does not pay off— if that scene, dialogue, or sequence doesn't really make sense or have a connection or meaning in light of your core theme—get rid of it. You have no time to waste. This essentially goes for feature films too but even more so for a short. So, use your screen time well, every moment, to convey that meaning.

Everything is valuable.

Nathan Vegdahl (Character Rigger)

If there's anyone who knows the Blender rigging system inside and out, it's you. How did your interest in rigging, specifically, develop?

Frustration, mostly. And I mean that really seriously. For me, rigging is mostly motivated by frustration as an animator. Most of the rigging that I do stems from wanting to animate and getting frustrated with rigs (often my own) that get in my way rather than get out of my way.

The first rigging I did was actually in XSI in college, and later a bit in Maya, also in college. In our animation classes we were often given pretty terrible rigs, so me and a friend of mine started covertly creating and distributing alternative rigs for the assignments, geared specifically to the exercise. These weren't character rigs but more like bouncing ball rigs or spinning top rigs, and so on. And it was really cool to see that almost without exception the people who used our rigs produced better animation. And there wasn't anything magical about the rigs. They just got out of the way and allowed people to focus on the animation instead of the rigs.

I did a bit of Blender rigging in college, the most notable being a rig I made for my dive animation in one of the BlenderArtists.org animation challenges. That rig was a very primitive predecessor to my simple biped rig. But most of my time was taken up by school, and we used XSI and Maya there.

For the beginners reading this, could you describe how you went from the level of being a complete newbie to being a top professional Blender user? How did you train yourself?

I'm rather proud to have been using Blender since 1998, pretty much right after it was first released online. So, a big part of it is just time spent doing 3D and time spent using Blender. I think it was really helpful that I got into it at such a young age, because then I wasn't so concerned with making things "good," and I didn't feel bad if I didn't finish projects. And that was really conducive to just exploring and learning.

My training in college was also extremely valuable. It didn't really matter that I wasn't using Blender in college. All the important concepts and techniques transfer between software packages. In fact, the most valuable animation class I took was a 2D hand-drawn animation class taught by Tony White. Software wasn't even relevant in that case. If you really want to learn animation, I highly recommend studying 2D animation. You don't even have to be good at it. I suck at it. But it really opened my eyes to a lot of things that I didn't expect, especially in terms of thought process and technique.

Big Buck Bunny was also huge for me. I think of it as my "lucky break." I honestly don't know where I would be right now without that project. Pretty much the only reason the Blender community even knows about me is because of that. I was really lucky to get on it, and I am forever grateful to Ton and Sacha for selecting me as part of the Peach team. I learned so much on that project, especially rigging. *Big Buck Bunny* was pretty much the first time I did any serious rigging at all. It was extremely scary, but somehow I pulled through without letting everyone down, and I came out the other end much better for it. And thanks to the fantastic reel material, it also really launched my career.

What do you think Blender's strongest and weakest points are in terms of rigging and animation, at present? Are there any areas left that you think need a complete overhaul, or is it now just a matter of debugging, tidying up features, and making incremental improvements in usability?

I think my biggest frustration with Blender is the armature system. It's kind of a cool concept, but I think in practice bones would be a lot better as objects than as data within an armature object. The reasoning for this is subtle and controversial. But as one minor example, you can't key controls from two characters at once. Thus, I feel really lucky that I haven't had to animate a swing-dancing scene in Blender. There are other things that the armature system makes inconvenient too.

Related to that is the limitation that actions can contain animation from only a single object/ID block. I think that's a big weakness in Blender's animation system right now. But it's also not easy to fix until the dependency graph system gets a big update. So, we'll see if it pans out at some point. But allowing arbitrary collections of animation data within a single action would make Blender's NLA system far more powerful and easy to work with, and I think would perhaps even allow some streamlining of the animation interfaces (we could drop the distinction between the DopeSheet and Action Editor, for example, which right now is subtle and confusing even to experienced Blender users).

But I think one of Blender's biggest strengths (at least, post-2.5) is its animation system actually. I've worked pretty extensively in both Maya and XSI, and in my experience Blender is generally better. For the most part, it's not due to a single major thing, but rather it's due to a lot of little things. Blender has always dealt with quaternion rotations far better than any other package I've used, for example. Quaternions are pretty much useless in Maya and XSI, but in Blender they just work, which is fantastic for things like ball-and-socket joints, where gimbal lock is a big issue in other packages. And Blender's Graph Editor does a lot of things right that many packages get wrong.

Are there any particular features that you think are especially underused? What are some of your favorite features that you think intermediate users might not know about?

Honestly, I'm not really sure. I don't know what other people do or don't use.

I think one of my favorite features for animating is hitting R twice to get trackball rotation. I often use that to pose a rig control without having to change the orientation of my view. I also hold down Shift a lot when moving rig controls, which slows down the transformation allowing for more precise positioning.

Blender 2.5's DopeSheet/Action Editor allows you to mark keys as primary keys, breakdowns, or in-betweens. And that can really help keep your animation organized, especially for someone like me who primarily animates in the DopeSheet editor (I pretty much use the Graph Editor only for polishing).

How can users find out more about advanced rigging theory, methods, and tools in Blender?

As with most aspects of 3D, I think the best resources tend to be pretty package-neutral. The basic rigging concepts between packages are pretty similar. They just have different names.

So, probably a lot of books on rigging in XSI or Maya or Houdini or whatever would be applicable to Blender. Though, you would have to know enough to be able to translate the concepts and techniques, which might not always be trivial. And some features won't transfer, of course (although they can still give ideas).

As far as Blender-specific resources go, I don't know if there's really much out there for advanced rigging. There are books that cover the basics but nothing I know of that covers advanced topics.

I'm toying with the idea of starting a video series. It's not for sure. But it's something I'd like to do.

If you could dream up some plausible new Blender feature for a version 10 years in the future, what would it be?

Node-based modifiers and node-based constraints.

I have very particular ideas about how I would want these to work, though. Maya's node system has some nasty limitations inherent in its design that I would like to avoid, for example.

Python modifiers would be great, too—slow, perhaps, but it would provide a great deal of flexibility.

I would also love to see Blender represent rotations internally with quaternions instead of with transform matrices. That may sound minor, but it would allow Blender to track 720 degrees of rotation in arbitrary spaces instead of just 360, which could be useful for both constraints and modifiers.

What advice do you have for people who want to seriously pursue rigging?

Animate. If you want to rig, you really should learn to animate. A rigger who doesn't animate is like a chair designer who doesn't have a butt. It can be done, but knowing what makes a rig good is going to be a lot harder if you don't use rigs yourself.

And whenever you're animating with a rig (especially your own!), take note of what pisses you off or frustrates you when you use it, because those are the areas that need to be improved. Don't just accept it. Get pissed off, and use that as motivation to figure out something better.

Also, don't get too caught up in being clever. I've had times before where I came up with a really clever solution to a problem, only to discover when using the rig that a simple FK chain is a lot easier to animate with. It's awesome to explore clever solutions and new ideas, but you have to be honest with yourself about whether they're actually improvements or not.

William Reynish (Character Animator)

Tell me a little bit about your animation and Blender background. Were you trained in traditional animation?

No, I did start with 3D. I've used Blender on and off since 2000. The real reason I started using it was because of its (for the time) unique game engine, which would let you piece together quite advanced logic and graphics without hiring a programmer.

As time passed, I got more interested in moviemaking and animation, so I took a hiatus and did some 2D animation at the Danish Film School. This turned out to be invaluable—I can recommend anyone interested in 3D animation to try doing a 2D project. It really helped me get a deeper understanding of how timing, spacing, framing, and acting works to create a finished animation.

I still love doing 2D, but it's really hard! First of all, you need to, like, draw and stuff. I like doing things really rough to get the feeling of movement right, but cleanup and in-betweening just isn't very fun in 2D.

On the other hand, there are times when I'm doing 3D where I just wish I could just draw the damn thing, instead of going through lengthy modeling, texturing, and rigging processes. In 3D character animation, deformations can drive you crazy, but you never have to consider that when doing 2D—you simply draw it. I'd love to be able to do certain deformations in a more fluid way in Blender, as part of the animation process rather than the rigging process.

Did you start out with other software tools, or did you develop your animation skills and Blender knowledge side by side?

Yes to both! In the 1990s I used a bunch of apps, such as Macromedia Director, which was an awesome multimedia tool. I used several Mac 3D apps such as Infini-D (used to create Rustboy), Strata 3D (Myst), Pixels 3D, and eventually Cinema 4D. As an animator, I've also always had a soft spot for Softimage, which I've used on a number of occasions. I usually think to myself that if I wasn't using Blender I'd probably use Softimage XSI with its awesome NLA.

I've never cared much for Max and Maya—both have always seemed unnecessarily clunky, complicated, and slow to use. I'm aware that they are extremely powerful tools, but they require too much setup and maintenance for my taste.

You've been a lead animator on two Blender Foundation open movies, and both of them have had a heavy emphasis on character animation, even while representing quite different animation styles. How much did the stylistic differences between Big Buck Bunny *and* Sintel *influence the practical side of animating the characters?*

It makes all the difference. The style of animation is interconnected with the visual style of the film. *Big Buck Bunny*, being colorful and silly looking, calls for some wacky animation. *Sintel* is more realistic, more subtle. Many conflicts are internal. There's lip sync.

I think doing something like *Sintel* is a good experience to have because it's harder to hide bad animation with such realistic characters. It forces you to be really careful about how you animate things like eyes, fingers, necks and so on. Everything had to be done more carefully.

In honesty, I'd have to say that I enjoy doing cartoony animation more. The *Sintel* style is almost too close to motion capture to be worth it. And when you do less realistic things, you can take more advantage of the unique things that animation can offer.

In what other ways did your experiences on the two projects differ?

Big Buck Bunny was a huge learning opportunity for me. I admit it was very daunting at first when I arrived in Amsterdam. I was (more or less) the only animator there. Nathan did some great animation, but most of his time was dedicated to rigging. Sacha did some, but he was constantly directing, storyboarding, and so on.

So, I just went with it and was determined to figure out how to animate this movie. It's incredible how quickly you can learn things when you feel like your life depends on it. And when you are the only one responsible for it, there's no one else to fall back on. So, I learned an incredible amount of stuff.

Sintel was different. First, I was asked to join the team six months into production. They already had worked for many months on the movie, and Lee Salvemini had done some awesome animation. It was more relaxed for me because I didn't have to carry the whole weight on my shoulders. And then Beorn and Jeremy arrived, and Nathan had some time to do animation too. It felt like being on a large team compared to *Big Buck Bunny*.

What were the biggest challenges of animating in Sintel? *How did you solve the problems that arose?*

I guess complicated body dynamics and facial animation were the biggest things. For whatever reason, I ended up with the bulk of the facial animation in the film, so that became my "thing" on *Sintel*. I did everything on the rooftop where Sintel meets the dragon, everything in the shaman hut, and the Sintel "realization" scene at the end. All these things were much more about acting than action.

In my experience, some of the hardest things to do in animation is where characters *don't* move a lot, because what then do they do? You can't hide them in fast-motion blur, and the viewers can see every detail. For the acting scenes, I ended up using video reference a whole lot, sometimes even importing into the Blender Sequencer to match timing from my video. I also did some video reference of interacting with director Colin Levy to get a feel for the scene. Some of these videos are quite embarrassing but helped a whole lot.

Are there any particular features of Blender or techniques that you think are underused?

Oh, yes! For animation I think the video sequencer, motion paths, and DopeSheet Extend (e-key) are underused. I also love using autokeying because it saves me hitting the I key every time I want to insert a key. Too few people use motion paths to track bones in 3D space. Use it to see if your arcs are nice and if your timing is off or jerky.

I think proxies are underused too. This is something quite unique to Blender, where you can define a character in a `.blend` file and then reference it in for every scene you need it. If you make a change to the character, it is automatically updated in all the scenes.

What are some of your favorite features or techniques that you'd like more intermediate users to know about?

For me, one of the most important and useful features to have been added in a long time is Rigify. Rigify is a fantastic autorigging system that creates incredibly powerful rigs for you, built into Blender 2.5. They can match up with any proportions you have and any number of limbs and features. Strangely, few people seem to know about Rigify's existence, but it really is great. For me, it's incredibly valuable. I like animation, but I'm always tired by rigging, which can take forever and is very technical and not that rewarding. Rigify makes rigging super fast and fun.

Some of those who know the feature exists don't know how to properly use it. Let me quickly explain. What you do is that you simply hit Shift+A and add a meta-rig. Go into Edit mode, and match that rig up with your character's proportions. Then, go to Armature properties and find the Meta-Rig Templates panel. Hit Generate, and Rigify generates a new armature complete with advanced constraints and controls. Then just parent your character mesh to this armature and use autoskinning. Done! Now you have attached a professional rig to your character, ready for animation.

How can users find out more about character animation and the animation tools in Blender?

Well, shamelessly I'll plug my training DVD I did a few years back called *Learn Character Animation with Blender*. There seems to be so many animation tools and workflows that too few know of, so I think there is a great need for more info on this. There really is missing a lot of training material here.

Every animator I know has a copy of the Richard Williams' *Animators Survival Kit.* If you're an animator and don't have it, then shame on you! Really, it's full of great tips and info.

If you could dream up some plausible new Blender feature for a version 10 years in the future, what would it be?

I'd start with a good NLA. The current one in 2.5 has the foundation to be really nice, but it's too limiting to be useful. It doesn't work correctly with rotations, which is a pretty basic requirement. I'd also love to have a good motion transformation system to transform motion from one character to another, even if bone names don't match and proportions are different. Softimage XSI has MOTOR for this, and it's really quite excellent.

In general, though, I feel that Blender's animation tools are under-appreciated. Blender has weak spots in modeling and rendering, but the animation tools are pretty darn great. Some of its features, such as proxies, motion paths, F-Curve modifiers, make users of other apps envious.

CHAPTER 16

Feifi the Canary— *Plumiferos* Takes Wing

In this chapter, you have a very special opportunity to take a glimpse inside *Plumiferos*, the world's first feature film to use Blender as its primary 3D animation software. The creators have kindly allowed me access to the rig of Feifi the canary, one of the main characters of the film, and I am very pleased to present an overview of this excellent example of cartoon-style rigging.

- Introducing Feifi
- Facial Deformations with Lattices
- Rigging a Cartoon Bird

Introducing Feifi

Plumiferos premiered in Argentina on February 18, 2010. The movie was Argentina's first-ever, all-CG 3D animated feature film and also the world's first Blender-made feature film. The creators of *Plumiferos* at Manos Digitales studio used a special branch of Blender to which they made their own modifications, which were later reintegrated into the open source trunk of Blender to appear as features in Blender 2.49 and Blender 2.5. Functionality developed during the *Plumiferos* project was used in the production of *Big Buck Bunny* and subsequent Blender Foundation projects.

Figure 16.1

Designs for one of the avian protagonists of *Plumiferos*

Production for *Plumiferos* overlapped with the production of *Elephants Dream,* and it's hard to imagine a better counterpoint to the Proog and Emo rigs discussed in Chapter 13 than the character of Feifi the canary (see Figure 16.1), the love interest of Plumiferos. Whereas the two protagonists of *Elephants Dream* are eminently unlovable, Feifi is as cute and charming as Proog and Emo are unsettling. Both for character and for style, the modeling and the rigging of Feifi are done in very different ways from that of *Elephants Dream.*

Stylistically, *Elephants Dream* is realistic and artificial in almost a diametrically opposed way to the way in which *Plumiferos* is cartoony and naturalistic. The creators of *Plumiferos* have created a natural-looking, convincing world to tell their story in. Lighting in *Plumiferos* is painstakingly naturalistic, whereas *Elephants Dream* is full of surreal glows and emanations. The directing style and camera work in *Plumiferos* is unobtrusive, whereas *Elephants Dream* often uses dramatic framing and camera angles to enhance the feeling of danger and unease in the film. In other important respects, however—particularly as concerns this chapter—*Plumiferos* is far less realistic, and far more cartoony, than *Elephants Dream.* This cartoon-quality completely informs the way the rig is set up, as you will see in this chapter.

The Feifi Mesh

Looking at the wireframe contours of the mesh in Figure 16.2, the differences in style and character between Feifi and the *Elephants Dream* protagonists are immediately clear. Feifi is rounded and smooth, with none of the jaggedness and incongruity of the *Elephants Dream* characters. Feifi is a classically cute cartoon character, complete with large head and very large eyes, puffy cheeks, small chin and mouth (in this case beak), and a small, rounded body. The mesh of the body is smooth, is clean, and at first glance appears comparatively simple.

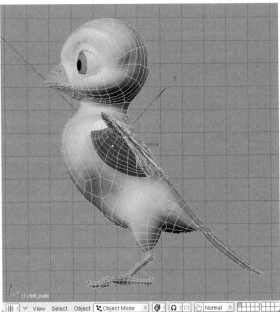

Figure 16.2

The Feifi mesh, front and side

Figure 16.3

Feifi's wings

In fact, although Feifi's head is clearly cartoony in its proportions, the body itself is actually not very exaggerated at all. The torso, legs, and feet are highly naturalistic. The most significant and complex concessions to naturalism in the mesh are probably in the wings, shown in their rest position in Figure 16.3. Clearly, they are based on considerable study of actual bird wings, and the component feath-ers are painstakingly organized to yield a naturalistic structure that can be animated in a convincing way; however, in keeping with the film's cartoon style, these wings are far more versatile and expressive than natural bird wings.

Feifi is not a single unbroken mesh. The wings and tail are built up of many mesh parts representing fea-tures that have been modeled separately and placed together, as in the exploded image of the Feifi mesh in Figure 16.4.

These segments were modeled separately for sev-eral reasons. It is more modular to do it this way than to have all the mesh pieces attached; similar wing structures are used for many of the bird characters in *Plumiferos*, and it is easier to reuse wing parts if they are separate. Also, using multiple mesh parts allows for

more materials to be applied to an object. Each unbroken mesh was limited to 16 different materials in the Blender 2.4x versions used in *Plumiferos*. As of Blender 2.5, this restriction has been lifted. This was generally not a particularly limiting restriction, because it is easy to use separate mesh segments within an object, as is done here. Lastly, separately modeling each of the large features that make up the wing yields very nice results and facilitates some interesting possibilities for wing posing—which you will look at a bit later in this chapter.

Figure 16.4

Separate feathers that make up the wings

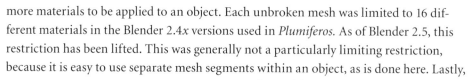

Facial Deformations with Lattices

In Chapter 10 you looked briefly at the use of lattices and their applicability to cartoon-style effects. One drawback of lattices in previous versions of Blender was some difficulty in animating them, because they relied on the deprecated relative vertex key system rather than the shape keys, which are typically used with meshes.

Blender 2.5 lets you create shape keys for lattices, so this situation is much improved. The Feifi rig takes the idea of using lattices for cartoon distortion to its logical extreme. A lot of mesh posing is done with lattices, and very little is done with shape keys. Even traditional armature deformation is minimal, particularly in the face area. Furthermore, Feifi uses hooks and bone parenting to allow complex lattice deformations to be controlled by armature, in the same way other meshes have done but without shape keys or drivers.

Figure 16.5 shows a view of Feifi's head with a complex scaffolding of multiple lattices. Each lattice covers a specific portion of the mesh and influences the part of the mesh defined by the vertex group named in the VGroup field in the Lattice modifier, as shown in Figure 16.6. They connect a hook to the parts of the lattice that will be deformed by going to Edit mode, selecting the lattice verts that the hook will influence, and then pressing Ctrl+H to create

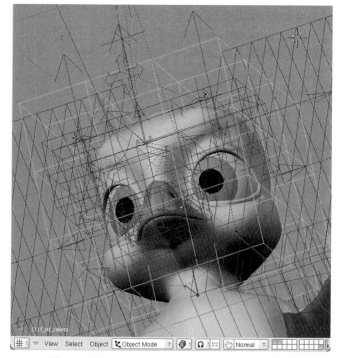

Figure 16.5

Lattices modifying Feifi's head

a hook. By default a new empty will be created as the hook object; in 2.5 a pop-up menu will come up asking you how you want to create the hook. This empty is then bone parented to the appropriate controller bone.

This approach results in a remarkably expressive face rig. In Figure 16.7 you can see a small sample of the kinds of deformations and facial expressions possible with this approach. The only portion of the face rig that involves weight-painted, bone-deformed mesh is the lower beak portion, which is opened by means of a bone. The only shape keys used are for opening and closing the eyelids. In these examples, once again, you can see the potential for lattices to create exaggeration and hence cartoon style.

Figure 16.6

The Lattice modifier applied to a vertex group

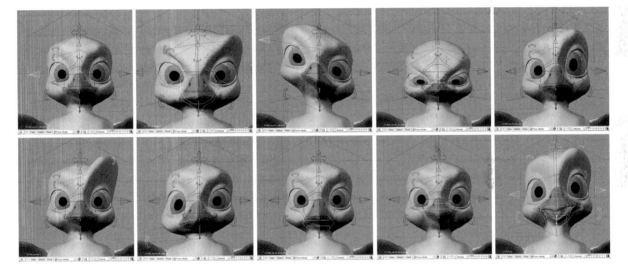

Figure 16.7

Facial deformations with a lattice/armature combination

Rigging a Cartoon Bird

The rest of the Feifi rig is equally interesting. You can see the entire bone armature structure in Figure 16.8. Although it is not clear from the black-and-white image, the Blender version used by the *Plumiferos* team allows custom bone colors as well as shapes. This feature, which is now standard in Blender, was developed specifically for this project by the *Plumiferos* team.

In the Feifi rig, the left wing and foot bone setups are colored red, and the right wing and foot are blue. Since animators may work in wireframe mode or without the mesh visible, it can be difficult to tell right from left when viewing the armature from the side. It is useful to have colored bones to distinguish the sides. Bone colors are available in current Blender versions by using the Bone groups feature.

Figure 16.8

The Feifi armature

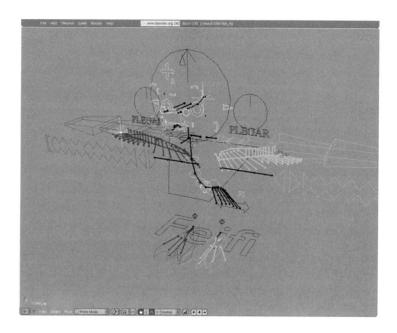

The rigging of Feifi's torso comes closest to using the rigging style you looked at elsewhere in this book. Feifi's spine is basically an IK chain that can be posed very flexibly by manipulating control points in the hip and neck area, as in Figure 16.9. This area, as well as the main posing bones for the head and legs, is rigged and skinned in a straightforward way using weight painting, as shown in Figure 16.10.

Figure 16.9

Posing Feifi's torso

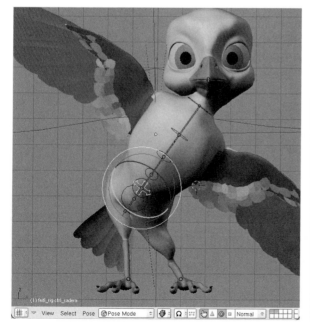 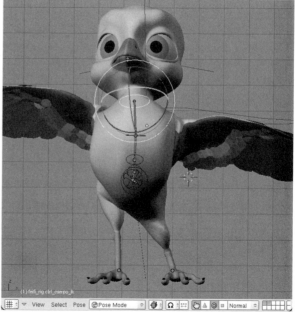

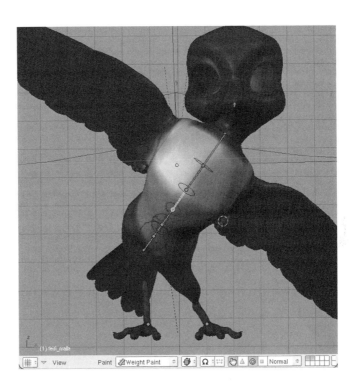

Figure 16.10

Feifi's torso weight painting

Wings

A place where the Feifi rig is especially interesting is in the wings. Modeling and rigging wings and feathers present a number of challenges that are not easily addressed using traditional armature-mesh deformation.

The Feifi rig basically breaks wing movement into components corresponding to something like flap, curl, and fan, with each of these components controlled mostly independently from the others, as shown in Figure 16.11.

Figure 16.11

The main components of Feifi's wing movement: flap, curl, and fan

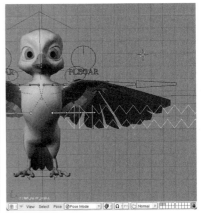

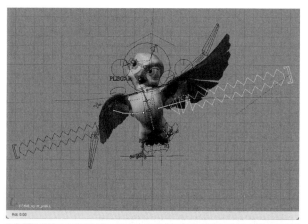

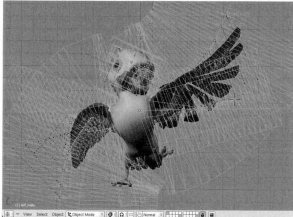

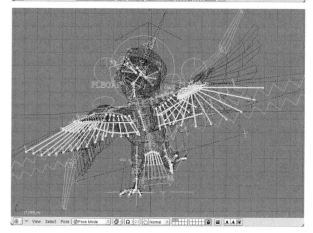

Figure 16.12

The posed mesh, lattices, and full armature: flap, curl, and fan

The angle of Feifi's wing to his body is determined by the rotation of a circular dial-like custom bone located over his shoulder. The curl within the wing is controlled by a chain of FK bones extending horizontally from the shoulder area; this setup allows for much more flexible posing than a natural bird wing, which is appropriate to a cartoon bird character that will likely have to use his wing as a hand from time to time. Finally, the fanning of the wing feathers, a key element of expressive wing posing, is controlled by *scaling* the accordion-shaped custom bones positioned horizontally beneath each wing.

This kind of flexibility would be difficult to accomplish using only weight painting and armature deformation. In fact, most of Feifi's wing posing is not accomplished with weight painting. Rather, as in the case of the facial deformations, the rigging of Feifi's wings is solved with lattices.

Feifi's wings are each modified by two lattices, one that controls flap and one that controls the curl of the wings. The lattices in turn are controlled by using hooks parented to the appropriate armature bones, like the facial deformation. A single wing's curl lattice is influenced by 25 separate hook modifiers. Figure 16.12 shows a wing pose, the accompanying lattice deformations, and a full view of all layers of the armature.

The only part of the wing's pose that is not controlled by lattices is the fanning mechanism. To fan the feathers, traditional armature deformation is used, in that each separately modeled feather is fully assigned to its own bone, as shown in Figure 16.13. Each feather follows the movement of its governing bone while remaining stiff.

The fanning itself is controlled by a very clever example of a kind of mechanical rigging that does not often find its way into character armatures. To understand how it works, it is helpful first to look at the setup in its rest position in Edit mode, as in Figure 16.14. Located at the tip of each deform bone is a small control bone (the bones named with the prefix tar_roja). These bones have no direct relationship via parenting to the feather deform bones; they are simply placed at their tips. The parent of the control bones is the str_proha.L bone.

In Pose mode, each of the feather deform bones is constrained using a Lock Track constraint to point toward the location of its respective control bone. Scaling the parent of this set of bones has the effect of scaling the control bones themselves and their distances from each other, while also changing the location of the point to which they are parented. As this happens, the tracking of the feather deform bones toward the control bones results in the deform bones spreading apart from each other, as shown in Figure 16.15.

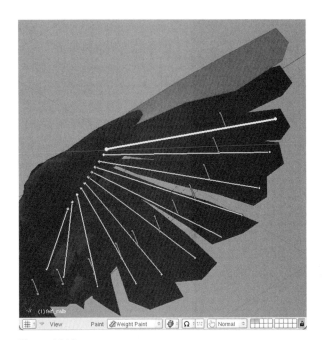

Figure 16.13

A feather mesh segment fully assigned to a deform bone

Figure 16.14

The wing fanning mechanism in Edit mode

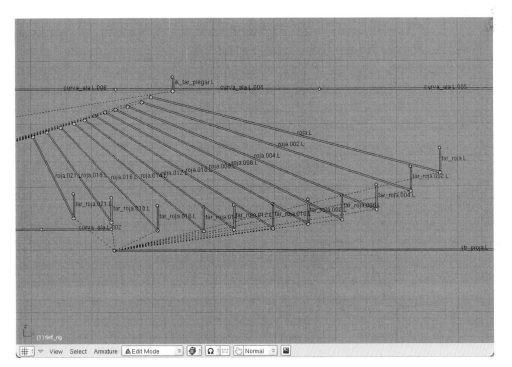

Figure 16.15

The feather-fanning mechanism in action

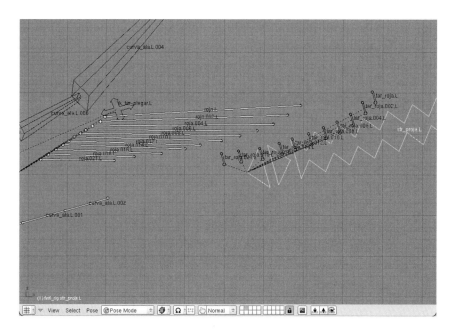

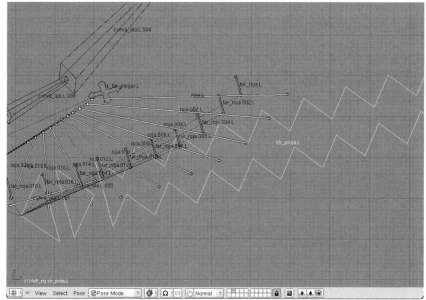

Figure 16.15

The feather-fanning mechanism in action

As you can see, in spite of the apparent simplicity of the Feifi character, the rig is a fairly complex construction. The result is a very expressive, poseable character that can allow an animator to create a wide range of actions and emotions quickly and easily. Although some of the techniques used in this rig certainly deserve to be described in greater depth, I hope that the approaches I've reviewed in this chapter will give you an idea of the possibilities available in Blender for rigging characters and perhaps point you toward some solutions of your own for your specific rigging needs.

Many of the core creative team members of the *Plumiferos* team have moved on to create Licuadora Studio and participated in *Sintel* as the "Team Argentina" off-site contributors. You can find out more about Licuadora's Blender animation work in my book with Claudio Andaur, *Blender Studio Projects: Digital-Moviemaking* (Sybex, 2010).

PART IV

Blender and Beyond

The material covered *in this book is far from the end of the story for aspiring Blender animators. This last part briefly covers some of the areas that are worthy of further study. Your work will benefit greatly if you have an understanding of other available software tools to complement Blender's functionality, so this part surveys some of the best free software options available.*

There is also a lot to learn about the craft of creating animation (this book only scratches the surface), so this part includes a chapter that contains recommended further reading on the topics of traditional animation and related computer graphics techniques.

CHAPTER 17 ■ OTHER SOFTWARE AND FORMATS

CHAPTER 18 ■ RESOURCES FOR FURTHER LEARNING

Other Software and Formats

As powerful and versatile as Blender is, no one program can do everything that the computer graphics animator needs to do. Certain tasks, such as creating 2D textures or editing sound, require a completely different sort of software. Even for tasks that Blender can perform, some people prefer (or are required) to use several 3D applications for different tasks.

This chapter briefly covers Blender's interaction with other software. First you will look at a variety of file formats that you can import and export to and from Blender. Then you'll learn about recommended open source software packages for various tasks in creating fully developed CG animations.

The chapter concludes with some changes currently in the works for Blender. Blender's development waits for no one; by the time this book is published, a new version may have been released or may be scheduled for release very soon. Here, you'll learn about scheduled updates and improvements so you have an idea of what to expect and how it relates to the version included on the book's downloadable companion files

- Importing and Exporting Other File Formats
- Useful Open Source Software for Blender Artists
- Blending into the (Near) Future

Importing and Exporting Other File Formats

Blender has traditionally had script-based import and export support for a wide variety of formats and software. The 2.5 recode has accompanied a complete overhaul of the Python API, so older scripts are currently in the process of being re-written and some formats may not be supported immediately. You should, of course, thoroughly test any scripts you intend to use before planning to place them into a production pipeline.

At the time of this writing, the second official Beta of the software, Blender 2.54 has just been released. Support for importing into this version is available for the following formats:

- COLLADA (.dae)
- Motion Capture (.bvh)
- 3D Studio (.3ds)
- Wavefront (.obj)
- Lightwave Point Cache (.mdd)

    Support for exporting from Blender is available for the following formats:

- COLLADA (.dae)
- Stanford (.ply)
- 3D Studio (.3ds)
- Autodesk FBX (.fbx)
- Wavefront (.obj)

Useful Open Source Software for Blender Artists

A huge amount of software can be useful at some point in a full 3D content creation pipeline—far more applications than I can cover here. Partly for space reasons, I am limiting this list to the most significant open source applications. I also assume that readers are familiar with at least the most well-known proprietary options in such areas as 3D content creation, image manipulation, and nonlinear video editing so I don't need to list them explicitly.

Most of what a 3D animator needs to do can be done using some combination of the software listed here. This is a very brief overview of open source alternatives in various areas, not necessarily a recommendation for any particular tool.

Video Playback

To play back the wide variety of video files available, you need a codec package and probably also QuickTime installed—although you do not necessarily need to use QuickTime Player. There are several better alternatives for players, but the VLC Media Player is my favorite. VLC is a cross-platform player capable of supporting a wide variety of codecs, and I have rarely come across a video file that it cannot play back nicely.

Collaboration

The following software packages are for use in collaborative projects, in which more than one person is involved in the work and potentially more than one application is being used.

Collada Collada is an XML-based format intended to be usable as an open standard, general representation schema for 3D information to allow the free exchange of this information between various applications. Using Collada (and the associated Blender-specific plug-ins), it should be possible to share data between Blender and Maya, 3D Studio Max, Softimage XSI, and a number of other supported applications.

Verse Verse is a tool for setting up a protocol to allow real-time interaction between various 3D environments, such as those of the software packages just mentioned. Collada and Verse are complementary in their goals and approaches. A Verse-based content creation environment can use Collada as its format, enabling users of multiple, 3D content creation applications to work on the same data simultaneously over a network. The Blender Foundation is actively involved in promoting development in Verse, but development of Verse currently lags behind the latest version of Blender, so users of Blender 2.5 and newer versions may need to be patient.

Blending into the (Near) Future

New features are already available in SVN development builds available at www.graphicall .org and some of them may be in an official release by the time this book is out. (It is no problem to run multiple versions of Blender side by side on the same machine, so if you want to experiment with an SVN build, you can do so without abandoning the release you have installed.)

Some exciting currently active projects include an overhaul of Blender's mesh modeling tools, a full integration of the powerful Freestyle non-photorealistic line renderer, advances in Blender's sculpting and physics functionality. You can keep abreast with what actual Blender developers are up to by checking the Blender developers blog at code.blender.org.

In the next chapter, you'll read about some further resources to learn about Blender's functionality and to keep up with what's happening in the world of Blender.

CHAPTER 18

Resources for Further Learning

At this point, you should know all you need to get started with character animation in Blender. There's plenty more to learn, though, both about Blender and about character animation. This chapter directs you to resources to continue your study of these topics.

First you'll get a rundown of freely available online tutorials in Blender and paid offerings from the Blender e-Shop. Some of the introductory tutorials overlap in coverage with this book and might provide another angle to learn from. Most of the intermediate-level tutorials and resources I'll be pointing to, however, cover aspects of using Blender that I haven't been able to address at all in this book. Becoming familiar with these resources can also help you stay on top of new features and functionality of future Blender releases.

Then you'll learn about a few of what I think are truly indispensable books on computer graphics and animation. If you are an experienced 3D animator already, you probably have all these books on your bookshelf; if not, you should. If you are just beginning in the field, these books will prove to be invaluable references.

- Selected Blender Resources

- Recommended Non-Blender-Specific Books

- On Becoming a Blender Master

Selected Blender Resources

In the past few years, there has been an explosion of learning resources for Blender, from freely available online tutorials to commercially published books and DVD training courses. This section will point you in the direction of the best of these resources.

The Blender e-Shop

Most of the best commercial training products for Blender are conveniently available in one place: the Blender Foundation's own e-Shop, located at www.blender3d.org/e-shop/. Better still, purchases at the Blender e-Shop go toward supporting the development of the software, making the e-Shop the ideal one-stop shopping resource for Blender training goods.

In the e-Shop, you'll find all the available Blender Open Movie DVDs as well as the spin-off training DVDs of the Open Movie Workshop. These are training DVDs created by the world's top Blender artists covering a wide variety of topics. William Reynish's *Learn Character Animation Using Blender*, Bassam Kurdali's *Mancandy FAQ*, Andy Goralczyk's *Creature Factory*, and David Revoy's *Chaos and Evolutions* are available as of this writing, and more titles may well have been added by the time you read this.

Of course, the Open Movie DVDs themselves, including the epic four-DVD set *Sintel* shown in Figure 18.1, are packed full of extra features including tutorials and Creative Commons–licensed assets that you can reuse in any way you like. The truth is that there are no better resources for intermediate and advanced Blender learning than those directly from the Blender Foundation.

Figure 18.1
The *Sintel* DVD package

You'll also find selected commercially published books (including this one) from various publishers covering a wide variety of Blender topics from animation to architecture to video editing and compositing.

When you stock up at the e-Shop, don't forget to toss some stickers and T-shirts into your order to support development and tell the world about your favorite 3D software!

Official Documentation

Even with the high-quality learning material available on the e-Shop, there will be times when you want to work with newer features or features that are not extensively covered in the available books and DVDs. To learn about these things, you will need to turn to the official documentation at the Blender website.

The best up-to-date information about the new features and functionality for each Blender release are the release logs for that release. You can find all the release logs here:

```
www.blender.org/development/release-logs/
```

For general documentation, look at the Blender Wikibook:

```
http://mediawiki.blender.org/index.php/Main_Page
```

These resources should take care of most of your Blender learning needs. But given the open source nature of Blender and the active community around it, there are often interesting things happening in the world of Blender that you won't learn about from any one wiki. For this reason, it's worthwhile to maintain contact with the wider Blender community to stay aware of new resources.

BlenderArtists Forum and BlenderNation

Blender has a very active, enthusiastic, and helpful community of users at `http://blenderartists.org/forum/`. This is where you should go first for technical questions about using Blender or any other Blender-related help. Use the search function first, and you will probably find the answer to your question immediately. Otherwise, post your question in the appropriate forum, and an answer will certainly come quickly, often within minutes.

BlenderNation at `http://blendernation.com` is a regularly updated source of Blender news. This is a good place to keep up with what's happening in the Blender world. It also has one of the best collections of tutorials and video tutorials available anywhere for Blender.

Other Recommended Online Resources

A huge number of tutorials and learning resources are available for Blender on the Web, and more are popping up daily. It is inevitable that I will fail to mention many excellent ones, but you will surely come across them if you read and search for specific topics in the BlenderArtists forum and BlenderNation. Still, there are a few outstanding sources of free and paid tutorials that are frequently updated with useful, novel techniques and presented with a high degree of professionalism.

Blender Cookie, located at www.blendercookie.com, is a very professional site where you can find a growing collection of top-notch video tutorials by a team of well-known Blender artists and teachers. There's good material for beginners and more advanced users, and Blender Cookie has been one of the leaders in putting out tutorials for Blender 2.5.

Andrew Price's Blender Guru website (www.blenderguru.com) is an ambitious and wide-ranging resource for Blender enthusiasts. Andrew's tutorials are very well presented and understandable and always yield compelling results. Best yet, Andrew is open to requests from the community. If there is an area you'd like to learn more about, let him know, and he just may delve into it for his next tutorial.

Kernon Dillon's Blendernewbies blog (http://blendernewbies.blogspot.com) has become one of the longest-running regularly updated sources for high-quality free tutorials. Kernon covers a lot of topics here, and in spite of the site's name, the material is often of interest to intermediate users.

cmiVFX (www.cmivfx.com) is an excellent subscription-based resource for top-quality streaming video tutorial content, including tutorials on modeling, texturing, shading and fur, compositing, and more. CartoonSmart (www.cartoonsmart.com) also provides introductory Blender video tutorials, with freely viewable samples available.

Recommended Non-Blender-Specific Books

CG animation is one of the most multidisciplinary art forms there is. To be a good CG animator, you must be technically inclined and also artistically gifted. You have to master modeling, texturing, posing, timing, lighting, rendering, and many other skills. And in addition to talent and practical skill, you must also have a wealth of knowledge. These books are a small selection of what I consider to be required reading for anyone wanting to create animations with Blender.

Character Animation

Animation has been around for about as long as cinema, but the art of character animation was perfected by the Disney studio in the 1930s and has not changed much since then. The techniques used to express motion and emotion in *The Incredibles* are not appreciably different from those used in *Snow White and the Seven Dwarves*. These books cover the principles of character animation, regardless of the technical tools you use to implement it.

Animation by **Preston Blair** (Walter T. Foster, current ed. 1987) First published in 1948, this book is pretty much the classic text on character animation. Almost everything in this book has since appeared elsewhere dozens of times, and anybody who grew up on Saturday morning cartoons has probably acquired most of the content of this book unconsciously by sheer osmosis. It has stood for half a century as an indispensable guide to the basics of character motion and is an important document of the period when animation came into its own as a fully developed art form.

The Illusion of Life **by Frank Thomas and Ollie Johnston** (Disney Editions, revised ed., 1995) This is a beautifully illustrated, hard-bound coffee table book that also happens to be very informative for animators. It presents the origins and methods of animation as created and used by Walt Disney and the Disney studio. It's interesting not only as a historical document of the art of animation but also as a guide to the principles and the ideas behind them. There's plenty in here that is not at all pertinent to CG work, but if you have any interest at all in how animation used to be done before the dawn of the Ipo curve, this is required reading.

The Animator's Survival Kit **by Richard Williams** (Faber & Faber, 2002) This book covers many of the same principles dealt with by the two other books I listed here, but it stands out in the wealth of visual examples included. There's hardly any printed text in the whole huge book. Every page is filled with drawn animation sequences with text handwritten on the illustrations. Richard Williams is a true master of the art of animation, and this is likely the closest most of us will ever get to peering over the shoulder of the likes of him.

CG-Related

I am deliberately leaving out references to a number of general digital character animation books because although there are many of them, I think that studying old-school character animation, combined with mastering one's own chosen software package, tends to make these books somewhat redundant. There are a lot of specific digital techniques that do need expanding on, though, so here I list a few CG books that mostly deal with issues not covered by this book or the tutorials to which I've referred:

Stop Staring **by Jason Osipa** (Sybex/Wiley, 2nd ed., 2007) This is the quintessential book on facial modeling and animation in 3D. Lip sync and emotional facial expressions are all dealt with in depth and in a way that is very practical for the digital artist.

Building a Digital Human **by Ken Brilliant** (Laxmi Publications, 2005) This book covers polygon modeling of a human figure from beginning to end in great detail. Realistic organic modeling with polygons is far from trivial, and this book does a good job of explaining the practice and the theory behind it.

Digital Lighting and Rendering **by Jeremy Birn** (New Riders, 2nd edition, 2006) This book does a great job of covering the topic of lighting and rendering. Pretty much everything you need to know about lighting and lights is in here, and most of it is fully applicable to Blender's lighting system. With regard to rendering, this book will leave you with a much clearer idea of the strengths and weaknesses of the Blender internal renderer and an understanding of the differences between the various rendering engines and ray tracers. The book also does an excellent job of highlighting the similarities and differences between digital lighting and traditional film lighting and is terrific looking to boot. The book's sister volume *Digital Texturing and Painting* by Owen Demers is also a beautiful and inspiring book, but in my opinion it lacks the practical focus of *Digital Lighting and Rendering*.

***Inspired 3D Short Film Production* by Jeremy Cantor and Pepe Valencia** (Course Technology, 2004) This book gives a nice overview of the full process of producing a 3D animated film. Although it doesn't go into the individual steps in great detail, it will give you an idea of what the process is and has a number of practical tips for people trying to get started with a 3D short. Even if you have no intention of doing all the work yourself, this book will help to give you an idea of where the animator fits into the larger scheme of such a project. It's also a nice-looking book with an accompanying DVD filled with entertaining and inspiring short animations.

On Becoming a Blender Master

If you've followed the steps in this book, sought help on the BlenderArtists forum, and investigated some of the other resources mentioned in this chapter, you are, without a doubt, well along the path to becoming a master of Blender. As your own skills improve, bear in mind that as a free software application with still-limited industry support, Blender relies heavily on the energy and enthusiasm of its users. Your own contributions to Blender and the community have a special weight. These contributions might come in a variety of forms. If you are a top-notch coder in C or Python, you might consider getting involved in coding Blender or creating useful scripts. Creating good, clear tutorials is also an excellent way to contribute to the community (and to learn!). Likewise, making yourself available at the BlenderArtists forum to answer questions from people less experienced than you is also an important contribution. And as an artist, simply creating work in Blender and letting that be known has great value for the Blender community at large.

I hope that you've gotten something out of what I have attempted to contribute with this book. I'm looking forward to seeing your work.

Happy Blendering!

Index

Note to the Reader: Throughout this index **boldfaced** page numbers indicate primary discussions of a topic. *Italicized* page numbers indicate illustrations.

A

abdomen of Captain Blender character, 62, *63*

accessing datablocks, **23**, *23*

Action constraint, 123

Action Editor

    facial animation, 263, 275

    key shapes, 271–272, *271*

    and NLA, 283–284, *284*, 286–288, *286*, 293, 295, 297

    posing and keyframing, **224–226**, *224*, *226*, **229**, *229*

    walk cycles, 239, 251

activating add-ons, **342–343**, *342*

active camera views, 14, *14*

active objects, 18

Add brush, 118

Add Curve add-on category, 344

Add Driver option, 166

Add Image Strip option, 274

Add Mesh add-on category, 344

Add Modifier option, 28, 37

add-ons, **342**

    activating, **342–343**, *342*

    example, **343–345**, *343–345*

    preferences, 24

Add-Ons panel, 136, *136*, 342–343, *342*

Add Sequence Strip menu, 337

Add To Group button, 23, *23*

additive painting, 154

additivity of shape keys, **163–164**, *164*

Adobe Premiere editing system, 424

After Effects editing system, 424

Align To View option, 51

Aligned handle type, 213

alpha channels, **335–336**

Alpha setting for hair, 119

Alpha Over setting, 340

Alpha Under setting, 338, *338*

ambient occlusion (AO), **332–333**, *333*

Andaur, Claudio, 417

anger, shapes for, 184, *184*, 186, *186*

angle-based flattening, 98

angles in linear extrapolation, 220

angry expression, 262

animation, **207**, **299**

    armature. *See* armature animation

    bouncing ball, **210–217**, *210–217*

    editing, **336–340**, *337–339*

    extrapolation, **220**, *220–221*

    F-Curves and F-Curve modifiers, **208**, **221–222**, *221–222*

    facial. *See* faces (biological)

    interpolation, **217–219**, *218–219*

    keyframes, **208–210**, *209*

    lattice modifiers, **306–309**, *307–309*

    lighting. *See* lighting

    mesh deform modifiers, **310–313**, *310–313*

    metaballs, **319–320**, *319–320*

    NLA Editor. *See* NLA Editor

    nonarmature, **297**, *297*

    props, **300–306**, *300–305*

    proxies, **278–282**, *278–283*

    rendering, **334–336**, *334*

    resources for, **430–431**

    softbodies, **314–317**, *314–318*

Animation (Blair), 430–431

Animation add-on category, 345

Animation screen, 209, *209*, 225, *225*

Animator's Survival Kit (Williams), 404, 431

anime style shading, **92**, *92*

anklerot bone, 367

ankles

    Captain Blender character, 60, *60*

    rigging, 364–367, *366*

ANT Landscape add-on, 344, *344*

AO (ambient occlusion), **332–333**, *333*

appending

    datablocks, 23

    proxies, **278**

Applications/Utilities directory, 4

Apply function, 31

area lamps, **330**, *330*

armature animation, **223**

bouncing

F-Curves, **233–234**, *233–235*

keyframing, **236–237**, *237*

line of action, **236**, *236*

preparing, **225–229**, *225–231*

previewing, **231–232**, *232*

DopeSheet and Action Editor, **224**, *224*

IK vs. FK posing, **246**, *246–247*

pose-to-pose, **250**

location, **250–255**, *251–255*

with speech, **255–259**, *257–259*

run cycles, **247–249**, *248–249*

walk cycles

setting up, **237–240**, *238–240*

upper body movement, **240–242**, *241–245*

Armature Deform With Automatic Weights option, 133, *133*, 147

Armature modifier, 30

meshes, 147–148, 201, *201*

rigging, 155

skinning, 134

softbodies, 317

armatures, **121**

animating. *See* armature animation

bones, **122–123**

building, **123–129**, *123–129*

Emo character, 362

Feifi the canary character, **411–412**, *412–413*

IK, **129–133**, *130–133*

meta-rig, **137–142**, *137–142*

shape key driver, 165

skinning, **133–135**, *133–135*

arms

in bouncing, 229, *230–231*

Captain Blender character, **62**, *63–64*

extruding, 127, *128*

FK posing, 246

posing, 157

walk cycles, **241–242**, *242*

weight painting, 152, *153*

artifacts

overlapping faces, 82, *82*

Subdivision Surface modifier, 45, *45*

aspect ratio, 334

assigning materials to faces, 90, *90*

asymmetry

facial animation, 262

shape keys, **177–178**, *177–178*

attaching meshes, **147–148**, *147–148*

Audacity sound editor, 255, **424**

Audio Scrubbing feature, 256, *256*

Auto handle type, 213

Auto Clamped handle type, 213

auto keyframing, **236–237**, *237*

AV-Sync option, 232, 273

AVI Raw format, 335

Avid editing system, 424

axes, restricting operations to, **17**

B

B-bones, 364, 372

background images

animation, 338

Captain Blender character, 54, *55*

human head modeling, 34–35, *35*

background matte paintings, 385

backlighting, 330–331, *331*

balls

bouncing, **210–212**, *210–212*

control points, **212–213**, *213*

Edit Mode, **213–214**, *214*

squash/stretch effect, **215–217**, *215–217*

picking up and throwing, **303–306**, *303–305*

Barton, Campbell, 383, **390–393**

Basis shape key, 160, *160*, 162, **164–165**

belly weight gain, **314–317**, *314–318*

belt for Captain Blender character

deformations, 200, *200*

material slots, 95

modeling, **68–70**, *68–71*

Berkeley Open Infrastructure for Network Computing (BOINC), 336

Berkeley Software Distribution (BSD) license, 356

Bezier curves, 212

Bezier interpolation, 213, **218**, *218*

biceps
   walk cycles, 242
   weight painting, 151–152
Big and Ugly Rendering Project (BURP), 336
Big Buck Bunny movie, **352–353**, *353*
   computational resources, 383
   nonhuman rigs, **370–372**, *371–372*
   production pipeline, 375, 379
bird character
   Big Buck Bunny, 370–372, 371
   canary. *See* Feifi the canary character
Birn, Jeremy, 431–432
black seams in mesh modeling, 81, *82*
Blair, Preston, 179, 236, 430
blend shapes, 160
Blender Artistic license, **357**
Blender Cookie site, 430
Blender desktop, 4–5, *4*
Blender Foundation, 350–351
Blender Guru site, 430
Blender Institute, **349–350**
Blender Open Movie Project, **349–350**, **359**
   Big Buck Bunny, **352–353**, 353
   Elephants Dream. See *Elephants Dream*
   nonhuman rigs, **370–374**, *371–374*
   production pipeline, **375–379**, *375–377*
   Project Mango and Project Gooseberry, **355**
   Sintel, **354**, *355*
   Yo Frankie!, **353**, 354
Blender Sequence Editor, 335
Blender Studio Projects: Digital-Moviemaking (Mullen and Andaur), 417
Blender units (BUs), **10**
Blender Wikibook, 429
Blender window, 5, *5*
BlenderArtists Forum, 345, 429–430
BlenderNation, 429–430
Blendernewbies blog, 430
blending in NLA Editor, 288
blinking in facial animation, 267
BOINC (Berkeley Open Infrastructure for Network Computing), 336
bones, **121–122**
   constraints, **122–123**, 132
   editing, **124–126**, *125–126*
   Emo character, 362
   extruding, 127–128, *127–129*
   facial rigging, **187–188**
   IK, **129–133**, *130–133*
   meta-rig, 139–141, *140–141*
   NLA Editor, **284–287**, *284–287*
   parenting, 18, 155, *156*
   picking up and throwing balls, **303–306**, *303–305*
   rigging, **142–146**, *143–147*
   shapes, **191–192**, *191–192*
   weight painting, **149–155**, *149–153*
boots for Captain Blender character, 95
bouncing ball, **210–212**, *210–212*
   control points, **212–213**, *213*
   Edit Mode, **213–214**, *214*
   squash/stretch effect, **215–217**, *215–217*
bouncing Captain Blender character
   F-Curves, **233–234**, *233–235*
   keyframing, **236–237**, *237*
   line of action, **236**, *236*
   preparing, **225–229**, *225–231*
   previewing, **231–232**, *232*
box modeling
   Captain Blender, **54**
      collar and belt, **68–70**, *68–71*
      hands and gloves, **65–66**, *65–67*
      head, **70–80**, *70–81*
      legs and feet, **54–60**, *55–62*
      torso and arms, **62**, *63–64*
   description, 33
Box Select tool, 15
   control points, 212
   doubled vertices, 84–85, *84*
   keys, 229
   vertices, 56, 58
Brilliant, Ken, 431
britches for Captain Blender character, 95
Brow Down (Left and Right) shape, 186, *186*
brow knit, 199
Brow Middle Up (Left and Right) shape, 185, *185*
Brow Outside Up (Left and Right) shape, 186, *186*
Brows Together shape, **183**, *183*

brushes for weight painting, 152
BSD (Berkeley Software Distribution)
   license, 356
buffer shadows, **327–328**, *327*
Building a Digital Human (Brilliant), 431
bump maps
   eyebrows, 104–105, *104–105*
   Proog character, 370, *370*
BURP (Big and Ugly Rendering Project), 336
BUs (Blender units), **10**
butterfly rig, 372, *373*

C

calves for Captain Blender character, 60, *62*
camera rotation, walk cycles with, **290–293**,
   290–294
camera views, 14, *14*
canary. *See* Feifi the canary character
Cantor, Jeremy, 432
Cap Ends option, 20
Captain Blender character, **54**
   animation, **299**
      lattice modifiers, **306–309**, *307–309*
      mesh deform modifiers, **310–313**,
         310–313
      metaballs, **319–320**, *319–320*
      props, **300–306**, *300–305*
      softbodies, **314–317**, *314–318*
   collar and belt, **68–70**, *68–71*
   eyebrows, **109–110**, *110–111*
   eyelashes, **106–109**, *107–109*
   eyes, **111–114**, *112–114*
   hands and gloves, **65–66**, *65–67*
   head, **70–80**, *70–81*
   jumping
      F-Curves, **233–234**, *233–235*
      keyframing, **236–237**, *237*
      line of action, **236**, *236*
      preparing, **225–229**, *225–231*
      previewing, **231–232**, *232*
   legs and feet, **54–60**, *55–62*
   pose-to-pose animation, **251–255**, *251–255*
   proxies for, **279–282**, *279–283*
   rigging. *See* rigging
   run cycles, **247–249**, *248–249*

shading and materials, **94–97**, *94–97*
shape keys. *See* shape keys
speaking, **255–259**, *256–259*, **294–296**,
   295–296
textures and UV mapping, **98–105**, *99–105*
torso and arms, **62**, *63–64*
walk cycles
   NLA Editor, **290–293**, *290–294*
   setting up, **237–240**, *238–240*
   upper body, **240–242**, *241–245*
CartoonSmart site, 430
cast shadows, **327**
Catmull-Clark subdivision surfacing, 28, 30
centers of objects, **17**
CG lighting. *See* lighting
CG-related resources, **431–432**
Chain Length setting, 132
chairs, 300
channels, bouncing ball, 212
Chaos and Evolutions training DVD (Revoy),
   354, 428
character animation
   Blender Open Movie Project. *See* Blender
      Open Movie Project
   Captain Blender. *See* Captain Blender
      character
   resources for, **430–431**
character animator interview, **387–390**, *388*,
   401–405
character rigger interview, **398–401**
cheats, lighting, **323**, 332
chest
   bones for, 126, *126*
   in bouncing, 229
   Captain Blender character, 62, *63*, 95–96, *95*
   weight painting, 149, *149*, 151–152, *152*
child bones, 126, *126*
child objects, 17
chin in human head modeling, 52
chinchilla character, *371*
Cinema 4D software, 402
Circle Select tool, 174
circles for utility belt, 69, *69*
Clear All Restrict Render option, 332
Clear Parent option, 130

Clip Cube option, 97
clipping, 32
    Captain Blender character, 58
    human head modeling, 37, 47–48, 51
clothing seams, 98
Cloud Generator add-on, 345, *345*
cloud texture, 113, *113–114*
cmiVFX resource, 430
collaboration
    open source software, **425**
    with Subversion, **378–379**
Collada open source software, **425**
collar for Captain Blender character, **68–70**, *68–71*
color
    eyes, 112
    hair, 119
    lamps, 324
    materials, 88–91, *89*
    texture, 96, 370, *370*
Comb brush, 117, *118*
command-line interface, 346, *346*
compositing, 336
    open source software, **424**
    overview, **338–340**, *338–339*
concentration expression, 186, *186*
Cone object, 20–21, 29, *29*
Connect Hair option, 139
Console editor, 8
constant extrapolation, **220**, *220*
constant interpolation, **219**, *219*
constraints
    bone, **122–123**
    cameras, 290–291
    eyes, 189–190
    IK, **129–133**, *130–133*
content, licenses for, **355–357**
context-sensitive menus, 9
contexts for properties, 9
control bones, 122, 144–146, *145–147*
control points, **212–213**, *213*, 216
controls for facial rigging, **187–188**, **194–200**, *195–199*, 262
CookTorr shader, 95
Copy Location/Rotation/Scale constraint, 122

copying drivers, 170, *170*
corner of eye, modeling, 42, *42*
Creative Commons license, 349–350, **357**, 383
Creature Factory training DVD (Goralczyk), 353, 428
cropping images, 36
crouch pose, 228, *228*
Ctrl+MMB keys, 10
cube, superhero from. *See* Captain Blender character
Cube object, 20–22, 28–29
curl
    Feifi the canary character, 413–414, *413–414*
    finger, 158, *158*
current state, saving, 25
Cursor To Selection option, 49
Curvaceous Galore add-on, 344, *344*
curves
    curve guides, 360
    function. *See* F-Curves
    NURBS, 31
custom bone shapes, **191–192**, *191–192*
Cut brush, 118
cyclical motion in walk cycle, **290–293**, *290–294*

D

Dansie, Ben, 382
datablocks
    description, **18–19**
    managing, **22–23**, *22–23*
Davidson, Jeremy, 383
default hotkeys, 24
default window arrangement, 5, *5*
Deflect Emitter option, 118
deform bones
    description, 122
    facial rigging, 187, **410–411**, *410–411*
    fingers, 363, *363*
    weight painting, **149–151**, *150–151*, 154
deleting vertices, 164
delight expression, 186, *186*
Demers, Owen, 432
Diffuse color field, 88, *89*
diffuse light sources, 328

diffuse shading, 91

Digital Lighting and Rendering (Birn), 431–432

Digital Texturing and Painting (Demers), 432

Dillon, Kernon, 430

Dimensions tab, 334

disbelief expression, 186, *186*

Disconnect Hair option, 139

dismay expression, 184, *184*

Disney, Walt, 208

Disney studio, 430–431

Distance setting for lamps, 324

documentation, official, **429**

DopeSheet, 7, **224–226**, *224*

doubled edges and vertices, **84–85**, *84–85*

dragon character, 370, *371–372*

    concept art, 374, *376*

    modeling, 388, *388*

Draw Normals setting, 82

drivers

    facial rigging, 197, *197*

    shape keys, **165**

        mesh deformations, **200–203**, *200–203*

        setting up, **165–168**, *165–168*

        tweaking, **168–172**, *168–172*

DrQueue software, 378

Durian project, 354, **382–383**, *382*

E

e-Shop, 428

ears for Captain Blender character, 75, *75*, 77

edge loops

    Captain Blender character

        eyelashes, 106–107, *107*

        gloves, 66

        head, 70, *71*

        legs, 60

        scalp, 76, *78*

        description, 43

        lips, 49, *50*

edges

    hairline, 75, *75–76*

    meshes, 28

    mouth, 184

    shaders, 92, *92*

Edit mode

    armatures, 125, 139

    bouncing ball, **213–214**, *214*

    human head modeling, 36

    IK, 130

    shape keys, 161, 163

editing

    animation, **336–340**, *337–339*

    bones, **124–126**, *125–126*

    meshes, 21, *21*

    User Preferences, 24

editing cages, 31

editor types, **7–8**

elbows, rigging, 142, *142*

Elephants Dream, **350**

    hand and foot rigging, **362–367**, *363–367*

    jacket, **368–369**, *368–369*

    learning from, **360–362**, *360–362*

    overview, **351–352**, *351*

    production pipeline, 375, *377–379*

    texturing, **369–370**, *370*

emitters, particle hair, 115–116

Emo character, 360–362, *360–362*

emotion, shapes for, **182–187**, *183–187*

Empty object, 95–96, *95*

Emulate 3 Button Mouse option, 10, 24

Emulate Numpad setting, 13, 24

End field in Timeline, 209–210

End frames for bouncing ball, 212

Energy setting for lamps, 324

equilateral triangles in subsurfacing, 29

exporting file formats, **422**

expressions, shapes for, **182–187**, *183–187*

extrapolation, **220**

    constant, **220**, *220*

    linear, **220**, *221*

extreme poses

    run cycles, 247

    walk cycles, 238–240, *238–239*

extrusions

    bones, 127, *127–129*

    circles, 69, *69*

    feet, 60, *61*

    forehead, 52, *53*

    human head modeling, 39, *39*

jaw bone, 195
legs, 60, *60*
lips, 49, *50*
mirrored faces, 48, *48*
unwanted, **84–85**, *85*
eye area, 74, *74*
eye sockets, 74, *74*
eyeballs
Captain Blender character, 111
human head modeling, 51–52, *51–52*
lattice deformations, **306–309**, *307–309*
eyebrows
Captain Blender character, 104, *104*, **109–110**, *110–111*
controls, 199
facial animation, 262
eyelashes, **106–109**, *107–109*
eyelids
Captain Blender character, 74, *74*
controls, 199
eyes closed shape, 175, *175*
human head modeling, 49, *50*
rigging, **188–192**, *188–192*
eyes
Captain Blender character, 71, *71*, **111–114**, *112–114*
human head modeling, 41–44, *42–43*, 49, *50*
rigging, **188–192**, *188–192*
scaling, 138
Squint shape, 185, *185*
eyes closed shape, **173–177**, *173–177*

F

F-Curves, 165, 208
bouncing ball, 212, 214, *214*, 216
grabbing and holding objects, 304, 306
jumping, **233–234**, *233–235*
modifiers, **221–222**, *221–222*
NLA Editor, 283, 294–295, 297
walk cycles, 292
face loops, 43
faces (biological)
Captain Blender character, 73, *73*
deformations with lattices, **410–411**, *410–411*

eyeballs in, 51, *52*
facial animation, **261**
lip-sync, **267–273**, *268–273*
playback, **273–275**, *274–275*
pose-to-pose vs. straight-ahead, **264–267**, *265–267*
posing, **262–263**, *263*
facial rigging
bones and controls, **187–188**
eyes and eyelids, **188–192**, *188–192*
shape key controls, **194–200**, *195–199*
tongue, **192–194**, *193–194*
faces (geometry)
human head modeling, 39, *39*, 46–47, *46–47*, 52, *53*
internal, **83**, *83*
meshes, 28
overlapping, **82**, *82–83*
fake users, 22, 89
fan bones
Emo character, 362
rigging, **367**, *367*
fanning component for canary character, 413–415, *413–416*
fearful expression, 262
feathers for canary character, **413–417**, *413–416*
feet
in bouncing, 228
Captain Blender character, **54–60**, *55–62*
Elephants Dream, **364–367**, *364–367*
IK, 130, 246
pose-to-pose animation, 251–255, *251–255*
walk cycles, 238, 240
Feifi the canary character, **407–408**, *408*
facial deformations, **410–411**, *410–411*
meshes, **408–410**, *409–410*
rigging, **411–412**, *412–413*
wings, **413–417**, *413–416*
File Browser editor, 8
files
data access from, **23**, *23*
importing and exporting, **422**
preferences, 25
production, **383–386**, *384–386*
fill lights, 330–331, *331*
filling faces, 44–45, *44*

Final Cut Pro editing system, 424
Final Fantasy: Advent's Children, 354
fingers
    Captain Blender character, 65–66, *67*
    curling, 158, *158*
    meta-rig, 141, *141*
    rigging, 363, *363*
FK (forward kinematics)
    bouncing, 226, *227*
    description, 129–130
    posing, 156–157, *157*, **246**, *246–247*
flap component for canary character, 413–414,
    413–414
flared gloves, 65–66
Floor constraint, 123
flying squirrel character, 353, *354*, 372, 374, *374*
footbot bone, 367
footmid bone, 367
foottop bone, 364, 367
forearms in walk cycles, 242
forehead modeling, 39, *39*, 46, *46*, 52, *53*
fork extrudes, 127
forward kinematics (FK)
    bouncing, 226, *227*
    description, 129–130
    posing, 156–157, *157*, **246**, *246–247*
Foundation Blender Compositing (Wickes), 424
Frankie the Flying Squirrel rig, 353, *354*, 372,
    374, *374*
Free handle type, 213
free software and licenses, 349, **355–357**
Freestyle renderer, 425
front views
    Captain Blender character, 54, *55*
    human head modeling, 40
frown controls, **196–200**, *197–199*
Frown (Left and Right) shape, 184, *184*
function bones, 122
function curves. *See* F-Curves
furniture, **300**, *301*
future of Blender, **425**

G

Gaze bone, 189–192, *189*, *191–192*
Generator Modifier panel, 168, *168*
geometry, **43**

Gimp open source software, 375, 377
    cropping with, 36
    description, **423**
    importing images with, 102, *103*
    open movies, 375, 377
GimpShop open source software, **423**
gloves
    materials, 95
    modeling, **65–66**, *65–67*
    weight painting, 152, *153*
GLSL viewports, 322–323, *323*
GNU Public License (GPL), **356–357**
Goedegebure, Sacha, 352, 375
Goralczyk, Andy, 353, 428
GPL (GNU Public License), **356–357**
grabbing
    keys for, 37
    objects, **301–306**, *303–305*
Graph Editor, 7
    bouncing ball, **210–217**, *210–217*
    shape key drivers, 165–166, *166–167*
gravity, 214, 216
gray checkerboard pattern, 100
groups
    light, **332**
    objects, **23**
Guenette, Angela, 382, 387

H

hair and hair particles, **115**
    Captain Blender character, 75, *76*, 115
    Elephants Dream, 360–361
    material and texture, 107, **119–120**, *119–120*
    scaling, 139, *139*
    styling, **117–119**, *118*
    system setup, **115–117**, *115–117*
    textures, 107
Hair particle modifier, 155
HairTex texture, 119, *119*
Hand Turkey studios, 383
handle types for bouncing ball, 213–214
hands
    Captain Blender character, **65–66**, *65–67*
    Elephants Dream, **362–363**, *363*
    walk cycles, **242**
happy expression, 262

head modeling
    bones for, 126, *126*
    in bouncing, 228
    Captain Blender character, **70–80**, *70–81*, 100, 105
    facial animation, 262
    Feifi the canary character, 412
    FK posing, 246
    poly-by-poly, **34–42**, *34–35, 37–43*
    rigging, 155, *155*
    run cycles, 249, *249*
    scaling, 138, *139*
    walk cycles, 241, *242*
headers for windows, 5
hemi lights, **328–329**, *329*
hips
    in bouncing, 228–229
    Emo character, 362
    extruding, 128, *129*
    mesh deformations, 201
    pose-to-pose animation, 251–255, *252–255*
    walk cycles, 238
holding objects, **301–306**, *303–305*
hotkeys, 8
    3D object interaction, **15**
    preferences, **24**, *25*
    working with, **10–12**
Human (Meta-Rig) option, 137
human skin textures, 98

IK. *See* inverse kinematics (IK)
Illusion of Life (Thomas and Johnston), **431**
Image Editor window, 334
Image Mapping panel, 96
Image Preview window, 337
images, background
    animation, 338
    Captain Blender character, 54, *55*
    human head modeling, 34–35, *35*
Import/Export add-on category, 345
importing file formats, **422**
in-betweens, 208
inconsistent normals, **81–82**, *82*
independent key shape drivers, 172, *172*
Infini-D software, 402

influence
    ball location, 303
    bones, 147, 149
    bump maps, 105, *105*
    F-Curves, 304, *304*
    hair, 119, *119*
    posing, 156–157, 246, *246–247*
    proportional editing, 40–41, 112
    shape keys, 162, *162*
    skinning, 133
    stencil texture, 114
    textures, 96, *97*, 108
    weight painting, 151–152
Info editor, 8
Inkscape open source software, **424**
input settings, **24**
Input tab for hotkeys, 12
Inspired 3D Short Film Production (Cantor and Valencia), 432
interface, **3**
    navigating. *See* navigating
    settings, **23–24**
    work areas and window types, **4–9**, *4–7*
internal faces in mesh modeling, **83**, *83*
interpolation, **217**
    Bezier, 213, **218**, *218*
    constant, **219**, *219*
    keyed values, 208
    linear, **218**, *219*
inverse kinematics (IK)
    bone constraints, 122
    bouncing, 226, *227*
    description, **129–133**, *130–133*
    hand rigging, **363**, *363*
    posing, 156–157, *157*, **246**, *246–247*
iris, eyes, 112, *112–113*
Ishtar scene, 383, *384–385*

jacket, **368–369**, *368–369*
jaw
    control, 200
    lip-sync, 268, 270
    rigging, **195–196**, *195–196*
Jaw Down shape, 180, *180*

Jaw Left/Jaw Right shape, 187, *187*
JLipSync open source software, **424**
Johnston, Ollie, 431
joints
    knees, 129, *129*
    meta-rig, 141
jumping by Captain Blender character
    F-Curves, **233–234**, *233–235*
    keyframing, **236–237**, *237*
    line of action, **236**, *236*
    preparing, **225–229**, *225–231*
    previewing, **231–232**, *232*

K

Keep Lengths option, 118
Keep Offset option, 188
Keep Root option, 118
key lights, 330–331, *331*
keyboard shortcuts, 8
keyframes, **208**, **224**
    jumping animation, **236–237**, *237*
    run cycles, 247
    Timeline, **209–210**, *209*
keying scale, **215–217**, *215–217*
keys, shape. *See* shape keys
knees
    Captain Blender character, 60, *62*
    joints, 129, *129*
knife tool
    faces, 71, *72*
    palm, 66, *66*
knuckles, rigging, 363
Kurdali, Bassam, 351–352, 428

L

Lambert shaders, 95
Lamp object, 19
lamps, **324–325**, *324–325*
    area, **330**, *330*
    hemi, **328–329**, *329*
    point, **325–326**, *325*
    spot, **326–328**, *326–328*
    sun, **329**, *329*

Lattice modifier, 30
lattices
    animation, **306–309**, *307–309*
    facial deformations with, **410–411**, *410–411*
layers
    light groups, **332**
    overview, **12–13**
    switching, 70, *70*
Learn Character Animation with Blender
    training DVD (Reynish), 353, 404, 428
legs
    Captain Blender character, **54–60**, *55–62*
    control bones, 144, *145*
    extruding, 128, *129*
    Feifi the canary character, 412
    FK, 246
    IK, 130, 132, *133*
    mesh deformations, 203, *203*
    rigging, 367, *367*
    walk cycles, 238, 241
Leonard, Beorn, 383, **387–390**, *388*
Levy, Colin, 354, 375, 382, 403
libraries
    linking, 278
    working with, **378**
licenses, 349–350, **355–357**, 383
Licuadora Studio, 383
lighting, **321**
    basics, **322–323**, *322–323*
    cheats, **323**, 332
    lamps. *See* lamps
    setups, **330–333**, *330–333*
    subsurface scattering, **106**, *106*
Limit Location constraint, 198, *198*
Limited GPL, 356
line of action in jumping animation, **236**, *236*
linear extrapolation, **220**, *221*
linear interpolation, **218**, *219*
linking
    actions to NLA, **283–287**, *284–287*
    proxies, **278–282**, *278–283*
lip sync, 261
    facial animation, 264, **267–271**, *268–270*
    open source software, **424**
    shape keys, **179–182**, *180–182*

lips
    controller, 200
    modeling, 40, **49**
Lips Together shape, 182, *182*
Lips Wide shape, 182, *182*
locations
    animation, **250–255**, *251–255*
    object, 19
Lodewijk, Martin, 375, 382
Logic Editor, 8
logo texture, 95–96, *96*
Loop Cut tool, 58, *59*, 62, *63*, 70
loops
    edge. *See* edge loops
    around eyes, 49, *50*
    human head modeling, 41–42
    overview, **43**
lower lip
    controller, 200
    lip-sync, 270
Lower Lip In shape, 181, *181*
Lower Lip Out shape, 181, *181*

M

Macromedia Director, 402
Maeter, Soenke, 382
Magpie editing system, 424
Make Vertex Parent option, 96
MakeHuman open source software, **423**
Mancandy FAQ, 352, 428
Manos Digitales studio, 408
manual keyframing, **236–237**, *237*
maps
    bump
        eyebrows, 104–105, *104–105*
        Proog character, 370, *370*
    texture, **96–97**, *97*
    UV, **98–105**, *99–105*
Mark Seam option, 98
mass in run cycles, 249
Mastering Blender (Mullen), 346, 424
Material Properties window, 88, *88*
materials and material slots, **88–91**, *88–91*
    Captain Blender characters, **94–97**, *94–97*
    hair, **119–120**, *119–120*

nodes, **93**, *93*, **109–110**, *110–111*
    properties, **91**, *91*
McCay, Winsor, 208
Measure add-on, 343, *343*
measurement units, **10**
media for animation
    adding, **337–338**, *337*
    compositing, **338–340**, *338–339*
    sound, **339**
Median Point, 17
menacing expression, 262
menus, context-sensitive, 9
Merge Threshold value, 84
merging windows, 5, *7*
Mesh add-on category, 345
Mesh Deform modifier, 30
Mesh Properties window, 99, 115
meshes and Mesh objects, **27**
    deformations
        animation, **310–313**, *310–313*
        driven shape keys for, **200–203**, *200–203*
    Feifi the canary character, **408–410**, *409–410*
    materials for, 88
    overview, **19–21**, *20–21*
    poly-by-poly modeling, **33–42**, *34–35*, *37–43*
    polygons and subsurfacing, **28–33**, *28–29*, *32*
    problems and solutions
        inconsistent normals, **81–82**, *82*
        internal faces, **83**, *83*
        overlapping faces, **82**, *82–83*
        unwanted doubles, **84**, *84*
        unwanted extrusions, **84–85**, *85*
    resizing, 138, *138*
    rigging, **147–148**, *147–148*
meta-rig armatures, **137–142**, *137–142*
metaballs, **319–320**, *319–320*
Metarig functionality, 10
mid-blink in facial animation, 267
Middle Mouse Button (MMB), **9–10**
Minnart shaders, 95
mirroring and Mirror modifier, 32, *32*
    Captain Blender character, 58, *59*, 69
    eyeballs, 51, *51*

facial animation, 262
human head modeling, 36–38, *38*, 40, 47–48
skinning, 134
in walk cycles, 239
working with, **54**
MMB (Middle Mouse Button), **9–10**
modifiers, **30–31**
effects, **32–33**, *32*
F-Curves, **221–222**, *221–222*
lattice, **306–309**, *307–309*
mesh deform, **310–313**, *310–313*
rigging, 148, *148*
skinning, 134, *134*
Modifiers tab, 28, *28*, 32
Morgenstern, Jan, 382
morph targets, 160
motion manipulators, 15
mouse, **9–10**
mouth
Captain Blender character, 71, *72*, 79, *80*
edges
control, 200
in shapes, 184
lip-sync, 268
modeling, 40–42, *40–41*
scaling, 138
movies
Open Movie Project. *See* Blender Open Movie Project
output formats, 335
moving edge loops, 60
MPEG4 format, 335
multiplicative blending, 288
multiplicative painting, 154

N

n-gons, 29
names for materials, 89, *89*
navigating, **9–10**
3D object interaction, **14–18**, *16–17*
Blender units, 10
hotkeys, **10–12**
layers, **12–13**
Middle Mouse Button, **9–10**
views and perspective, **13–14**, *14*

neck
bones for, 126–127, *126*
Captain Blender character, 68, *68*, 79, *79*
facial animation, 262
modeling, 52, *52*
nervous anticipation expression, 262
NLA Editor, 7, **283**, *283*
linking to, **283–287**, *284–287*
nonarmature animations, **297**, *297*
strips, 283
walk cycle repetitions, **293**, *293–294*
walk cycle with camera rotation, **290–293**, *290–294*
walking and talking, **294–296**, *295–296*
working with **287–289**, *287–289*
Node Editor window, 8, 93, *93*, 339, *339*
nodes
composite, **339–340**, *339*
materials, 93, *93*, **109–110**, *110–111*
Noise F-Curve modifier, 221, *221–222*
nonarmature animations, **297**, *297*
nonhuman rigs in Blender Open Movie Project, **370–374**, *371–374*
nonlinear video editing and compositing software, **424**
nonsymmetrical modeling, 36
nonuniform rational B-splines (NURBS), **31**
normals in mesh modeling, **81–82**, *82*
nose
Captain Blender character, 71, *72*
facial animation, 262
modeling, 47–48, *47–48*
nose crinkle control, 199
Nose Crinkle shape, **183**, *183*
nostrils, modeling, 47–48, *48*
NURBS (nonuniform rational B-splines), **31**

O

Object add-on category, 345
Object mode
IK, 130–131
shape keys, 161
skinning, 133
weight painting, 151

objects
   centers, **17**
   datablocks, **18–19, 22–23**, *22–23*
   grabbing and holding, **301–306**, *303–305*
   interacting with, **14–15**, *16–17*
   meshes, **19–21**, *20–21*
off-site rendering, **336**
official documentation, **429**
omnidirectional light, 325–326
one-to-one shape key relationship, 168
Open Content license, 357
open mouth for lip-sync, 268
Open Movie Project. *See* Blender Open
   Movie Project
open source software and content, **422**
   collaborative projects, **425**
   free and open licenses, **355–357**
   modeling, **423**
   nonlinear video editing and
      compositing, **424**
   Sintel, **383**
   sound and lip sync, **424**
   texturing and 2D, **423–424**
   video playback, **425**
OpenGL render button, 232
Optimal display option, 210
optimistic expression, 262
oral cavity in Captain Blender character, 79
Orange movie, 350
Orange project, 352, 375
order of modifiers, 148, *148*
orthogonal views, 34
Osipa, Jason, 179, 431
Outliner window, 8, 22, *22–23*
output formats, **335–336**
Output tab for facial animation, 274, *274*
overlapping faces in mesh modeling, **82**, *82–83*

P

painting, weight
   mesh deformations, 201
   overview, **149–155**, *149–153*
   shape keys, 177
   softbodies, 315–316, *316*
palm, cutting, 66, *66*
Papagayo open source software, **424**

parent-child relationships in IK, 130, *131*
parent objects, 17
parenting, **17–18**
particle hair, **115**
   material and texture, **119–120**, *119–120*
   styling, **117–119**, *118*
   system setup, **115–117**, *115–117*
Particle Properties window, 116, 120
Path Edit mode, 118
paths in animation, 250–251
Peach team, 352–353
perspective, **13–14**, *14*
phoneme sets, **179–180**
Photoshop program
   cropping with, 36
   vs. Gimp, 423
picking up balls, **303–306**, *303–305*
pinched effect, 83, *83*
pipeline, production, **375–378**, *375–377*
   collaboration, **378–379**
   libraries, **378**
pivot points, 17, *17*
Pixels 3D software, 402
plastics, shaders for, 95
Play button on Timeline, 209
playback
   facial animation, **273–275**, *274–275*
   open source software, **425**
Plumiferos. See Feifi the canary character
point lamps, **325–326**, *325*
Point Select mode, 118–119
poly-by-poly modeling, **33–42**, *34–35, 37–43*
polygons, **28–33**, *28–29, 32*
Pose mode
   IK, 130–131, *131*
   rigging, 155
   skinning, 133
   weight painting, 151
pose-to-pose animation, **250**
   location, **250–255**, *251–255*
   with speech, **255–259**, *257–259*
   vs. straight-ahead, **264–267**, *265–267*
posing, **224**
   facial, **262–263**, *263*
   rigging, **156–158**, *157–158*
   weight painting, 154

previewing animation, **231–232**, *232*
Price, Andrew, 430
production files, *Sintel*, **383–386**, *384–386*
production pipeline, **375–378**, *375–377*
    collaboration, **378–379**
    libraries, **378**
production schedules, *Sintel*, 386, *386*
Project Apricot, 353
Project Gooseberry, **355**
Project Mango, **355**
Proog character, 351, *351*, 360, *360–361*
    in clay, *375*
    foot rigging, 364, *364*
    jacket, **368–369**, *368–369*
    texturing, **369–370**, *370*
Properties window, **8–9**
proportional editing, 40–41, *41–42*, 112
props, **300**
    furniture, **300**, *301*
    grabbing and holding objects, **301–306**,
      303–305
proxies, **278–282**, *278–283*
Puff brush, 118
pupils for eyes, 112
Push tool, 389
Python scripts, 3, 136, **341**
    add-ons, **342–345**, *342–345*
    API, **345**, *345–346*
    tutorials, **346**, *346*

Q

QuickTime software, 425

R

radians, 168–169
Ramp panel for hair, 119, *119*
ray shadows, **328**, *328*
Receive Transparent option, 109
Recover Last Session option, 4
relationship lines in rigging, 144, *144*
Relax Pose tool, 389
Remove Doubles option, 82, 84
renaming materials, 89, *89*
Render add-on category, 345

rendered frames, sequencing, **273–275**,
    274–275
rendering
    animation, **334–336**, *334*
    hair, 120, *120*
    off-site, **336**
    output formats, **335–336**
    properties, **334–335**, *334*
resizing
    meshes, 138, *138*
    windows, 5, *6*
resources, **427**
    Blender, **428–430**
    non-blender, **430–432**
ResPower services, 336
Restrict Render Unselected option, 332, *332*
Revoy, David, 354, 375, *375–377*, 382, 428
Reynish, William, 353, 383, **401–405**, 428
RGB color setting, 324
ribs
    in bouncing, 228
    run cycles, 249, *249*
rigging, **121**
    Captain Blender, **135**
      finishing off, **155**, *155–156*
      generating, **142–146**, *143–147*
      meshes, **147–148**, *147–148*
      meta-rig armatures, **137–142**, *137–142*
      posing, **156–158**, *157–158*
      Rigify add-on, **135–136**, *136*
      weight painting, **149–155**, *149–153*
    Elephants Dream, **362–367**, *363–367*
    Emo character, 362
    facial. *See* faces (biological)
    Feifi the canary character, **411–412**,
      412–413
    proxies for, **279–282**, *279–283*
Rigging add-on category, 345
Rigify add-on, 404
    bone shapes, 191
    installing, **135–136**, *136*
    meta-rig armatures, 137
    rig generation, **142–146**, *143–147*
Rings setting, 51
Rip tool, 65

roll of bones, 141, *141*
Roosendaal, Ton, 349, 351, 382
Rotate Around Selection option, 24
Rotate Edge tool, 75
rotating
    3D objects, 15, *16*
    bones, 124, *125*
    cameras in walk cycles, **290–293**, *290–294*
    edge loops, 60
    edges, 75, *75–76*
    eye constraints, 189–190
    keys for, 37
    objects, 19
    views, 41
Rotobezier add-on, 345
Round shape, 182, *182*
run cycles, **247–249**, *248–249*

S

Sad Sad Song project, 387
sadness expression, 184, *184*
Salvemini, Lee, 382–383, 403
saving changes, 4
scaling
    3D objects, 15, *16*
    armatures, **137–139**, *137–139*
    arms, 62
    bones, 363, *363*
    edge loops, 60
    human head modeling, 36–37, *37*
    keys for, 37
    squash/stretch effect, **215–217**, *215–217*
    wings, 414
scalp for Captain Blender character, 75–76, *77*, 115, *115*
screenplay for *Sintel*, 386, *386*
screenwriter interview, **393–398**
scripts, 3, 136, **341**
    add-ons, **342–345**, *342–345*
    API, **345**, *345–346*
    tutorials, **346**, *346*
scrubbing, 256, *256*, 267
seams, clothing, 98
Segments setting, 51
Select Grouped menu, 138

Sequence Editor, 8
    benefits, 424
    editing in, **336–340**, *337–339*
    facial animation, 264, *265*
    rendered frames, **273–275**, *274–275*
    sound, **256**, *256*
Set Keyframe Handle Type menu, 213
shaders, 91, *91*
    for plastics, 95
    toon, **92**, *92*
shading
    anime style, **92**, *92*
    Captain Blender characters, **94–97**, *94–97*
    materials, 91, *91*
    options, 28, *29*
shadows from lamps, **324–328**, *327–328*
Shape Key Editor mode, 271–272
shape keys, **159**
    additivity, **163–164**, *164*
    basics, **160–163**, *160–163*
    Basis shape, **164–165**
    Captain Blender character, **172–173**
        asymmetry, **177–178**, *177–178*
        emotion, **182–187**, *183–187*
        eyes closed, **173–177**, *173–177*
        lip syncing, **179–182**, *180–182*
    drivers, **165**
        mesh deformations, **200–203**, *200–203*
        setting up, **165–168**, *165–168*
        tweaking, **168–172**, *168–172*
    Emo character, 361, *361*
    facial animation, 262
    facial rigging, **194–200**, *195–199*
    lip-sync, **271–273**, *271–272*
    vertices, **164**
Shift+MMB keys, 10
shortcuts, keyboard, 8
shot breakdown spreadsheet, 386, *386*
shoulders
    bones for, 127, *128*
    extruding, 62
    facial animation, 262
    walk cycles, 241
    weight painting, 152, *152*
Show Alpha option, 108

side views, 54, *55*
Single Bone option, 124
single-vertex parenting, 18, 96
Sintel movie, **354**, *355*, **381**
    Barton interview, **390–393**
    Durian project, **382–383**, *382*
    DVD package, 428, *428*
    Leonard interview, **387–390**, *388*
    nonhuman rigs, **370–374**, *371–374*
    open content, **383**
    production files, **383–386**, *384–386*
    production pipeline, 375, *375–376*, 379
    Reynish interview, **401–405**
    tutorials, **387**, *387*
    Vegdahl interview, **398–401**
    Wouda interview, **393–398**
size
    meshes, 138, *138*
    objects, 19
    vertices, 33
    windows, 5, *6*
skin textures
    applying, 98
    subsurface scattering, 106
skinning, 121, **133–135**, *133–135*
slots, material, **88–91**, *88–91*
smile controls, **196–200**, *197–199*
Smile (Left and Right) shape, 184, *184*
Smooth brush, 118
Smooth shading option, 58, *59*
Smooth tool, 76
Snap Cursor To Selection option, 188
Soft Body Cache Collision setting, 317, *317*
Soft Body Edges setting, 317, *317*
Soft Body Self Collision setting, 317, *317*
softbodies
    animation, **314–317**, *314–318*
    jacket, 368, *368*
Softimage XSI software, 402
software, open source. *See* open source
    software and content
Solid OpenGL Lights settings, 322
sound
    in animation, **255–259**, *256–259*, **294–296**,
        295–296

lip sync. *See* lip sync
    open source software, **424**
    Sequence Editor, **339**
Specular Intensity setting, 108
specular shading, 91
speech
    in animation, **255–259**, *256–259*, **294–296**,
        295–296
    lip sync. *See* lip sync
spheres for eyeballs, 111–113, *114*
Spider-Man 2, 378
splitting windows, 5, *6*
Spot Shape panel, 324
spotlights, **326–328**, *326–328*
squash/stretch effect, **215–217**, *215–217*
squint controls, 199
Squint (Left and Right) shape, 185, *185*
squirrel character, 353, *354*, 372, 374, *374*
SSS (subsurface scattering), **106**, *106*
Stallman, Richard, 356
Start field on Timeline, 209–210
Start frames for bouncing ball, 212
state, saving, 25
stencil textures, 114, *114*
steps in walk cycle
    setting up, **237–240**, *238–240*
    upper body, **240–242**, *241–245*
stillness in animation, **250**
stills output formats, 335
Stop Staring (Osipa), 179, 431
straight-ahead animation, 250, **264–267**,
    265–267
Strand material, 119
Strata 3D software, 402
Strength setting for weight painting, 152
stretch keys for bouncing ball, 217
Stretch-to constraint, 123
strips, NLA, 283
    walk cycle repetitions, **293**, *293–294*
    walk cycle with camera rotation, **290–293**,
        290–294
    walking and talking, **294–296**, *295–296*
    working with **287–289**, *287–289*
styling, hair, **117–119**, *118*
Subdivide Smooth option, 56, *56*, 70, *70*

Subdivision Surface modifier, 30
subdivision surfacing, 28, 45, *45*
subsurf modifier, 28, 45, *45*, 134
subsurface scattering (SSS), **106**, *106*
subsurfacing, **28–33**, *28–29*, *32*, 74, *74*
subtractive blending, 288
subtractive painting, 154
Subversion system, **378–379**
sun lamps, **329**, *329*
superhero character. *See* Captain Blender
    character
surfaces, NURBS, 31
surprise expression, 186, *186*
suspicion expression, 186, *186*
symmetrical modeling, 36
symmetry
    facial animation, 262
    lip syncing, 180
    shape keys, 177
syncing
    cyclical motions in walk cycle, **290–293**,
        290–294
    lip sync. *See* lip sync
    sound in animation, **255–259**, *256–259*,
        294–296, *295–296*
System add-on category, 345
system preferences, **25**

T

tables, 300
tail in FK posing, 246
talking
    in animation, **255–259**, *256–259*, **294–296**,
        295–296
    lip sync. *See* lip sync
technical director interview, **390–393**
teeth
    Captain Blender character, 79
    in lip syncing, 182
Text add-on category, 345
Text Editor, 8
Texture Paint mode, 100, *101*, 104
Texture Paint Shading option, 100
Texture Properties window, 96, 105

textures
    basics, **95–97**, *95–97*
    eyelashes, **106–109**, *107–109*
    eyes, **111–114**, *112–114*
    hair, **115**, **119–120**, *119–120*
    materials for, 88
    open source software, **423–424**
    Proog character, **369–370**, *370*
    UV mapping, **98–105**, *99–105*
themes
    preferences, 25
    vertex size, 33
Thomas, Frank, 431
3D cursor, 10, *10*, 49, *49*
3D space navigation, **9–10**
    3D object interaction, **14–18**, *16–17*
    Blender units, **10**
    hotkeys, **10–12**
    layers, **12–13**
    Middle Mouse Button, **9–10**
    views and perspective, **13–14**, *14*
3D View add-on category, 343
3D View editor, 7
3D view windows, 9
3D viewports, 34, *34*, 37–38
three-point lighting, **330–332**, *330–332*
three-vertex parenting, 96
throwing balls, **303–306**, *303–305*
thumbs, extruding, 65, *65*
Timeline, 7, **209–210**, *209*
Tip Select mode, 118
To Active Bone option, 131
toe bones rigging, 364
toggling layers, 13
tongue
    lip-sync, 270
    modeling, 79
    rigging, **192–194**, *193–194*
Tool Shelf, 17, 20, 28, *29*
toon shaders, **92**, *92*
topology, **43**
torso
    Captain Blender character, **62**, *63–64*
    Feifi the canary character, 412, *412*
    weight painting, 151–152

TrackTo constraint, 123, 290–291
Transform Channel option, 172
Transform Properties window
    jaws, 195
    meta-rig, 141, *142*
    for rigging, 365
translating 3D objects, 15, *16*
transparency of textures, 108
triangles in polygon modeling, 29, *29*
triple-vertex parenting, 18
tutorials
    facial rigging, **387**, *387*
    Python scripts, **346**, *346*
tweening, 208

U

U coordinate, 98
Uncompressed file formats, 335
underarm in weight painting, 152, *152*
unwanted doubles, **84**, *84*
unwanted extrusions, **84–85**, *85*
unwrapping UV, 98–99, *99–100*
upper body in walk cycles, **240–242**, *241–245*
upper lip controls, 199
Upper Lip In shape, 181, *181*
Upper Lip Out shape, 181, *181*
user objects, 22
User Preferences window, 8
    Add-Ons panel, 136, *136*, 342–343, *342*
    auto keying, 237, *237*
    hotkeys, 12
    settings, **23–25**, *24*
    vertex size, 33
users of materials, 89
utility belt, 69, *69*
UV/Image Editor, 7, 98, 102–103
UV mapping, **98–105**, *99–105*
UV Test Grid option, 103
UV Texture panel, 99

V

V coordinate, 98
Valencia, Pepe, 432
van Lommel, Brecht, 383
Vazquez, Pablo, 353, 383

Vector handle type, 213–214
Veenliet, Dolf, 383
Vegdahl, Nathan, 136, 382, **398–401**
Venom's Lab training video (Vazquez), 353
Verse open source software, **425**
vertex groups
    shape keys, 177–179, *178*
    skinning, 133
    softbodies, 315–316, *315*
    weight painting, 154
vertex parenting, 18, 96
vertex weighting, 149
vertices
    doubled, **84–85**, *84–85*
    human head modeling, 42, *42–43*
    lattices, 306
    legs, 60, *60*
    lips, 49
    meshes, 28
    neck, 68, *68*
    particle systems, 116, *116*
    shape keys, **164**
    size, 33
    weight painting, 151
    wireframe mode, 180
video, open source software for
    editing and compositing, **424**
    playback, **425**
Video Sequence Editor. *See* Sequence Editor
viewpoints, 14
viewports, 34, *34*, 37–38
views
    Captain Blender character, 54, *55*
    navigating, **13–14**, *14*
visibility of bones, 149, *150*
VLC Media Player, 425
VSE. *See* Sequence Editor

W

walk cycles
    with camera rotation, **290–293**, *290–294*
    pose-to-pose animation, **251–255**, *251–255*
    setting up, **237–240**, *238–240*
    upper body movement, **240–242**, *241–245*
walking, IK for, 130
Wardiso shaders, 95, 114

.wav files, 255

Weight brush, 118

weight gain, softbodies for, **314–317**, *314–318*

weight in run cycles, **249**, *249*

weight painting

    mesh deformations, 201

    overview, **149–155**, *149–153*

    shape keys, 177

    softbodies, 315–316, *316*

White, Tony, 399

Wickes, Roger D., 424

widgets, manipulator, 15, *16*

Williams, Richard, 404, 431

windows

    defined, 9

    types, **4–9**, *4–7*

wings

    deformation, 372, *373*

    Feifi the canary character, 409–410,
        409–410, **413–417**, *413–416*

Wings3D open source software, **423**

Wire display, 312, *312*

wireframe view

    Captain Blender character, 58

    human head modeling, 36

    mesh modeling, 85, *85*

    vertices, 180

words

    in animation, **255–259**, *256–259*, **294–296**,
        295–296

    lip sync. *See* lip sync

work areas

    human head modeling, 34

    overview, **4–9**, *4–7*

World Properties window, 333

Wouda, Esther, 375, 382, **393–398**

wrinkles, 183

wrists

    for glove, 66, *67*

    meta-rig, 142, *142*

X

X-Axis Mirror feature

    activating, 127, *127*, 139, *140*

    softbodies, 315

X Mirror editing

    eyes closed shape, 174

    lip syncing, 180

    shape keys, 177

X offset setting, 35–36, *35*

X-Ray box, 124, *124–125*, 139, *140*

Y

Yo Frankie! game, **353**, *354*

Z

Z Location curve for bouncing ball, 212,
    214, 216

Zierhut, Anthony, 377